Working on the Dock of the Bay

Working on the Dock of the Bay

Labor and Enterprise in an Antebellum Southern Port

MICHAEL D. THOMPSON

THE UNIVERSITY OF SOUTH CAROLINA PRESS

© 2015 University of South Carolina

Published by the University of South Carolina Press
Columbia, South Carolina 29208

www.sc.edu/uscpress

Manufactured in the United States of America

24 23 22 21 20 19 18 17 16 15   10 9 8 7 6 5 4 3 2 1

Library of Congress Cataloging-in-Publication Data

Thompson, Michael D.
  Working on the dock of the bay : labor and enterprise in an antebellum Southern
port / Michael D. Thompson.
     pages cm
  Includes bibliographical references and index.
  ISBN 978-1-61117-474-8 (hardcover : alk. paper) — ISBN 978-1-61117-475-5 (ebook)
  1. Stevedores—South Carolina—Charleston—History—19th century. 2. African American stevedores—South Carolina—Charleston--History—19th century. 3. Labor—South
Carolina—Charleston—History—19th century. 4. Charleston (S.C.)—Race relations—
History—19th century. 5. Charleston (S.C.)—Economic conditions—19th century.
6. Charleston (S.C.)—Social conditions—19th century. I. Title.
  HD8039.L82U695 2015
  331.7'6138710975791509034—dc23
  2014044829

Cover illustration: Henry Alexander Ogden (after his original), *South Carolina—Our Great
National Industry—Shipping Cotton from Charleston to Foreign and Domestic Ports—A Scene
on North Commercial Wharf.* From *Frank Leslie's Illustrated,* November 16, 1878. Courtesy of
Deborah C. Pollack.

For my wife, Melissa,
my children, Ben and Lily,
and my mentor, Jim

Contents

Illustrations

Acknowledgments

Like any long-term project, this book benefitted from the support and assistance of many selfless individuals. My most profound thanks goes first and foremost to my mentor, Jim Roark, who generously and patiently has guided my professional and scholarly development over the past decade. I similarly owe a debt of gratitude to David Gleeson for taking an early interest in my work and for offering regular encouragement ever since. I am grateful as well to my editor, Alex Moore, for fielding the countless questions of a first-time author and for offering thoughtful and always constructive feedback. The writing and revising of this book also was facilitated by much appreciated comments and suggestions from Jonathan Prude, David Eltis, Bernard Powers, Jeffrey Bolster, Dylan Penningroth, James Schmidt, Leon Fink, Brian Luskey, Wendy Woloson, Glenn Gordinier, Kerry Taylor, Graeme Milne, and the anonymous peer reviewers for the University of South Carolina Press and the National Endowment for the Humanities.

Meanwhile it was my privilege to encounter many of the nation's most outstanding and professional archivists and librarians while conducting the research for this book. I especially would like to thank Allen Stokes, Henry Fulmer, Robin Copp, Graham Duncan, Brian Cuthrell, Charles Lesser, Faye Jensen, Mary Jo Fairchild, Mike Coker, Jane Aldrich, Nic Butler, Harlan Greene, Eric Emerson, Carol Jones, Janice Knight, Laura Clark Brown, and Amy McDonald. Both the research and writing of this book received generous financial support from Emory University's Department of History and Laney Graduate School; the University of Tennessee at Chattanooga; the South Caroliniana Library and the Institute for Southern Studies at the University of South Carolina; the Avery Research Center for African American History and Culture and the Program in the Carolina Lowcountry and Atlantic World (CLAW) at the College of Charleston; the Munson Institute of American Maritime Studies at Mystic Seaport; the Southern Historical Collection at the University of North Carolina at Chapel Hill; and the John Hope Franklin Collection for African and African American Documentation at Duke University.

Finally, I am appreciative and thankful for the abounding friendship of former graduate school classmates as well as many colleagues at the University of Tennessee at Chattanooga, particularly Zeb Baker, Aaron Althouse, James Guilfoyle, and Will Kuby. But without the unwavering love and support of my family—my wife, Melissa; my son, Benjamin; my daughter, Lily; my father, Howard; my mother, Rochelle; and my brother, Matt—the completion of this book would not have been possible. Thank you, and I love you.

Introduction

On October 28, 1869, hundreds of dockworkers gathered for an emergency meeting along Charleston's commercial waterfront. George B. Stoddard, a forty-seven-year-old Massachusetts-born stevedore who had settled in the city during the 1850s by way of Mobile, had been fired while loading the ship *A. B. Wyman*. A skilled and experienced cotton stower, Stoddard was dismissed not for professional deficiencies but because he was a white Republican and a member of the port's mostly black Longshoremen's Protective Union Association. Notwithstanding the mounds of cotton bales blanketing the wharves and awaiting shipment, Charleston's exporters refused to any longer engage those vessels employing Stoddard. Either the ship or the stevedore had to go. In the wake of Stoddard's discharge, fellow union members immediately initiated a strike and then assembled to discuss further actions. Convinced that this conflict was "but the first move of a determined effort to crush out the longshoremen who have demanded and received higher wages" in recent years, the attendees agreed to prolong the work stoppage "until the shippers withdraw all discrimination against longshoremen on account of their political sentiments, whether such members be Republicans or Democrats." Utterly dependent upon these dockworkers' vital labor and confronted with united resolve, the exporters quickly capitulated and the longshoremen—including George B. Stoddard—returned to work by November 2.[1]

This episode is remarkable not least because G. B. Stoddard just years prior had led Charleston's white master stevedores in public remonstrations against enslaved black competitors, many of whom as freedmen risked their livelihoods in 1869 to aid their former rival and to save their now common labor union.

But most extraordinary is the very existence of this robust association of class-conscious wharf laborers. Waterfront unions, such as that of New Orleans's highly skilled white cotton screwmen, founded in 1850, were rare in antebellum southern ports. Certainly no formal organization of dockworkers—white or black, free or enslaved, native or immigrant, skilled or unskilled—existed in Charleston before the Civil War. And yet, less than two years after the collapse of the Confederacy and the institution of slavery upon which it was built, many of the South Carolina port's workers joined in walkouts and to form the Longshoremen's Protective Union Association. The state legislature granted incorporation to this union in 1869, and by January 1875 the *Charleston News and Courier* reported a membership of eight hundred to one thousand "of the bone and sinew of the colored workingmen of Charleston." One historian has contended, "During Reconstruction and throughout the remainder of the [nineteenth] century, the longshoremen launched the most ambitious, aggressive, and well-organized campaign to secure their interests as workingmen," and "were a force to be seriously reckoned with on every wharf in Charleston." Other scholars have pointed out, "It was among the longshoremen that the first successful Negro labor organizations were formed," and shortly after the war this union "was referred to in the press as 'the most powerful organization of the colored laboring class in South Carolina.'"[2]

How was such an effective association, predominantly made up of former slaves, possible so soon after the Civil War? Southerners' unbudgeable commitment to the extensive ownership and employment of black slave laborers, as well as racial, ethnic, social, political, and occupational divisions among workers, had precluded the formation of waterfront labor organizations in antebellum Charleston. Though these schisms and contests at times persisted after the Civil War and the abolition of slavery, the city's postbellum dockworkers united—and struck—often and long enough to extract employer concessions ranging from regular work hours and higher hourly wages to overtime pay and the exclusive use of union members.[3] Even on war's eve a few years earlier, such explicit workplace demands and negotiations remained muffled and latent, and such tangible and collective advances proved unattainable. But far from passively accepting their exploitation, those toiling along Charleston's waterfront and elsewhere in the urban and maritime Old South audaciously laid the groundwork for astounding triumphs in the otherwise tragic New South.

This long and arduous struggle to shape the terms of wharf labor neither began nor ended during the early to mid-nineteenth century, however.[4] Still today the mostly black members of Charleston's Local 1422 of the International Longshoremen's Association (ILA) contend daily with limited community support and unabashed anti-union hostility from many officials in Columbia. In January 2000, state and municipal authorities unleashed hundreds of heavily armed law enforcement personnel in an unsuccessful attempt to break the dockworkers' association for daring to resist one shipping line's use of non-union laborers within the port. The subsequent indictment of five Charleston longshoremen—one white and four black union members—on trumped-up and ultimately dismissed felony charges of conspiring to incite a riot drew national attention, and serves as a contemporary exhibition of the trials and tribulations with which those laboring on southern waterfronts have grappled for over three hundred years.[5]

Impactful and relevant far beyond Charleston and the South, this pre–Civil War confrontation and its complicated dynamics of race, class, and labor relations should be viewed through the street-level experiences and perspectives of the workingmen, and occasionally workingwomen. Like their postbellum and present-day counterparts, those laboring on the wharves and levees of antebellum cities—whether in Charleston or New Orleans, New York or Boston, or elsewhere in the Atlantic World—were indispensable to the flow of commodities into and out of these ports.[6] So crucial were these workers, in fact, that government authorities and employers everywhere wrestled with balancing on the one hand the necessity of free movements and communications among the labor force, and the impulse on the other hand to manage those who worked, especially if coerced or enslaved. But despite their large numbers and the key role that waterfront workers played in these cities' pre-mechanized, labor-intensive commercial economies, too little is known about who these laborers were and the work they performed. Though scholars have explored the history of dockworkers in ports throughout the world, they have given little attention to waterfront laborers and dock work in the pre–Civil War American South or in any slave society. Labor, however, can be further used as a prism to elucidate the borders of slavery and freedom, restriction and agency, reaction and progress, and workers' liminal position betwixt and between.

Such an approach also informs our understanding of waterfront laborers in free northern ports such as New York, Boston, or Philadelphia by demonstrating how the institution of slavery fundamentally altered the working-class experience and environment. White men toiling on antebellum northern waterfronts, for instance, may have encountered labor competition from a few free black workers; but they never contended with large numbers of slaves deemed naturally suited to the work and better "acclimated" to local diseases. Dockworkers north of the Mason-Dixon Line were aware of and sometimes participated in debates over abolition, emancipation, and slave insurrection; but they never were required to navigate the rival security and commercial interests of southern slaveowners, merchants, and legislators. Nor were they forced to consider the risks and rewards of laboring as free men amid a deluge of laws and regulations intended to control and exploit free black and enslaved fellow workers, but which frequently swept up whites as well. As with much in the southern past, then, the distinctive experiences of the region's antebellum dockworkers reveal much about the working conditions, mores, and lives of laborers throughout the nation and the Atlantic World.

Even the trajectory of Charleston's antebellum commercial economy is altered when viewed from the workers' perspectives. At the time of Charleston's founding in the late seventeenth century, sailing vessels conveying goods to and from Europe, Africa, and the Americas followed a clockwise route dictated by the prevailing winds of the North Atlantic and the flow of oceanic currents. Advantageously located along the western edge of this flourishing beltline of Atlantic World trade, Charleston basked in a "golden age of commerce" as ship captains throughout the eighteenth and early nineteenth centuries called at the port to unload and load cargo before proceeding to cities farther north along the American coast and then on to Europe. But the ruinous Panic of 1819 marked the end of Charleston's halcyon days as the preeminent seaport in the American South. The 1820s ushered in a forty-year period of relative economic decline that culminated in the waterfront's devastation during the Civil War.[7]

Several factors contributed to the passing of the city's commercial reign. The launch of faster steamships brought down the curtain on the age of sail, with trading vessels no longer having to follow a circular path around the perimeter of the Atlantic. Ships thereafter could navigate directly between Europe and northern American ports, thus bypassing Charleston. The shallow bar across the entrance to Charleston Harbor also hindered an increasing number of larger vessels from reaching the city's wharves. Other shipowners and captains boycotted or were driven away by the city's and state's ever more contentious political and sectional stances.

Above all, Eli Whitney's invention of a new cotton gin in 1793 and the subsequent cotton boom prompted a decades-long westward migration of planters and slaves from the depleting soil of Charleston's vast hinterlands to the rich lands of Alabama, Mississippi, Louisiana, and Texas. South Carolina, as a result, went from being the nation's leading cotton producer in 1821 to the fourth ranked in 1850 and the seventh in 1860.[8] Planters in these new southwestern states shipped their cotton out of Gulf Coast ports like Mobile and New Orleans. Making matters worse for South Carolina's commercial gentry, New York shippers began operating regular coastal packets in the early 1820s to transport cotton from Charleston to the northern port, where the bales were transferred to larger oceangoing vessels and shipped to European ports such as Liverpool, London, and Le Havre. Though Charleston continued to export some of its cotton directly to Europe, New York interests pocketed a substantial portion of the profits for those bales conveyed across the Atlantic via New York, a major financial loss for lowcountry merchants and businessmen.[9]

It is understandable, then, why scholars routinely have depicted mid-nine-teenth-century Charleston as a peripheral port with a sluggish, dilapidated commercial waterfront absent of the hustle, bustle, and relevance of its past. Even the city's national census ranking slid over time, descending from the fourth most populous municipality in 1790 and the sixth in 1820, to only the fifteenth in 1850 and the twenty-second in 1860. But most economic studies of Charleston after 1819 focus on the waning fortunes of South Carolina's planters, factors, wharf owners, bankers, and other elites. This inquiry considers instead how waterfront workers were affected by and reacted to Charleston's struggles to keep pace with more rapidly expanding southern cotton ports.

Population and National Ranking of Charleston,
South Carolina, 1790–1860

Year	Whites	Slaves	Free Blacks	Total	Rank
1790	8,089	7,684	586	16,359	4th
1800	9,630	9,819	1,024	20,473	5th
1810	11,568	11,671	1,472	24,711	5th
1820	11,229	12,652	1,475	25,356	6th
1830	12,828	15,354	2,107	30,289	6th
1840	13,030	14,673	1,558	29,261	10th
1850	20,012	19,532	3,441	42,985	15th
1860	23,376	13,909	3,237	40,522	22nd

Source: Coclanis, *Shadow of a Dream*, 115, table 4.4; www.census.gov.

Charleston's commercial decline was chiefly comparative. The state's production of cotton actually increased significantly between 1800 and 1860. White and black South Carolinians cultivated approximately 20 million pounds of cotton in 1801, 40 million pounds in 1811, and 50 million in 1821. By 1850 the state's plantations and farms turned out over 150 million pounds of the staple, and nearly 177 million in 1860. Rice production also was on the rise in South Carolina. On the eve of the American Revolution at least 73 million pounds of rice were grown in the state each year. By 1850, over 104 million pounds of rice were produced, and a decade later planters generated more than 117 million pounds of the staple.[10]

Escalating cash crop production triggered a corresponding rise in rice and especially cotton exported from Charleston. The transportation and market revolutions in the first half of the nineteenth century—highlighted in South Carolina first by the opening in 1800 of the Santee Canal connecting the upcountry to the lowcountry, then by the completion of the South Carolina Railroad linking the plantations along the Savannah River to Charleston in 1833—further facilitated the upsurge of cotton arriving in the port.[11] Between 1822 and 1829, an average of 172,000 cotton bales were exported annually from Charleston. An average of about 225,000 bales were shipped each year in the 1830s, 309,000 in the 1840s, and 451,000 in the 1850s. Over half a million bales of cotton were loaded onto vessels at Charleston's docks in 1855, 1856, and 1860. In addition, tens of thousands of rice tierces and hundreds of thousands of bushels of rough or unmilled rice were shipped from the port each year during these decades.[12]

Unimpressed visitors filled letters and diaries with stinging remarks about ramshackle warehouses, unpaved streets, and austere lodgings they encountered in Charleston between 1820 and the Civil War.[13] Waterfront property owners and employers wrung their hands over dwindling profits and "the drudgery of the wharf business."[14] It is true that an increasing proportion of cotton shipped from Charleston was stowed aboard vessels bound for New York City rather than directly for Europe, rendering the trade less remunerative for many Charlestonians than previously. And it is undeniable that by 1820 New Orleans dethroned Charleston as the "Queen City of the South," exporting over a million bales of cotton a dozen times between 1843 and 1859, and over 2 million bales in 1860.[15] But to a drayman, wharf hand, or stevedore in Charleston, the city's comparative standing to other southern ports, the number of cotton bales being shipped from competing entrepôts, and the commodity's price and destination were irrelevant. Mounting quantities of cotton, rice, and other goods for export, to say nothing of ample imports, meant more work and more workers on Charleston's docks. As the city's Chamber of Commerce reported in 1828, by boosting the number of cotton bales arriving in the port, "you necessarily give more employment to labour, which diffuses a general benefit throughout all classes of society . . . drayage, porterage, mending, weighing, commissions, &c. every department of industry would be benefited."[16] Regardless of the shipping route or final port of call, every bale had to be transported to the wharves, pressed, marked, and weighed, stored into warehouses and then removed to shipside, hoisted onto vessels and into ships' holds, and finally stowed skillfully and laboriously into place. For waterfront workers, what mattered was that more cotton than ever before was arriving at the commercial wharves, generating a heightened and empowering demand for their essential labor.

By focusing on Charleston's commercial decline relative to ports such as New Orleans and then turning their scholarly attention elsewhere, historians have neglected the worker's-eye view of crucial events and developments in one of the Atlantic World's most historically significant cities. Alternative southern ports—Baltimore, Norfolk, Wilmington, Savannah, Pensacola, Mobile, Biloxi, New Orleans, Galveston—too could be examined to study shifting interpretive frameworks of race, class, and labor, as well as the transition from slavery to freedom, in an enticement-filled urban waterfront environment.[17] But aside from the prodigious assemblage of both primary and secondary sources pertaining to South

Carolina's foremost entrepôt, the city's and the state's import between the end of the American Revolution and the beginning of the Civil War is incontestable. Even after the sun had set on the port's commercial heyday and the city entered a period of relative populational decline, Charleston remained almost continuously in the regional, national, and international spotlight. It was in Charleston, after all, where Denmark Vesey plotted one of the South's most expansive and enduringly compelling slave insurrections in 1822. In response to this abortive revolt, South Carolina became the first of the southern Atlantic and Gulf Coast states to pass "Negro Seamen Acts" designed to thwart seditious communications between northern and foreign free black sailors and seaboard slaves in ports such as Charleston. It was South Carolina too that championed the doctrine of nullification and pushed the nation to the brink of constitutional crisis and war in Charleston Harbor in late 1832 and early 1833. And in December 1860, of course, it was in Charleston where prominent South Carolinians gathered to become the first southern slaveholding state to secede from the Union, and where Confederate forces fired upon Fort Sumter in April 1861 to commence the Civil War. Far less known are the concurrent and entwined struggles of those laboring and living along the docks of this consequential port city. But when relocating waterfront workers and their labor from the margins to the center of such a momentous past—reframing their role from mere observers to critical actors in that antebellum history—the ability and intrepidity of recently unshackled freedmen to swiftly organize and take on the challenges of their new yet familiar postbellum employment environment is not so surprising and puzzling after all.

Chapter One

"Using violent exercise in warm weather"

The Waterfront Labor
Experience and Environment

Black and white all mix'd together,
Inconstant, strange, unhealthful weather
Burning heat and chilling cold
Dangerous both to young and old
Boisterous winds and heavy rains
Fevers and rheumatic pains
Agues plenty without doubt
Sores, boils, the prickling heat and gout
Musquitos on the skin make blotches
Centipedes and large cock-roaches
Frightful creatures in the waters
Porpoises, sharks and alligators
Houses built on barren land
No lamps or lights, but streets of sand
. . .
The markets dear and little money
Large potatoes, sweet as honey
Water bad, past all drinking
Men and women without thinking
Every thing at a high price
But rum, hominy and rice

. . .

Many a bargain, if you strike it,
This is Charles-town, how do you like it.

> Captain Martin, 1769, quoted
> in Edgar, *South Carolina,* 155

Not long after Charleston's relocation in 1680 to the peninsula formed by the confluence of the Cooper and Ashley rivers, commercial wharves began protruding from the walled city's eastern fortifications (see figure 1). Though only 68 trading vessels dropped anchor within the harbor in 1706, 217 ships moored at the port's eight wharves in 1739. By the 1760s and early 1770s more than 500 oceangoing and hundreds of additional coastal and plantation vessels docked at the waterfront each year.[1] Benefiting from a capacious harbor with docks located only a few miles from the open Atlantic Ocean, Charleston was British North America's third busiest seaport in 1770, surpassed in total annual tonnage by only Philadelphia and Boston. As the number of commercial vessels calling at the port increased, new and impressive wharves sprouted. On the eve of American independence, local revolutionary leader and merchant Christopher Gadsden undertook the seven-year construction of Gadsden's Wharf, a landing that extended nearly a thousand feet into the Cooper River and accommodated up to thirty vessels at a time (see figure 2).[2]

Writing in the twilight of the colonial era and amid the erection of Gadsden's impressive wharf, Captain Martin vividly captured in verse many of the harsh realities of waterfront labor and life in South Carolina's principal entrepôt. Rebuffing many visitors' idyllic depictions of refinement, opulence, and gentility among the lowcountry elite, this British naval commander instead described his littoral surroundings in unromantic and uncensored terms. Those struggling to earn a living along the water's edge—whether black or white, enslaved or free—faced daily drudgery, discomfort, and danger. Assisted during the first half of the nineteenth century by only the most rudimentary of equipment and techniques, waterfront workers toiled long hours hauling goods to and from the wharves, unloading and loading vessels, and stowing cargo into cramped and stifling ships' holds. They sang work songs to hasten the passage of time and to synchronize and energize their efforts, but also as an outlet for their collective lamentations and grievances about their labor conditions and environment. Not just taxing and unpleasant, wharf labor was exceptionally dangerous, with a great many ways to become injured, maimed, or even killed. But fully conscious of these pitfalls and far from passively resigned to their unenviable fate, Charleston's dockworkers doggedly forged conventions and laid claim to a host of customary rights that vexed local and state authorities for decades to come.

Though contemporary accounts of waterfront labor and laborers are rare, travelers often were attentive to the diverse array of commercial vessels and goods all about Charleston's early-to-mid-nineteenth-century wharves. French botanist François André Michaux reported in October 1801, for instance, that the port was "generally full of small vessels from Boston, Newport, New York, and Philadelphia, and from all the little intermediate ports." Other observers extended this list into the Caribbean and across the Atlantic to include ships from Havana, London, Liverpool, Manchester, Glasgow, Greenock, and Le Havre.[3] In November 1839 seaman Charles Barron wrote to his father in Maine that, in addition to many steamboats, there were approximately two hundred sailing vessels within the harbor.[4] And surveying a scene that stretched over half a mile along the city's Cooper River waterfront, the editor of the *Illustrated London News,* Scotsman Charles Mackay, commented in March 1858, "The wharves of Charleston . . . present an animated spectacle, and the port is filled with vessels" (see figure 6).[5]

But what most fascinated those strolling along East Bay Street or down the many cobblestone lanes and alleyways that ran toward the Cooper River were the immense quantities of commercial goods piled upon the wharves. "Nothing but bales of [cotton] and barrels of rice are seen in the lower part of the city," wrote Swedish scholar Carl David Arfwedson. "The streets and quays are sometimes so filled with them," he added, "that the agility of a sailor is required to effect a passage."[6] Apart from this maze of merchandise, one anonymous traveler took note of the many "Spacious & substantial" brick storehouses that could accommodate tens of thousands more parcels of cotton and rice.[7] By 1847 the City Council proudly reported that Charleston's warehouses could hold 100,000 cotton bales, and that it was common for between 40,000 and 50,000 bundles to be stored there at any one time. Cotton factors Oswell Reeder and John B. DeSaussure wrote to Camden planter A. H. Boykin in March 1856 that over 60,000 bales of the staple were in the port and awaiting shipment (see figures 16 and 24).[8]

Charleston's commercial trade extended far beyond cotton and rice, however. Journalist Walter Thornbury noticed "brown sheaves of tobacco . . . black casks of tar, pitch, and turpentine, from the North Carolina and western forests," whereas fellow Englishman Robert Russell highlighted the considerable exportation of lumber. Others found imports most intriguing. The Frenchman Michaux enumerated provisions such as flour, salt, potatoes, onions, carrots, beetroots, apples, and oats, as well as planks and other building materials. State and local officials, meanwhile, established rates of wharfage, storage, and weighing for hundreds of mercantile goods ranging from indigo, hemp, lime, and coal to toys, tea, chocolate, and cigars.[9]

One of the most detailed, though much romanticized, descriptions of "the great seaport of Charleston" and its commercial articles was penned in 1828 by Scottish author and Royal Navy officer Basil Hall:

I was much struck with the sort of tropical aspect which belonged more to the port of Charleston than to any other I saw in America. I remember one day in particular, when, tempted by the hopes of catching a little of the cool sea breeze, I strolled to the shore. In two minutes after leaving the principal street, I found myself alongside of vessels from all parts of the world, loading and unloading their cargoes. On the wharf, abreast of a vessel just come in from the Havannah, I observed a great pile of unripe bananas, plucked from the trees only four or five days before in the Island of Cuba. Close by these stood a pyramid of cocoa nuts, equally fresh, some with their husks still on, some recently stripped of their tough wiry coating. The seamen were hoisting out of the hold of a ship, bags of coffee and large oblong boxes of sugar. . . . On every side the ground was covered, in true commercial style, with great bales of cotton, boxes of fruit, barrels of flour, and large square cases of goods, built one upon the top of another, with the owner's initials painted upon them within mystical circles and diamonds, visible between the crossings of the cords which had held them tight on their voyage from Europe or from India. The whole scene, though anything but new to me, was certainly not on that account less pleasing. The day, also, was bright and sunny, and the numerous vessels which fringed the wharf, or were scattered over the ample bay, were lying with their sails loosed to dry. I almost fancied myself again in the equatorial regions; a vision which brought many scenes of past voyages crowding upon my recollection.[10]

Many contemporaries, however, lacked Hall's intimate familiarity with the maritime environment and thus his favorable and nostalgic sensory reaction. Visitors more typically were struck by the commercial waterfront's putrid odors and relentless din than its semitropical and invigorating qualities. The inviting smells of fresh coffee and fruit mingled with those of tobacco juice, fish, and bilgewater. The sun's rays beat upon a mixture of exposed pluff mud and decaying matter beneath the wharves, saturating the air all along the docks with a distinctive funk.[11] Some of the cargo too was especially noxious. The stench of guano was so pungent and offensive, for example, that Charlestonians living on East Bay Street near the commercial wharves petitioned the City Council in June 1854 "complaining of the annoyance and inconvenience" of having the fertilizer unloaded and stored so near their residences.[12]

Nor was the waterfront a tranquil place. Coopers and ship carpenters hammered away at their trades, the wheels of drays and carts rumbled noisily over cobblestone streets and the wooden planks of the wharves, and scores of hucksters—men, women, and children—tenaciously hawked their wares and services.[13] Cotton and rice brokers similarly beseeched prospective buyers to sample the port's principal staples. "The ear is continually annoyed with sounds proclaiming the price of these articles," the Swede Arfwedson grumbled in 1832.[14] Wharf managers (known as wharfingers), merchants, and ship masters, meanwhile, barked orders to the throngs of laborers and seamen scurrying hither and thither. As mariner Henry P. Burr wrote to his family in 1838, "My ears have been so long grated" with the profane language of his captain, who was "often heard in his out-breakings to every ship 2 or 3 docks on each side of us." So loud and persistent was the swearing, in fact, the captain had "become notorious."[15]

But since maritime commerce was seasonal, such hubbub waxed and waned under the dictates of nature's clock. The wharves boomed with activity when there were cotton, rice, and other exports to be shipped, and slid into relative sluggishness during the growing season when cash crops were yet to be harvested.[16] The shipping season began in October when bales of cotton and tierces of rice began flowing into the port, and roared on until Christmas when waterfront commerce momentarily came to a standstill.[17] But with the New Year also arrived the annual peak of the trading season, which continued into the spring and through the end of April. Robert Russell remarked during his visit to the city in January 1855, "The greater part of the business being transacted in winter, the wharves were covered with bales of cotton, and the harbour crowded with ships." During the summer, however, waterfront activity slowed until the fall and the beginning of a new commercial cycle.[18]

Cotton's long journey to Charleston's wharves began on thousands of Carolina and Georgia plantations and farms, where field hands picked, ginned, and baled the cash crop, and then hauled the bundles to the nearest navigable river and loaded them onto small plantation boats or schooners bound for the port (see figure 8). When the cotton arrived at the entrepôt's commercial waterfront, boat hands and dockworkers unloaded or "landed" the bales and any other cargo. Some planters alternatively sent their cotton to Charleston on carts or wagons down bumpy rural roads. And after 1833 an increasing proportion of the cotton exported from Charleston was conveyed to the city by train, with draymen transporting the bales from the railroad depots to the Cooper River wharves (see figures 7, 13, and 17). But whether via plantation boat, country cart, or railcar, when the hundreds of thousands of cotton bales and barrels of rice reached the waterfront, as one clerk later put it, "work was on."[19]

Cotton in particular required many tenders, and the wharves bustled six days a week from dawn until dusk as various persons sampled, classed, priced, and marketed the staple.[20] Though sometimes crudely pressed on the plantation, cotton bales were compacted again in the city. "After the bales come from the planters to a seaport like Charleston," Englishman John Henry Vessey explained during his visit in 1859, "they are compressed by steam power, or they would take up too much space on shipboard." Walter Thornbury described a cotton press in 1860 New Orleans. When the bales first arrived on the Crescent City's levee from plantations along the Mississippi River, they were "fluffy on the edges, and white handfuls of cotton bunched out at the tears of the sacking." But when subjected to the "creaking and groaning" press, the bales were transformed from "a mere disheveled bundle of loose cotton" into "a neat, hard, square parcel, even and compact." Sailor Charles Nordhoff maintained that, after compressed to half its original size, a bale was "as solid, and almost as hard as a lump of iron."[21] In addition to conveying goods around the city and between the railroad yards and the wharves, many of Charleston's draymen found employment shuttling bales to and from the various cotton presses located near or on the waterfront. Fitzsimons's Wharf factor John Schulz frequently paid free black drayman Alexander Harleston and other transportation workers in the 1810s and 1820s for "Drayage to [Cotton] Screw & back."[22] North Boyce's Wharf factor and commission merchant Charles T. Mitchell likewise engaged the services of another free black drayman, Thomas Cole, who in the 1850s and early 1860s collected hundreds of dollars in cash each year for hauling cotton and other goods consigned to Mitchell.[23]

Charleston's waterfront employers also hired laborers, both male and female, to stitch torn cotton bagging. "Cotton on account of its being thrown several times from one boat into another," explained a Chamber of Commerce report, "arrives in bad order . . . and is then subject to much expense for mending."[24] John Schulz, for example, "Paid Negro hire Mending Cotton Bales" 50 cents on May 31, 1819, and between 1856 and 1861 Charles T. Mitchell made cash payments ranging from $1.60 up to an astounding $202 to a slave mender named Berney.[25] Charlestonian Daniel E. Huger Smith clarified how such a menial but necessary task could be so costly. "The mending was done by a gang of cotton menders to whom this charge was paid over," the exporter recalled, "they supplying their own twine and bagging as well as the labor."[26] At some point, meanwhile, cotton bales were weighed, and goods of all types marked with symbols and numbers indicating their owners or consignees. English painter Eyre Crowe, who accompanied novelist William Makepeace Thackeray to Charleston in March 1853, was captivated by a young slave, who "with brush in hand, dipp[ed] it into a tar-pot, in order to mark the proper hieroglyphics upon the side of the compressed cotton bale. There he sits enthroned—not a bad emblem of the saying 'Cotton is king'" (see figures 12, 24, and 25).[27] It was, of course, the enslavement rather than the elevation of southern blacks on both rural plantations and urban waterfronts that enabled the preeminence of cotton.

Goods not immediately required at shipside for loading were either piled upon the open wharves or placed in storage. Once drayed or rolled to waterfront warehouses, the hefty burdens often were manually hoisted to an upper story with the assistance of little more than a rope and tackle or inclined plane.[28] When needed for shipment, this painstaking and strenuous process was reversed, with the goods being removed from storage and drayed or rolled to awaiting vessels. Waterfront employers, in the meantime, engaged local workers to unload and load the freight. When the brig *Alexis* arrived at Gadsden's Wharf in July 1823, for instance, factor Charles Edmondston hired an unspecified number of "labourers for discharging the Cargo & relading" the vessel. He also paid a drayman to transport turpentine and cotton unloaded from the *Alexis* to a warehouse or store in the city.[29] In February 1833 the captain of the *Robin Hood,* Joseph Nickerson, similarly hired anywhere from two to eleven slaves each day to assist his crew in discharging ballast and loading the ship with rice and cotton.[30]

Not all ports utilized the same methods to unload and load vessels, and Charleston lagged many European seaports in the adoption of waterfront innovations. But not everyone was aware of Charleston's technological backwardness. As early as 1742, merchant Robert Pringle wrote to Englishmen William Cookson and William Welfitt that the packages they had shipped from Hull were so huge that they "Occasion'd a great Deal of trouble, [and] Inconveniency in landing them." According to Pringle, one bale of their goods was equal in size to four standard bundles in Charleston; he even declared, "Never was so Large a Bale seen here." So too with the English merchants' casks, which were "so ponderous & so Large." Colonial statutes permitted wharf owners "to build and erect . . . Cranes, Crane Houses, and Ware Houses" beginning in 1725. But, the Charlestonian explained, "We not being provided with Cranes & Such Convenienys [*sic*] for Landing goods as in England," the attempt to discharge the oversized cargo ended in disaster. While hoisting the first bulky cask out of the vessel's hold using Charleston's customary techniques and equipment—consisting of "canocks" or a basic tackle—the rim of the barrel broke under the massive weight and fell back into the hold and burst into pieces, causing damage to other goods awaiting discharge. Pringle therefore advised that, in the future, "Goods in the Smallest Packages are most Proper for this Place, [and] are always Landed in the Best Order."[31]

Indeed, very few if any dockside cranes were used in Charleston until long after the Civil War.[32] Dozens of plats depicting the city's waterfront in the late eighteenth and early to mid-nineteenth centuries reveal the locations and dimensions of not only the wharves, docks, and adjacent streets and passageways, but also warehouses, sheds, scales houses, and offices. But only two plats, both produced in 1824, portrayed cranes: three on Kunhardt's Wharf and one on Magwood's Wharf (see figure 5).[33] Unclear is whether these depictions were of existing or proposed devices; and regardless, a ship's spars and a block and tackle powered by dockworkers, sailors, and horses were the far more common means to unload and load ships in the South Carolina port.[34] Many trading vessels similarly were fitted with a jib hoist or a derrick, a simple lifting device consisting of a tackle fixed to the end of a beam that pivoted back and forth above the wharf and the vessel's hold. When Captain Nickerson docked the *Robin Hood* at a Charleston wharf in 1833, the first mate noted in the ship's log getting the vessel's derrick ready to discharge ballast.[35] The following description illustrated how this apparatus was used to load cotton in nearby Savannah: "Then a derrick from the ship let down a great hook and hoisted a bale on which knelt a Negro to balance the load. Up went the hook, while cotton and Negro moved slowly through the air; then down through the open hatch into the hold the bale was lowered, to be seized by the waiting packers and stowed away while the hook swung up and out again with the dangling Negro clinging to it. Bale after bale with its human ballast was thus lifted and dropped."[36] Dockworkers, both enslaved and free, participated in similar scenes along Charleston's antebellum waterfront.

A sketch of Charleston appearing in *Harper's Weekly* depicted another convention by which cotton and other goods were loaded in the port (see figure 23). Several drays line the wharf along the length of a ship. With the assistance of dockhands, draymen remove from their vehicles the large and weighty bales and maneuver them close to the vessel. But rather than ship's tackle or derrick, three inclined planes or gangplanks reach from the vessel's deck to the wharf below. The wharf laborers position a bale at the bottom of the nearest gangplank, where they prepare to attach a rope. This rope leads up the plank to the deck, where either the ship's seamen or other dockhands pull the bundle upward. In some cases the rope was connected to a hoisting device on the deck, such as a capstan or a windlass, which workers operated by pushing or pumping handles attached to the respective apparatus.[37]

A second instructive image from *Harper's Weekly*, a dock scene in New York City, showed workers unloading a vessel (see figure 22). Prominent in the foreground are two white horses connected to a system of ropes and pulleys. As the horses strain forward, a large bale rises out of the ship's hold and perches above the deck waiting to be lowered to the adjacent wharf.[38] Hoisting horses also were employed, of course, in antebellum Charleston to discharge and load trading vessels (see figures 8 and 21). An auction in May 1856 advertised horses that had "been used by stevedores for hoisting on the wharves." Many waterfront employers invested in horses of their own, including the proprietors of Adger's Wharves, who owned two horses in the years before the Civil War. When not themselves utilizing these horses, their owners often hired out the animals for three dollars a day, about three times the wages of many common laborers.[39]

Though the raw muscle of men and horses continued to power these relatively basic methods of unloading and loading ships in the years both before and after the Civil War, new tools, techniques, and technologies occasionally appeared on Charleston's waterfront. The late antebellum years, for instance, witnessed the advent of small mobile steam engines to assist with hoisting the unprecedented quantity of ever more unwieldy cotton bales arriving at the wharves.[40]

Charleston's 1859 city directory included an advertisement for A. L. Archambault, a manufacturer of portable steam engines in Philadelphia. These machines generated between four and thirty horsepower, and were mounted "On wheels with Tongues for Horses" to move them about the waterfront. On the market since July 1849, among the engines' diverse utilities was the unloading of cargo from commercial vessels.[41] It is impossible to know how many such hoisting devices were purchased and employed in the South Carolina port. But Archibald McLeish, a local machinist and wheelwright, informed Charlestonians in the pages of the 1860 city directory that he repaired items such as iron axles for drays and carts, weighing scales, and "Hoisting Machines for Stores."[42]

Back on the docks, after discharging imports and loading exports, a gang of laborers went to work stowing cotton and other outbound goods into a vessel's cargo hold. Consisting of five hands, one being the "header" or foreman, these work gangs toiled together to tightly pack compressed cotton bales into the hold using large jack screws.[43] When in Mobile Bay in the late 1840s or early 1850s, mariner Charles Nordhoff meticulously captured the work of these cotton screwmen, who were determined "to get into the ship as many pounds as she could be made to hold" by squeezing "three bales into a space in which two could be barely put by hand."

> It is for this purpose the jack-screws are used. A ground tier is laid first; upon this, beginning aft and forward, two bales are placed with their inner covers projecting out, and joining, leaving a triangular space vacant within. A hickory post is now placed against the nearest beam, and with this for a fulcrum, the screw is applied to the two bales at the point where the corners join, and little by little they come together, are straightened up, and fill up the triangular space. So great is the force applied, that not unfrequently [*sic*] the ship's decks are raised off the stancheons [*sic*] which support them, and the seams are torn violently asunder. . . . Cooped up in the dark and confined hold of a vessel, the gangs tug from morning till night at the screws, the perspiration running off them like water, every muscle strained to its utmost.

Nordhoff deemed cotton screwing not only "the most exhausting labor that is done on ship board," but also a task "requiring, besides immense strength, considerable experience in the handling of bales, and the management of the jackscrews." Proper and skillful stowage could increase the cargo capacity of a ship by about 15 percent. In this fashion, hundreds and even thousands of cotton bales were packed into a single vessel's hold.[44]

In Charleston and ports throughout the antebellum South, work songs were an integral and customary component of the waterfront labor process, especially the stowing of cotton. Whether in a plantation field or a ship's hold at a wharf, slaves in the American South employed work songs to coordinate and invigorate their movements, pass the time, and challenge their labor environments.[45] For those toiling on the wharves and stowing cotton, synchronized movement often was essential and therefore was the primary purpose of dockworkers' songs. As one early scholar of African American folk music explained, "To the Negro, to work in unison means to sing; so as the men strained at their task, a laboring chant arose whose fine-toned phrases were regularly cut by a sharp high cry, '*hey!*', which emphasized the powerful twisting of the [jack] screws by the rhythmic muscular movement of the singers. Verses without number were made up, and many were the cotton-packing chants." Offered as a typical example was the "Cott'n-Packing Song," which slaves sang "*ad infinitum*" while working on Savannah's riverfront. Not unlike field labor on many plantations, dock work had a cadence, and thus this song was described as "Absolutely rhythmic and rather slow, with regular and monotonous emphasis."[46]

> Screw dis cott'n,
> > *hey!*
> Screw dis cott'n,
> > *hey!*
> Screw dis cott'n,
> > *hey!*
> > Screw it tight—*hey!*
>
> Screw dis cott'n,
> > *hey!*
> Screw dis cott'n,
> > *hey!*
> Screw dis cott'n,
> > *hey!*
> > Wid all yo' might—*hey!*
>
> Here we come, boys,
> > *hey!*
> Here we come, boys,
> > *hey!*
> Here we come, boys,
> > *hey!*
> > Do it right—*hey!*
>
> Don't get tired,[47]
> > *hey!*

> Don't get tired,
> > *hey!*
> Don't get tired,
> > *hey!*
> > Time ain't long—*hey!*
>
> Keep on[48] workin',
> > *hey!*
> Keep on workin',
> > *hey!*
> Keep on workin',
> > *hey!*
> > Sing dis song—*hey!*[49]

The consistent and predictable rhythm of such songs kept the work gang in unison and the slaves' recurring retort of "*hey!*"—which accompanied the turning of the screw—was "a sharp, rather aspirant ejaculation," both of which rendered their physical efforts more forceful and efficient.[50]

New England ship captain James Carr recorded the lyrics of several work songs he heard on Charleston's docks in August 1815. "As you approach the wharves," the observant visitor wrote in his diary, "the Song of the negroes at work greet your eer [*sic*] cheerfully from every quarter." After discharging a cargo of lumber from Bangor, Maine, Carr rented four jack screws and hired four gangs of five slave dockworkers for five days to "work on board the ship stowing cotton" bound for Liverpool. The captain accompanied the slaves into the hold, where he facetiously remarked upon "the savoury smell that may be supposed to arise from twenty negroes using violent exercise in warm weather, in the hot and confined hold of ship and you may imagine what a delicious treat I enjoyed." But the singing "made such an impression on my mind, as to enable me to give a few specimans [*sic*] of the African working songs in Charleston." When toiling in gangs, Carr noted, the slaves "work & sing with all their might & whither hoisting, hauling, rowing or heaving at the Jack screw, they keep in perfect time in all their motions—this gives them more force as they are united & simultaneous in their exertion."

> Cheerly up, and cheerly down;
> > hey boys hey.
> Cheerly up, and cheerly down;
> > ho boys ho.
> Cheerly up, and cheerly down;
> > high land a.

> Cheerly up, and cheerly down;
> > high land o.[51]
>
> Sing talio, Sally is a fine girl, sing talio;
> Sally is a good girl, sing talio, sing talio;
> > hoora, hoora, sing talio.
> Sally in the morning, Susan in the evening;
> > Sing talio, sing talio;
> Sally is a sweet girl, Susan is a beauty;
> > sing talio, sing talio,
> > hoora, hoora, sing talio.[52]

One worker—typically the gang's header or foreman—sang "what they consider the words of the song," and then the entire gang belted out the chorus. According to Carr, the underscored words were the chorus, and those double-scored were "sung more loud & strong, in which the whole gang join with all their force, and generally much glee." Down in the hold amid this cacophony, the captain vividly recalled how "it often happened that they all had their throats open at the same time as loud as they cou'd ball." But he added, "The blacks having remarkable [*sic*] nice ears for music, are very correct in their time & pauses."[53]

Charles Nordhoff captured a similar soundscape several decades later in Mobile. With the cotton bales and jack screw in position,

> The gang, with their shirts off, and handkerchiefs tied about their heads, take hold the handles of the screws, the foreman begins the song, and at the end of every two lines the worm of the screw is forced to make one revolution, thus gaining perhaps two inches. Singing, or chanting as it is called, is an invariable accompaniment to working in cotton, and many of the screw-gangs have an endless collection of songs, rough and uncouth, both in words and melody, but answering well the purposes of making all pull together, and enlivening the heavy toil. The foreman is the chanty-man, who sings the song, the gang only joining in the chorus, which comes in at the end of every line, and at the end of which again comes the pull at the screw handles. One song generally suffices to bring home the screw, when a new set is got upon the bale, and a fresh song is commenced.

Among the four cotton-screwing songs that Nordhoff selected to chronicle was "Fire Maringo," variations of which could be heard throughout the mid-nineteenth-century Atlantic World as seamen transported the lyrics and tunes of this and scores of other waterfront and shipboard work songs from port to port.

Lift him up and carry him along,
    Fire, maringo, fire away,
Put him down where he belongs,
    Fire, maringo, fire away.
Ease him down and let him lay,
    Fire, maringo, fire away,
Screw him in, and there he'll stay,
    Fire, maringo, fire away.
Stow him in his hole below,
    Fire, maringo, fire away,
Say he must, and then he'll go,
    Fire, maringo, fire away.[54]

Because efficiency and a quick and steady work pace resulted in greater output and profits, ship captains and other waterfront employers recognized and appreciated the functional advantages of these ritual work songs. Both Nordhoff and Carr highlighted the "shrewd management" and central role of a gang's header or foreman, who led the singing as well as the work. Having studied the origins and history of African American music, Booker T. Washington wrote, "Whenever companies of Negroes were working together," including on antebellum southern wharves and levees, "some man or woman with an exceptional voice was paid to lead the singing, the idea being to increase the amount of labor by such singing."[55] Early twentieth-century ethnomusicologist Natalie Curtis Burlin too remarked that so widespread was the belief among employers that "the Negro labors best when he labors with song, that in old days a man who could lead the singing of a gang of workmen was well worth extra pay."[56] But, as traveler Charles Peabody discovered, a gang could become perturbed with this leader if the tempo of the selected songs became too brisk and the labor too arduous.[57] The pace of the work, after all, was among the most salient aspects of the labor process that enslaved and free dockworkers alike aimed to manipulate and even control.

But, between the time James Carr and Charles Nordhoff made their respective observations of southern cotton stowing, a new class of master stevedores emerged to superintend even the most proficient of the ports' manual laborers. During the early nineteenth century, Charleston's wharf hands, screwmen, and other marginally skilled waterfront workers sometimes were referred to as "stevedores," as on February 27, 1833, when Captain Joseph Nickerson's mate noted that local "stevedores [were] employed part of the day stowing cotton" aboard the *Robin Hood*.[58] Though the term continued to be conflated with and used by some contemporaries to describe more common dock laborers, the local meaning and function of the stevedore changed dramatically during the 1830s and 1840s. In these workers' own words, they explained, "I mean by stevedore the responsible man; the one who makes the contract and directs the work. He is the stevedore. Those that are in his employ are headers, foreman [*sic*], screw hands, &c."[59] Adept at properly, efficiency, and quickly stowing the maximum amount of cargo into a vessel's hold, stevedores both hired and supervised the port's dockhands in carrying out this vital and difficult task.[60]

These waterfront managers—who effectively paralleled white plantation overseers, with both black drivers (that is, the headers or foremen) and field slaves (the screwmen) beneath them—at first lacked guidelines on stowage based on scientific principles and requisite knowledge of ship construction, center of gravity, capacity, and so forth. But by the mid-nineteenth century, stevedores could study manuals such as John McLeod Murphy and W. N. Jeffers's *Nautical Routine and Stowage, with Short Rules in Navigation,* and Robert White Stevens's *On the Stowage of Ships and their Cargoes,* often simply referred to as *Stevens on Stowage.*[61] The authors of the former text pointed out in 1849 that it was only in the second quarter of the nineteenth century that "stowage became not only a distinct department by itself, but subsequently indeed, a separate profession." These books accordingly sought to educate the "professional stower" in the rules and practices—including "a few 'Yankee notions'"—that governed the adroit stowage of vessels.[62] *Stevens on Stowage,* for instance, detailed the correct preparation of a hold's ballast and dunnage for the receipt of cotton before issuing the following warning: "Great attention is required to see that as much as possible is put into the hold, but when screwed too tightly it has been known to rend a ship at sea." Former merchant seaman and scholar Stan Hugill contended that transatlantic cotton vessels came to be known as "coffin ships," since "Cotton, if it becomes damp, swells a great deal, and for this to happen to the bales, already jammed to their utmost capacity by the great jackscrews, was extremely serious. These wooden ships would virtually come apart at their seams and founder in the middle of the Atlantic, miles from port, all hands going to Davy Jones' Locker." With others' lives and property under their expert care, stevedores also were trained in averting the spontaneous combustion of the highly flammable bales.[63]

By the 1850s a cadre of highly skilled, compensated, and increasingly white stevedores had not only reshaped the hiring, work, and wage payment processes on Charleston's waterfront, but also ascended as a force in the city's political, economic, and labor struggles. Wharfingers, merchants, factors, and ship captains still engaged many waterfront laborers; but the employment of shipboard work gangs increasingly was entrusted to master stevedores intimately familiar with the physical strength, experience, and work habits of the individual hands. After being contracted to oversee the loading or unloading of a vessel, a stevedore personally selected, hired, and supervised his work gangs throughout the job. As for the disbursement of wages, shipowners or captains typically paid the stevedore in cash once a week while the work progressed, then gave him the balance when the stowage was complete. The stevedore subsequently distributed cash wages among his labor gangs either weekly or in a lump sum at the end of a job.[64]

Mercantile accounts track this payment process. The cash book of factor Charles T. Mitchell not only listed the payments he made to draymen and cotton menders, but also the money he doled out and took in for his clients. Many of these cash transactions were on behalf of shipowners whose vessels called in Charleston to fill with cotton bound for destinations such as New York or Liverpool. Though Mitchell usually did not specify the names of the stevedores who worked on his patrons' vessels, he meticulously recorded the payouts he made to them over a period of several years. Under an account for the owners of the ship *Home,* for instance, Mitchell entered a payment of $200 to a "stevedore on a/c [account] for Stowing"—which included both the transfer of goods from the dock onto the vessel and packing the cargo into the hold—on February 13, 1858. This disbursement was followed by an additional $200 on February 20, and finally the "Stevedore Bal[ance]. of Bill" of $203.84 on February 27. In all, this stevedore received $603.84 for overseeing the stowage of the *Home* over about a three-week period.[65] Even as the stevedore and his labor crew squeezed the last bales of cotton and other goods into the *Home*'s hold, another stevedore was beginning work on the ship *Alexandrine.* On February 20, Mitchell paid this second contractor $200, followed by installments of $280 on February 27, $170 on March 6, and finally $46.19 on March 13 for the "Bal of a/c for Stowing Cargo."[66]

Some stevedores were hired to discharge a vessel, which generally was less difficult, time consuming, and remunerative than stowing. This task nonetheless could require great effort and skill, and potentially was very dangerous. When a gang of Liverpool stevedores boarded Charles Nordhoff's vessel to unload the cotton screwed into the hold in Mobile, "it took fifteen men and two tackles an entire hour to break out six bales in the tier next the main hatchway."[67] Some of Charleston's discharging stevedores—men such as John Torrent and John Symons—doubled as riggers and possessed their own horses to assist with hoisting goods out of ships' holds.[68] In December 1858, for example, Charles T. Mitchell settled "Torrents [*sic*] Bill for discharging" the ship *Minnesota* totaling $145.28, in addition to nearly $800 paid out over five installments to another stevedore for stowing the vessel.[69]

The records of another merchant, Charles O. Witte, help elucidate these loading costs. When the Dutch bark *Nederland* was in Charleston in January 1860, the stevedore collected 23 cents for the stowage of each bale of cotton, 9 cents for tierces of rice, and 5 cents for barrels of rosin. It took the stevedore and his screw gangs twenty-seven days to stow 1,452 cotton bales, 220 tierces of rice, and 335 barrels of rosin, labor that cost the owners of the *Nederland* $402.01. Compensating the stevedore based upon the number of items stowed, rather than the time spent working, rewarded the skillful and efficient loading of the vessel. After all, the ability to pack an extra 100 cotton bales into a hold at 23 cents per bale put $23 more into the stevedore's pocket.[70] This arrangement, however, did not benefit those under the stevedore's supervision who toiled at the jack screws to squeeze in those additional bales. Most hired dockhands were paid a fixed daily or hourly rate and thus had an incentive to slow the pace of work and thus increase their wages. But stevedores were rewarded for speed. In the case of the loading of the *Nederland,* for instance, the contractor would have received the same total payment whether it took him and his screwmen two weeks or four weeks to complete the job. But if it only took two, the stevedore was able to pay his crew a smaller share of the earnings and then move on to the stowage of another vessel.

Shipowners and captains also embraced a fast work pace, since less time in port meant lower dockage charges and other costs and enabled additional revenue-generating voyages during the course of the year. Port rules or shipping contracts often specified a limited number of "running days" or "lay days" (Sundays usually excepted) to unload and load vessels, and required those captains who failed to clear the wharf in time to pay hefty demurrage fees.[71] It therefore was generally in the financial interest of merchants, factors, shipowners, and captains to have cargo discharged, loaded, and stowed as quickly as possible, and profits were slashed when slow work or bad weather delayed the departure of vessels. Charleston merchant and wharf owner Christopher Fitzsimons assured one client in 1810, "Your ships are loading as fast as circumstances will admit," and when the stowing of approximately 1,800 cotton bales was complete, "you will have two of the best cargoes of upland cotton ever shipped from this port." In 1859 Captain Henry C. Keene admitted to his ship's owners in Bath, Maine, that due to the difficult work of compressing and stowing cotton the stevedore was "progressing rather slowly in loading." Nonetheless, Keene promised that "we shall fill up as fast as possible" and attempt "to put away nearly 800,000 lbs." of the article, which was bound for Kronshtadt, Russia.[72] A stevedore and gang with a reputation for skill, efficiency, and speed, on the other hand, sometimes garnered public praise, surging contracts, and occasional bonuses. In April 1853, for example, the owners of the brig *Jessie Miller* paid a two-dollar "Gratuity to [the] stevedore's foreman" for a job well and quickly done.[73]

But chief among the drawbacks of working rapidly in such a strenuous and hazardous environment was the exacerbation of already too frequent waterfront injuries, accidents, and even deaths. Back injuries and hernias were ubiquitous among dockworkers. According to the city's wharf owners, the typical weight of a bale of cotton in 1790 was 200 pounds; but by 1856 that average had ballooned to 450 pounds. Cotton bales had become so cumbersome, in fact, that two and sometimes three dockhands were needed to handle and roll the bundles about the wharves, whereas only one worker sufficed in previous decades.[74] Meanwhile, Charleston's Chamber of Commerce standardized barrels of rice at 600 pounds, though some weighed even more.[75] Merchants' and factors' account books often documented the weight of each bale of cotton or barrel of rice handled, bought, or sold, and Charles T. Mitchell's records include a bale of cotton weighing a gargantuan 746 pounds.[76] Draymen had to lift and roll these burdens as well. Mayor Charles Macbeth reported to the City Council in 1858 that the "heavy loads which were carried by the carts, drays, &c."—many totaling 3,000 pounds—were so great that the vehicles' narrow wheels were breaking the streets. As one former slave drayman in Mississippi attested to a WPA interviewer, "dat wurk wus so heavy it most broke me down in my [loins]" (see figures 15, 17, and 25).[77]

The perils of waterfront labor included far more than injuries from excessive physical exertion, however. Those toiling on ships' decks, for instance, had to take care not to tumble through an open hatch. In April 1840 free black stevedore Archibald Cooler—the first stevedore, black or white, to appear in Charleston's city directories in the early 1830s—died after falling into a cargo hold.[78] Similarly, an Englishman named William Baxter was working for stevedore John Torrent in March 1856 when he "accidently fell through the forward hatch into the hold" of the steam packet *George's Creek,* which was being unloaded at Brown's Wharf. The fall fractured Baxter's skull, and after about four hours "death relieved him of his sufferings."[79]

All those who frequented the waterfront, in fact, had to take care where they walked and stood. Warehousemen and wharf hands rushing to remove goods from storage did not always exercise appropriate caution. In September 1804 the City Council passed an ordinance "to prevent the pernicious practice of throwing cotton in bales, goods, or any other articles from the second or upper floors of ware-houses, stores, or other buildings within the city of Charleston." Prompted by "several distressing accidents," the measure further prohibited cotton bales and other articles from being lowered "without a good and sufficient tackle and rope." Violators of this ordinance, including those permitting workers under their employ to throw goods from upper stories, were subject to a fifty- to hundred-dollar fine.[80] But it was much more costly, both in time and labor, to properly lower rather than simply heave cotton bales and other goods from the upper floor of a waterfront warehouse to the wharf or street below. As a consequence, a slave was killed instantly at the East Bay Street store of a merchant when a stack of iron bars fell on the bondsman in October 1835. Then on the afternoon of December 29, 1838, Irish-born merchant Samuel Patterson was standing near a wharf storehouse when a bale of cotton was "thrown on him from the upper story." Badly injured, the fifty-three-year-old Patterson was taken home but died a few hours later.[81]

Such tragic episodes prompted the periodic enforcement of the law. Factor John Lewis and wharfinger John Elford, for instance, were brought before the City Court and fined fifty dollars each in July 1840.[82] Some offending wharf managers, held accountable for the actions of their workers, petitioned the City

Council for relief from the penalty resulting from what they claimed was "an accidental violation of the Ordinance."[83] In June 1844, alderman Robert Seymour proposed a bill allowing goods to be lowered with a parbuckle—a sling usually made of rope that could be used to roll or pull barrels and bales of goods up or down an inclined plane—"or some other safe mode other than the one now prescribed." In December 1845 the council indeed amended the 1804 ordinance to permit the use of parbuckles to "lower Cotton in Bales, Goods, or any other articles in bales, from the second floor of warehouses, stores, or buildings, situated to the east of East Bay Street."[84]

Not even horses could withstand a descending cotton bale. In one stunning accident, the *Charleston Mercury* reported, "A horse attached to a dray belonging to Mr. McClue, was instantly killed yesterday morning by the cotton, with which the dray was loaded, falling on him. It appears that another dray being driven rapidly along the Bay, the two came in contact; and in attempting to get clear of each other, the tail of one of the drays struck the legs of Mr. McClue's horse, causing him to fall; and the cotton rolling off the dray on him, crushed him to death."[85] Draymen too encountered life-threatening perils while working on or near the wharves. One slave drayman was killed instantly near the Exchange Building at the corner of East Bay and Broad streets after his horse spooked and the bondsman jumped or was thrown to the ground.[86] During all steps of the waterfront labor process, from the draying of goods to the stowing of cotton, speed meant heightened danger for the workers.

When waterfront accidents did not end in death, the injuries could be devastating nonetheless. When the horse of a slave carter took fright in 1847, the driver's leg was broken and had to be amputated.[87] One ship captain had his leg snapped "by a bale of cotton falling on it," and Adger's Wharf commission merchant T. L. Wragg "had his foot crushed so severely, that amputation was necessary."[88] Alms house hospital records showed waterfront workers being treated for injuries including a broken tibia, fractured cranium, sprained ankle, bruises, and wounds of the side, head, and sternum.[89] In addition to medical care from the alms house, some injured workers turned to local charities for aid. In December 1845 the Hibernian Society's Committee on Relief gave ten dollars to Mrs. Sweeney after her husband—probably Irish drayman John Sweeney—broke his leg. And in March 1852, Charles Patrick and his wife similarly received fifty dollars from the New England Society "to procure a comfortable passage home" to Westport, Connecticut, after Patrick had been "disabled by an accident from getting a livelihood" in Charleston.[90]

Drowning was another common risk for those who entered the hustle and bustle of the waterfront. In all, death records cataloged 310 drownings among whites, free blacks, and slaves in Charleston between August 1819 and April 1865. Of those 310 deaths, 293 or 94.5 percent of the victims were male; and of the 293 men who drowned during those years, 248 or 84.6 percent were sixteen years of age or older. In other words, 248 or exactly 80 percent of the 310 people officially recorded as drowning in Charleston over a period of nearly half a century were men of working age. Some of these victims, of course, died while fishing, bathing, or swimming, and others perished during flash floods or hurricanes. A few no doubt fell into a dock or mill pond while in a drunken stupor. But scores were men who drowned while toiling as wharf hands, stevedores, seamen, captains, clerks, and merchants on the city's commercial wharves.[91]

In January 1832, for example, a slave fell from Gibbs's North Wharf and his body was not recovered until the next day. One of factor and wharf owner George Chisolm's bondsmen was found drowned in a dock in September 1834. Likewise, three slaves belonging to Accommodation Wharf owner Joseph Prevost drowned in March 1855, and two "valuable negroes" owned by captains Barlin and Brooks drowned "off from the Wharf where the Steamer Gordon was laying" in August 1859.[92] Waterfront clerks as well were prone to falling or being knocked into the docks. Zamba, a slave who claimed to be an African king, worked as a porter in his master's auction store on Vendue Range. He recalled saving a young Scottish clerk named Mr. Thomson in the early years of the 1800s. Zamba and Thomson had been ordered to go down to the wharf and arrange for some goods to be unloaded from a vessel for a sale the next day. According to the slave's account, "The ship lay across the end of one of the wharves, and was a few feet distant from the land; in walking up the plank which reached to the ship's gangway, Mr. Thomson unfortunately slipped his foot, and was instantly swept by the tide, which runs pretty strong here, astern of the ship, and in a few minutes would have been far out in the harbour. At this season, sharks were tolerably plentiful about the harbour, ranging about for prey at all times; so that poor Mr. Thomson, who could only swim a few strokes, was in imminent danger." Able to "swim like a seagull," Zamba quickly jumped into the water and reached Mr. Thomson just as he was about to sink below the surface. With Thomson "in a state of insensibility" and Zamba "well ducked and completely out of breath," a boat soon came alongside and pulled the two men to safety.[93]

As this narrative suggests, drowning was not the only threat to life and limb if a worker fell off a wharf or docked vessel. Merchant John Holland's young slave slipped off of Crafts's Wharf in September 1810, and while being swept away by the tide was "dragged down by a shark." When the predator was caught, pieces of the slave's arm and coat were found in its maw.[94] The *Charleston Courier* announced in August 1818 that a shark measuring twelve feet long and six feet around had been caught at Daniell's Wharf, and advised readers, "This should operate as a caution to persons who are in the habit of bathing at the different wharves in the city."[95] Nor was the proximity of these sharks to the wharves a mere fluke. During the 1840s and 1850s, master cooper Jacob Schirmer frequently noted in his diary the capture of large sharks "off Southern Wharf" or "near the Wharves," some measuring over eleven feet long.[96]

Severe weather oftentimes posed a threat to exposed dockworkers. Captain Henry P. Burr wrote to his sister in July 1845 about "the enervating effect of the weather" in Charleston, and described how "the oppressive heat disinclines one from any exertion beyond what necessary business calls for." But for those living hand to mouth, waterfront wage labor was a necessity that transcended any disinclination or debilitation brought on by searing summer heat. One month prior to Burr's letter, Schirmer recorded that a seaman had died on Magwood's Wharf "by Heat internally & externally." Nor was Burr entirely immune to the effects of the heat, complaining to his father during a later trip to the city in June 1847 about "a most severe headache . . . brought on by exposure to the sun."[97]

Charleston was no stranger to brutal and dangerous heat waves.[98] When scorching temperatures swept through the city in July and early August 1854, scores of workingmen died. The *Charleston Standard* reported that "men and animals have been overcome and dropped lifeless in the streets," including one inhabitant who "fell upon the pavement as though he had been shot." Michael Kennedy, "a native of Ireland, and employed as a drayman by Mr. Woodside," suffered sunstroke and died within half an hour. Another Irishman, named Carey, expired shortly after he "was overcome by the heat on Union wharf."[99] On July 4, 1860, Jacob Schirmer observed that, despite a pleasant morning, the day was "very hot and so intense was the heat that an unusual number of deaths have taken place by Sun Stroke." After the Independence Day festivities concluded and the well-to-do retreated to the relative cool of their piazzas and parlors, working people remained exposed. On July 6, the *Charleston Mercury* declared, "It has been terrible; for eight long days our citizens have panted and sweltered." Temperatures reached as high as 102 degrees, resulting in "a record of deaths from exposure, sun strokes, &c., unexampled in the history of Charleston." In addition to those reported dead on previous days, the *Mercury* informed readers that a cooper on Gadsden's Wharf named Peter Dolan, who "had been complaining of the heat on Monday and Tuesday," died suddenly on Wednesday afternoon. Also "prostrated from the excessive heat," a drayman named Myers was stricken and taken to the ice house, where he was revived. The newspaper continued "the sad record of the unfortunate and often fatal results from this terrific term" on July 7, including three laborers being treated at the city's Roper Hospital.[100]

Bitter cold also made for miserable and sometimes dangerous work conditions. Christopher Fitzsimons wrote to Gustavus and Hugh Colhoun in Philadelphia in February 1803 explaining that "a heavy fall of snow has so completely inundated our streets that it would be almost impracticle [sic] and certainly injurious to ship cotton at such a crisis." In January 1834, Schirmer observed that freezing rain had created icicles that were hanging from the trees. A few weeks later,

Vanderhorst's Wharf manager John Crawford wrote to owner Elias Vanderhorst that one of the enslaved dockhands, Dublin, had been unable to work for some time. "During the late Icy weather," Crawford elucidated, "he fell down & broke one or two of his Ribs."[101] Such treacherous work conditions were not unusual. Jacob Schirmer recurrently noted the "stinging cold," "thick Ice," sleet, and snow he encountered on the waterfront.[102] "Raw Rainy & Cold. . . . weather very unpleasant, looks like snow," he wrote on January 19, 1851. And on New Year's Day 1856, the cooper complained that "the weather was so unpleasant that very little work could be done."[103]

If all of these risks were not enough, waterfront laborers also had to beware of lightning strikes, hailstorms, ship and cotton fires, bursting steamship boilers, and the falling walls of dilapidated warehouses, not to mention a regular traffic of drunkards, pickpockets, and violent criminals.[104] Stray dogs roamed the wharves, and "wild cattle dash[ed] madly about the streets" while being driven from the southernmost landings to butcher pens in the city's northern neighborhoods.[105] Vessels docked at the waterfront with captains and crewmen sick with yellow fever and other deadly diseases. Ships' holds were moldy, damp, and dirty, and home to pests such as mosquitoes, cockroaches, and rats.[106] Perishable cargo sometimes arrived rotten and rancid.[107] Rubbish, offal, dead animals, and other "nuisances" were cast onto the wharves and into the docks, where they lingered before being flushed out with the tide.[108] Some citizens urged that the docks be cleaned more regularly, "as the filth collected in many of them emits effluvium" thought to be "greatly injurious to health."[109]

But despite municipal and state authorities' efforts to shield inhabitants from the waterfront's most prejudicial aspects, continuously exposed were hundreds of wharf laborers daily toiling amid the myriad perils of their wage-earning environment. So acute were the risks, in fact, some slaveowners considered dock work too dangerous for their costly slave property.[110] Other masters purchased life insurance for particularly valuable bondsmen. Though most free black and white wharf hands earned too little to afford a policy, life insurance advertisements targeted "Persons who possess but limited incomes . . . and all others whose families might be in danger of being reduced to poverty and distress, by the death of those on whose daily exertions they are dependent"—a description befitting nearly all who engaged in waterfront wage labor.[111]

Notwithstanding its reputation among visitors and local elites as a place to catch cool and salubrious sea breezes or observe the spectacle of Atlantic World trade, Charleston's commercial wharves clearly were neither a safe nor easy place to make a living. But waterfront work had its advantages, especially for the city's enslaved blacks. Hiring out one's own time and collecting cash wages along the frenzied and cosmopolitan seaboard was, after all, far preferable to picking cotton under the watchful gaze of whip-wielding slave masters, overseers, and drivers on interior plantations. With certain aspects of dock slaves' labor and lives indisputably beyond their command, they stove nonetheless to overcome challenges, better their circumstances, and maintain hard-earned customs and conventions despite long odds and untold attempts to maximally exploit their industry.

Chapter Two

"This very troublesome business"

Actions, Reactions, and
the Pursuit of Mastery

From the colonial period through the middle decades of the nineteenth century, black workers, enslaved and free, dominated common dock labor along
Charleston's waterfront. "The laborious business is here chiefly done by black
slaves of which there are great multitudes," observed Philadelphia merchant
Pelatiah Webster in the midst of the Stamp Act Crisis in May 1765. During the
ensuing American Revolution, a Hessian officer in British-occupied Charles
Town[1] noted, "Everything is done by Negroes, whom one finds in great numbers
in all houses, and to excess in many." Antebellum visitors to the port too recorded
the ubiquity of black slaves, especially on and near the waterfront. One traveler
was forcibly struck by the sheer proportion of blacks in the city. "The streets
are thronged with them," he wrote to a friend in Newburyport, Massachusetts.
"They are the draymen, the market tenders, the carriers of burdens, hewers of
wood and drawers of water." Liverpool merchant G. T. Fox made similar observations, noting in 1834, "In the city almost the whole of the working population
are Negroes, all the servants, the carmen & porters," an oft-used term for general
dock laborers. In the mid-1840s, Scottish journalist Alexander Mackay remarked,
"Charleston has many peculiarities to remind the stranger of its latitude, but
none so striking or so constantly before his eyes, as the swarms of negroes whom
he meets. They are everywhere, in the capacity of domestic servants within and of
labourers out of doors, about the wharves and shipping, and in the streets, toiling, singing or whistling and grimacing." Some travelers were repulsed by what

they encountered. Despite prefacing his comments with a reminder to readers that "all of my sympathies are enlisted on the side of the poor slaves," abolitionist Philo Tower demurred during his 1850s visit to Charleston that "one of the most disgusting sights presented to a Northerner, in walking the streets of a Southern city, and one that meets him at every corner, not only in the streets, but on the quays, levees, and on all the public walks and squares, is the mighty, rolling, headlong mass, or tide of negro servants."[2]

Such contemporary remarks clearly document black workers' near monopolization of Charleston's waterfront labor force during all but the last of the antebellum years. But they also inaccurately depict an unregulated horde of autonomous slaves roaming the city's thoroughfares, docks, and alleyways entirely unchecked. Though living and laboring for wages in an urban and littoral environment unquestionably bestowed tremendous advantages and opportunities, bondsmen in southern coastal cities were not left unmolested and unconstrained. Largely unbeknownst to most outside observers, an incessant contest was taking place for the control of black dockworkers' time, movements, earnings, and culture. State and municipal authorities—who usually were also local slaveowners and employers—continuously passed laws and implemented policies designed to subjugate the port's most essential laborers and their most subversive conventions. Aimed primarily at blacks, such efforts ranged from slave badges and hiring stands to fixed wages and even the censuring of work songs. Often unsuccessful, these restrictions were met with day-to-day, and sometimes clever and intrepid, resistance from many of the city's enslaved dockhands who fought to preserve their long-held customary rights as urban wage earners.

Even as the port's black waterfront workers cultivated these embryonic seeds of robust postbellum labor organization and class formation, divergent factions of white Charlestonians were struggling to achieve unity in the face of a latently insurgent black majority population. Following both the bloody 1739 Stono Rebellion that commenced roughly twenty miles south of colonial Charles Town and the abortive Denmark Vesey conspiracy in 1822, South Carolinians adopted extensive slave codes that not only constricted the many social and economic latitudes and mores of the lowcountry's slaves but also hindered the free and smooth flow of commerce through the region's most consequential port. For some white inhabitants the fear of murderous servile insurrection triggered a siege mentality that justified absolute mastery whatever the cost. But others rejected the closed, insular society of a police state, instead championing judicious authority over the entrepôt's myriad bondsmen without hobbling waterfront workers' capacity to efficiently seek and gain employment when needed. This wrangling between the proponents of security and prosperity persisted until the onset of the Civil War, presenting those enslaved blacks firmly entrenched as the city's predominant seaboard labor force with a labyrinth of laws and regulations that were intermittently enforced, then neglected, tightened then loosened. Amid this ebb and flow, slaves discerned and sought to capitalize on openings and occasions to exercise their agency and maintain their dignity and traditions as critical, and oftentimes valuable and skilled, workingmen.

Black slaves were employed to labor on Charleston's waterfront from the building of the first wharves in the late seventeenth century until the waning months of the Civil War. Some wharf owners purchased enslaved dockworkers or leased them from their masters for extended periods of time. But many urban bondsmen alternatively secured permission from their owners to hire themselves out to wharfingers, merchants, factors, ship captains, or dray owners. As former slave John Andrew Jackson noted, it was conventional in Charleston "for the masters to send their slaves out in the morning to earn as much money as they can, how they like." Those hired-out slaves who did not work on the docks toiled at a wide array of jobs, including as tradesmen or mechanics, butchers, barbers, chimney sweeps, house servants, washerwomen, and hucksters. Though pecuniary arrangements varied, employers often paid hired slaves for their labor directly, and the bondsmen subsequently were expected to turn over a substantial portion of their earned wages to their masters. Robert Smalls, who described himself in an 1863 interview as "a rigger and Stevedore," hired out his own time in Charleston during the 1850s and paid his master Henry McKee $15 of his earnings each month, keeping the rest for himself. According to Jackson, hired-out dockworkers—many of whom lived out on their own as well—earned $1.25 a day in the mid-1840s stowing cotton at the wharves and had "to maintain themselves, and clothe themselves, and pay their masters two-and-a-half dollars per week out of this," or they would "receive a severe castigation with a cat-o'-nine-tails." Slaves who resided on their masters' urban property or had their clothing and food provided were expected to give up a greater proportion of their wages.[3]

Many waterfront employers extolled the advantages of hiring or leasing rather than owning their workforce. To be sure, hirers had to take care not to be too negligent or cruel. If a slave leased for a fixed term of service became ill, was injured, or ran away, the hirer not only sustained the loss of the bondsman's labor but also remained responsible for the payment of the slave's wages for the duration of the contract.[4] In addition, many agreements stuck the employer rather than the master with costs such as food, clothing, shelter, and medical bills.[5] Casually engaging workers by the day, though rather costly, conveniently avoided such obligations. But temporarily hiring or even leasing labor for an entire month or year also did not require the considerable and long-term capital commitment of buying slaves. Prime able-bodied wharf hands were not cheap, with an average price of $500 in 1807 and $1,000 in 1858.[6] And these purchase costs were merely the beginning of lifelong expenditures for the maintenance of owned workers. Former South Carolina governor Thomas Pinckney pointed out in 1822 that employers of hired servants did not have to care for the "superannuated, the infirm, or the indolent, who are now so heavy a tax on the proprietor." Furthermore, an employer could select a hired-out worker with the requisite skills that matched a specific job. As Pinckney put it, the hirer could "contract for efficient service," which, he added, "if the person employed, should be incapable or unwilling to perform, he would be discharged, and a more suitable subject engaged."[7] Hired bondsmen, meanwhile, could be worked harder since the temporary employer had little interest in the slaves' long-term well-being or value. "Hired slaves are commonly treated more harshly, or with less care and attention, than those in possession of their owner," explained a South Carolina judge in 1839, and "their moral qualities are almost always deteriorated."[8]

Despite these potential risks to their human chattel, masters frequently offered their slaves for short-term employ on the city's hazardous waterfront. "TO HIRE. THREE prime wharf hands," read a May 1835 advertisement in Charleston's *Southern Patriot*. The same newspaper announced the availability in July 1846 of a "WHARF HAND AND LABORER TO HIRE." And a "prime able bodied" twenty-year-old slave carter and laborer was advertised for employ in August 1841.[9] In great need of experienced but relatively cheap and nonpermanent labor, especially during the peak commercial season, wharf owners and managers snatched up available bondsmen. "Wanted.—Ten Able Bodied NEGROES, for Wharf Hands, whose wages will be punctually paid," declared one such employer in December 1841.[10] And as evidenced by James Carr's hire of twenty slaves in 1815 to stow his vessel with cotton or Charles Edmondston's engagement of dockhands to unload and load the brig *Alexis* in 1823, ship captains and merchants also secured waterfront workers as needed.

Though this hiring-out system proved gainful for many waterfront employers, masters, and bondsmen alike, most antebellum southern wharves and levees were worked by a combination of hired, leased, and owned slave hands.[11] Among the throng of enslaved blacks swarming Charleston's docks were those variously employed on Vanderhorst's Wharf. Obtaining the waterfront property in the late 1780s and selling it in the early 1890s, the Vanderhorsts generated an extensive collection of extant business papers that provided an extraordinary and detailed view into the management of both the family's wharf and black dockhands for three-quarters of a century between the end of the American Revolution and the beginning of the Civil War.[12] For most of this period the Vanderhorsts owned at least one, and as many as five, slaves consigned to toil along the Cooper River. Sure to keep a substantial share of any profits for themselves, father Arnoldus and son Elias Vanderhorst annually rented the wharf to urban managers who were required to hire the family's enslaved wharf hands during the term of the lease.[13] But even as these chattel laborers were being bought, sold, retired, and occasionally buried, they regularly were joined by ancillary bondsmen leased for several months or an entire year, as well as slaves hired by the hour, day, or week. Take February 1837, when perennial wharfinger John Crawford reported to Elias Vanderhorst that present labor expenses consisted of "9 negroes hired (exclusive of your two) at 14$ pr. month each," plus $50 every month for additional "Transient negro hire." Whereas Crawford had employed the Vanderhorsts' wharf hands, eight leased slaves, and casual hires for approximately $1,150 per year in the 1810s, the annual cost of employing a similar amalgamation of workers two decades later had reached upwards of $2,000.[14]

Meanwhile, an account from October 1806 through September 1807—one of the first documents in the collection explicitly mentioning workers—included $468.64 paid out over the course of the year for "Victualling the 5 Wharf Negroes, also negro hire, & other small expenses attending Wharf."[15] Individual expenditures indeed may have been "small" or trifling, but they could add up. Aside from miscellaneous outlays (for example, city slave taxes and sporadic fines or workhouse corrections) and the hiring of short-term labor when needed, the Vanderhorsts' personal wharf slaves had to be sheltered, fed, and clothed.[16] Family patriarch, Revolutionary War veteran, and former city intendant[17] and state governor Arnoldus Vanderhorst plausibly housed his enslaved hands in tenements he constructed on the wharf property fronting East Bay Street. Though its apartments primarily were rented to white Charlestonians, "Vanderhorst Row" included servants' quarters and kitchens and would have furnished not only proximity to the workplace but also the means to monitor and control the whereabouts and habits of the valuable hands.[18] Providing sustenance, and sometimes alcohol, also kept slaves close to work and home. In 1817 a kitchen was rented for $3 per month along with a "Cook for Negroes" for $6 monthly. Other disbursements recorded during the same decade included "finding said negroes in meat at 31 1/4 ct. pr. day" and "paid 210.00 for rice, 1 quart each per day." And in the last six months of 1830, $290 was spent on "Food for Whf. Hands & others."[19] Numerous accounts over the decades, meanwhile, captured the frequent purchase and distribution of clothing ranging from cotton and flannel shirts, trousers, drawers, and shoes to jackets, hats, stockings, and blankets. Summer clothing typically was issued in May, whereas winter attire most often was doled out in November.[20]

Medical care also cut into the profits of the wharf business, regardless whether a lease obliged the Vanderhorsts or the tenant wharfinger to pay the expenses. Apart from labor time and productivity lost due to illnesses and the resultant cost of replacement workers, habitual payments were made for doctors' visits and medicine. In 1824, for instance, Dr. Grimke billed the wharf $12.21 for attending to Dublin, an African-born dockhand Arnoldus Vanderhorst purchased from fellow wharf owner William Smith for $530.75 in 1810. The same physician was called upon to care for the Vanderhorsts' other longtime wharf slave, Will, in 1827.[21] After Robert necessitated medication in April 1820, Dr. Johnson and Dr. Maynard were paid for "stopping Hemorrhage for Robert" in July. Far less dire treatments included "a phial Harlem Oil for Dublin's Toe" in 1823, and the extraction of his tooth in 1836. When Dublin fell on the icy wharf and broke his ribs in January 1834, Crawford wrote to Vanderhorst that the "Doctor is attending him & I believe he is doing well. I afford such comforts as are necessary."[22] Other accounts indicated that such convalescent assistance included extra blankets and provisions such as meat, sugar, and tea.[23]

But slaves long exposed to such difficult and dangerous work did not always recover. When Will died in September 1836 the Vanderhorsts, who perceived themselves as model paternalists, purchased a coffin and paid for the funeral expenses.[24] London, who Elias Vanderhorst acquired in 1835 for $400 and employed on the wharf after Will's death, passed in April 1844 despite months of medical attention from Dr. W. C. Ramsay. The family again covered the burial costs of their enslaved wharf hand.[25] Dublin, who city death records listed as a remarkable one hundred years old at the time of his death in 1851, was effectively retired from dock duty during the mid-to-late 1840s. Still periodically provided with a suit of clothes, shoes, and blankets, Dublin further received from the Vanderhorsts a cash "allowance" of 75 cents per month—raised to $1 in the final year of his life—to secure his own victuals. But with cotton exports booming and the demand for waterfront labor unrelenting, Elias Vanderhorst and his wharfingers gradually turned to the exclusive and costly employ of temporarily hired slaves. With Dublin on the verge of retirement and London on the precipice of death, Mr. Crawford conferred with Mr. Vanderhorst on the "very heavy labor and great expense" of running the wharf, remarking that "very few unacquainted with the business would suppose the expense so great."[26]

Like the city's wharf and mercantile firms, the South Carolina Railroad needed scores of laborers at the company's Charleston depot to unload cotton bales from the cars and roll the massive bundles about the rail yard in preparation for transport to the Cooper River wharves (see figure 17).[27] In the early 1840s the company's leaders debated whether to hire or purchase slaves for these menial but indispensable tasks. President Tristam Tupper opposed calls for ownership, arguing in July 1840 that the railroad lacked the capital means for such a substantial expenditure. Tupper furthermore pointed out that ownership brought additional responsibilities while sacrificing the benefits of hiring. Unable to demand the intervening redress of a master, the railroad would be solely responsible for the vexatious corrections and sales of misbehaving or indolent workers. "The privilege of promptly dismissing an inferior, vicious, or otherwise worthless negro from our service," also would be lost if slave laborers belonged to the company.[28]

But when James Gadsden assumed the presidency of the South Carolina Railroad later in 1840, he sought to reverse course. As the owner of Gadsden's Wharf, he not only advocated for the company's purchase of slave workers but also called for the company to acquire a Cooper River wharf and then extend the railroad tracks to the waterfront. Gadsden calculated, "If labor owned could be substituted for labor hired, and we could own a wharf," the railroad could reduce its overall expenses by 20 to 25 percent. Acknowledging Tupper's concerns about the initial cost of such an investment, Gadsden insisted that he was "not for spending any more money uselessly," but stated that he was confident that a relatively small outlay in the short term would be rewarded with considerable savings and profits.[29] To James Gadsden's dismay, however, he was unable to persuade the Charleston City Council to allow the railroad tracks to be extended to the waterfront, and the company's fiscally conservative board of directors restricted the acquisition of slaves "to single Fellows, who can only be purchased at great risk as to character and for Cash."[30]

But just months after businessman and banker Henry Workman Conner replaced Gadsden as company president, the railroad reorganized its Charleston cotton-yard labor force. On September 20, 1850, the directors resolved to hire black laborers for up to $12 per month; but if workers could not be procured for that rate, then five or six slaves were to be purchased. Evidently unable to hire enough slaves for this amount, Conner was authorized two months later "to purchase 10 Male Negroes, on the best possible terms."[31] By the spring of 1852 the railroad had fully embraced the purchase policy, buying fifty-four additional slaves at a sale in Aiken on April 27. The Charleston city assessor reported in November 1858 that the company's property tax bill included twenty-six slaves and a "House and Lot occupied by the Negroes."[32] Nor was the South Carolina Railroad the only transport firm in the state buying up workers. The owners of Railroad Accommodation Wharf Company, which gained incorporation from the South Carolina General Assembly in December 1856, expended a staggering $10,541.50 to purchase ten enslaved wharf hands.[33]

Owned slaves, clearly, were substantial financial assets as well as a wharf's labor force. Like other investment capital, enslaved workers were bought, sold, and otherwise transferred as necessary.[34] When Charles Edmondston sold his wharf, stores, and warehouses in November 1837, also auctioned were fifteen slaves said to be "accustomed to work on the wharf."[35] Cooper Jacob Schirmer similarly noted in July 1853 the sale of West Point Rice Mills and all of the attached mill and wharf hands to factor and commission merchant Thomas Bennett Lucas, who already owned a portion of Cannonsboro (sometimes spelled Cannonsborough) Wharf and Mill Company located on the Ashley River.[36] In 1860 the West Point property again was sold, including about 180 slaves, "most of them bought by the parties who purchased the Mill."[37] Lucas and C. M. Furman, meanwhile, sought in February 1859 to buy out the share of Cannonsboro "and the negroes thereon" owned by the late J. C. Blum. During negotiations the representatives of Blum's widow reminded Lucas and Furman that the mill property, which like the city's other rice facilities included wharves, warehouses, and worker housing, had appreciated greatly in value over the years. But they specifically pointed out that, aside from the company's real estate, "negroes are selling much higher than they did at the time they were purchased."[38] Finally, when Otis Mills and E. M. Beach petitioned the state legislature for the incorporation of Atlantic Wharves to form the Atlantic Wharf Company in 1859, they transferred "the said wharves with the Wharf hands" to the corporation, which was valued at $400,000. Tax records from 1858 showed that Otis Mills & Co.—the proprietors of Atlantic Wharves—owned eighteen slaves, while the grain merchant firm Mills, Beach & Co. that operated on Atlantic Wharves possessed an additional thirteen slaves.[39]

Slaves who remained the private possessions of wharf owners frequently were deeded to heirs along with the wharves upon which they labored.[40] When Arnoldus Vanderhorst divvied up his substantial property holdings in 1810, he bestowed to his two younger sons (John Stanyarne and Elias) Vanderhorst's Wharf "with all the Stores and buildings thereon . . . [and] Together with the Negro Slaves usually attached to the said Wharf."[41] William Pritchard Jr. granted his wife the use, rent, and profits of his wharf and "Wharf Negroes" for her support after his death in 1817.[42] In 1835 Simon Magwood prescribed that Magwood's Wharf be given to his son Charles, along with nine male slaves who likely worked on the family's wharf.[43] And Irish-born merchant James Adger left to his wife all of his enslaved house servants, but not "the slaves that may be attached to and employed upon the Wharves now usually called Adgers [*sic*] North and South Wharves." These slave wharf hands, along with the houses, stores, furniture, and other personal property "attached or appertaining to the said Wharves," were bequeathed equally to his four sons.[44] Though Adger did not specify how many of his city slaves worked on the docks, he owned eighteen bondsmen in Charleston in 1850 and sixteen at the time of his death in 1858.[45]

Wharf owners' wills often distinguished between what was to be done on the one hand with "Wharf Negroes" or "Wharf Servants," and on the other with their "plantation Negroes" or field hands.[46] According to Daniel E. Huger Smith, who was born in Charleston in 1846 and split his own childhood between the city and the family's plantation, country slaves were "quite distinct" from those who labored in Charleston.[47] Slaves said to be "attached" to the wharves occasionally were employed off the docks. John Crawford, for instance, collected twenty-five dollars in October 1832 for hiring Will back to Elias Vanderhorst to paint the wharf owner's house. Will again was put to painting his master's residence for eight months in 1833, for which Vanderhorst similarly reimbursed Crawford for the labor lost upon the wharf.[48] But most slaves who were designated as "Wharf Negroes" possessed specific knowledge and skill sets for waterfront work that precluded their casual employment elsewhere in the city or their habitual transfer back and forth between the urban and rural labor environments.[49]

Wharf-owning families, meanwhile, certainly were not the only beneficiaries of slaves' waterfront toil. English traveler John Lambert noted of Charlestonians in early 1808, "Those who are unable to give 500 or 600 dollars for a slave, which is the usual price of a good one, generally hire them, by the month or year, of people who are in the habit of keeping a number of slaves for that purpose. Many persons obtain a handsome living by letting out their slaves for 6 to 10 dollars per month. They also send them out to sell oysters, fruit, millinery, &c.; or as carmen and porters." G. T. Fox likewise observed during his visit to the port in November 1834, "Many persons invest their property in slaves & let them out . . . & draw from their wages nearly their whole income."[50] Lydia Jane Ball Waring, whose name alone announced her familial connections and affluence, owned eleven urban slaves and hired out as many as seven to various employers in Charleston at one time. Shortly after Waring's death, for instance, the owners of Southern Wharf paid her estate $47.67 in cash for the hire of Frederick for a total of five months and ten days in 1841.[51] One of Waring's contemporaries, Miss Juliet Georgiana Elliott, began hiring out slaves in Charleston as a substantial if not sole source of income as early as 1844. At the end of each year Elliott recorded in her personal account book the income generated by her slaves' wages. In 1853, for example, Elliott collected $865.25 from seventeen slaves. She raked in $1,130 from her urban bondsmen in 1860, and was still living off such wages as late as 1864.[52] With Dublin superannuated and the family's other owned dock-hands deceased, three separate masters received a total of $144 from Vanderhorst's Wharf in 1848 for "Negro hire."[53] Chisolm's Rice Mill paid Mary Fraser Davie $47.48 in July 1855 for her hired-out slave William's wages, and the widow received a total of $138 in 1859 from Southern Wharf for Fred.[54] Meanwhile, Commercial Wharf paid $169.60 to the wife of well-off factor John Colcock for the hire of her hands.[55] And Colcock's business partner, James Legare, received a total of $192 from Commercial Wharf between July 1856 and July 1857 for the wages of his slave wharf hands James and Jim.[56]

Some white Charlestonians were far more impecunious and relied upon the monthly wages of one or two hired-out waterfront slaves just to make ends meet. For example, the General Assembly received a request for assistance in 1800 from a widow named Mary Norton, who was "in indigent circumstances" after her valuable slave Cuffy—"from whose labor she derived so much of her support"—was executed for larceny and attempting to cut the throat of a white man.[57] Naomi Smith, who was nearly sixty years old and "very infirm," found herself in a similar situation in November 1822 after her slave Caesar was executed for alleged involvement in the Denmark Vesey conspiracy. Caesar had been "a prime healthy able bodied negro" of about twenty-five years of age who clothed and supported himself at his own expense and regularly paid Smith ten dollars each month out of his wages working as "an active drayman." The woman's only other source of income was four dollars per month from a fourteen-year-old slave boy and an annual hundred-dollar stipend from the charitable St. Andrews Society. Though Smith did not object to Caesar's death sentence, this "peculiarly severe personal loss" forced her to turn to the state legislature for aid.[58]

The transgressions of slaves like Cuffy and Caesar perpetually reminded southern masters, whether rich or poor, of the inherent perils of allowing their bondsmen to labor for wages in the relatively autonomous and potentially corrupting urban port environment. Though the "nominal rate of wages in town seems in favor of employing them there" rather than in the countryside, Thomas Pinckney argued in 1822, the "intemperance and debauchery so generally prevalent [in Charleston], diminish in an extraordinary degree the profits of his labor, while it ruins the constitution and morals of the slave." Planters living in Christ Church Parish near Charleston complained to the legislature in 1829 that the mere temporary exposure of rural slaves to "free blacks and low and worthless white people" in the city "has infused into the minds of the negroes ideas of insubordination and of emancipation, which they carry with them when sold into every part of the State." Back in 1764, in fact, merchant and planter Henry Laurens felt compelled to remove one of his urban bondsmen, Abram, "from some pernicious connexions that he has made with Slaves in Charles Town."[59]

In 1819 factor Charles Kershaw counseled Charlotte Anne Allston, a Georgetown District planter and widow who already had several bondsmen hiring out in Charleston, not to continue employing her slave James in the city. Kershaw had spoken to a Mr. Black (likely merchant Alexander Black) about hiring James, but Black offered only ten dollars per month. The factor therefore advised Allston to put James to work in the plantation fields, where "he will earn more than double what he will do in this place." Besides this financial consideration, Kershaw warned Allston about the pitfalls of urban wage labor. "James may perhaps go on very well with Mr. Black for a few months," he explained, "but after that he will have bad notions put into his head—he will want to work out and pay Wages which is much the same as giving him his freedom." Kershaw then stated that as Allston's factor in Charleston he would collect and forward James's pay from Mr. Black if she chose to hire the slave in the city, but added, "you may be assured, James will not be obedient or attentive to his Work."[60]

Charles Kershaw had good reason for this foreboding admonition. Charleston's hiring-out arrangement no doubt was remunerative to masters such as Charlotte Anne Allston and convenient to waterfront employers like Mr. Black. Any such gains, however, came at the cost of loosening, and sometimes losing, control over thousands of valuable enslaved laborers. City and state lawmakers therefore devised precepts to keep the port's crucial yet volatile workforce in check. But many slaves disdained a system that dangled the promises of relatively autonomous urban wage labor, then often deprived their choice of employment and employer, robbed them of the great preponderance of the fruits of their industry, exposed them to difficult and dangerous work conditions, and above all denied their very freedom and liberty. Aware of the perquisites of laboring and living in a dynamic Atlantic port, slaves like Cuffy, Caesar, and James did not relinquish without a struggle those comparative advantages inaccessible to most of their black brothers and sisters drudging on inland plantations. Slavery was neither inherently nor inevitably incompatible with the urban environment: the individual and collective agency and boldness of the enslaved rendered it so.

Whether owned by a wharf or mercantile company or hired by the day, month, or year, the ubiquitous slaves who effectively monopolized common dock labor (often referred to in Charleston as "porterage") from the colonial period through the early nineteenth century toiled under a tightly regulated employment structure that extended far beyond the forfeiture of wages. Badges, for instance, became an integral component of the city's slave-hiring governance.[61] Though authorities first introduced a ticket or pass requirement for slaves in the late seventeenth century, legislation enacted in 1712, 1722, and 1740 repeatedly chastised those who allowed their bondsmen "to do what and go whither they will, and work where they please," and prohibited slaves from hiring out without a certificate or note from their masters.[62] But soon ceasing to entrust this consent solely to individual slaveowners, city officials decreed in 1751 that no slave could hire out in Charleston as a porter or laborer "until the Owner or Person having Charge of such Slave, shall have obtained a License from the Commissioners of the Streets for so doing." The order continued that, "if any Person hire or employ any Negro, not having a Badge or Ticket," the offender was to be fined ten shillings.[63] A 1764 colonial statute repeated the prohibition against slaves hiring out as porters and laborers without a license, and added that the ticket or badge had to be worn publicly.[64]

These latter two measures addressed more than hiring badges, however. As historian Robert Olwell recounted, "In 1746, the grand jury complained of 'the slaves of Charles Town, who act as porters & who refuse to work for a reasonable hire, when they are frequently found Idle, & often insist on as much for an hour or two as pays their Masters for a whole day.' In 1750, the jurors again objected to the slave porters, particularly 'that it is left in their power to chuse [*sic*] or refuse such work as are required and the exorbitant wages demanded by them.'" Then during the early 1760s slave porters and common laborers conspired to boost their wages.[65] The 1751 decree and 1764 act forcefully responded by empowering city authorities—the so-called Commissioners of Streets—to regulate or fix "the rates of porterage and labour of such slaves, and also, to appoint the places where such slaves shall ply" for hire. Soon after it was determined that slave porters and common laborers were to "ply at the <u>Curtain-line</u>, between the <u>Watch-House</u> and the <u>Gap</u> opposite to Col. <u>Beale's</u> house, and not elsewhere."[66] The "curtain line" being the fortification and sea wall just to the east of East Bay Street, slaves seeking to hire out in colonial Charles Town thus were required to wait along a prescribed four-hundred-foot stretch of the Cooper River waterfront; no longer were they permitted to freely roam the wharves seeking employment, as they traditionally had for over three-quarters of a century (see figures 1 and 2).[67]

As for wages, the local administrators stipulated in 1764 that slave porters engaged in "Labour in Ships at the Wharves" were to receive ten shillings per day, whereas the less skilled "rolling of rice [barrels], or other common porterage" on the docks paid seven shillings and six pence a day. As for more casually hired common laborers, those who worked for two hours earned two shillings and six pence, between two and four hours brought three shillings and nine pence, and half a day's work garnered five shillings. Slaves who failed to comply with these set wages were to receive up to twenty lashes; culpable white employers were left unpunished.[68] The 1764 act also regulated transportation workers plying for hire. Draymen and carters—under this clause, black and white, enslaved and free—were required to obtain a license, and Charleston's commissioners were authorized to fix the rates of drayage and cartage, which were to be published in the local newspaper and "hung up in some public place in the said town." Anticipating worker resistance, any carter, drayman, or wagoner accepting more than the established rates were to be fined £5, which was to be given to the overcharged party. But not deterred by threats of whippings and fines, and perhaps emboldened by the era's revolutionary ideals, the city's slaves defiantly continued to "refuse to work, unless it be such work as shall be agreeable to themselves and such pay as they may require."[69]

After the Revolution and the incorporation of Charleston in 1783, the waterfront and its largely enslaved labor force remained too vital to the city's and state's economic fortunes to operate according to laissez-faire principles. The new municipal and state governments therefore recommenced the enactment of laws regulating the employment and wages of black dockworkers.[70] Though unnoticed or unacknowledged by many visitors and inhabitants who instead emphasized an efficiently functioning port amid its commercial heyday, the back-and-forth informally negotiated contest for control raged on between capital and labor, employers and employees, masters and slaves, statutes and customs.[71] But within the waterfront's counting houses, the City Council chamber, and the halls of the state legislature, a simultaneous debate persisted between commercial boosters most concerned—whatever the risks—with the port's progress, prosperity, and competitiveness, and those haunted by the specters of slave rebels past, present, and future. Caught in the middle were Charleston's intractable waterfront workers, obliged to navigate constrictive state laws and city ordinances passed and then episodically enforced at the behest of the latter faction, and recurrently ignored and undermined by the former.

Notwithstanding these concurrent struggles, the City Council embraced the badge requirement and updated the procedures periodically between 1783 and 1843.[72] The basic system, however, remained unchanged through the end of the antebellum era and the institution of slavery. Slaveowners who wished to hire out bondsmen in the city were required to annually purchase slave badges, upon which were inscribed the year, a general occupation—usually porter, servant, mechanic, fruiterer, or fisher—and a badge number. Porter badges—which cost two dollars before 1837 and four dollars thereafter—were worn by not only slave porters but also day laborers and draymen, most of whom worked on the waterfront.[73] Vanderhorst's Wharf manager John Crawford, for instance, regularly procured two badges to enable dockhands Will and Dublin to labor on the family's wharf. The aforementioned Juliet Georgiana Elliott, meanwhile, purchased numerous slave badges from the city each January for her multitude of hired-out bondsmen; Mary Fraser Davie's personal accounts also included recurrent badge purchases to legitimize William and Fred's hire to employers such as Chisolm's Mill and Southern Wharf.[74] These tags beneficially enabled masters to avoid cumbersome contracts each and every time their slaves were hired for hourly or daily labor on the docks.[75] In some years, 1801 and 1802 for instance, porter badges were larger in size than those of other hired-out slaves, such as mechanics and servants. This helped an employer to quickly scan the designated segment of waterfront and identify and summon an available dockworker.[76]

Aside from expediting the hiring process and tracking the whereabouts and supply of wharf laborers, the city's badge program helps scholars to deduce the number of black slaves who toiled on the docks during the first two-thirds of the nineteenth century. Charleston's city directories did not list slaves; and though U.S. Census records decennially reported the total number of bondsmen residing in the city, they failed to reveal slaves' occupations. But since masters were obliged to purchase tags anew annually for their hired-out slaves, badge production and sales figures divulged the approximate number of bondsmen who hired out on the waterfront and elsewhere in the city between 1800 and 1865. According to one study, estimates range from as few as 302 badges sold in 1809 to a prolific 5,196 in 1860.

By 1807, each occupational category of slave badges was numbered separately. So, for example, if an extant fisher badge from 1820 was stamped or engraved with the number 100, then it can be ascertained that at least 100 slaves worked as fishermen in that year. In the early twentieth century, Charleston journalist and lay historian John Bennett reported seeing a porter badge numbered 1,376 from 1842. A surviving 1847 porter badge is numbered 1,283.[77] Twice in the early

Slave Badge Sales, 1800–1865

Year	Badges Sold	Year	Badges Sold
1800	2,116	1835	3,508
1805	1,354	1840	4,191
1810	656	1845	3,843
1815	1,898	1850	4,135
1820	2,050	1855	3,834
1825	3,269	1860	5,196
1830	3,459	1865	88

Source: Greene et al., *Slave Badges*, 86, 99, 108, 119, 133–34, 157, 167.

1850s the city furthermore published the number of badges produced for each occupational category. In 1850, 4,480 total slave badges were made, 1,400 or 31.3 percent of which were for porters.[78] And of the 6,350 tags made for 1851, 1,600 or 25.2 percent were porter badges.[79] This evidence suggested that during the 1840s and 1850s well over one thousand slaves were lawfully employed on or near Charleston's waterfront as porters, day laborers, draymen, and carters.

Badge statistics also provided an idea of how many drays and carts operated for hire in antebellum Charleston. Though slave draymen wore porter badges, the city also required all persons leasing or driving for hire a dray, cart, or wagon to obtain badges or tags to be placed on the vehicles. In 1850 municipal officials ordered the production of 415 dray and 145 cart badges.[80] Over time the number of drays and carts—and thus the number of draymen and carters—had increased as the amount of cotton passing through Charleston's waterfront swelled.[81] According to a report of a South Carolina Railroad stockholders' meeting held in the mid-1840s, there were 206 drays and 81 carts licensed in the city in 1831; in 1842 there were 231 drays and 107 carts; and as of May 1845, 311 drays and 127 carts.[82] Despite labor competition from an influx of lowly skilled white immigrants during the 1840s and 1850s, the demand for slaves to labor on the city's docks and drays remained robust until the Civil War and emancipation.

Municipal authorities in the early nineteenth century, meanwhile, engaged in schemes far more aggressive and intrusive than slave badges to centralize and circumscribe waterfront employment. An ordinance passed in September 1801 sought to further "regulate the Wages of Licensed Porters, and other Day Labourers" and to fix the locations of their hiring "stands." As in the decades before the Revolution, this ordinance was prompted by continued "exorbitant and varying demands made by licensed porters, and other day labourers." White hirers, remarkably, still necessitated economic and legislative protection from defiant black slaves who virtually cornered the waterfront labor market during this period. In order to "prevent further imposition" upon employers, the law declared that dockworkers—now including any free blacks or whites—were not to demand and were not "entitled to receive any other than the following rates, to wit":

> For a full day's labour, or the lading or unlading of the cargo of any vessel, or for any other employ in which a porter or day labourer may be engaged,
> 85 cents.

> For a half day's labour,   42 cents.
> For a quarter of a day's labour,   25 cents.

Any slave who asked for, demanded, or received wages higher than those stipulated still could receive up to twenty lashes on the bare back. If the offender was a free man—black or white—he was to be fined up to five dollars.[83]

This latest attempted crackdown tightened other aspects of laborers' lives and habits as well, including the number and length of mealtimes. The ordinance, for instance, defined the hours of a full day's labor as lasting "from sun rise to twilight in the evening," with a one-hour break permitted for breakfast and another hour for dinner. In the summer months of June, July, August, and September—which were those with the most daylight and thus the longest workdays—the ordinance allowed for a two-hour dinner. The harbor master was required to familiarize ship captains with these various regulations regarding the fixed "wages of porters and laborers on hire."[84]

The ordinance, moreover, called on the city marshal "to fix proper stands" where porters could offer themselves for hire. It took over two years for Marshal James Browne to announce the locations of these porter stands, but when he did so in November 1803 all were situated on or near the waterfront: "No. 1, at the lower end of Tradd-street, below the curtain line; No. 2, the north side of Beale's wharf; No. 3, fronting Mr. Cambridge's vendue store [on Exchange Street]; No. 4, the north side of the Exchange [at the corner of East Bay and Broad streets]; No. 5, fronting Mr. Cochran's wharf" (see figures 2, 7, and 13).[85] This increase from one hiring location in 1764 to five in 1803—and their continued proximity to the wharves—attests to the physical and commercial growth of the waterfront, and to the rising demand for and supply of slaves seeking employment as porters or day laborers on the city's bustling docks. This bourgeoning of waterfront labor coincided with Charleston's commercial golden age, which was fueled by the export of rice and then cotton and lasted until the devastating Panic of 1819. One visitor remarked in the early 1810s that Charleston was "destined to be the Emporium of Trade for an extensive & valuable Part of the Southern Continent of North America." And indeed, the city was first among southern ports with $6 million in cotton exports in 1815.[86]

But as the number of slaves working on the wharves increased, so too did some white leaders' impulse to structure, police, and control waterfront labor and laborers. Confined in 1764 within a four-hundred-foot tract of East Bay Street, dockhands awaiting hire now were tethered to specific and fixed points. Workers were warned that these five stands were the only places within the city where they could "offer themselves for work as Porters," and violators were liable to receive as many as ten stripes.[87] Aiming also to severely limit the movements and activities of slaves, the City Council obliged wharf laborers to remain at these stands even "while they are not engaged or employed to work."[88] If the enslaved were to be mastered and if the urban environment was to be made perfectly compatible with the institution of human bondage, slaves could not be permitted to wander aimlessly or drift into nearby houses, alleyways, or grog and gaming shops between jobs. In public view at a street-corner porter stand, slaves were harder pressed to get drunk, gamble away their masters' wages, exchange illicit goods, or plot insurrection. Not solely a slave management and safety mechanism, however, this measure also better ensured that wharf hands were readily available and in abundance when needed. As with slave badges, such dictums bridged the divide between white Charlestonians' dueling interests in commercial ascendancy and racial security, and thus elicited support from both factions.

But slaves long had exercised the freedom to pick and choose those employers for whom they did and did not wish to work. Like slaves on the auction stand manipulating the outcome and terms of their own sales, bondsmen at the porter stand stubbornly insisted on having an influence over their own labor conditions. As with the later practice of the waterfront shape-up, the assemblage of workers at the porter stands was supposed to enable hirers to select the most vigorous, skilled, experienced, hard-working, and obedient—that is, "docile" and "contented"—slaves, while rejecting the old, the weak, the indolent, and the rebellious. Instead, the enslaved dockhands had taken to sizing up the employers: Who was known to treat his workers most fairly and leniently? Who acquiesced to longer breaks or slipped higher wages or a dram to the industrious? Who permitted the hands to sing loud and bawdy work songs, or control the pace of labor? Who, in short, allowed those slaves who were afforded the opportunities of urban waterfront work to enjoy those relative advantages as well as the mores of their workplace culture? The 1801 law therefore again aimed to strip this incredible decision-making power from the enslaved and place hiring authority fully into the hands of the white master class. If a licensed slave waiting at one of these porter stands refused or neglected "to work for any person that applies to him, and tenders him the established rate for his hire," the guilty bondsman now could be placed in the stocks for up to one hour or receive up to ten stripes. The porter or laborer was authorized to decline a solicitation for work only if he was "previously employed, or actually engaged to work for some other person."[89] This was a law, though long flouted, that both commercial pragmatists and security hawks could honor and enforce.

The Charleston City Council reiterated these hiring and wage rules in a comprehensive ordinance "for the government of negroes and other persons of color" passed in October 1806. There were, however, some amendments and additions implemented in response to actual practices and to close loopholes in the law. Despite increasingly tighter legal constraints on their already limited autonomy, enslaved waterfront workers seized opportunities to buck domination and maintain some control over the terms of their own labor. For example, compelled under the 1801 law to accept a job if offered, slaves resolved to take their time in getting to the work site. Amid this interval between the moment of hire and arrival at the specified wharf or warehouse, freedom of movement, communication, and action temporarily were restored. Unshackled from the porter stands, slaves were taking advantage of the liberating power of both market demand for their vital labor and masters' insatiable desire for wage income. Thus forced to partake in the same type of give-and-take cycle of action and reaction, accommodation and resistance, as white masters and overseers on rural plantations throughout the slave South, municipal authorities proclaimed in 1806, "as soon as any porter or day laborer is engaged to work, he shall immediately depart from his stand to such place as shall be ordered by the person engaging him." Any black laborer who failed to promptly leave the stand and report directly to the designated place of employment was liable to punishment.[90] Though the penalties for those workers who refused to accept a job offer or demanded or received higher wages were elevated to coerce compliance, the wage rates were not.[91] Finally, the section pertaining to meals was refined, further tipping the financial scales in favor of white employers. If the hirer provided a day laborer with food and drink, now 6 ¼ cents—regardless of the amount or quality of the victuals—could be deducted from the worker's wages for each meal, up to 18 ¾ cents per day if the employer furnished breakfast, lunch, and dinner. Supplying meals, legislators assumed, kept workers on the job site and out of trouble.[92]

Meanwhile, the laws regulating the hiring process and wage rates of hired-out draymen and carters also were updated. Ordinances passed in 1805 and 1807 adopted the concept of the porter stands, directing that "No carts or drays shall stand or ply for hire in any of the streets, lanes, or alleys, but be divided and placed by the City Marshal . . . at such place or places as may be appointed out by him." As with dockworkers, draymen and carters were required to remain at these hiring stands "while not engaged or actually employed," and therefore were not to loiter in adjacent neighborhoods or drive their vehicles around town soliciting employment, or engaging in immoral, illegal, and seditious activities. Transportation workers too were obliged under threat of fine to accept a job when offered, unless "pre-engaged to work for some person immediately."[93]

But despite intentions, these various provisions did not ensure that employers in need of a drayman, porter, or wharf hand were certain to find one. Both the 1764 statute and the 1805 ordinance had declared that all draymen and carters plying for hire in the city were required to accept work "at all times of the day," Sundays excepted.[94] These laws failed to stipulate, however, the precise hours that workers had to remain available. As a result, when one ship captain set out in September 1835 in search of drays to transport twenty-six packages from Roper's Wharf to a warehouse, "he was not successful, it being late in the afternoon."[95] With a sizable share of slaves' wages destined for their masters' pockets and with the enticements of the city all about, it is little wonder why many unengaged workers knocked off early.

To manage compensation and enable the standardized measure of distance from one area of the city to another, the 1805 law divided Charleston into twelve cartage and three drayage zones. Draymen and carters were paid by the job—defined as the loading, transporting, and unloading of goods—and the rates or wages were fixed based on the distance traveled and, for cartmen, the type of freight carried. Since the great preponderance of Charleston's transportation workers were employed conveying goods to and from the waterfront, all but three of the sixty-one possible distances or routes enumerated in this ordinance began or ended at the wharves. For example, if a carter hauled a load of lumber from any of the wharves to the zone bounded by Meeting, Broad, Church, and South Bay streets, he was due 43 cents. If the same load was taken from the wharves to the area of the city confined within Meeting, Broad, King, and South Bay streets, he was to be paid 50 cents for having driven a little farther. Likewise, the drayage of a hogshead of tobacco from the inspection station to the waterfront brought either 42 or 62 cents depending on whether delivered to a wharf located to the north or to the south of the Governor's Bridge (at present-day East Bay and North Market streets).[96] This pricing scheme confirmed not only the ubiquity of draymen and carters on the wharves, but also the central and indispensable role these workers played in the smooth and efficient flow of goods through the port. But as with similar regulations for other waterfront laborers, this ordinance was designed not only to systematize transportation rates within the city but also to restrain the economic and bargaining power of the workers. Draymen and carters who demanded or received higher wages than those expressly legislated therefore were subject to punishment.[97]

For decades the hiring practices and wage rates of Charleston's dockworkers were regulated by these ordinances enacted in the late eighteenth and early nineteenth centuries. The City Council, however, granted itself the authority to annually assess and if necessary alter these fixed wages. In the case of dockhands, such a change was allowed "if there be any essential rise or fall in the necessary articles of life," such as rent, food, and clothing. Modification to the pay of draymen and carters, on the other hand, was determined not solely by fluctuations in the cost of living in Charleston, but also "any material rise or fall in the price of grain, fodder or other articles of life."[98] In addition to the sum surrendered to their masters, enslaved draymen and carters regularly handed over a portion of their wages to the dray owners or companies responsible for providing and maintaining draft animals, vehicles, and other requisite equipment.[99]

In any case, waterfront workers' pay remained static until February 7, 1837, when on the eve of the Panic of 1837 the City Council amended both of the wage-fixing ordinances. Unlike in 1801 when the wages of enslaved, free black, and white porters and day laborers were prescribed equally, after 1837 the minority of white dockworkers—empowered and emboldened by the franchise since 1810—were free to demand and receive as high a rate as possible.[100] As for a "negro or other slave" hiring out as a porter or day laborer, his wages were increased in 1837 from 85 cents to one dollar for a full day's labor, which still was defined as lasting from sunrise until twilight, "allowing one hour for breakfast and one hour for dinner." This wage hike was implemented not for the welfare of the slave laborers, but to assist urban masters in offsetting increased expenses ranging from shelter and sustenance to the cost of slaves themselves. Even the annual price of porter badges doubled from two to four dollars the month after this change.[101] But employers too benefited from the revised ordinance. Rather than being assigned rates for a half or quarter day's work, black laborers employed on the docks for less than a full day now were to be paid 12 ½ cents per hour.[102] Gone were the days, in other words, of a half-day's wage for less than a half-day's labor. Meanwhile, the amended transportation ordinance updated the city's drayage rates and routes as well.[103]

Though authorities imposed these laws to limit the movements, personal incomes, and individual autonomy of hired-out slaves, bondsmen nonetheless endeavored to preserve what they deemed customary rights as pivotal port workers. Nearly a century after grand jurors first bemoaned slave porters spurning work and demanding higher wages, for instance, city marshals reported draymen to municipal authorities in 1839 for "refusing to take a load," despite the proper payments being tendered. And amid the Civil War in January 1862, city police arrested the driver of dray number 598 "For exorbitant Charges for drayage from East Bay to Rutledge Street."[104] Though some workers were caught and penalized, many surely exercised this prerogative without detection.

Others found alternative ways to work the system to their own benefit. When former Charleston merchant Thomas Napier moved back to the city from New York in 1857, he wrote to factor John P. Deveaux with specific instructions for the handling of his furniture, a portion of which was shipped in nine boxes aboard the schooner *Robert Caldwell*. Napier directed Deveaux to engage a drayman to deliver the boxes to his house on Rutledge Street near Montague Street and to "drive into the large Gate and go around to the Kitchen." He also instructed the factor to hire "two hands to help in with the Boxes, and get the hands to agree to put them into the places pointed out, even though we should have to pay them extra for it."[105] Exploiting Napier's apparent unfamiliarity with the current wage rates, not to mention his old age and blindness, these three hired slaves brashly acted. Napier described to Deveaux what transpired: "On Saturday the men commenced carrying up the Furniture to my House, and took the whole day to carry four Boxes, for which the Drayman charged 75 cents per load, and the two men who assisted in loading and unloading charged at the rate of 18 ¾ cents per hour apiece from 9 O'clock A.M. to 6 O'clock P.M. amounting in all for Drayman, and men to $6.25 which I paid them on last Saturday evening." In other words, only four of Napier's nine boxes of furniture were delivered to his house over a period of nine hours. Granted, the slaves had to load the heavy and cumbersome containers onto the dray, drive over half a mile from the wharf to the house, remove the boxes from the vehicle and carry them into the residence through the back kitchen, and finally unpack and situate the furniture as directed. But these bondsmen also embraced the chance to control and slow their pace of work and to maximize their wages.

According to the rates established in 1837, draymen who transported goods "From any of the wharves from the north side of Broad-street to Ashley river, north side of Beaufain-street, west side of King-street"—which included Napier's new house—were to receive only 31 ¼ cents per load, not 75 cents. The two day laborers hired from the waterfront porter stands to assist this crafty slave drayman were duplicitous as well, charging 18 ¾ cents per hour rather than the 12 ½ cents stipulated in 1837. And even though these hourly workers undoubtedly paused for one or two meals during the long workday, they charged Napier for the full nine hours.[106] Had Thomas Napier been better apprised of the prevailing wages, he might have challenged the workers' claim and refused payment. An irritated Napier instead paid the slaves in full at the end of the day, then instructed John Deveaux to make changes for the delivery of the other five boxes: "I think that it would be better to employ two or three Drays so that they could help each other on and off with the Boxes, and dispense with the two hands to assist." Since draymen were paid to load, haul, and unload their freight to earn their wages, even at the extravagant rate of 75 cents Napier only would have had to pay $3.75 for the conveyance of the remaining five containers. But since he needed the furniture carried into the house as well, Napier suggested that the factor pay the draymen "a little extra for putting away." The affair was far from over, however. Thirteen more boxes were on their way to Charleston aboard another vessel, to be followed by a third shipment yet to leave New York, "which will close this very troublesome business."[107]

Troublesome business indeed. Over the preceding decades, slaves' labor and lives had been tightly prescribed by law. The practice of roaming the wharves and seeking the most favorable task and pay had been eroded and replaced by restrictive slave badges, hiring stands, and fixed wages. The freedom to accept or refuse employment or a particular employer was stripped under pain of punishment. Work hours, commutes from hiring locations to job sites, and even meals all were regulated; meanwhile, the labor itself had become increasingly onerous and hazardous as the cotton bales and rice barrels became weightier. But persistently conscious of advantageous opportunities and especially the liberating power of demand for their own indispensable labor, enslaved workers seized the customary rights and privileges that rendered urban waterfront employment unique and seductive.

Though detached from the port's day-to-day hiring and wage-earning practices, owned dockhands appreciated the immense need for their labor as well. With many aspects of their lives on the wharf managed, these slaves sought ways to push back against the most objectionable facets of governance. The long commercial season busied these waterfront workers with moving, weighing, marking, storing, lading, and unlading the burdens of trade. But any hopes for the unhurried and dull summer months, or even fleeting lulls during the peak period, frequently were dashed by still more grueling tasks. The first explicit reference to the owned hands attached to Vanderhorst's Wharf came in 1800 when a rental agreement with George and Alexander Chisolm stated, "it is also understood that when the negro laborers on said wharf can be spared they are to be permitted to assist in the works carrying on, on the Said wharf." Subsequent wharfinger contracts contained similar stipulations. The three 1808–11 leases between Arnoldus Vanderhorst and his son John noted, "It is also agreed that when the four negro men, are not employed on the immediate business of the Wharf, that they shall assist in digging out the Cellars of the Stores now building and clearing out the dirt, Stones and brick bats, from the same and the Lott [*sic*]: and remove the same to where it may be wanted to fill up the Wharf and Stores."[108] The want of repairs and improvements was unremitting for an active and competitive wharf business, and the relatively sluggish trade of the off-season presented an annual opportunity to perform this work. Unless hired out to other Charlestonians during this downtime, wharf hands were expected to help. After a gale badly damaged the wharf, manager John Crawford wrote to Elias Vanderhorst in January 1833 requesting restorations to stay the resultant loss of business and reputation. The project would not be too costly, the wharfinger argued, since "you have the carpenters who with the assistance of the wharf hands and employing about 6 other axe men, could go on well."[109]

Unable to decline this auxiliary work outright, the Vanderhorsts' permanent dockhands possessed other means of dissent. Whereas some slaves stole or absconded from their overbearing masters and employers, Will and Dublin may have opted for feigned ailments.[110] The toll of a worker's absence from the wharf due to ill health, whether real or contrived, was lost labor, productivity, and profits, as well as the costs of substitute hires and medical bills. When itemizing the wharf's dealings in 1817 and 1818, Crawford recorded his mandatory hire of the "two fellows" Will and Dublin, but "deducting time lost during sickness." A similar credit was noted in the 1822 account, followed by the cost of two weeks' lost labor for each enslaved wharf hand in 1824. Instances of "cost time" remained frequent throughout the 1820s: Dublin was sick the entire month of June 1826; both hands were ill in January and December 1827; Will missed fourteen days of work in August 1828; and Dublin was laid up seventeen days in December 1828. But the peak came in 1829, when the "absent time of Will & Dublin this y[ea]r. on acct. sickness" totaled thirteen weeks. Five more weeks were lost in 1830, four weeks in 1832, and finally "3 weeks sickness of Dublin June, July, and August 1833," the last being in the midst of John Crawford's requested repairs.[111] These recurrent and costly bouts with illness simply may have been due to legitimate infirmity and age.[112] Will, after all, died in September 1836, and the octogenarian Dublin was nearing retirement. But one ought not rule out resistance as an alternate or simultaneous interpretation of such extensive truancy.[113]

This incessant struggle between a controlling master class and resistant black slaves, meanwhile, also was waged over matters as seemingly innocuous as waterfront work songs. But here, too, the city's various white factions and special interests disagreed whether the songs were principally placatory or seditious. Whereas the commercial lobby emphasized their mollifying and synchronizing benefits, those more concerned with order and security feared Trojan horses of rebellion. Noted scholar of African American folk music Newman Ivey White argued in 1928 that the primary purpose of work songs was not physical, but mental. Rather than to increase the force and efficiency of the laborers' united efforts, the songs, White claimed, chiefly were intended "to keep the singer's thoughts from interfering with his work, to pacify his mind with the semblance of thought without yielding to any of the distractions which more serious thoughts would involve." In other words, the primary function of these ostensibly lighthearted tunes was "to keep the worker's mind contented with at least the illusion of thought while his body is allowed to work mechanically."[114] Work songs surely helped slaves to pass the time and instituted a measure of camaraderie among the laborers.[115] If their purpose was pacification, however, one should not presume that these songs produced contented slaves. But some white contemporaries drew exactly that conclusion. Observing wharf hands stowing cotton in Charleston in 1815, New England ship captain James Carr deduced not only that work songs made the slaves' "tasks go off hand more cheerily," but also that since "a Negro alone, seems a solitary being—he delights to work in large gangs—is loquacious & appears perfectly happy." Visitor N. M. Perkins, just prior to describing "a stevedore, on board ship," wrote in November 1841 to a business associate in New York, "One thing is certain, the slaves are happy; no man but an idiot, even if looked the opposite direction, but would notice."[116]

Slaves knew better. One slave in Charleston later reflected on his first impressions of his fellow bondsmen when he arrived in the city in the early nineteenth century: "Draymen, porters, and workmen of every description, seemed generally merry and hearty; and, in the loading of ships with cotton, rice, &c., a stranger would think the negro one of the merriest creatures in the world: such continual singing and bawling going on, as if there were no such thing as care in the world." Time and personal experience revealed, however, that he "had yet only seen the bright side of the picture," and had "observed few of the evils of slavery."[117] The editor of the magazine *The Nation*—which was founded by abolitionists in July 1865—likewise cautioned in 1867 that the outwardly jocular lyrics and buoyant tone of slave work songs misleadingly could suggest "the easiness of the yoke of bondage." The songs, the editor argued, rather were "the embodiment of the mental and physical anguish of a bruised race—the safety valve of their complaining and revolt against oppression."[118] In other words, just as plantation and city slaves alike broke tools, played the fool, faked injury or illness, or subtly altered the pace of labor, work songs served as still another means to protest grueling and perilous work conditions, long hours, and paltry or no wages without directly confronting the overwhelming force of slaveowner power.[119] An episode aboard the brig *Chili* during the 1830s exemplified enslaved wharf hands' thinly veiled verbal critiques of domineering employers. After the ship's captain beat a resilient white cabin boy, Henry B. Hill of Massachusetts, slaves unloading the vessel were heard "vigorously" retorting, "Thank God, Massa Captain ain't conquered him yet."[120]

White Charlestonians also knew better than to assume that singing meant happy slaves. Whereas some visitors like James Carr thought the slaves' songs charming curiosities, locals found them increasingly menacing, repulsive, and jarring. Charleston's Grand Jury entreated the legislature in January 1793 to "prevent the scandalous practice of profane Swearing"; among the jurors' complaints in September 1799 was "the noise, and disturbance made by Domestics thro' the Streets."[121] Even the city's commercial leaders eventually had enough of the custom and joined the call for curtailment. In September 1801 the City Council passed an ordinance aimed in part to regulate and suppress the loud, bawdy, and seditious work songs that permeated the waterfront. The law was said to be justified because "it has of late become a practice with slaves, to be whooping and hallooing indecently about the streets, or on the wharves, and to sing aloud obscene songs, in which practice they more especially indulge while working on board shipping, to the great hindrance of those who are engaged in business, on the wharves, and to the general disturbance of the citizens." It was this same ordinance—passed amid the ongoing Haitian Revolution, the aftermath of

Gabriel's failed rebellion in Virginia, and Thomas Jefferson and the Democratic Republicans' "Revolution of 1800"—that again cracked down on slaves' "exorbitant and varying demands" by fixing waterfront workers' wages and establishing the five stationary porter stands. The audacity of the city's enslaved wharf hands thus extended well beyond boisterous and crude singing; yet municipal officials did not take this destabilizing workplace din lightly. Offenders were to receive up to ten stripes at the workhouse, the expense of which was to be paid by the slaves' owners. But if the transgression took place on a ship at the wharves, then "the master, mate, owner, or consignee of the vessel, on board of which such whooping, hallooing, or obscene singing is heard" was obligated to pay for the correction. As with workers' fixed wages, the harbor master was assigned the duty of familiarizing every captain who docked at the wharves with this clause.[122]

City authorities understood that work songs served a useful and even indispensable function in their port's efficiency and prosperity. But like talking vociferously or cursing publicly, singing bawdy lyrics while unloading or loading a vessel at the wharves was a long-prevailing way for overworked and underpaid urban slave wage laborers to challenge their work conditions and meager earnings as well as their enslavement. Lawmakers therefore targeted the disruptive, irreverent, and potentially rebellious features of these waterfront songs, rather than the singing itself. But whether owing to worker defiance, lack of enforcement, or the law's subjective nature, the 1801 ordinance failed to eradicate the disagreeable behavior. Another measure passed as part of the comprehensive black code in October 1806 reaffirmed the prohibition against blacks "whooping or hallooing any where in the city, or of making a clamorous noise, or of singing aloud any indecent song." The punishment for those who violated this ordinance was increased to a maximum of twenty lashes. And if the crime took place on a vessel, now the ship master was to be fined twenty dollars for each offense.[123]

Collections of slave work songs reveal the obscenity and temerity of some tunes. Songs about sex, hard drinking, gambling, and other riotous behavior were common among southern work gangs.[124] Charlestonians long had bemoaned the dram and grog shops of the city that illegally sold or traded liquor to slaves and allegedly corrupted their morals and encouraged laziness and pilferage. Various city ordinances had sought to eliminate these shops and slave drinking. But slaves boldly pushed back against white control and persisted in their desire and quest for alcohol. Indeed, two of the work songs James Carr heard in the hold of his vessel in Charleston in 1815 explicitly referred to liquor:

> Ceasar should you like a dram;
> Ceasar boy Ceasar.
> Ceasar will you have a dram;
> Ceasar boy Ceasar.

Ceasar is a smart fellow,
  Ceasar boy Ceasar.

Tis grog time o day,
  huzza my jolly boys, tis grog time o day;
Back like a crow bar, belly like a tin pan,
  huzza my jolly boys, tis grog time o day;
Tis grog time o day; tis grog time o day;
  huzza my jolly boys, tis grog time o day.
Tis time for to go, tis time for to go;
  huzza my jolly boys, tis time for to go;
Haul away so tis time for to go,
  huzza my jolly boys, tis time for to go.[125]

Fully cognizant of whites' efforts to stamp out blacks' consumption of alcohol, the enslaved waterfront workers aboard Captain Carr's vessel nonetheless sang openly and subversively about grog and dram. Despite longs hours of exhausting work, these bondsmen laboring in Carr's hold boasted of their strong backs and stomach muscles, while motivating themselves with the prospect of a drink during an impending break or at the end of the workday. Extant accounts, in fact, showed that some wharf owners illicitly provided their slave workers with alcohol. When Vanderhorst's Wharf required repairs between July and December 1823, among the expenses was $22.62 "paid for Rum for hands during time of Work." It likewise cost $386 in one year to purchase "food & Liquor" for the eight enslaved wharf hands regularly employed on Vanderhorst's Wharf.[126]

Though James Carr captured these references to alcohol and commented on the volume of the singing, he did not describe or complain of any profane or otherwise inappropriate lyrics being sung by the twenty slaves he hired to pack cotton into his vessel's hold.[127] Nonetheless, the prospect of twenty lashes, and the potential fines imposed on the owners of hired-out slaves or ship masters such as Carr, again failed to curb the much maligned "whooping and hallooing" early in the nineteenth century. Just a few years after Captain Carr's observations, the City Council was compelled in July 1819 to further amend and toughen the 1801 and 1806 ordinances. "Whereas, public decorum and due observance of public decency are at all times worthy of the attention of this Council," the 1806 law had "been found inefficient to secure these objectives." Still under pain of twenty stripes, blacks were barred from using "any blasphemous or indecent words, or crying out in a blasphemous, obscene or indecent manner." Those who carried out "any loud or offensive conversations" on street corners or other public places in the city—such as slaves awaiting hire at the designated porter stands—were subject to between five and twenty lashes.[128] This gulf between these laws' goals

54

and their efficacy in practice persisted through the remainder of the antebellum period, as white authorities struggled both against unruly slaves and with one other to simultaneously achieve economic and racial dominion.[129]

Work songs, of course, were not the only means by which bondsmen harnessed everyday aspects of their waterfront labor and culture to fulminate against enslavement. Unlike wharf hands, who typically toiled in pairs or gangs, slave draymen frequently worked alone. Though cut off in the midst of a task from one's fellows, these vital port workers nonetheless possessed their own unique and effective tools of protest and resistance. Armed with horses, whips, and wheeled vehicles, the city's enslaved draymen were expected to transport goods swiftly and adeptly. Not solely beneficial to Charleston's commercial interests, such efficiency also advantaged many of the laborers themselves. Draymen, such as those who fleeced Thomas Napier in 1857, occasionally profited from slowing their pace. Some merely received a flat weekly or monthly wage from their masters regardless how much they worked. But others secured more favorable terms, pocketing all wages earned beyond a predetermined amount. Such draymen, then, possessed the drive to complete as many jobs as possible in a given day to enable the purchase of food, clothing, shelter, alcohol, entertainment, and sometimes freedom for themselves or a family member. Speed, then, was essential to the fulfillment of both the city's commercial interests and numerous workers' individual sustenance and aspirations. But just as hastiness on the docks increased workplace danger, accidents, injuries, and deaths, fast driving frequently precipitated reckless driving, putting at risk workers and nonworkers alike.[130]

Travelers' erroneous observations went beyond surmising that the port's workers were unchecked and contented and their waterfront songs harmless and appealing. One northerner wrote in 1835 that slaves "seem to be in perpetual awe of the whites" and "stop to let you pass." "Is a drayman passing through a street, which crosses your path," the visitor continued, "he does not, like ours, let you clear yourself if you can, but pauses at a most respectful distance."[131] But many resident Charlestonians would have been perplexed by this comment, including Jacob Schirmer, who had recorded in his diary ten months earlier that "a little daughter of Mr. Allender was carelessly run over by a Drayman and had her leg broke." In April 1839, four years to the day of the northerner's published remarks, Schirmer again tragically noted that a "Jury of Inquest served over a Child of Mr. Davidson," who was knocked down, trampled upon, and "Killed by a Horse [and] a Dray."[132]

Far from isolated, however, such injurious and deadly incidents were epidemic in the streets of Charleston, prompting authorities to act. The 1764 colonial statute regulating the employment of waterfront workers enunciated penalties for improper and fast driving. The 1805 and 1806 transportation ordinances again barred the fast and reckless driving of drays and other vehicles, specifying the appropriate pace of conveyance through the city as no "faster than a walk."[133] A separate 1806 measure even prohibited the driving of drays and carts—not to mention the rolling of heavy commercial barrels—on the foot pavements in the effort to better protect pedestrians and municipal infrastructure alike.[134] The "melancholy" occurrences continued nonetheless. Reverend John B. Adger recalled how in the mid-1810s his young brother, future merchant and wharf owner James Adger III, was run over by a dray carrying a hogshead of tobacco on Boundary Street (renamed Calhoun Street in 1850).[135] Fed up, Charleston's Grand Jury complained in October 1821 about the manner in which slaves and free blacks rode through the streets at breakneck speed, endangering children and other pedestrians.[136]

Many perpetrators were, indisputably, held to account. City Attorney John Wroughton Mitchell prosecuted cases of "riding fast" in 1819, and his law records include a free black drayman compelled in 1831 to pay medical expenses to the owner of a slave woman he ran over.[137] City Council minutes from the late 1830s and early 1840s, meanwhile, document dozens of slave—and occasionally free black and white—draymen and carters who were arrested and then either fined or lashed for improper and reckless driving. Marshal Prendergast, for example, reported to the mayor and council in January 1840 the driver of dray number 96 for breaking a lamppost on George Street, that of number 200 for injuring the pavement, of dray 67 for overturning a stone step on King Street, and a slave carter for driving fast.[138] Though one Charleston "Citizen" acknowledged municipal officials in the pages of the *Charleston Courier* for enforcing the laws against fast-driving carters and draymen, unclear is whether the steady stream of pecuniary and physical punishments actually altered workers' behavior.[139] Pressure from masters, dray owners, employers, merchants, and commercial boosters—not to mention the incentives of working rapidly and earning increased wages—eroded the administration of justice and public safety over time. By the late 1840s it became necessary for the City Council to resolve, "That the Ordinance respecting fast driving be most rigidly enforced, as several instances have occurred where the draymen have most wantonly driven over persons, and very serious consequences have ensued."[140]

As the years passed and casualties mounted, many white Charlestonians adopted this air of suspicion that not all of these abundant episodes were mere accidents. In May 1860 the *Charleston Tri-Weekly Courier* remonstrated against "the existence of an evil that our community has too long patiently borne," and renewed calls for executing the law. "Rapid and reckless driving in open violation of a City Ordinance," the writer claimed, "is indulged in to a fearful extent by many of our merciless and spirited drivers." Earlier that week a slave named John ran over and killed a four-year-old girl with his loaded dray just blocks from the waterfront. "The unfortunate little creature had its arm and back broken, and was otherwise mangled in a frightful manner," the newspaper reported. The previous June another child was, in the words of Jacob Schirmer, "Run over on the Bay by a horse and Dray and almost instantly killed." Dismissing those who blamed the carelessness of victims, the *Courier* insisted that ladies in the town frequently were forced to dash back to the sidewalk when attempting to cross the street.[141] Savannah's *Daily Morning News* reported similar outrages in March 1859, alleging that some draymen "seem to take a delight in seeing how near they can come to driving over [some]one, without actually doing it." Just during the preceding week several local women, as in Charleston, "had to run for their lives" to avoid falling victim.[142] The implication that such incidents were, in fact, deliberate and malicious attacks on white Charlestonians raised the prospect that some transportation workers were exploiting the distinct instruments of their employment to object to their circumstances and bondage. Whereas plantation slaves "accidentally" wrecked tools or crops and wharf hands "clumsily" damaged valuable commercial goods or mishandled a cotton bale, urban draymen and carters opposed control over their lives by willfully imperiling the lives of others.

Though black laborers most often overcame or circumvented the attempted mastery of their labor and lives from within the institution of slavery, some elected to exit the system altogether. Like bondsmen throughout the early national and antebellum South—whether on remote cotton plantations or in populous urban centers—many of Charleston's enslaved dockworkers ran away, prompting frequent notices in the city's newspapers from white slaveowners. In 1799, for example, Archibald Calder announced the absconding of his slave Cyrus, who was "well known upon all the wharves in Charleston, as a drayman." Wharf owner George Chisolm offered twenty-dollar rewards in 1812 and 1821 for capturing and lodging his runaway wharf hands in the workhouse. Sam Polaskey, according to Chisolm, was "a stout, strong made black fellow . . . and for several years a wharf hand on the wharf of the subscriber," whereas another "stout, well sett [*sic*] Fellow" named Jack was "generally well known as one of my wharf hands for many years."[143] Wharf owners' business papers revealed the flight of other waterfront workers. When tallying the income for Vanderhorst's Wharf between October 1, 1806, and September 30, 1807, the costs of "Sickness & Running away" among the five wharf slaves was deducted from the year's profits. A detailed accounting of expenses showed that, after Marcus ran away in late 1807, Arnoldus Vanderhorst paid to capture and lodge the enslaved dockhand in the workhouse before buying him "a suit cloths [*sic*]" and selling him in early 1808. Taffey similarly was apprehended and punished in the workhouse in early 1810. Around the same time, wharf owner Christopher Fitzsimons sold one of his slaves, Sambo, who absconded three times within four months.[144]

Obviously a means to escape bondage, at least temporarily, running away also served as an effective form of protest and resistance against the persistent efforts of employers, masters, and city officials to control nearly every facet of water-front employment, conventions, and culture. Daily struggling to make ends meet within the confines of badge laws, fixed hiring locations, capped wage rates, and censured work songs, aggrieved dock laborers strove to reclaim the promise and advantages of urban waterfront work along the shores of the Atlantic World. By withholding crucial physical labor from their employers, hiring out with-out their owners' knowledge or consent, or refusing to hand over wages to their masters, absconded waterfront workers fended off subjugation and insisted on benefiting from the rewards of their own back-breaking exertions. Even while presiding over South Carolina's revolutionary Provincial Congress convened in 1775 to champion liberty and independence from the ostensible tyranny and en-slavement of Great Britain, Henry Laurens chastised his brother's slave Ishmael who—though not absconding—attempted to conceal £30 he earned working as a porter without Laurens's permission.[145] Slaveowner John Smith warned readers of the *Charleston Times* in January 1808 "not to employ my two fellows, ABRAM and JACOB—the first a carpenter, the other a stevadore [*sic*]," both of whom had been hiring themselves out despite lacking Smith's consent.[146] And opting not to continue laboring on the docks, a thirty-five-year-old wharf hand named Natt conspired with two other runaways in the early 1830s to subsist through the illicit sale of moss and "hoop poles" to stores near the city's Ashley River rice mills.[147]

In one remarkable case, Thomas C. Marshall, a perennially cash-strapped wharfinger on Crafts's Wharf, complained to his cousin in New York about the prolonged absence of one of his waterfront slaves. "I am in close pursuit of my fellow Anthony, who has been away now upwards of Two years," Marshall wrote in October 1839.[148] Two months later Marshall expressed confidence that An-thony still was in South Carolina, having "heard he was busily employed in the [Santee] canal boats, between Columbia & the lower locks." The wharfinger's source for this valuable information was a captured runaway at Charleston's workhouse, who himself claimed to have remained on the lam for years "working at times as a laborer on the wharves and at other times in the canal boats between Charleston, Columbia, & Camden." Having toiled on Charleston's docks along-side Anthony—who as a work gang foreman or header "used to lead the singing at the fall, while hoisting rice"—the apprehended bondsman revealed that he had last seen Anthony on the Santee Canal earlier that autumn. "He seldom comes to the city," the slave explained, "but when he does, he hires some one in his place to hoist the cotton & conceals himself until the return of the boat & goes on board again at Gadsden wharf." Armed with this tip and hoping to recover hundreds of dollars in lost wages, Thomas Marshall vowed to capture Anthony during the winter: "My Bull Dogs are wide awake & feel desirous of obtaining the $100 I offer for lodging him in the work house."[149]

Unwilling or unable to devote such resources to the apprehension of their human property and principal sources of income and labor, other slaveowners sought to utilize the city's badge system to track down recalcitrant slaves. Aside from generating revenue for the municipal government, badges were yet another means by which city authorities regulated and monitored urban slave labor. Since slaveowners were required to purchase a new tag for their hired-out slaves each year, the badge laws aimed to curtail the number of slaves working out without the knowledge or consent of their masters. The system also endeavored to prevent nonresident runaways from finding work in the city.[150] To better ensure efficacy and enforcement, an ordinance passed in 1786 reiterated the colonial-era requirement that hired-out slaves "wear the Badge . . . on some visible part of their dress," and permitted constables or other authorized persons "to command any negro applying for hire or working out, to produce his or her badge." Slaves refusing or failing to present a badge upon request were to be taken immediately to the workhouse.[151] Thus when Peter Bee offered a ten-dollar reward in April 1807 for the return of his twenty-eight-year-old runaway Sancho, he added that the slave "Had on when he went away . . . his Badge as a Porter No. 20, by which means he gets work about Gadsden's Wharf, as he was seen there last Monday."[152] To the physical descriptors typically used to identify runaway slaves—age, height, build, color, speech, markings, scars, piercings, clothing, and so forth—was added the specific occupational category and number of the badge that the law required Sancho to wear (and if requested, proffer to authorities) to legally continue hiring out on the docks.

Further stacking the odds of detection and re-enslavement against absconded slaves like Sancho was an ordinance ratified in July 1807 obliging city marshals to check the badges of hired-out slave porters and day laborers at least once a month, and entitling these officials to half of any fees levied.[153] In 1821, perhaps following one such workplace inspection, the city fined wharf owner Otis Mills sixteen dollars for employing four slaves without badges. Municipal authorities too found wharf owner Charles A. Magwood in violation of the badge laws in 1834.[154] City Council minutes from the 1840s contained not only scores of petitions from slaveowners and employers requesting relief from badge penalties, but also marshal reports of bondsmen caught for various badge infractions.[155] The councilmen, in fact, awarded Marshal Wallace fifty dollars in June 1842 "as a compensation for his exertions in detecting Negroes working out with improper Badges."[156] So though Captain Richard Clark claimed in an 1836 runaway ad that a description of his servant Ely was "needless, as he is well known," the master was sure to mention that the slave "had a badge to work on the wharves generally, [and] was also hired by Mr. W[illiam]. Patton, to work on the Steamboat wharf."[157] Clark presumed that the city's constrictive badge system would assist in the identification and recovery of his valuable waterfront property.

But as with other attempts to manipulate and control waterfront workers, slaves also regularly evaded badge laws and boldly defied the aims of the tightly circumscribed hiring regime. Though the tags were devised as emblems of ownership, dominion, and shame, slaves hiring out their own time along the waterfront bore them as manifest symbols of their independent earning power, autonomy, and freedom as urban laborers.[158] Rather than being identified and arrested, runaways possessing badges just as often employed this licensing scheme to persist in laboring on the docks and earning wages fully for themselves. Using the master class's own system "as a protection against being committed" in 1827, a runaway drayman named Frank wore and presented his slave badge when posing as a free black man did not suffice.[159] One former slave recounted his elusion of capture while working on the docks as a runaway in the 1830s. The day after this fugitive arrived in Charleston, he walked to the waterfront and waited at a "stevedore's stand" with other hands seeking work. After being hired without a badge to stow cotton, the slave described how he found a tag during a lunch break:

> One day in going from the cook-shop to the vessel, I was walking along among the bales of cotton on the wharf and saw something shining on the ground. I did not know what it was, but picked it up and put it in my pocket. It had a chain to it and some marks on it. That night, when we were all at work, the policeman came on board the vessel with a paper in his hand and said, "Holloo, have you got any runaway niggers here?" The stevedore said "no,—no runaways in this lot." Then the police man said he must see badge. So he made them all show badge. When he came to me, I took the thing that I had found out of my pocket, because I saw it looked just like the rest. I was very much frightened, because I did not know as it would do, but he looked at it and said it was right, and then I felt mighty glad. If I had not had that badge I should have been carried straight to the [work] house.[160]

Even when under the scrupulous eye of municipal authorities, slaves found ways to slip the system with a combination of attentiveness, resourcefulness, and sometimes luck.

With or without badges, runaways and other workers seeking to hire themselves out without their owners' permission oftentimes found willing white collaborators. Though city officials strictly enforced the regulations on occasion, waterfront employers in need of labor frequently undermined the laws and, risking heavy fines, illegally hired slaves lacking tags. As a contemporary white city resident put it, even runaways "who will work, may get employ."[161] Charleston slaveowner A. B. Wilson exhibited little faith that the city's stringent hiring protocols would prevent his young slave Henry—described as having "a countenance somewhat grum"—from finding dock work in the city. Though the runaway "has no ticket or badge from me," Wilson explained, he nonetheless "is supposed to be working on the wharves, driving a dray or hack, or employed by some one in the Upper Wards."[162] Empowered by the very same appetite for labor that, ironically, kept them enslaved in the antebellum South, the city's black dockhands deftly exploited white Charlestonians' competing interests in surveillance and security on the one hand and productivity and profitability on the other.

By performing Charleston's most essential labor, waterfront workers became the master class's foremost targets of exploitation and control. But being situated along the seaboard also rendered that domination most difficult. In 1832, in fact, Charlestonian Edward R. Laurens included slave stevedores, wharf laborers, and draymen among those occupations "the very nature of which relieves [slaves] in a great measure from the wholesome restraint of a master's eye."[163] Given the opportunity to toil in the most crowded, hurried, cosmopolitan, and outward-looking locale within an already relatively autonomous urban environment, enslaved dockworkers were not contented with limiting their defiance and agency to working without a badge, refusing to hand over wages, declining a job, altering the pace of labor, feigning illnesses, singing loudly, driving recklessly, or overcharging for their services. Access to the circulating flow of goods, people, and information about the expansive Atlantic World offered so much more, and Charleston's enslaved waterfront labor force took full advantage.

Chapter Three

"Improper assemblies & conspiracies"

The Advantageous Enticements of Wharf Labor

In 1862 a former South Carolina slave named John Andrew Jackson published an account of his enslavement and escape from bondage during the winter of 1846–47.[1] In this narrative Jackson claimed to have become aware of the geographical limits of slavery from northern travelers passing through rural South Carolina. "The 'Yankees,' or Northerners, when they visited our plantations," the former slave explained, "used to tell the negroes that there was a country called England, where there were no slaves, and that the city of Boston was free; and we used to wish we knew which way to travel to find those places." John Andrew Jackson often had been tasked with driving his master's cattle to market in Charleston, located approximately 150 miles away, and it occurred to Jackson that "if I could hide in one of the vessels I saw lading at the wharfs [sic], I should be able to get to the 'Free country,' wherever that was." During a three-day Christmas holiday in 1846, Jackson slipped away from the festivities of the slave quarters and made his way to Charleston on a pony. Recalling that it was the custom in the city for masters to hire out their bondsmen, he joined a gang of slave wharf hands on the docks and—despite lacking the mandatory badge used to visibly identify and regulate the city's enslaved workers—earned wages "without arousing any suspicion."[2]

After laboring on the docks for several weeks, Jackson boarded a ship and inquired of the free black cook whether the vessel was bound for Boston. After the cook affirmed that it was, the runaway asked, "Can't you stow me away?" The free black seaman immediately said that he could, but having second thoughts he asked Jackson, "Did not some white man send you here to ask me this?" The cook elucidated that under the provisions of South Carolina's controversial Negro Seamen Acts—passed between 1822 and 1856 and designed to prevent seditious communications between southern slaves and northern or foreign free blacks— the black members of the crew had been in jail since the vessel's arrival, but that in preparation for departure the captain had paid to release them from confinement the day before.[3] Despite his misgivings, the free black cook agreed to look for a place to hide Jackson, but beseeched the fugitive not to betray him.

When Jackson returned to the vessel the next morning, the cook again expressed apprehension and told the slave to go ashore and that he wanted nothing to do with him. Jackson obeyed, but sneaked on board after the cook entered the ship's galley. Tiptoeing to the cargo hatch, the runaway waited there for the captain or mate to emerge from the cabin. When the mate appeared, Jackson asked permission to remove the hatch, and "He thinking that I was one of the gang coming to work there, told me I might." Jackson descended and soon was joined in the hold by a gang of slave laborers, who began questioning him about his occupation and owner. "Just then they were all ordered on deck, and as soon as I was left, I slipped myself between two bales of cotton, with the deck above me, in a space not large enough for a bale of cotton to go; and just then a bale was placed at the mouth of my crevice, and shut me in a space about 4-ft. by 3-ft., or thereabouts. I then heard them gradually filling up the hold; and at last the hatch was placed on, and I was left in total darkness." Cramped, dehydrated, and nearly asphyxiated—conditions not unlike those experienced by millions of enslaved Africans during the Atlantic crossing—John Andrew Jackson was forced to reveal himself en route to Boston. The captain, like the free black cook, was convinced that he was being entrapped and that a white Charlestonian had ordered Jackson to stow away in the vessel. The captain therefore resolved to return the runaway aboard the first southward ship encountered; "however, he met no vessel." On the evening of February 10, 1847, the ship and stowaway docked in Boston and Jackson obtained his freedom.[4]

As evidenced by John Andrew Jackson's account, laboring on an urban waterfront had its advantages, even for the enslaved. The antebellum South's bustling wharves and levees offered slaves more than the capacity to hire out one's own time, earn wages, and claim a measure of autonomy. Situated on the western rim of the Atlantic World—in what might be characterized as an amphibious or littoral borderland—slaves toiling along Charleston's seaboard also were afforded ample occasion to interact with northern and foreign mariners, stow away in dockside vessels and abscond to northern ports, and steal or pilfer valuable commercial goods.[5] These labor and life experiences were in many ways unique. Due to the nature of their indispensable work, enslaved dock laborers in this coastal port were daily subject to outside influences and presented with remarkable opportunities and enticements not accessible to most plantation slaves or even other urban bondsmen not employed along the water's edge. Not even the slaves of New Orleans's crowded levees or those manning the hundreds of steamboats plying the Mississippi enjoyed quite all of the potential and inherent benefits of perpetual exposure and access to oceangoing vessels of the nearby Atlantic and their crews. Consequent legislation such as South Carolina's Negro Seamen Acts and the 1841 New York Ship Inspection Law aimed to further control the communications and movements of the city's bondsmen. But as with those measures censuring work songs and prescribing slave badges, hiring stands, and fixed wages, enslaved dockworkers were not so easily dominated and found ways to resist and circumvent such restrictions.[6]

Such episodes and legislation not only failed to preclude black agency and indefatigability, but also had unintended consequences for Charleston's ailing commercial economy and its waterfront workers, sowed discord among local whites, and fanned the flames of the sectional divide on the eve of the Civil War. White Charlestonians' hopes to revitalize their port's prosperity while simultaneously endeavoring to restrain its most vital yet latently seditious labor force moreover highlights an antebellum South and broader mid-nineteenth-century American and Atlantic environment fraught with numerous contradictions and tensions—between the forces of progress and reaction, federal power and states' rights, and especially freedom and slavery.

The Negro Seamen Acts were a series of laws enacted in southern coastal states beginning in the early 1820s intended to halt abolitionist and insurrectionary contact between urban slaves and northern or foreign free black sailors. Although South Carolina's Negro Seamen Acts have received the most scholarly attention, similar laws also were passed in Georgia (1829), North Carolina (1830–31), Florida (1832), Alabama (1837, 1839, 1841), Mississippi (1842), Louisiana (1842), and Texas (1856), suggesting that the subsequent findings and analyses reach far beyond Charleston and inform the history of many antebellum southern ports. Though much has been written over the past eighty years about the diplomatic, political, economic, and legal repercussions of the various Seamen Acts, conspicuously absent has been a discussion of how the acts affected waterfront work and workers.[7] Given that these laws sought to forestall the "evil consequences" of free black seamen maliciously mingling with and contaminating the city's slaves, it is important to consider their impact upon the hundreds and perhaps thousands of enslaved waterfront workers who were most exposed to the influences of mariners from all over the Atlantic World.[8]

The Negro Seamen Acts were prompted by the discovery and preemption in 1822 of the alleged slave revolt led by free black Charlestonian Denmark Vesey. Among the thousands of slaves said to have been recruited for the Vesey plot were "600 men on the Bay" and "some hundred Draymen."[9] Dozens of meetings among the plot's leaders and participants furthermore took place on the Cooper River waterfront.[10] Perault Strohecker—who "had worked out and paid his wages with extreme punctuality"—recruited merchant Benjamin Hammet's slave Bacchus "whilst hauling cotton to the wharf" from Hammet's storehouse.[11] "George a Stevidore [sic]" reportedly attended a meeting at Vesey's house on Bull Street, and "met Perault twice upon the Bay."[12] Adam Bellamy "was a Carter and worked on Williams's Wharf when Paris Ball [a stevedore], Pompey Lord, James Clement and Nero [a cooper] worked, all of whom were engaged in the conspiracy."[13] Among other waterfront workers joining in this endeavor were drayman Jack Cattell—who while "down upon the Bay" pointed out his master and vowed to kill him—and William Garner, who was "to command the Draymen" and himself "had got twelve or thirteen draymen to join."[14] Enslaved cotton packers, porters, coopers, ropemakers, ship carpenters and caulkers, and mariners also were implicated in the extant trial record.

White Charlestonians suspected that visiting free black seamen—while docked at the Cooper River wharves and afforded extensive interactions with these hundreds of waterfront rebels—had encouraged Vesey and intended to assist the rebellion. One slave conspirator, for instance, claimed that "a brown man, the steward of [a] cutter, had stolen some of the arms" for use in the plot.[15] Monday Gell, a ringleader and principal court informant during the subsequent trials, maintained that he had walked with Vesey to Vanderhorst's Wharf, where Vesey asked a black ship cook named William to carry a letter addressed to Haitian president Jean-Pierre Boyer to Port-au-Prince.[16] An African-born slave cooper, John Enslow, testified that "Gell also wrote letters to St. Domingo by the steward of a Brig lying at Gibbes [sic] & Harpers [sic] Wharf" in the effort to gain assistance from the black inhabitants of that island.[17] And South Carolina governor and Charlestonian Thomas Bennett—who himself had seven slaves implicated in the conspiracy—contended that this bearer of Monday Gell's correspondence was "a negro from one of the northern states."[18]

White sailors too were tried and convicted "on indictments for attempting to excite the slaves to insurrection."[19] Among four white men brought before a Charleston court of sessions in early October 1822 were William Allen and John Igneshias. Allen—described as "a tall, stout, fine looking sailor, a Scotchman by birth, about forty-five years of age, and who had recently arrived in Charleston"—was accused of urging the execution of the Vesey plot and volunteering to participate in the revolt. Despite assuring local blacks that "though he had a white face, he was a negro in heart," this white mariner told authorities that his motives were pecuniary and that black liberation "was an object of no importance to him." Concluding that Allen "was not actually engaged in the conspiracy," the court nevertheless sentenced the sailor to a one-year imprisonment and a $1,000 fine.[20]

John Igneshias, a tall, athletic, "Spaniard, a sea-faring man, about forty or forty-five years of age," was overheard conversing with a slave along the waterfront and exhorting blacks to slaughter the city's white residents. Found guilty, Igneshias received a three-month sentence and a hundred-dollar fine.[21] South Carolina's attorney general elected to prosecute these "degenerate white men" for the "Misdemeanor in inciting Slaves to Insurrection" rather than the capital offense of engaging in actual rebellion. But municipal officials were convinced that the similar and "perhaps more aggravated" crimes of many other "desperate" white men, including additional white sailors, remained undetected and unpunished.[22]

Free black mariners, meanwhile, were presumed to have fomented the revolt by importing and circulating the "injudicious speeches" and pamphlets of northern abolitionists.[23] Denmark Vesey reportedly possessed a pamphlet opposing the slave trade, whereas Monday Gell was said to have "read several speeches, and pamphlets" which convinced him "that the *Northern Brothers* would assist them" in the conspiracy.[24] Mary Lamboll Beach wrote to her sister in Pennsylvania of "the voluminous papers found" in possession of the conspirators, while Governor Bennett maintained, "Materials were abundantly furnished in the seditious pamphlets brought into this state, by equally culpable incendiaries."[25] Anticipating the passage of the Negro Seamen Acts almost exactly five months later, another Charlestonian dramatically vowed in the immediate aftermath of the plot's discovery, "We will throw back on them all these black free incendiaries."[26]

The South Carolina General Assembly responded swiftly and, amid the broader struggle to control enslaved waterfront workers and regulate their access to information, passed the first series of Negro Seamen Acts on December 21, 1822. Under the provisions of the legislation, free blacks employed aboard vessels docking at a South Carolina port from any other state or foreign nation were to be seized and placed in jail until their vessels were ready to depart. Furthermore, the captains of these vessels were required to pay for the expenses of these confinements, and if they failed either to remove the free black seamen from the port or refused to pay for their detentions, the captains could be fined at least one thousand dollars or imprisoned for two months, and the free black seamen could be sold as slaves.[27] Though "white men of the lowest characters" such as sailors William Allen and John Igneshias had been implicated in the Vesey plot less than two months prior to the passage of the Negro Seamen Acts, the legislation omitted provisions concerning foreign or northern white mariners.[28]

Proponents of the Negro Seamen Acts insisted that the laws were "a necessary precaution to prevent [black seamen] access to our slaves" and that South Carolina had a right to self-preservation.[29] The South Carolina Association—a group of prominent white Charlestonians formed in 1823 to maintain order and implement stricter controls over the city's black population—warned, "To permit a free intercourse to exist . . . between our slaves and [northern] free persons of colour, would be, to invite new attempts at insurrection." Members of the association, which included many wharf owners and merchants, also decried the "abundant opportunities" northern free black mariners had "for introducing among our slaves, the moral contagion of their pernicious principles and opinions"—namely, freedom, abolition, sedition, and rebellion.[30] In fact, the Negro Seamen Acts frequently were compared to maritime quarantine regulations enacted to inhibit the importation of deadly infectious diseases, and free black seamen accordingly were likened to "clothes infected with the plague."[31] One Charleston merchant summed up the sentiments of the acts' defenders when he averred, "we think it necessary, and the niggers and the Yankee merchants must learn to put up with it."[32]

Despite the fervent defense of the Negro Seamen Acts, they encountered widespread opposition and generated endless controversy. Critics argued that the acts were ineffective and failed to prevent dangerous interactions with the city's slaves. Some Charleston merchants labeled the laws "totally useless and inefficient" and contended that they were "liable to perpetual evasion and infractions."[33] One Charleston Grand Jury expressed concern that free black seamen detained under the Negro Seamen Acts nevertheless were coming into contact with slave prisoners in the city jail, thus negating the laws' segregationist intent.[34] Opportunities for subversive exchanges, such as that between John Andrew Jackson and the free black cook from Boston, also existed during the interval between a sailor's release from confinement and his vessel's departure. Some foreign observers simply thought the legislation perplexing. "And how can such a measure be useful? I should be at a loss to reply," wrote the Marquis de Lafayette's secretary Auguste Levasseur during the Frenchmen's visit to Charleston in March 1825.[35] The British consul for the Carolinas, George Mathew, concurred with Levasseur, pointing out that, given the thousands of free blacks living in the city and the state and the constant presence of foreign visitors in Charleston, it was unlikely that any of the city's slaves were yet unaware of black freedom and the geographical limits of slavery.[36]

Steady and fervent salvos against the acts, in fact, were launched from representatives of the British government, who decried the treatment of free British subjects and argued that the laws violated the free trade provisions of the 1815 Commercial Convention between the United States and Great Britain. Northern state governments responded likewise. But when Massachusetts agent Samuel Hoar arrived in Charleston in late 1844 to initiate legal suits challenging the arrests of free black citizens of the Bay State, the South Carolina legislature condemned him as a seditious danger to public safety, and Hoar was compelled to flee under the threat of mob violence. South Carolina authorities similarly derided the Massachusetts legislature in 1845 for its increasing hostility toward the institution of slavery and lamented the potential "downfall of our once happy union."[37]

Opponents of the Negro Seamen Acts, moreover, questioned and challenged the laws' constitutionality. Within weeks of the acts' passage both a local district court and the South Carolina Court of Appeals upheld their constitutionality. But then in August 1823, the U.S. Circuit Court ruled that the laws violated the federal government's exclusive right to regulate commerce and therefore were unconstitutional. The acts' apologists declared that the court's decision violated the state's sovereignty, thus placing the doctrine of states' rights at the heart of the defense of the Negro Seamen Acts. Officials in South Carolina accordingly disregarded the ruling and continued to imprison free black seamen, igniting what some scholars have considered the first crisis between the state and the federal government.[38]

Meanwhile, foreign and American ship captains alike complained that the Negro Seamen Acts engendered significant cost, inconvenience, and delay, and deprived them the labor of their free black crewmen. British captain Peter Petrie, for example, protested in January 1824 that "the release of these unfortunate men from jail, fees and loss of their services put me to considerable expense."[39] Another captain wrote to Boston shipping merchant Thomas Lamb, "you will sea [sic] by our bill of disbersments [sic] that it is two [sic] expencive [sic] to bring blacks here after this."[40] One Charlestonian estimated that the costs incurred from the acts amounted to a "tax" of twenty thousand dollars annually on those trading in Charleston rather than other southern ports.[41] Such sentiments prompted members of Charleston's Chamber of Commerce to remonstrate that the laws were impoverishing the city by driving trade to competing ports such as Savannah and were threatening to "Shackle the commerce of Charleston."[42] Despite Georgia passing its own (albeit less severe) Negro Seamen Acts in December 1829, Savannah annually exported more cotton bales than Charleston between 1825 and 1838, with a total advantage of over 766,000 bales during this thirteen-year period.[43]

The Negro Seamen Acts indeed contributed to Charleston's relative economic decline during the four decades before the Civil War. The severity, expense, and inconvenience of the laws dissuaded vessels with free black seamen from entering Charleston Harbor and impeded attempts to revive the city's commercial prosperity. But with the real export of cotton generally on the rise despite the acts, hundreds of vessels employing black mariners continued to dock at the city's wharves.[44] Even after factoring in the cost of confinement while in Charleston, captains could hire free black cooks, stewards, and seamen for lower wages than white mariners.[45] The South Carolina Association pointed out that "scarcely a vessel which arrives in our port from the North, which has not two or three, or more black persons employed," while some dropped anchor with all black crews.[46]

Once vessels arrived in Charleston and their black seamen were removed to the jail, replacement crews had to be found. White seamen sometimes were used to fill the vacated positions. In November 1839 mariner Charles Barron wrote to his father in Maine that he was the steward of his vessel for twelve days in Charleston. "They took our Cook and Steward and put them in jail," Barron explained, adding "The Captain wanted me to act as Steward and I did."[47] But not all seafaring and native working-class whites were as willing or able as Barron. Members of the Chamber of Commerce insisted that local whites were not innately suited for such work: "very few if any whites . . . are qualified to act as cooks and Stewards whilst numerous persons of colour have been regularly bred to those offices, and are capable of performing them with great dexterity." These mercantile men further contended that passengers were distressed when whites served in these traditionally black positions. White replacements not only were "extravagant and extortionate in their demands," but also often quit without notice.[48]

With free black seamen in jail and most native southern whites inept or indisposed to performing waterfront and shipboard labor, visiting ship masters frequently had little choice but to hire local black workers to temporarily take the place of detained free black crewmen. Responding in 1823 to protestations that "seamen are instruments of commerce" and that the laws therefore restrained and impaired free trade, the state's legal counsel contended that since "loading & unloading may be done by stevedores"—meaning local free black and enslaved dockworkers—the Negro Seamen Acts did not infringe upon the federal government's exclusive right to regulate commerce.[49] Henry B. Hill, who in the 1830s left Massachusetts and went to sea as the cabin boy of the brig *Chili*, recalled that, when a northern vessel arrived in Charleston, "her crew would leave her, cook and all," and "The place of cook would be supplied by parties on shore who kept slaves that they let for that purpose."[50] And thirty years after the passage of the Negro Seamen Acts, British Consul George Mathew reported allegations that "the owners of wharf and dock laborers" in Charleston had lobbied for and long supported the acts to reap the financial gains that accompanied the expanded need for their waterfront slaves.[51] The Negro Seamen Acts therefore increased demand for local enslaved dockworkers and further solidified black slaves' domination of wharf labor in early nineteenth-century Charleston.

Such potentially profitable circumstances and schemes did not come without risk, however. Mathew also observed that much ill-will and "deep irritation" were generated among northern and foreign white seamen who sometimes were forced to unload and load their vessels alongside hired black slaves. Though a vessel's white crewmen may have been used to laboring shoulder to shoulder with free black men, many considered it demeaning to work with black slaves. What's more, Mathew warned that placing enslaved waterfront workers in such close contact with aggravated white seamen "might be productive of the very danger [the acts] are designed to preclude."[52] One of the white mariners implicated in the

1822 Vesey plot, John Igneshias, had publicly proclaimed in the presence of black slaves that he "disliked everything in Charleston, but the negroes and the sailors," and promoted the violent overthrow of slavery.[53] And yet, South Carolina's resultant Negro Seamen Acts failed to suppress such seditious and abolitionist-minded communications between enslaved Charlestonians and white sailors, and in fact inadvertently facilitated such perilous associations.

Meanwhile, the extensive criticisms leveled against the Negro Seamen Acts prompted several alterations to the laws over the years. The General Assembly passed the first modifications in December 1823, repealing the enslavement provision and allowing free blacks employed on naval vessels to remain aboard while in port. But the 1823 law also enacted more severe penalties for free black offenders, and in 1835 the enslavement provision was reinstated.[54] Seeking to close a loophole, legislators amended the 1823 act in December 1825. The 1825 statute called for free black seamen to be removed and jailed, but lawmakers believed that black mariners were evading the law by passing as "free Moors, Indians and Lascars."[55] It therefore required vessels arriving with free black cooks, stewards, and seamen to drop anchor in the stream of the Cooper River at a distance of at least 150 yards from the wharves and to unload and load cargo using lighters—an expensive, inconvenient, and time-consuming process.[56] The amendment presumed that forcing vessels arriving with free blacks—or alleged free blacks—to remain in the river would avert dangerous contact between the city's slaves and any such deceitful black mariners. Lawmakers inexplicably did not account for the fact that lightermen, like other dockworkers in early nineteenth-century Charleston, were overwhelmingly black slaves. Consequently, scores of enslaved lightermen daily rowed out to vessels in the stream, where they mingled with not only potentially sympathetic white captains and crewmen but also any masquerading free black seamen. Under far less local white supervision than shoreside slave stevedores and wharf hands, enslaved lightermen discharging and loading ships in the river were more easily told about freedom, slipped an abolitionist pamphlet, or stowed away in the hold of a northern-bound vessel. Planter Alexander Mazyck may have been correct when he pointed out in 1851 that a slave rebellion had not occurred in Charleston in the nearly thirty years following the Vesey conspiracy and the passage of the original 1822 Negro Seamen Acts.[57] This coincidental absence of manifest insurrection, however, was not attributable to the acts' capacity to terminate contact with free black mariners.

The Negro Seamen Acts again were altered in 1856, permitting vessels to dock at the wharves and allowing free black seamen to remain on board rather than being removed to the jail. Captains were required to provide bonds to assure that their black mariners would not go ashore.[58] But this amendment too had unintended consequences. One ship captain petitioned the City Council in March 1858 asking relief from a fine after free black members of his crew had been "decoyed on shore by parties eager for the half penalty which goes to the informant."[59] Visiting captains also sometimes took advantage of unforeseen loopholes in the 1856 law. Henry C. Keene, master of the bark *Burlington,* wrote to his ship's owners in Maine that, since sailors were scarce in Charleston, "I get $1.12 ½ per day for my black boys, at work on cargo." Though prohibited from going ashore, Keene's free black seamen may have been moving from ship deck to ship deck and perhaps even laboring on the docks, and thus were competing for work with Charleston's slave wharf hands.[60]

Like the 1825 amendment's provision requiring lighters, the 1856 alterations failed to inhibit contact between Charleston's enslaved dockworkers and all free black seamen. Charleston's mayor, Charles Macbeth, expressed his opinion to the City Council in November 1858 that he did not think the 1856 amendment to the Negro Seamen Acts fulfilled its intended purpose: "The object of the bond was to prevent any communication with our slaves, but while our slaves, in the capacities of stevedores and laborers, worked on board of vessels in which [free blacks] were, that object was so far frustrated. The evil which it was the purpose of the legislation on the subject to guard against . . . was but little lessened." Furthermore, whereas in the recent past an average of only 140 free black seamen had arrived annually in the port, 220 entered the harbor between December 1856 and December 1857.[61] And the eight months preceding Macbeth's report—"during which there was but little trade," chiefly being the commercial off-season—had witnessed the arrival of no fewer than 233 "colored" seamen. Fearful of the corrupting influence of these increasing numbers of free black mariners upon enslaved stevedores and other waterfront laborers, the mayor pronounced that "it would be prudent for [the] Council to request the Legislature to repeal the Act of 1856."[62]

Macbeth's suggestion was disregarded, and the 1856 provisions remained in effect. Then in 1859 a small but assertive group of white master stevedores alerted the General Assembly that "Ships having Collerd [*sic*] Crews from 14 to 16 Men Commanded by Northern Men and owned at the North, hire your Slaves as Stevedores to Load and unload their Ships, and place your Slaves in direct communication with any emisary [*sic*] the North may think propper [*sic*] to send amongst us. Collerd [*sic*] persons are prohibited from colecting [*sic*] together for any purpose, but on board Ships they can collect from 40 to 60 at any time without any White Person among them, from 10 to 20 feet below decks, and 50 to 60 feet from the Ladder to go below decks." Due to the 1856 amendment to the Negro Seamen Acts, such ill-intentioned northern emissaries included not only white abolitionists but also free black mariners permitted to remain on board while in port.[63] The white stevedores underscored this point in a letter to the editors of the *Charleston Courier* in January 1860. They argued that though "free negros [*sic*] arriving in our port cannot come on shore and mingle with your slaves," the city's enslaved waterfront workers "are permitted to go on board by fifties, and then have uninterrupted intercourse with them, and not a white person present but the officers of the vessel, and perhaps they are too much occupied to pay any attention to what passes between the crew and laborers."[64]

But were such claims plausible? Or was this simply another example of the hackneyed rhetoric of hysteria and paranoia? As early as 1797 prominent white Charlestonians—including wharf owners Arnoldus Vanderhorst and Simon Magwood—petitioned the state legislature concerning the "dangerous designs and machinations of certain french [*sic*] West India Negroes" and other "nefarious and pernicious" slaves who might be introduced into the city under the guise of free black mariners. To inhibit the spread of the Haitian Revolution to the Carolina lowcountry, the memorialists suggested requiring that bonds be paid "to secure their re-exportation." A quarter-century before Denmark Vesey and the first Negro Seamen Acts, city residents clearly dreaded "improper assemblies & conspiracies" among foreign sailors and local slaves, especially urban waterfront laborers.[65]

Subsequent to the Vesey affair, when hundreds of enslaved dockworkers allegedly were exposed to the "unreflecting zeal" and "indiscreet conduct" of "abolition emissaries from St. Domingo and New York," white Charlestonians had associated free black sailors with the introduction and dissemination of "insurrectionary tracts" and subversive ideals along the waterfront.[66] It was not uncommon during the antebellum period for inhabitants to warn of the evil of "foreign philanthropy" or interference intended to "incite our people to rebellion."[67] When in December 1860 South Carolina articulated the causes and justification for the state's secession from the federal Union, delegates emphasized citizens' constitutional "right of property in slaves" and the failure of non-slaveholding states to return fugitive bondsmen. More specifically, the declaration continued, the northern states "have permitted the open establishment among them of societies, whose avowed object is to disturb the peace and to eloign the property of the citizens of other States. They have encouraged and assisted thousands of our slaves to leave their homes; and those who remain, have been incited by emissaries, books and pictures to servile insurrection."[68] But again, did northern "abolitionists spies and conspirators" really have designs against Charleston and the South?[69] Did visiting seamen ever demonstratively distribute "inflammatory" and "incendiary" publications to Charleston's enslaved waterfront workers?[70]

In 1809 city officials arrested the free black steward of the New York ship *Minerva* for importing hundreds of antislavery pamphlets. Though Charleston authorities recovered only a handful of the offending booklets, the accused seaman avoided a capital trial and punishment by consenting to permanently depart the state.[71] Many incidents, however, did not implicate free black mariners. A mob of Charlestonians, for instance, attacked a Methodist abolitionist in 1800 and destroyed his pamphlets. J. J. Negrin—a Swiss immigrant and the printer of several of Charleston's city directories during the first decade of the nineteenth century—was accused of disseminating subversive literature after his publication of the Haitian declaration of independence on July 4, 1804.[72] The persistence of such episodes prompted state lawmakers in December 1820 to legislate a thousand-dollar fine and one-year imprisonment for any white persons "convicted of having, directly or indirectly, circulated or brought within this State, any written or printed paper, with intent to disturb the peace or security of the same, in relation to the slaves of the people of this State."[73] Free blacks guilty of importing or distributing seditious materials were to be fined one thousand dollars for the first transgression, and lashed up to fifty times and banished from the state for a repeat offense. And yet, despite presumptions that free black sailors had incited the 1822 Vesey conspiracy with the spread of subversive literature, evidently no mariner—black or white—was prosecuted under this 1820 law in the aftermath of the aborted plot, further calling into question whether such threats were real or imagined.

Then on the evening of Saturday, March 27, 1830, the ship *Columbo* from Boston arrived in Charleston and docked at the wharves. "[W]hen the Negroes came on board to discharge the cargo," Edward Smith, the white steward of the northern vessel, anxiously handed one of the slave dockworkers a pamphlet. Taking notice, other slave laborers aboard the vessel approached Smith and asked him for copies, and the steward quickly gave away his two remaining booklets. Suspecting that Smith was "engaged in distributing some pamphlets of a very seditious & inflammatory character among the Slaves & persons of color" on the city's waterfront, the captain of the City Guard, Frederick Wesner, concealed himself and eavesdropped on a conversation between Smith and "a Negro fellow." According to Wesner, when the slave asked Smith for a pamphlet, the white steward replied that he did not have any additional copies but that he could get more in Boston.[74]

Smith was arrested and taken to the guard house, where he explained that on the day before departing Boston "a colored man of decent appearance and very genteely [*sic*] dressed"—who Smith took for either a minister or a bookseller—boarded the *Columbo* and asked Smith whether he would do him a favor. Smith said that he would, so long as "it would not bring him in trouble." Handing Smith a packet of pamphlets, the black Bostonian instructed Smith to "give them secretly to the Black people" in Charleston and "not let any White person know any thing about it." Smith dubiously claimed that he did not know what the pamphlets were about, that he only distributed them because he had promised to do so, and that he was unaware that he had done anything wrong or had violated the law.[75]

The grand jury rejected Smith's excuses and indicted him under the 1820 law for "falsely and maliciously contriving and contending to disrupt the peace and security of this State and to move a sedition among the Slaves of the people of this State with force and arms at Charleston." The pamphlets in question were none other than David Walker's "Appeal . . . to the Coloured Citizens of the World," which first was published only months earlier in September 1829 and promoted violent rebellion.[76] Smith, described in the *Charleston Courier* as a "foreign steward," was convicted of seditious libel on May 17, 1830, sentenced to the maximum twelve months in prison, and fined one thousand dollars.[77]

The Smith affair—occurring amid dissension over the "Tariff of Abominations" and on the eve of a Nullification Crisis that pitted states' rights against federal power and southern agriculturalists against northern manufacturers—refueled anxiety about potential slave revolts and exemplified the type of seditious communications the city's white residents most feared. Given the ease with which Edward Smith furtively slipped Walker's "Appeal" to Charleston's most accessible bondsmen, the white stevedores were justified when warning years later that northern emissaries and free black seamen might conspire with enslaved dockworkers in unsupervised ships' holds; recollections of this 1830 case perhaps induced such admonishments. The revelation that the *Columbo*'s white captain and mate were aboard the vessel at the time Smith distributed the pamphlets to the enslaved workers—as during the 1847 exchanges between John Andrew Jackson and the black Boston cook—furthermore legitimated these stevedores' exhortation that ship officers often were too preoccupied with their duties to notice interchanges between crewmen and local black workers.[78]

But Charleston was not the only southern destination for David Walker's "Appeal." Typically trafficked by sympathetic northern mariners, both black and white, the contentious pamphlet also appeared in or near Savannah, New Orleans, Wilmington, and Richmond in what many southerners interpreted as a systematic plot to spark insurrection.[79] This broad and nearly simultaneous distribution of the "Appeal," one scholar contended, "did much to regionalize a concern that had long been a hobby of South Carolina radicals," most notably evidenced by Georgia and North Carolina hastily adopting variants of the Negro Seamen Acts in the immediate aftermath of the pamphlet's appearance.[80]

For many white Charlestonians, this episode vindicated their state's Negro Seamen Acts and confirmed the laws' continued necessity. Smith's confession stated that "A short time after his arrival, a colored Cook or Steward was one day taken from a vessel lying near the Columbo," indicating that city officials were enforcing the Negro Seamen Acts in early 1830.[81] But Edward Smith was a white mariner, and the acts made no attempt to prevent interactions between slaves—especially those working on the waterfront—and white seamen or other whites visiting the city.[82] Only the far less proactive 1820 law under which Smith was convicted stood between omnipresent white sailors and the latent slave rebels laboring along the port's docks. Northern abolitionists such as David Walker consequently preferred and sought out white mariners like Edward Smith—as well as the northern ship steward who imported Walker's pamphlet to Savannah in December 1829—to carry seditious literature into Charleston and other southern ports because they attracted far less attention than their free black shipmates.[83]

Yet the aftermath of the Smith discovery witnessed an even more rigorous enforcement of the Negro Seamen Acts, an inexplicable reaction given that the perpetrating sailor was white.[84] With the seditious importations of most white mariners still going undetected—not to mention the Negro Seamen Acts' failure to halt contact with all free black seamen—Charleston's enslaved waterfront workers exploited the laws' numerous defects and loopholes, persistently resisting and circumventing efforts to control their labor and lives and to circumscribe their unmatched access to information from outside the South's peculiar—and porous—institutional walls.

John Andrew Jackson's 1840s slave narrative, meanwhile, demonstrated that northern and foreign seamen, again both black and white, sometimes encouraged and assisted slaves desiring to flee Charleston and bondage via the "Maritime Railroad." With thousands of vessels annually entering and exiting Charleston Harbor during the antebellum era, the remonstrations and reactive measures of perturbed white slaveholders and employers ultimately failed to forestall resistant maritime runaways.[85] As with the Negro Seamen Acts, legislation such as South Carolina's 1841 New York Ship Inspection Law also complicated efforts to boost the port's relative share of the cotton export trade, drove a wedge between the city's commercial and security interests, and further heightened sectional tensions.

Runaway slaves were drawn to Charleston's waterfront. In fact, countless bondsmen had escaped enslavement by stowing away in northern-bound vessels during the colonial period, and maritime runaways continued during and after the American Revolution. In an August 1781 runaway advertisement, William Sams announced that his slave Will "has been seen about the wharfs [*sic*] in town."[86] James Lynah similarly informed readers in May 1784 that his man Guy "has been frequently seen about Rose's wharf."[87] Some slaveowners plainly stated their fears, such as William McWhann, whose "stout made negro lad named SAM" was supposed to be "lurking about till he gets an opportunity of going on board some vessel."[88] Slave masters were so concerned that their absconded slaves would stow away and sail to freedom, hundreds of runaway advertisements issued warnings to ship captains. A typical notice read, "Masters of vessels are hereby cautioned against suffering such a slave to be harboured by their crews, concealed on ship board or carried off."[89]

Though "inveigling, stealing and carrying away" slaves became a capital offense in South Carolina in 1754, the problem remained so acute that Charleston's Grand Jury—which included wharf owners Florian Charles Mey and John Blake—complained in September 1797 that "great numbers of Negroes and other Slaves, are carried off the State to the great injury of the Citizens thereof."[90] Taking notice, Governor Charles Pinckney called upon the General Assembly to pass legislation requiring all departing vessels to stop at Fort Johnson—located on James Island near the mouth of Charleston Harbor—and be searched for runaway slaves (see figures 18 and 19). A legislative committee subsequently reported that laws formerly designed to thwart such "mischief" had fallen into disuse after the Revolution. The committee therefore recommended that a new act be passed "to prevent the Evil complained of."[91]

Lawmakers failed to enact such legislation, and hundreds of slaves continued to run away on the Maritime Railroad. Leaders of the South Carolina Association, including Elias Vanderhorst, again warned the state legislature in the early 1820s that there were increasing attempts to "inveigle away our slaves." So many packet lines now existed between Charleston and New York, not to mention other northern ports, that "the opportunities for embarking are occurring almost every day in the year," and consequently there was "no security, that our slaves, will not be seduced from the service of their masters, in greater numbers than heretofore."[92] When in 1821 three enslaved sailors fled their vessel anchored in the Cooper River, the ship's captain surmised that the runaways would attempt "to get on board some vessel bound to the northward."[93] A free black New Yorker named Joseph Lawrence, meanwhile, had arrived in the lowcountry aboard the schooner *Fair Play* in June 1822, and was convicted and imprisoned for "endeavoring to inveigle" a slave named Macklin.[94] And Augusta slaveowner Jonathan Hand was convinced in July 1828 that his slave Harry, an absconded drayman, would "probably endeavor to escape out of the country, either by the way of Charleston or Savannah."[95] The historical record therefore demonstrated that most runaway slaves were not, in fact, unwillingly "inveigled" or "seduced, swerved from their allegiance to their masters." That slaves were no more passively acted upon than they were contented and docile, slaveowners privately knew well. "Slaves are . . . capable of evil purposes as well as good," admitted a Charleston judge in January 1860. "They are, to a certain extent, free agents. They have brains, nerves, hands, and thereby can conceive and execute a malignant purpose," including freeing themselves from bondage.[96]

But rather than merely loitering about the wharves and awaiting a chance occasion to slip into a ship's hold, many runaway slaves actively sought waterfront work that presented these "opportunities for embarking," especially when screwing cotton or hoisting rice below decks. Waterfront employment, in other words, was an ideal halfway house on a runaway's road to freedom. In an account similar to that of John Andrew Jackson's escape from bondage, *The Emancipator* chronicled the firsthand narrative of another slave's flight from Charleston's waterfront during the winter of 1837.[97] This unnamed bondsman detailed the beatings and abuse he had received while working for a railroad company in rural South Carolina. The day after a particularly severe whipping, he slipped away and into some nearby woods. That night, under the cover of darkness, the slave returned to the railroad, boarded a car, and hid among cotton bales bound for Charleston. After arriving in the city, the runaway made his way to the waterfront and—though without the requisite slave badge—"waited there with the rest of the hands to get work."[98] Before long a stevedore approached and offered the fugitive a job, and he followed the employer to a wharf where he worked alongside other slaves "stowing away cotton in a vessel" from Boston.

Each day the slave wharf hands went to a cook-shop for meals. But lacking money, the runaway returned to the vessel where he became acquainted with the white steward, who gave the slave something to eat. When asked one day "how much of your wages do you have to give your master," the slave answered all, to which the steward responded that "it was not so where he came from," and "There the people are all free." Apparently having never heard of black freedom, the former slave recalled, "When he told me this I began to think that there was a free country, and to wish that I could get there." During subsequent conversations, the steward proposed assisting the slave to run away to the North: "He said the vessel was all loaded and would sail next morning. That day was Saturday, and he told me that after I knocked off work and had got my pay, I must stay about there till it was dark and all the people in the ship were asleep and that he would wait for me. He said he had got a place made to hide me in, and that if I was sure not to cough, or make any noise, he thought he could get me away safe." After dark, the fugitive crept along the wharf to the vessel where he was greeted by the white steward, who hastily opened the scuttle and instructed the slave to quietly jump in. Once the hatchway was closed, the stowaway "crowded in between the bales." After a harrowing four-week voyage to Boston, the steward assisted the runaway out of his hiding place and directed him to walk up the street and inquire for a colored boarding house. The newly freed slave soon encountered a black man who quickly perceived "from my dress and the cotton on my head and clothes" that he was a runaway, and saw to it that he was cared for.[99]

Another episode of waterfront labor facilitating escape from bondage comes from the WPA interview of former slave Susan Hamlin. Hamlin's father, Adam Collins, was a slave coachman on Edisto Island, located about twenty miles south of Charleston. The day after Collins received a whipping, the slave drove his master four miles into the woods, tied him to a tree, "an' give him de same 'mount of lickin' he wus given on Sunday." Collins frequently had been permitted to go to Charleston on errands, so he made his way to a landing and boarded a boat taking agricultural products to the city. Once in Charleston, "he gone on de water-front an' ax for a job on a ship so he could git to de North." Evidently not required to present a slave badge or provide proof of free status, Collins was hired and eventually sailed to New York where he worked as a store clerk.[100]

Meanwhile, slaveowner A. J. Huntington of Augusta offered an eye-catching thirty dollars for the arrest of his mulatto slave Ben Elliott, who had absconded in October 1834. In advertisements continuously appearing in the *Charleston Courier* between February 4 and April 9, 1835, the master expressed concern that Ben had returned to Charleston, the city in which the slave was raised and his mother still "sells fruit in the market." Prior to being sold to Huntington eighteen months before—and despite being "rather dandyish"—Ben was "in the habit of working about the wharves and on board vessels as a Stevedore or an Assistant." This slave having disappeared into the relative anonymity and liminality of Charleston's waterfront, the runaway ad, paradoxically, reemerged in the New York abolitionist newspaper *The Emancipator* in May 1836. After nineteenth months of searching for his valuable bondsman, A. J. Huntington reasonably concluded that Ben was no longer in South Carolina and likely had exploited his employment and familiarity on Charleston's docks to stow away to freedom in New York City.[101]

Many slaves, of course, were not successful in their attempts to run away via Charleston's waterfront.[102] Wharfinger Thomas Marshall, in fact, reported that one of his slaves—who "writes well enough & has the capacity to write his free papers, passes &c."—was confined in the workhouse after attempting "to take his departure for the north" by engaging with "the Yankey [*sic*] Capt. of a fishing smack."[103] In June 1837 two slaves owned by lawyer and legislator Langdon Cheves were discovered at sea aboard the brig *New York* and transported back to Charleston on a pilot boat.[104] Under the title "Another Attempt at Escape," the *Savannah Georgian* reported in May 1845 that a slave named James, the property of Charleston's mercantile firm Williams and McBarney, was "fortunately discovered" hiding between a water cask and a cotton bale aboard a British bark anchored off Long Island and bound for Liverpool.[105] This English seaport also was the intended destination for Billy, who City Guard officer Moses Levy found "concealed in the long boat of the British ship *Coronet* . . . prepared to make his escape." A year earlier the same slave had made it over the bar of Charleston Harbor before being discovered and returned to town. Conceding that "the city of Charleston render[ed] it comparatively easy for the said slave to accomplish his purpose to abscond in some future attempt," Billy's master resolved to sell the "unruly" but valuable bondsman.[106] And master cooper Jacob Schirmer recorded in his diary the daring but failed attempt of a slave who stowed away on the steamer *S. R. Spaulding*, which was bound for Boston and carried delegates from the Democratic National Convention held in Charleston in late April and early

May 1860. This fugitive was discovered at sea, transferred to a vessel that took him to Baltimore, and returned from there to Charleston by rail.[107]

Evidence suggested that New York and Boston—the latter being the cradle of the American antislavery movement and home to prominent abolitionists such as David Walker and William Lloyd Garrison—were the preferred destinations of Charleston's maritime runaways. Though many seafaring New Yorkers and Bostonians offered aid to stowaways ranging from benign neglect to active assistance, not all in these northern ports were abolitionists. In April 1852—less than one month after the publication of Harriet Beecher Stowe's *Uncle Tom's Cabin* unleashed a firestorm of sectional enmity and contentious debate over the federal Fugitive Slave Act of 1850—the *Charleston Courier* printed with "considerable gratification" a letter sent from a Boston merchant house to one of the firm's ship captains in Charleston: "See that you do not bring any negroes—slaves—away. If you find any secreted after you get to sea, no matter if in Boston Bay, we wish you to return to [Charleston] and deliver any such slaves to their owners, or the proper authorities. We would spare neither expense or [*sic*] trouble in restoring to our Southern friends their slaves." These Bostonians, it seemed, valued commercial trade relations and prosperity more than freedom for black southerners. The newspaper commended these "Northern brethren" for their "praiseworthy conduct" and for exercising the "right spirit."[108] When a Charleston slave was discovered hiding aboard a New York–bound steam packet in October 1836, the *Courier* similarly announced, "The Commanders and Managers of these boats have in every such instance, taken effectual means to restore such property—no matter at what risk or inconvenience."[109] Such sectional harmony, however, was the exception rather than the rule, a fact that was no more evident than during the aftermath of the "Virginia Controversy."

In the summer of 1839 the schooner *Robert Center* sailed into Norfolk, Virginia, for repairs with three free black seamen aboard.[110] As an enslaved ship carpenter named Isaac worked on the schooner, these three black sailors advised the slave that he was "foolish to remain in Virginia as he could get good wages in the north."[111] After the *Robert Center* was repaired and had departed, the slave carpenter could not be found, prompting his owner, John G. Colley, to suspect that the skilled and valuable bondsman had escaped on the New York–bound vessel. Colley immediately dispatched a party to travel to New York City and recover the absconded slave, who indeed was found hiding in the ship's hold. The runaway was returned to Virginia, but New York governor William Henry Seward—an antislavery Whig—refused to arrest and extradite the three black mariners for prosecution in the Old Dominion.[112]

Then in May 1840, the New York state legislature passed a fugitive slave act that was viewed by some south of the Mason-Dixon Line as "manifestly designed . . . to throw obstacles in the way of the recovery by Citizens of the Southern states of their fugitive slaves." This New York law granted runaways the right to jury trials and provided them with legal counsel and representation. The legislation furthermore required payment of a thousand-dollar "penal sum" from those suing for recovery of supposed fugitive slaves to cover legal fees in unsuccessful cases.[113] Outraged authorities in Virginia responded with an appeal to fellow slaveholding states for support and collaboration.[114] Legislators in Columbia answered this call and on December 17, 1841, passed "An Act to Prevent the Citizens of New York from Carrying Slaves or Persons Held to Service out of this State and to Prevent the Escape of Persons Charged with the Commission of Any Crime," more commonly known as the New York Ship Inspection Law. This law, which was similar to one enacted in Virginia, was said to be a "retaliatory measure" against New York and "was passed in testimony of the high confidence which South Carolina reposed in the Counsels of Virginia and as a manifestation of her determination to cooperate with the Commonwealth and other States in maintaining by all proper methods an institution in which she has a common interest."[115]

South Carolina's 1841 New York Ship Inspection Law stipulated that vessels owned in any proportion whatsoever by a citizen of New York could not depart Charleston before undergoing an inspection for runaway slaves or fleeing criminals. Given that valuable slaves had long used northern-bound vessels to escape bondage, this legislation struck many slaveowning South Carolinians as imperative and commonsensical policy. The law seemingly would have been more practical and effective, however, had it also obliged the examination of vessels owned by Bostonians and northerners besides those from New York. But as a reactive rather than proactive measure, southern legislators targeted New Yorkers for reasons other than the Virginia Controversy: It was the New York–based American Anti-Slavery Society that had mailed thousands of abolitionist tracts to slaveholding Charlestonians in July 1835, prompting a mob to seize the offending pamphlets and publicly burn them along with effigies of Arthur and Lewis Tappan; other New York abolitionists and moral reformers in 1839 established the Colored Sailors' Home, where hundreds of fugitive slaves were secreted and free black mariners—such as those who assisted slave stowaways and disseminated seditious literature to bondsmen in southern ports like Charleston—were encouraged to join the struggle against the institution of slavery; abolitionists founded the nation's first antislavery political party, the Liberty Party, in New York City in 1840; and in 1841 New York lawmakers reversed a longstanding law permitting southern slaveholders to bring their bondsmen into the Empire State for up to nine months without surrendering their human property.[116] As abolitionist attacks on the southern institution intensified, slavery's defenders responded with vigorous and pointed salvos aimed directly at their harshest northern critics—in this case, New Yorkers.

Like the Negro Seamen Acts, meanwhile, the sectionally divisive New York Ship Inspection Law also had local detractors and unintended consequences for Charleston's commercial waterfront and its workers. And arguments similar to those both for and against the black sailor laws often were applied to this 1841 legislation. Opponents insisted that the New York Ship Inspection Law was unconstitutional, inefficient, and ineffective; inhibited free trade; and drove much-needed business to competing ports. Each mandatory inspection cost $10, which amounted to an annual expense of $120 for packet vessels monthly conveying passengers and goods between Charleston and New York.[117] Shipowners complained that, in addition to this inspection fee, they were required to execute a $1,000 bond—not coincidently the exact amount as the New York fugitive protective law's "penal sum"—to secure compliance with the law and cover "all damages which may be assessed against them, if a slave should be found on board."[118]

Critics also protested that payment of this $10 "tax" was required even if the inspector did a poor job and failed to detect a stowaway—not an improbable outcome given the abundant nooks and crannies of a loaded ship's hold.[119] Indeed, if a fugitive slave was later discovered, the vessel's owner was fined $500 for violating the law.[120] In 1845 Charleston's shipowners asked the state legislature to repeal the act and reminded lawmakers of the city's economic decline relative to other southern ports: "Our aim should be, not to close our ports, but to open every avenue, and widen every channel that would lead us once again to that commercial pre-eminence which once marked our City but has so long departed from us."[121] Any hindrance to commercial trade affected not only those at the top of Charleston's waterfront hierarchy—merchants, factors, wharf and dray owners, and stevedores—but also the enslaved laborers whose diminished employment opportunities curtailed the extraordinary autonomy and access that urban wage earning and the littoral environment made possible.

Measured in terms of actual ship arrivals and departures, total tonnage, and export figures, Charleston's commercial economy impressively withstood events ranging from the Nullification Crisis and Panics of 1837 and 1839 to the passage of the Negro Seamen Acts and New York Ship Inspection Law.[122] Despite the latter piece of legislation, for instance, ship arrivals at Charleston's docks rose from 1,673 in 1841 to 1,718 in 1842, with departures increasing from 1,610 to 1,713.[123] Twenty-eight packet vessels regularly transported freight and passengers between Charleston and New York in 1848, more than double the number with any other Atlantic, Gulf, or West Indies port.[124] And in addition to the climb in overall cotton and rice exports, the number of cotton bales shipped coastwise north of Charleston—that is, primarily to New York and New England—increased from 61,519 in 1840–41 to 70,783 in 1841–42; the number of rice tierces shipped, meanwhile, rose from 20,773 to 29,140.[125] Charleston's mercantile interests, therefore, may have overstated the negative impact of controversial legislation on Charleston's commercial trade.

There is some evidence, however, of both real and relative commercial decline in Charleston and other South Carolina ports immediately following the passage of the New York Ship Inspection Law in December 1841. Whereas $1,557,431 of goods was imported to South Carolina in 1841, that figure dropped steadily to an antebellum low of $822,602 in 1845. Despite broader economic recovery by 1843 from the previous decade's devastating financial panics, the total tonnage of vessels engaged in foreign commerce calling at the state's ports declined from 25,394 in 1841 to 19,515 in 1845. Relative to other southern ports, Charleston exported 230,000 bales of cotton in 1841—roughly 90,000 fewer than Mobile and nearly 600,000 fewer than New Orleans, but 81,000 more than Savannah. Given a choice between two rival southern Atlantic ports a mere hundred miles apart, New York shipowners and captains could punish Charleston's fire-eaters by loading their cotton in Savannah. Many planters along the Savannah River also may have elected to float their cotton to the Georgia port rather than transport it via railroad to South Carolina's more sectionally militant entrepôt. And indeed, while Charleston exported 269,007 bales of cotton in 1842—39,000 more than the previous year—Savannah's shipment of the staple rose dramatically to 299,173 bales—150,000 more than in 1841.[126] Though such disadvantageous short-term trends cannot be attributed to the 1841 ship-inspection law alone, these figures contextualize the remonstrances of the port's competing security and commercial interests.

Also controversial was the legislation's provision that required an inspection even if New Yorkers owned only a small percentage of a vessel and South Carolinians owned the remainder.[127] The law furthermore was in effect if a ship owned entirely by citizens of South Carolina was commanded by a New Yorker. Stockholders in the Charleston–New York packet lines—including wharf owners and employers of enslaved waterfront workers such as James Adger, Otis Mills, and Charles T. Mitchell—reminded legislators that they too were slaveowners and were "interested in all laws tending to the security of slave property."[128] They nevertheless joined with other shipowners and merchants to ask for relief from the act's "exceedingly onerous" tax burden, and argued that South Carolinians were being "made to bear all the weight of the retaliation that was intended for the people of New York" after the enactment of that state's 1840 fugitive slave law.[129]

Champions of the law answered that it was "a wise and necessary protection to [South Carolina's] citizens" from northern abolitionists who sought "to tamper with our slaves, to seduce them from their obedience, and to protect them when fugitive."[130] During the January 1860 sentencing of Francis Michel, a young white porter aboard the New York steam packet *Marion* who was convicted "of aiding any [sic] assisting in the escape of a runaway slave" belonging to a Charleston butcher, Judge T. J. Withers contended, "There is a peculiar duty on the part of a Government which holds slaves to protect that description of property."[131] Blaming the abolitionist "crew such as now infests the Northern part of the United States," the judge argued that the 1754 law under which Michel was convicted was "a wholly insufficient barrier to the multitudinous thieves who have been spawned upon this country by a fierce fanaticism on the part of some, by a cheap, hypocritical, pretensive, vagabond philanthropy, on the part of many more, inspired by the numerous Pharisees of Northern pulpits, the 'unco good and rigidly righteous,' all seized upon and moulded into a homogeneous but corrupt mass by the greedy lovers of political power and general plunder." The ease with which Charleston's slaves could stow away—"through the instrumentality of those who may come from New York or other places, tainted and corrupted by such men as the Cheevers and Beechers"—compelled the state legislature to pass a special ship-inspection law that, admittedly, "involv[ed] heavy expense and much trouble."[132] Despite such candid concessions from supporters and more severe critiques from opponents, legislative committees in Columbia assigned the task of reviewing grievances regarding the 1841 New York Ship Inspection Law repeatedly rejected calls for repeal.[133] The Committee on Federal Relations even doubled down, calling for "the adoption of more stringent and effectual measures to protect our Citizens from the outrages of New York on our Slave property."[134]

But as time passed and Charleston's export economy continued to lose ground to rival ports such as Savannah, Mobile, and especially New Orleans, legislators acknowledged that alterations were advisable. In 1848 the members of the Committee on Federal Relations had a temporary change of heart and agreed that the law was "only productive of injury to individuals" and failed to efficiently curtail slave stowaways.[135] As John Andrew Jackson's remarkable escape via the Maritime Railroad the year before attested, a steady stream of waterfront workers and other bondsmen also continued flowing to less scrutinized northern ports. Just as the Negro Seamen Acts inadequately and inexplicably neglected the threat of white sailors, the New York Ship Inspection Law futilely omitted Boston, Philadelphia, and other destinations attractive to maritime runaways. And even if the law was an effective—though severely limited—means of deterrence and detection, slaves who were doggedly resistant to mastery nonetheless found indirect waterborne routes to New York. Reminiscent of the 1838 account in *The Emancipator,* for instance, a slave named Alick who had been hired out to a drug store in Columbia absconded in 1850 to Charleston aboard a railcar. Having made it safely to the waterfront, the runaway secreted himself on a steamboat bound first for Wilmington and then on to New York.[136]

The Committee on Colored Population maintained in 1851 that if the law was fully and faithfully enforced it was sufficient to prevent waterfront runaways, but too conceded that amendments were needed.[137] And twice the Committee on Federal Relations suggested that the inspection fee be reduced—in one instance to five dollars and in the other to only one dollar—in the effort to relieve the burden upon Charleston's shipowners and to increase both the number of vessels owned by South Carolinians and those trading in Charleston.[138] The 1841 act nevertheless remained on the books essentially unrevised until the Civil War rendered the matter of stowaway slaves moot. As with the Negro Seamen Acts and the port's web of hiring, wage, and employment laws—and much as we will observe when examining struggles over waterfront labor competition and the prevention of yellow fever epidemics—Charleston's oft-conflicting yet overlapping mercantile, slaveholding, and security interests proved unable to fully accomplish any of their individual objectives. Failing to restore the commercial "golden age" of what historian George C. Rogers Jr. characterized as an increasingly "closed" and inward-looking city, municipal and state leaders as well exacerbated the sectional chasm that soon engulfed the Cooper River waterfront and ultimately shattered the chains so long designed to control the labor and lives of the port's enslaved workers.[139]

But even as slaveowners fretted over "foreign" tampering with their principal source of wealth and the port's primary labor force, internal threats also loomed. "How long are we to submit to these worse than abolitionist enemies?" asked Charleston's grand jurors in May 1851, warning state legislators of the "disastrous effects" ignominious local whites were having upon slaves, slaveholders, and the entire institution of slavery. Concerned about those who resorted to the "disreputable mode of gaining a livelihood" by trafficking liquor to bondsmen, the grand jury complained that such degraded men "induce the slave to drink drugged beverages, which speedily destroy his health and encourage him to pilfer as a means to pay for the poison."[140] Similarly decrying those "unprincipled white men" who seduced slaves "into crimes and practices, calculated to destroy them, and despoil their owners," yet another grand jury insisted that, if laws prohibiting the receipt of stolen goods were not enforced, "we shall soon be overrun by a lazy, drunken, and pilfering set of slaves."[141]

The theft and pilferage of cotton, rice, and other valuable commercial goods from Charleston's waterfront was rife during the antebellum period. Also typical was the tendency to assume that blacks were natural thieves and were the perpetrators of these crimes. But unwilling to acknowledge that slave theft contradicted proslavery claims that the South's bondsmen were contented, docile, and mastered, many white Charlestonians rationalized that thieving slaves simply did not know any better. Despite punishing guilty slaves—whether by sending them to the workhouse, by relocating them from the relative autonomy of the city to a more isolated and constricted rural plantation, or even by selling the most troublesome miscreants—slaveholders simultaneously portrayed black offenders as passive victims of "unscrupulous" white shopkeepers who depraved the city's slaves and enabled their theft and pilferage by purchasing the purloined goods. Slaves, of course, were conscious of their actions, and often stole from the docks as partial and customary redress for expropriated freedom, wages, and other grievances.[142]

In an antebellum southern economy built upon the ownership and employment of valuable slave labor, debased and thieving bondsmen were a concern to security scolds and commercial boosters alike. According to Charleston's grand jurors, "Slave property in this District, and especially in this City is every day decreasing in value . . . in consequence of the corrupt influence" of the white liquor dealers.[143] One South Carolina judge explained that slaves' market values were determined by their habits, character, and behavior, and that vice could render even the strongest and most skilled slaves worthless and dispensable. Much also depended upon "the opportunities [a slave] has to commit crimes, and the temptation to which he is exposed."[144] In July 1807 wharf owner Christopher Fitzsimons felt compelled to ship an African-born bondsman named Jim to the New Orleans slave market. "He is a very sensible handy fellow and can turn his hand to any work," Fitzsimons explained, "but is a most notorious thief and as I wanted him on the wharf I found he would not answer to that employ."[145] Enslaved dockworkers like Jim did not steal all of the goods that disappeared from Charleston's antebellum wharves. But as with stowing away and exposure to free black seamen and seditious literature, no occupation surpassed the degree of access, opportunities, and enticements to steal and pilfer as afforded the city's waterfront laborers. In response to workers' efforts to exert customary rights and privileges, protest and resist enslavement, and make ends meet, the master class instituted yet more measures in the incessant struggle to restrict slaves' agency and to control their labor and lives.

Large quantities of commercial goods were stored uncovered and unprotected on Charleston's open wharves. Not just subject to the elements of nature, merchandise piled on the waterfront also was accessible to thieves. As early as 1740, merchant Robert Pringle advised John Erving of Boston that bricks were "the worst Commodity a Ship Can bring here" since "There is always a very great Breakage on them & as they Lye [sic] expos'd on our Common Wharfs [sic] after Landing are Lyable [sic] to be Stolen and Embezell'd [sic] by all Comers." Planter and wharf owner William Smith Jr. testified on December 1, 1808, that "two barrells [sic] of tar of the value of seven dollars, were on this morning feloniously stolen, taken and carried away from his wharf." And in June 1823, fifteen barrels of flour valued at $108.75 and belonging to bakers James and William Maynard were stolen from the wharves. Unsure who to blame for the theft, Chamber of Commerce arbitrators simply concluded "that it must have been carried off by some person or persons, who had no right to the said flour."[146]

Thieves also targeted waterfront stores and warehouses. Five hundred pounds of bacon were purloined from Samuel Davenport's store on Elliott Street in July 1822. Entering at night either through a window or the roof, the unidentified plunderer was assumed to have been black. The *Charleston Courier* reported in May 1830 that two bags of coffee were burgled from a store on Depau's Range near Chisolm's Wharf. On the evening of August 22, 1833, the store of J. C. & C. Burckmyer & Co. at 140 East Bay Street was broken into, and two barrels of flour were stolen. The barrels soon were recovered from a boat at Magwood's Wharf, and two of the vessel's crewmen were found guilty of the crime and sentenced to twenty-five lashes in the city market. But according to Jacob Schirmer, these men purchased the flour from a slave owned by David B. Lafar, a cooper on Magwood's Wharf.[147]

As this last case suggested, waterfront workers frequently stole merchandise from the wharves. In October 1823, for example, black draymen abetted the theft of ten barrels of rice from Prioleau's Wharf, and in February 1826 a slave carter named Abraham heisted a parcel of three hundred new bricks from Mey's Wharf.[148] But with cotton the king of Charleston's export economy, so too was it the primary target of waterfront theft and pilferage. In 1825 approximately 159,327 bales of cotton were shipped from Charleston; one decade later 204,119 bales were exported, and in 1840 the number had risen to 307,679.[149] With such an immense amount of cotton piled on the city's waterfront, it should come as no surprise that the late 1820s and early 1830s witnessed a sharp increase in the theft—and subsequent sale—of cotton from the wharves (see figures 16 and 24).

Some of the attempted cotton thefts were simply astonishing, such as a scheme in January 1830 to roll an entire bale away from Fitzsimons's Wharf.[150] Not all cotton thieves were as brazen or stole on such a grand scale, however; indeed, the embezzlement and sale of small amounts of cotton was most common. On May 9, 1835, for instance, a slave named Lewis sold an eight-pound bag of cotton to Elizabeth Mills for only 8 cents—less than 6 percent of the commodity's prevailing value on the legal market.[151] But for the purchasers of this purloined cotton, such relatively small and not easily detectable parcels could add up to a substantial and gainful traffic, even if resold under the going rate. The sellers, often pilfering dockhands exercising workplace prerogatives and mores, augmented paltry and garnished wages.

Waterfront plunder became so pervasive, in fact, that during the 1830s over forty wharf owners, wharfingers, and merchants petitioned the South Carolina Senate.[152] "The evil has at length gone so far that Your Memorialists . . . are now induced to come before your Honourable Body for [the] relief and protection . . . of the Cotton and Rice lying upon the Wharves of Charleston," they explained. The petitioners elucidated that "Cotton especially, from the immense quantities received, and the little injury it sustains from exposure to the weather, is frequently not Stored, and is always in large quantities lying upon the wharves."[153] Thus exposed, the unstored bales were "liable to continual depredations by Slaves and free persons of Colour who frequent" the waterfront, and in this way "Rice, and Cotton especially, to an immense amount, are plundered upon our wharves." The wharf owners estimated, "As Startling as the fact may appear," the equivalent of at least 500 bales of cotton were purchased illegally each year by Charleston's storekeepers from thieving slaves and free blacks.[154] In addition to unprincipled and greedy shopkeepers, the wharf owners blamed such extensive theft on the widespread forging of slaves' trading passes or tickets and ineffective laws prohibiting traffic with slaves and free blacks. "[T]he Laws as they exist against trafficking with Slaves, admit of such easy expedients for evading their applications," the petitioners argued, "that they are equivalent to no laws at all."[155]

Though disregarding the wharf owners' impractical call to prohibit all commercial exchanges with slaves and free blacks, the General Assembly in 1834 decreed it "sufficient for the conviction" of storekeepers who unlawfully traded with slaves to prove that a bondsman entered a shop with an article and then left without that same item.[156] This act still allowed storekeepers to trade with slaves bearing tickets purportedly signed by their masters; but by significantly lowering the burden of proof in illicit trading cases, the new law facilitated legal proceedings against unscrupulous white buyers. Authorities indicted State Street traders John and Mary Daniels for as many as fifteen counts of purchasing parcels of stolen cotton from dozens of slaves between May 1 and August 14, 1835. In one instance, "a Slave supposed to be the property of John Fraser"—a wharf owner and factor who employed slaves as dockhands—sold a bag of cotton weighing about twenty pounds and worth four dollars to John Daniels. The Danielses pled guilty in October 1835, and were sentenced to an imprisonment of three months and a hundred-dollar fine.[157] During the same month the court also found fellow and aforementioned illicit cotton buyer Elizabeth Mills guilty of "Negro Trading."[158]

Despite an increase in the prosecution and conviction of white cotton dealers after the passage of the 1834 act, the law was not a panacea. On August 21, 1835, Jacob Schirmer recorded in his diary that "Lynch Law was exhibited this morning on the person of a Mr. Carroll, who has been carrying on the business of a Barber, but who has attended more to the purchase of Stolen cotton." The *Charleston Courier* explained that R. W. Carroll—an alias for Richard Wood—had used his shop at 4 Queen Street near East Bay Street and the Cooper River wharves to receive "stolen goods, from negroes," and to export "about 60 bales of cotton annually." Schirmer reported that Wood shipped as many as 75 bales in one season. Richard Wood had been prosecuted many times for carrying out this illicit trade, but had been "shielded . . . from *legal* punishment" as a result of unspecified technicalities of the law. Though the "Lynch Club"—the same radical group that seized and burned the American Anti-Slavery Society pamphlets mailed to Charleston the previous month[159]—had advised Wood to leave the city by August 20, he greeted such warnings with "contempt and defiance" and persisted in "his dishonest traffic." Taking matters into their own hands, a number of citizens assembled on August 21 and removed the culprit from his shop. According to the *Courier,* "[Wood] was immediately marched down to Price's wharf, tied to a post, and there received about twenty lashes on his bare back; a tub of tar was then emptied upon his head, in such a manner as to cause it to extend over his whole body; and the *gentleman* was properly decorated with a covering of loose cotton, the principal material in which he had carried on his illicit traffic, with much advantage to his purse." After being "tarred and Stuck with Cotton," Wood was escorted up East Bay Street and marched through the market and other public thoroughfares "in order that others guilty of the like practices should take warning by his fate." Afterward, Wood was lodged in the city jail for his own protection before being "put on board of a vessel & sent to New York."[160]

Extant sources made no mention of punishing the thieving slaves who were said to have stolen and then sold cotton to Richard Wood or other black-market cotton traders. Charleston's records from the Court of Magistrates and Freeholders, which heard the cases of free blacks and slaves, have been lost or destroyed. It also was much easier to identify the location of a purchaser's shop or residence than to recognize a slave seller in the cover of darkness. Though slaves employed the theft and pilferage of waterfront cotton as an agent of survival, entitlement, and active resistance, the city's master class portrayed complicit bondsmen as manipulated victims of this unscrupulous white cotton trader. "It is sincerely to be hoped that this exhibition of the popular feeling," declared the *Courier,* "will operate as an effectual warning to all engaged in the nefarious practice of corrupting our colored population, by purchasing stolen property from them, to desist from their illegal and dishonest course," adding that it was "the fixed determination of the inhabitants of Charleston no longer to submit quietly to such a system of spoliation and robbery." Frustrated by the law's failure to rein in a particularly egregious offender who had acted "in perfect defiance of the community," one group of Charlestonians turned to extralegal and summary justice.[161]

But the city's wharf owners and merchants did not wholly lose faith in legislative action. In 1836 approximately forty petitioners, including Otis Mills, James Adger, and Ker Boyce, asked members of the state senate to pass an act permanently closing Mitchell's Alley in Charleston. Running three hundred feet in length from East Bay Street to Bedon's Alley, Mitchell's Alley was said to be a "receptacle of much filth and trash of every description," and thus was "frequently a nuisance." Only eight feet wide at one end and five feet at the other, the "Alley is too narrow to admit the passage of any carriage or cart, and is, in fact, of no advantage to the public, as it is not used by the citizens generally who live in the neighborhood of [the] said alley as a passage way." But most importantly, the memorial declared "That [the] said Alley being little frequented, and, at night, very dark, is the resort of negroes and disorderly white persons, and it has not infrequently facilitated the escape of negroes who have been detected in Stealing from the wharves." Blacks—often dockworkers—again were the presumed perpetrators of waterfront theft. On December 21, 1836, legislators in Columbia authorized the Charleston City Council "to cause Mitchells' [*sic*] alley . . . to be permanently closed up at that end . . . which terminates at Bedon's alley." In late February 1837 the City Council formed a committee "to adopt such measures as might be deemed expedient for shutting up Mitchell's Alley," and by the end of the year this waterfront escape route was eliminated.[162]

The crackdown on the illicit cotton trade initiated in the mid-1830s curtailed theft of the cash crop from the wharves. But short of complete eradication, Charleston's mercantile community relentlessly endeavored to further master and control waterfront larceny—and the alleged black thieves—during the 1840s and 1850s. Some owners of waterfront property sought to slow down plunderers with barriers, whereas others employed night watchmen.[163] Wharf owners and merchants convinced the City Council to add more street lamps on the waterfront and "to organize an efficient Wharf Watch."[164] In 1845 the city spent $220 for "the temporary increase of the City Guard for special duty on the wharves, during the accumulation and pending the shipment of Cotton."[165] And a special committee reported to the City Council in February 1847 that the protection of the property piled on the open wharves "required seven men of the guard detailed specially for this duty," costing the city an additional $1,300 annually.[166]

Despite increased security and surveillance, the theft of cotton and other valuable commercial goods from the wharves did not cease entirely. In fact, worker pilferage—that is, the stealthy and habitual theft of small quantities of goods by those laboring on the waterfront—defiantly persisted as it had for decades. Just as waterfront workers flouted badge laws and fixed wages, sang vociferous and indecent work songs, exchanged seditious communications, and escaped bondage via the Maritime Railroad, warehousemen, cotton weighers, and other wharf hands had only to slip a handful of loose cotton into their pockets while merchants, factors, and wharfingers were preoccupied or busy elsewhere (see figures 12, 16, 24, and 25). The city's wharf owners complained in the 1830s that "after the Cotton is weighed and before it is shipped the weights have fallen short . . . repeatedly."[167] Noted in the account book of factors Ker Boyce & Co. on January 17, 1837, were "125 lbs. cotton Robbed from 1 B[ale] C[otton]."[168] At 17 cents per pound, this purloined cotton afforded the thief with as much as $21.25 worth of cash or traded goods. For a hired-out slave collecting $10 or $12 a month—most of which had to be turned over to his master—this sum often equaled the net earnings of an entire year. Thus continued the endless struggle between slave workers seeking to preserve customary rights and entitlements, supplement meager incomes, and resist bondage, and hegemonic whites determined to control nearly every aspect of these vital workers' labor and lives.

In 1849 the City Council passed an ordinance deeming it illegal "to pack, bale up, or otherwise prepare for sale" loose cotton without having received a license, or for anyone (whether licensed or not) to transport loose cotton to any location west of East Bay Street "unless the same be in original packages, or has been packed at a licensed press." Indicative of the severity of the pilferage problem, wrongdoers could be fined $1,000 for each violation. Furthermore, "If any person or persons, within the City, shall steal loose Cotton, or shall buy or receive stolen loose Cotton, knowing the same to be stolen," the offender—if white or a free person of color—was to be fined $250, whereas slaves were to be apprehended and either tried and punished by a Court of Magistrates and Freeholders or turned over to their masters for private correction. And, finally, licensed cotton presses were to place a brand and number on every bale of cotton, with a $100 fine to be doled out to anyone caught altering, erasing, or obliterating such identifying marks.[169]

Apart from packers, pressers, and weighers, menders especially had ample occasion to pilfer loose cotton. Employed to stuff protruding strands back into bales before sewing up the torn bagging, cotton menders were able to pilfer small amounts of the article from each bale.[170] Legislation ratified by the City Council in September 1855 sought to remedy this very behavior. Entitled "An Ordinance to Prevent Depredations upon Cotton," this law explicitly decreed that "it shall not be lawful for any mender or menders of cotton bags or cotton bales, to carry with him, her or them, any basket, bag or other vehicle, for the purpose of taking away . . . any sample or samples of cotton, or any loose cotton, from any bags or bales they may be employed to mend." The measure went on to outlaw menders from taking or pulling out cotton from any bag or bale, unless the cotton was damaged and the mender was directed to pick it out by the owner. Targeting illicit buyers as well, the ordinance declared it illegal for licensed cotton packers to purchase loose or sample cotton from anyone other than a factor, a shipping merchant, or the head clerk or salesman for such persons.[171]

"For the purpose of detecting and reporting offenders," the mayor was to assign a police officer "who shall keep watch on and along the wharves of the city, at least three hours each day," from October 1 through June 1. And to keep menders and other pilfering dockhands on their toes, this officer was to "change his hours of watch from time to time, for the more effectual enforcement of his duty." White cotton menders caught violating this ordinance were to be fined $50. Free black and slave menders were fined only $25, but also received at least twenty-five lashes if they failed to pay. This most recent design for mastery on the wharves paid dividends. The *Charleston Mercury* reported in February 1856, for instance, that "Jim, a colored boy, the property of Mr. Magrath"—an Irish merchant who in 1850 owned four male slaves in Charleston, some or all of whom likely were employed assisting Magrath on the waterfront—"was arrested by Officer Levy, for stealing two large sample baskets of cotton."[172]

Of course, police patrols and the threat of fines and corporal punishment could not deter all cotton bandits, and only the careless or unlucky were caught and prosecuted. Most dockworker pilferage, like their other illicit and rebellious activities, remained undetected and unsolved. For every documented loss, scores and perhaps hundreds of items disappeared from the docks without a trace; an absent item frequently was the only evidence of the surreptitious act. In one major case of waterfront pilferage in 1857, the equivalent of five hogsheads worth of sugar valued at $500 went missing from casks in Otis Mills & Co.'s warehouse on Atlantic Wharves, from which "divers quantities were at divers times abstracted." Otis Mills & Co. owned and employed numerous slaves on Atlantic Wharves, most or all of whom had access to the company's warehouses where this sugar was stored and ample occasions to embezzle it.[173]

The relative seclusion of ships' holds likewise afforded slave laborers abundant opportunities and temptations—not only to stow away, engage with northern and foreign seamen, procure abolitionist literature, and even plot insurrection, but also to pilfer cargo. In late February 1857, John Fraser & Co. paid East Bay Street grocer James Bancroft Jr. $11.38 to cover the cost of a cask containing seven dozen pints of porter "Short delivered," or missing, from the vessel *Gondar*. Two and a half years later, the agents of the *Ann & Susan* paid Bancroft 84 cents "for 6 Bottles Ale taken out of one of the casks," which was a portion of the 114 bottles purchased by the storekeeper.[174] All manner of merchandise and cargo remaining at the bottom of the hold or dropped on the wharf also routinely made its way into the pockets of stevedores, dockhands, draymen, and nonworkers who gleaned the waterfront to make ends meet.[175]

Laborers sometimes intentionally damaged goods and broke open barrels to gain access and enable pilferage. The logbook of the fittingly named ship *Robin Hood* recorded that on February 9, 1833, the vessel's crew and four local hired slaves were employed discharging ballast and loading 1,790 bushels of rough rice. Tasked with stowing the rice in the ship's hold, the enslaved wharf hands "broached 1 barrel of pork."[176] In 1853 Charleston grocer John H. Graver sued the agents of the steamer *Palmetto* over a splintered and spoiled barrel of bacon. Even after the bacon had been repacked in a new container, Graver protested that it lacked the proper marks and was "ranced [sic] and bad, inferior in quality, and of a smaller sized flitch than that in the other four casks" consigned to him. Though the barrel of bacon might have been damaged in transit, it is equally feasible that stevedores and dockhands engaged in discharging this tasty commodity from the hold broke open the cask and pilfered a portion of the meat. Graver pointed out, after all, that some of the bacon seemed to be missing from the barrel in question.[177]

Draymen and carters too broke into cargo and pilfered waterfront articles. The Chamber of Commerce adopted a rule in February 1839 prescribing that, "When goods are to be delivered to a drayman," consignees were to create a written order complete with the drayman's name and license number.[178] Though intended to clamp down on pilferage and assist authorities, such procedures failed to dissuade all workers. "The slave Gadsden," for instance, "was hired as a drayman by . . . the agent of a line of vessels between New York and Charleston, to transport goods and merchandise from the vessels to the Rail Road depot." Untethered from a hiring stand and entrusted with the conveyance of valuable articles through the city's streets and alleys, Gadsden—like the enslaved laborers who overcharged for the drayage of Thomas Napier's furniture in 1857—seized on this opportunity to supplement his income. According to court records, "He broke open two boxes of hats and carried part of the contents" to a white grocer named Tiedeman, who was found guilty in January 1850 of receiving the stolen goods.[179]

Largely unsupervised, draymen and carters also joined their fellow waterfront laborers in helping themselves to fistfuls of cotton, rice, and other readily concealable commodities (see figures 4, 10, 14, 16, and 17). Coal, for instance, was an easy target for pilfering workers seeking fuel for cooking or to warm an ill-constructed dwelling on a cold night. But so much imported coal disappeared over the years that the City Council passed an ordinance in 1848 to reduce the amount pilfered. After being discharged from ships' holds and placed onto carts, each load of coal was to be weighed and then issued a certificate stating its mass (measured in tons) and specifying either the name of the cart owner or the number of the cart. Anyone suspecting the improper removal of coals could demand the reweighing of a vehicle. If ten or more pounds of coal were found to have been taken from the cart, the driver—if a white man—was to pay 10 cents for every missing pound and was to be fined twenty dollars. If the offender was a slave, the owner of the cart was to pay these penalties. When fifty or more pounds of coal were absent, a white carter was to pay fifty dollars, lose his license, and be disqualified from receiving a carter license in the future; if a slave, the cart owner again was to suffer the consequences. Municipal officials, in other words, assumed that, if coal was missing, especially in relatively small amounts, the waterfront workers who transported it were either pilfering or making illicit exchanges or sales. The weight of a load also could decrease if wet coal dried or if pieces were jolted out on an unpaved and rutted street. But given carters' access and opportunities, they almost certainly were pilfering the fuel. And since the ordinance turned a blind eye if fewer than ten pounds of coal were unaccounted for, it almost behooved laborers to craftily slip handfuls into pockets and pouches for the survival and comfort of themselves and their families.[180]

But not merely rational economic behavior, worker theft and pilferage were part and parcel of the much broader contest for dignity and dominion along antebellum southern docks. So willfully disruptive to commerce and menacing to Charleston's security were this plunder and other unruly conventions, in fact, that some inhabitants advocated the gradual replacement of the port's mostly enslaved labor force with free white immigrants. Whites too sometimes stole from wharves and warehouses.[181] But it was inherent and instinctive for black slaves to steal, concluded many employers and masters, who pejoratively defined a "thieving" bondsman as "one who stole much more than the average."[182] As state jurist John Belton O'Neall put it in 1839, "Occasional thefts among the tolerably good slaves may be expected."[183] Withdrawing bondsmen from the still outward-looking water's edge and away from the seductive and corrosive urban and littoral environment, thought a few, would resolve far more problems than would be produced. Such an improbable revolution in the racial constitution of Charleston's essential waterfront workforce, however, faced long-entrenched interests and age-old propensities for black enslaved dock labor.

FIG. 1. "A Plan of the Town & Harbour of Charles Town," 1711. "A compleat description of the province of Carolina in 3 parts: 1st, the improved part from the surveys of Maurice Mathews & Mr. John Love: 2ly, the west part by Capt. Tho. Nairn: 3ly, a chart of the coast from Virginia to Cape Florida / published by Edw. Crisp; engraved by John Harris." Library of Congress, Geography and Map Division.

FIG. 2. (FACING) "Ichnography of Charleston, South-Carolina: at the request of Adam Tunno, Esq., for the use of the Phoenix Fire-Company of London, taken from actual survey, 2d August 1788 / by Edmund Petrie." Library of Congress, Geography and Map Division.

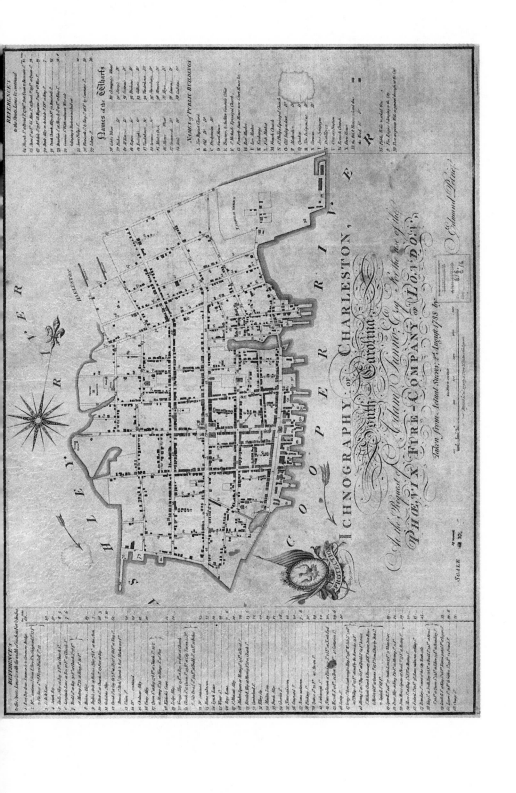

ICHNOGRAPHY of CHARLESTON, South Carolina

At the Request of Adam Tunno Esq: for the use of the
PHŒNIX FIRE-COMPANY of LONDON,

Taken from Actual Survey, 2d August 1788 by Edmund Petrie.

SCALE

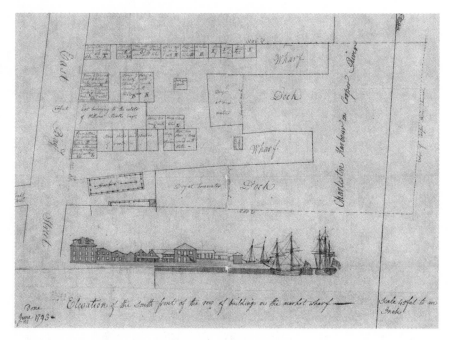

Fig. 3. Plat of Craft's, Motte's, and Greenwood's Wharves, 1793. Charleston County Register Mesne Conveyance, McCrady Plat Collection, 0541.

Fig. 4. Drayman in Charleston. John Rubens Smith, "View of a Street in the City of Charleston, South Carolina, with a Church at Center," ca. 1812. Library of Congress, Prints and Photographs Division.

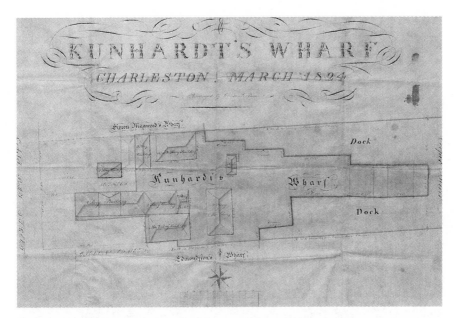

FIG. 5. Plat of Kunhardt's Wharf, 1824. Simon Magwood Papers, 1810–70. Courtesy of South Caroliniana Library, University of South Carolina, Columbia.

FIG. 6. "City of Charleston, South Carolina, looking across Cooper's River / painted by G. Cooke; engraved by W. J. Bennett," ca. 1838. Library of Congress, Prints and Photographs Division.

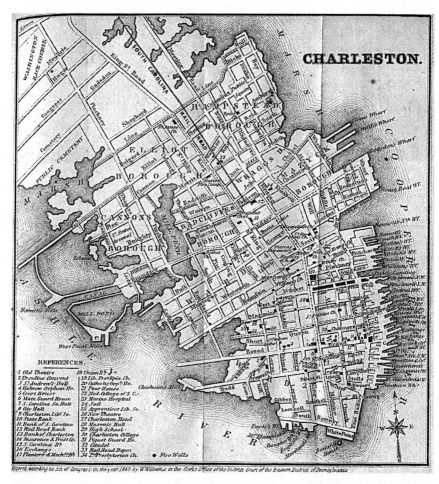

REFERENCES.
1 Old Theatre	18 Union Bk
2 Ursuline Convent	19 Lib. Prot.Epis. Ch.
3 St.Andrew's Hall	20 CatholicOrp.ⁿHo.
4 Hebrew Orphan Ho.	21 Poor House
5 Court House	22 Med.College of S.C.
6 Main Guard House	23 Marine Hospital
7 S. Carolina So.Hall	24 Jail
8 City Hall	25 Apprentices Lib. So.
9 Charleston Lib^y So.	26 New Theatre
10 State Bank	27 Charleston Hotel
11 Bank of S. Carolina	28 Masonic Hall
12 Rail Road Bank	29 High School
13 Bank of Charleston	30 Charleston College
14 Insurance & Trust Co.	31 Piquet Guard Ho.
15 S. Carolina B^k	32 Citadel
16 Exchange	33 Rail Road Depot
17 Planters & Mech.^cB^k	34 2^d Presbyterian Ch.

● Fire Wells

FIG. 7. Charleston, 1849. Perry-Castañeda Library Map Collection, University of Texas at Austin

FIG. 8. (FACING) "Panorama of Charleston," 1851, by John William Hill (American, 1812–1879). Hand-tinted lithograph on paper. Image courtesy of the Gibbes Museum of Art, 1918.001.0005.

FIG. 9. "At the Charleston Hotel," 1853. Eyre Crowe, *With Thackeray in America* (New York: Charles Scribner's Sons, 1893), 149.

FIG. 10. Drayman near St. Michael's Church, 1853. Eyre Crowe, *With Thackeray in America* (New York: Charles Scribner's Sons, 1893), 154.

FIG. 11. Wharf hands in Charleston, 1853. Eyre Crowe, *With Thackeray in America* (New York: Charles Scribner's Sons, 1893), 155.

FIG. 12. Wharf hand marking a cotton bale, 1853. Eyre Crowe, *With Thackeray in America* (New York: Charles Scribner's Sons, 1893), 157.

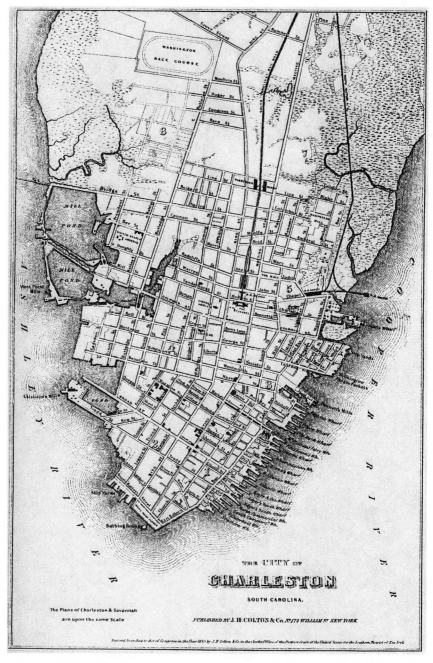

FIG. 13. "The City of Charleston, South Carolina, Published by J. H. Colton. Includes Streets, Wharves, and Race Course, Wards and Rail Lines," 1855. Charleston County Public Library.

Fig. 14. Draymen at the corner of East Bay and Broad Streets, 1857. Samuel Smith Kilburn Sketchbooks, 1855–60. Courtesy of the American Antiquarian Society.

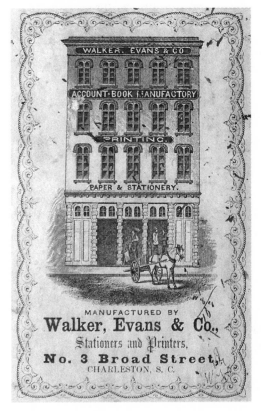

Fig. 15. Walker, Evans & Co. advertisement, ca. 1860. Court of General Sessions, Criminal Journals, Charleston District, 1857–64. South Carolina Department of Archives and History, Columbia.

Fig. 16. Cotton Drayman on Union Wharf. "Rush of Cotton, Union Wharf, Charleston, No. 37." in Views of Charleston and Vicinity stereograph series by F. A. Nowell, Charleston (Photographs 11921.10 Nowell). Courtesy of South Caroliniana Library, University of South Carolina, Columbia.

Fig. 17A. Waterfront workers on South Carolina currency.

FIG. 17B. Bank of the State of South Carolina one-dollar bill, 1860. Canceled currency. South Carolina Department of Archives and History, Columbia.

FIG. 17C. South Carolina Railroad Company fare ticket. Courtesy of South Caroliniana Library, University of South Carolina, Columbia.

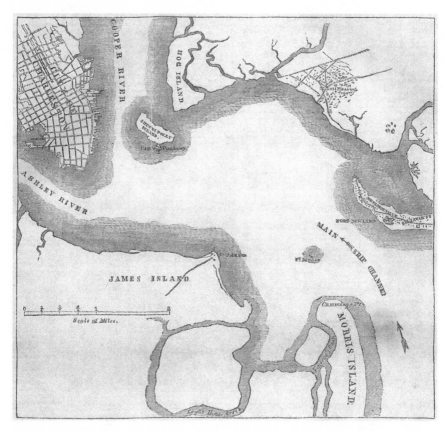

FIG. 18. "Map Showing the Forts, Islands, Etc., of the Harbor of Charleston, South Carolina." *Harper's Weekly,* January 19, 1861. Courtesy of Irvin Department of Rare Books and Special Collections, University of South Carolina Libraries, Columbia.

Fig. 19. "Charleston, S.C. and Its Vicinity," in Robert Tomes, *The War with the South: A History of the Late Rebellion with Biographical Sketches of Leading Statesmen and Distinguished Naval and Military Commanders, Etc.* (New York: Virtue & Yorston Publishers, 1862), vol. 1, opp. 58. Courtesy of Irvin Department of Rare Books and Special Collections, University of South Carolina Libraries, Columbia.

FIG 20 A
Civil War damage
on Vendue Range,
1865. "Charleston,
South Carolina,
Vendue Range,
looking east from
near the corner of
East Bay Street."
Library of Con-
gress, Prints and
Photographs
Division.

FIG. 20 B
Civil War damage
on Vendue Range,
1865. "Charleston,
South Carolina,
Vendue Range."
Library of Con-
gress, Prints and
Photographs
Division.

Fig. 21. "Bird's Eye View of the City of Charleston, South Carolina, 1872." Library of Congress, Geography and Map Division.

FIG. 22. "Scene on a New York Dock—Stevedores Unloading a Ship." Drawn by
I. P. Pranishnikoff. *Harper's Weekly*, July 14, 1877. Courtesy of Irvin Department
of Rare Books and Special Collections, University of South Carolina Libraries,
Columbia.

FIG. 23. "Loading Cotton at Charleston, South Carolina." Photographed by George
N. Barnard. *Harper's Weekly*, January 19, 1878. Courtesy of Irvin Department of Rare
Books and Special Collections, University of South Carolina Libraries, Columbia.

FIG. 24. "South Carolina.—Our Great National Industry—Shipping Cotton from Charleston to Foreign and Domestic Ports—A Scene on North Commercial Wharf.—From Sketches by H. A. Ogden." *Frank Leslie's Illustrated Newspaper,* November 16, 1878. Courtesy of Avery Research Center for African American History and Culture, College of Charleston, S.C.

FIG. 25. "Weighing an Invoice of Cotton Before Consignment to a Foreign Port. South Carolina.—Our Great National Industry—Scenes on the Cotton Wharves of Charleston.—From Sketches by H. A. Ogden." *Frank Leslie's Illustrated Newspaper,* November 16, 1878. Courtesy of Avery Research Center for African American History and Culture, College of Charleston, S.C.

Chapter Four

"Laborers from abroad have come to take their places"

The Racial and Ethnic Transformation of the Waterfront Workforce

During a visit to South Carolina in early 1808, Englishman John Lambert observed, "There are no white servants in Charleston. Every kind of work is performed by the negroes and people of colour." "From the nature of our Society," members of Charleston's Chamber of Commerce affirmed in 1826, "menial occupations are necessarily confined to colored persons—White men disdain and are unwilling to undertake them." A white Virginian similarly explained to northern journalist Frederick Law Olmsted that even destitute white laborers refused to do "certain kinds of work" typically reserved for slaves, and that "if you should ask a white man . . . to do such things, he would get mad and tell you he wasn't a nigger."[1] Unskilled urban wage labor was considered not only the province of black slaves, but also dishonorable and a blot on the character of anyone aspiring to upward socioeconomic mobility in the Old South.[2] During three years of travels through eleven southern states, abolitionist Philo Tower indeed observed that whites who made a living performing manual wage labor could "scarcely gain admittance into the [aristocratic] class, any sooner than the poor slave himself, of the regular woolly-heads, simon pure."[3]

Stigmatized as "nigger work," common waterfront employment indeed was shunned by the vast majority of native white South Carolinians and southerners.[4] One study found that less than 2 percent of whites born in the South undertook unskilled wage labor of any type in late antebellum Charleston.[5] Another scholar of labor in the city contended that whites "invariably" eschewed the crude and arduous tasks of loading and unloading ships as "an anathema and demeaning."[6] Prior to the 1840s, blacks, mostly slaves, indisputably dominated menial dock work as well as the transport of commercial goods to and from Charleston's commercial wharves. Even as late as 1842, visiting Briton Charles Lyell wrote unequivocally, "the slaves have at present a monopoly of the labour-market."[7] But soon thereafter the city's waterfront workforce revolutionized as millions of Irish and other white immigrants crossed the Atlantic and settled in port cities all along the Eastern Seaboard and Gulf Coast. By the eve of the Civil War, dock labor in Charleston no longer was cornered by one race or invariably avoided by another.

To the complex and often factional struggles pervading the city's waterfront, then, can be added a contest among the laborers themselves. Significant friction, and sometimes violence, accompanied the racial and ethnic transformation of this most vital workforce, as white newcomers endeavored to reduce or eliminate their free black and enslaved competitors. In addition to utilizing the electoral power of universal white male suffrage, the more skilled and articulate of the white workingmen employed legislative petitions and public appeals in the effort to gain occupational protections and make further inroads against black rivals. But aside from proving largely unsuccessful, many of these entreaties exposed and exacerbated socioeconomic and vocational rifts between a cadre of professional white stevedores and the waterfront's lesser skilled and often destitute common white laborers. Yet despite these workers' diversity of position, ability, compensation, class, origin, and culture, they all shared the challenge and "otherness" of being free and white wage earners in the urban slaveholding South.

Before the 1840s white waterfront workers were few and far between. Cart owners seeking to hire drivers to convey goods to and from the wharves in late colonial Charles Town noted, "there is but very few white people who will follow that Employment in this Town."[8] Of the 1,620 white Charlestonians listed in the 1790 city directory—the first to include any free transportation workers—only 13, or less than 1 percent of the enumerated inhabitants, were draymen or carters.[9] These figures were relatively high, however. In the eleven subsequent city directories published between 1794 and 1819, fewer than six white draymen and carters combined appeared on average. And the eight directories published between 1822 and 1840–41 included no white draymen or carters. The 1816 directory, meanwhile, was the lone city guide between 1782 and 1848 to include porters, and only two white men—Henry Clime and P. Crevier—were listed.[10] Likewise, only one white stevedore—H. C. Cortea in the 1837–38 edition—appeared in the city directories prior to the 1850s.[11]

Other sources, however, captured a handful of those whites who performed waterfront labor in Charleston during the late eighteenth and early nineteenth centuries. Commission merchants Rowland Hazard and Peter Ayrault, for example, regularly patronized at least two white draymen during the 1790s. Every five to ten months between August 1796 and July 1798 Hazard and Ayrault settled drayage accounts with Henry Hyer and John Woodmancy, with payments ranging between $12.30 and $35.75.[12] City records showed that fifty-three-year-old native Charlestonian and drayman Samuel Williams was admitted to the alms house—generally reserved for whites only—on March 26, 1825, and died four days later.[13] And several of the previously mentioned legislative acts from the late colonial and early national eras—specifying matters such as workers' wages and hiring locations—included references to whites engaged in drayage, cartage, and porterage along the docks.[14]

The minority of southern whites willing or financially obliged to endure the indignity of vital but servile seaboard labor often suffered slavish wages as well.[15] Beginning in 1764 the wages of both black and white draymen and carters were capped equally; though white transport workers could request and accept less than the established rates, they rarely could compete with the legion of hired-out slaves and still make ends meet.[16] White porters and day laborers had their pay regulated only from 1801 to 1837, freeing them before and after this time period to earn as high a wage as employers were willing to dole out. Some wharfingers, ship captains, and merchants—like Rowland Hazard and Peter Ayrault—exercised a racial predilection for white waterfront workers, but most hired the more numerous and often cheaper blacks.

Blacks and whites engaged in unloading and loading cargo or other dock labor were limited after 1801 to 85 cents per day. In 1837, when the wages of white wharf hands were loosed from regulation, blacks' daily pay rose to $1. Draymen and carters, again, were compensated based on the distance of conveyance. But Charleston architect Robert Mills reported in 1826 that white workmen in the city more generally earned $2 per day, whereas enslaved blacks received $1. Mills also calculated that white mechanics—including skilled coopers, riggers, and ship carpenters—earned an average wage of $1.37 ½ per day, compared to 82 ½ cents per day paid to slave artisans. Blacks had an even clearer advantage over whites in the eyes of hirers when engaged by the month.[17] During the 1830s, the City of Charleston employed both black and white laborers for public works projects. A white worker reportedly earned about $26 each month, but a slave only cost the city $12 monthly plus $1 each week for food. In the aftermath of the Panic of 1837, Mayor Henry L. Pinckney urged the City Council to cut the number of municipal workers and to employ blacks rather than whites to save money.[18] According to Mills, slaves could be hired for $10 to $12 per month; but sometimes slaves could be found for even less. In August 1846, for example, one master advertised his "PRIME young Negro" wharf hand and laborer for only $8 per month. As Scottish traveler James Stuart noted when in Charleston in March 1830, "the prodigious saving [*sic*] by employing slaves is obvious."[19]

Despite these significant disadvantages, Charleston's white workers competed with slaves for waterfront and other employment for nearly two centuries. And though their efforts were often futile, these free and white men frequently appealed to legislators for occupational and economic protection from their black rivals. A proposal circulated in South Carolina's colonial assembly in 1735 pondered a prohibition on slaves being "employed for Hire as Porters, Carters or Fishermen" in Charleston, but the ban was stripped from the broader bill prior to final passage. Early the next decade, in the aftermath of the Stono Rebellion, a committee of the same body recommended outlawing "the bringing up [of] Negroes and other Slaves to mechanic Trades in which white Persons usually are employed."[20] The committee's suggestion came on the heels of a 1742 petition from Charleston's white artisans—perhaps the first official grievance from the city's white workers—complaining of "the want of a law to prevent hiring out of Negro tradesmen to the great discouragement of white working men coming into the province."[21]

Though it took until 1755 for lawmakers to adopt such a prohibition, it was only the first of many measures over the years aimed at skilled bondsmen.[22] The slave code enacted in 1764 declared it unlawful for slaves "to carry on any mechanick [*sic*] or handicraft trade of themselves, in any shop or otherwise in Charlestown," language that the new state legislature adopted in a 1783 act.[23] In 1796 the Charleston City Council passed an ordinance barring slave mechanics from hiring out their own time, and another municipal regulation in 1806 outlawed slaves from practicing any mechanical pursuits on their own accounts.[24] The city's slaveowners, meanwhile, were forbidden in 1751 from having "more than two Male Slaves to work out for Hire, as Porters, Laborers, Fishermen, or Handicraftsmen in Town," a proscription repeated in 1764. These were the same laws that required waterfront slaves to be licensed and identified with badges.[25] And like those restrictions, these prohibitory measures were irregularly or weakly enforced in the face of staunch opposition from income-hungry masters, efficiency-minded commercial boosters, and the defiant slaves themselves who continued to struggle against white laborers for urban waterfront work until the Civil War.

Aggrieved by a dearth of employment opportunities and slumping wages, Charleston's white workers nonetheless persisted in their endeavor to eradicate or at least reduce slave competitors. The initial petition in 1742 against enslaved tradesmen was followed two years later by a similar objection from white shipwrights. When after the Revolution a lack of construction work in Charleston made it difficult for white bricklayers and carpenters to support their families, they appealed in 1783 to the South Carolina General Assembly for relief from "jobbing negro" competitors who casually moved from job to job and accepted paltry wages.[26] It was later that same year that the legislature reaffirmed the colonial-era ban on autonomous slave mechanics and handicraftsmen. And yet in 1793 the city's white master coopers fulminated against the "very great and growing evil" long perpetrated by slaves who illegally carried out various trades and occupations "free from the Direction and Superintendance [*sic*] of any White person whatever," and worked for wages much lower than whites could "possibly afford." As Robert Mills reported decades later, white coopers and other skilled workers earned nearly twice the daily wages of their enslaved rivals, which whites argued was necessary to meet their higher standard and cost of living.[27] But wary lawmakers—many themselves slaveholders with hired-out bondsmen earning wages in the city—declined to incorporate the Society of Master Coopers of Charleston, created not only "for the Purpose of general Utility" and mutual aid but also as a means "of discouraging and utterly preventing those Practices of Slaves" which threatened the white coopers' livelihoods.[28] Down but not out, Charleston's white mechanics again pressed state leaders in 1794 to enforce or "pass a Law for regulating [the] exercise of Mechanic trades by slaves in the City of Charleston." Though a bill to circumscribe slave mechanics in both Charleston and Georgetown was introduced and debated, the measure was defeated in the South Carolina Senate by a vote of sixteen to eleven.[29]

White workers did have a few prominent advocates in their late-eighteenth-century campaign for refuge and recognition. One leader of the state Constitutional Convention held in Charleston in 1788, for instance, openly contended that "cheap negro labor was steadily undermining the white artisan class" in South Carolina.[30] And in September 1795, Charleston's Grand Jury presented state legislators with the "very great grievance, that Slaves that are Mechanics are allowed to carry on various handicraft Trades on their own account to the great prejudice of the poor [white] Mechanics in this City."[31] Buoyed by such support and the 1796 city ordinance against enslaved artisans hiring themselves out to employers, members of the nascent Charleston Mechanic Society resolutely petitioned the legislature for incorporation in 1798. But mindful of past setbacks, especially the coopers' failed accreditation bid only a few years before, the artisans changed tactics. Though this association of white workingmen would continue to play an active and vocal role in the crusade against black labor competition, their petition for incorporation was devoid of any mention of slaves or free blacks. Focused instead on the desire to pool funds for the support of sick and injured fellow workers, the city's white mechanics curried enough favor with slaveholding state legislators to gain a five-year charter.[32]

By not granting permanent incorporation, however, lawmakers revealed a cautious distrust of these white workers' true intentions. Ever vigilant for threats to the institution of slavery in general and to individual masters' sovereignty, property, and income in particular, authorities furthermore were intolerant of any efforts to organize or boost wages, as black porters had done in the early 1760s. The Charleston Mechanic Society therefore again steered clear of the issue of black labor competition when asking for a perpetual charter in 1803. Once more appealing to legislators' humanity, the members emphasized the society's objective of benevolent financial and material support for the destitute families of unemployed, ill, injured, and deceased tradesmen. Then imploring to be put on an equal footing with the state's other charitable institutions—such as the aristocratic South Carolina Society and the German Friendly Society—the white workers asked, "are your Petitioners less useful Citizens than any other Class of men? are they less orderly or less moral or less attached to the Constitution or Laws of their Country? and if they are not, why should a badge of Suspicion distinguish them while others are cloathed [*sic*] in honor?" Acutely aware of their vulnerable and peculiar status as free wage laborers in a slave society, these workingmen also were staking claim to justice and their rights as free and white men.[33] Evidently not convinced that this collection of white workers was interested in solely charitable pursuits, the General Assembly refused a permanent charter in 1803 but renewed the incorporation of the Charleston Mechanic Society through 1817.[34]

The Denmark Vesey conspiracy of 1822 finally presented Charleston's white mechanics and other workingmen with a golden opportunity to strike boldly and decisively at their black competitors. Just months after the alleged plot was foiled, South Carolina Association member and former governor Thomas Pinckney published his "Reflections, Occasioned by the Late Disturbances in Charleston," in which he suggested measures aimed at preventing future slave revolts in the city. Pinckney, writing under the pseudonym Achates, began by including among the causes of the Vesey conspiracy the ease with which black Charlestonians, free and enslaved, were able to obtain money "afforded by the nature of their occupations . . . as mechanics, draymen, fishermen, butchers, porters, hucksters, &c." Blacks thus employed not only spent their wages in pursuits of drunkenness and debauchery, but also were "willing instruments of any delusive plan of mischief which may be presented to them." According to Pinckney, the knowledge acquired through these occupations as well as the requisite tools of employment—such as horses, vehicles, and even knives—"increase[d] their ability to do mischief," as evidenced by the reckless and sometimes malicious driving of drays. An official report further claimed that the plot's recruits were "principally confined to Negroes hired or working out, such as Carters, Draymen, Sawyers, Porters, Labourers, Stevidores [*sic*], Mechanics, those employed in lumber yards, and in short to those who had certain allotted hours at their own disposal." But admitting the impracticality of directly preventing these "ill effects," Pinckney sought to remedy the one "evil" that was within the control of city and state authorities: "The disparity of numbers between white and black inhabitants of the City."[35]

In 1800 there were 1,213 more blacks than whites in Charleston. By 1820 the black majority had increased to 2,898, with 14,127 black and 11,229 white Charlestonians (see table in introduction). This "rapidly increasing evil—this sine qua non of insurrection," had to be reversed. But, Pinckney asked, "what substitute can be obtained to occupy the employments now filled by the Negroes?" The notion of being placed on the same footing with black slaves, let alone working shoulder to shoulder with them, repulsed most free white men. As a result, white immigrants supposedly were deterred from settling in Charleston. The solution, Pinckney argued, was to entirely eradicate blacks from certain occupations and wholly replace them with whites.[36]

First and foremost among the former governor's arguments in favor of free labor was the increased security and diminished risk of slave revolts that would accompany an elimination of Charleston's black majority. An inflow of free white laborers simultaneously would enlarge the ranks of the city's militia and offer better protection in wartime. The reduction in blacks would lead to less idleness and depravity, such as theft and pilferage, while whites' superior morals would provide a more wholesome example to the city's impressionable children. Moreover, the burden on local government and charitable institutions would decline as impoverished whites found employment, and the labor would be better and more industriously performed. After all, Pinckney intimated, what incentive did slaves have to work hard and efficiently if the bulk of their wages had to be turned over to their masters? Black laborers similarly mistreated their work tools and equipment, including horses and other animals, thus causing much unnecessary expense and waste. It further was suggested that hiring white workmen actually could prove cheaper than employing slaves, who—as with the Vanderhorsts' wharf hands—often had to be fed, clothed, housed, and treated when ill, injured, and old. And even if whites were more expensive, their advantages far outweighed the cost of the extra wages. Pinckney concluded, in short, that jobs including waterfront draymen and porters "would be more advantageously filled by white men."[37]

But before Charlestonians could "get rid of the blacks" and their occupations turned over exclusively to free white workingmen, white substitutes had to be recruited. Pinckney insisted that the supply would follow the demand; that is, once it was known "that Charleston requires any number of mechanics, draymen, &c. who will be liberally paid for their services," white laborers would come to the city like moths to a flame. And fully a quarter of a century before Ireland's Great Famine, the impoverished and oppressed Irish were thought ideal candidates for recruitment. Pinckney asked,

Who that contemplates the unhappy condition of Ireland, where impoli-
tic regulations, and the enormously unequal distribution of property have
reduced a brave, industrious, and honest peasantry to perish by famine in
a fruitful country, when at the time there is no real scarcity of provisions,
can doubt that from that ill-fated Island alone an accession might soon be
received, of active, industrious mechanics and labourers, to a City, where
are already comfortably established, so many of their countrymen, who having passed through their seasoning, and now understanding the precautions
necessary to be taken on change of climate, would with their accustomed
benevolence and hospitality, effectually advise and assist the new-comers
to establish themselves with safety and advantage[?][38]

This exchange of black laborers for white, Pinckney conceded, would not be easy,
convenient, or without cost. Time would have to be allowed for slaveowners to
sell, hire, or transport their bondsmen out of town, and employers would need
time to advertise and fill vacated positions. The question was, "whether the object
be worth the cost?" History and experience had shown that "nothing good and
valuable can be obtained without exertion and expense."[39] In other words, the
disadvantages of such a fundamental change ought not to overshadow the immense advantages, the principal being greater security and the removal of terror.

Thomas Pinckney failed to win the broad support of white Charlestonians for
his plan to wholly replace urban slave laborers with immigrant whites and relegate
slavery to a rural institution in South Carolina. But most inhabitants agreed that
something had to be done to better control and perhaps reduce the city's black
majority. Shortly after the discovery of the Vesey plot, Intendant James Hamilton
and the members of the City Council petitioned state legislators recommending,
among other things, that "the number of male slaves [in Charleston] be greatly
diminished," including "all those who hire themselves out or are hired by their
owners." In October 1822 Charleston's Grand Jury proposed reviving the ineffec-
tual laws passed in 1751 and 1764 limiting the number of slaves each master was
permitted to hire out in the city. Endorsing such a rule, one resident called for
"all that useless class of Servants," including day laborers and draymen, to be sent
away to the countryside.[40]

This public policy debate culminated in December 1822 with a reactionary
slave code that included the first of the state's Negro Seamen Acts. But significantly, the statute also outlawed all male slaves from hiring their own time, that
is, making labor agreements with employers without the direct involvement of
their masters. Under the new law, slaveowners who permitted their bondsmen to
do so were liable to the seizure and forfeiture of their valuable human property.[41]
Previous regulatory measures, such as slave badges and waterfront porter stands,

had been designed in part to render the short-term hire of bondsmen more convenient and efficient; but these schemes had failed miserably in their surveillance function. This 1822 law therefore was intended to limit the ability of urban slave workers to act as if they were free, and thus to lessen their overall autonomy and the threat of future slave insurrections. After all, one of the plot's alleged leaders, slave drayman William Garner, boasted prior to his execution that he was "master of his own time, as good as free."[42]

According to the act, a master wishing to hire slaves out now was obligated to roam the wharves and workshops of the city to identify and contract each job on behalf of his slaves. It was common for Charleston's slaveowners to sign contracts hiring out slaves for a month or a year. But this 1822 law made it impractical and bothersome to hire out bondsmen for shorter periods. In other words, the letter of the law required that the master personally make the employment arrangements each time a slave was needed to haul a dray load of cotton from the railroad depot to a dockside vessel, or a wharfinger or ship captain wanted to hire a slave awaiting work at a waterfront porter stand. This tedious and time-consuming task clearly would not have been worth the hassle for the majority of Charleston's slaveowners, and would have opened the labor market for many waterfront occupations to white workingmen.[43]

But it soon was evident to all in Charleston, and especially the city's white workers, that authorities were not enforcing this central but onerous provision of the 1822 law. In a petition to the General Assembly just a few years after the passage of the act, more than one hundred white mechanics bluntly protested that this potentially salutary statute "fell dead-born" and had "never been in any manner carried into execution." Self-interested masters routinely evaded the law, the petitioners contended, by providing their slaves with notes or certificates stating that the bondsmen were permitted to work out. The mechanics went on to object that "such is the indolence of Mankind, that there are but few owners who do not prefer turning loose their Slaves upon the Community, with such a Certificate, to hunt for Work . . . than put themselves to the trouble of making the contract." Hard hit by Charleston's recent "decay of Trade" and relative economic decline, the white workers claimed that, due to competition with enslaved and free black workmen, their situation had become "so unprosperous, as to hold out to those who would be willing to . . . gain their livelihood by honest and laborious Industry in their avocation, a prospect full of gloom, and almost of Despair."[44]

Meanwhile, contrary to Thomas Pinckney's hope that the disparity between blacks and whites in the city could be corrected with an influx of white laborers, the petitioners claimed that the number of white workers in Charleston actually was decreasing. Some white mechanics had to turn to more menial employment, perhaps including common dock labor. Harkening back to the Denmark Vesey affair and the fear that first prompted both Pinckney's essay and the 1822 law, the white workingmen warned that "Charleston, already swarming with a population of Free Blacks, and of Slaves, more Licentious than if they were Free, must, in a very short time, be in the condition of a West India Town, which it will be impossible to defend without a Regular Military Force."[45] As the contest between advocates of prosperity and security heated up, the specter of insurrection and slaughter was a new dart in the white workers' quiver that would be employed often in the decades to come.

Planter and Charleston resident Edward R. Laurens played on his neighbors' fears when he championed the city's struggling white workingmen in an address to the Agricultural Society of South Carolina in September 1832. Like Thomas Pinckney, Laurens expressed views and policies that he readily acknowledged were "heterodox and unpopular" among the vast majority of South Carolinians and especially fellow slaveholders. But rather than calling for the replacement of blacks with whites in the city, Laurens argued, "slaves should not be allowed residence within the city in greater numbers than are actually necessary." He conceded that the use of urban slaves in occupations such "as draymen, stevedores, wharf-labourers, and mechanics" had been too long established to accomplish their entire removal from the city. The employment of slave labor on Charleston's waterfront, in other words, had passed a point of no return. Still, there was the potential to reduce the "great redundancy" of slaves engaged in these crucial yet abundant positions by offering payments to entice white emigrants. If this were done, Laurens argued, within only a few years Charleston would have a much more effective and wholesome workforce and population. Laurens rejected the claim that an unhealthy climate explained why few white laborers had immigrated to Charleston, and echoed Pinckney in maintaining that the supply of free and white draymen, laborers, and mechanics would meet the demand if only the city offered a little "liberal encouragement."[46]

Slaveowning interests had precluded any serious or sustained attempt to recruit white immigrants in the decade after Thomas Pinckney's 1822 essay. In fact, the 1830 U.S. Census had confirmed that the gap between Charleston's black and white populations had increased by over 1,000.[47] Laurens claimed that recent laws "honestly intended to benefit the mechanic interest" had produced the opposite effect by placing "further difficulties in the path of the poor young white man." He was particularly critical of an act that exempted from "extra taxation" (that is, hiring badges) the slaves of white master mechanics who worked under the direction of their owners.[48] This measure not only "operated to make the rich richer," but also led to the exclusion of white journeymen in favor of cheaper slave apprentices. Many of the city's white workers consequently were being "driven from their honest trades to earn their bread by other means." Some simply were packing up and moving on. But rather than blaming slaves for this "ultimate exclusion of the bone and sinew of our population," Laurens fingered Charleston's "intermediate class" of free blacks.[49]

By 1832 it was clear to Edward Laurens and many other advocates for free labor in Charleston that a war against urban slavery—even after Vesey—was not just an uphill battle but a losing one. With the Nullification Crisis underway and controversial legislation such as the Negro Seamen Acts sparking both sectional and international tensions, southerners accelerated their evolving defense of slavery. No longer a "necessary evil," the institution was rebranded as a "positive good" focused on the beneficial and paternalistic nurturing of an inferior race.[50] In addition, the seats of power in Charleston and Columbia were occupied by slaveowners who long had enjoyed the fruits of their hired-out urban slaves' wage labor.[51] Free people of color, on the other hand—a "third class in our community"—had fewer defenders and thus were much more vulnerable than slaves. "By far the greatest evil . . . which slave-holding communities have to contend with," free blacks not only deprived jobs from hard-working whites but also planted notions of freedom and insurrection in the minds of Charleston's slaves. Denmark Vesey, Laurens reminded his audience, was a free black man. And if nothing was done about the ongoing exodus of white laborers from the city, "worse than savage massacre may yet be the consequence of their absence." The remedy to this free black "nuisance" was their "entire extinction" or banishment from the city and state. Though Charleston's free people of color lived a precarious existence and frequently had their rights and very liberty threatened, it was not until the eve of the Civil War that white South Carolinians mounted a concerted effort to drive free blacks from the city.[52]

Arguments similar to those of Thomas Pinckney and Edward Laurens resurfaced from time to time in 1830s and 1840s Charleston. James Gadsden and other leaders of the South Carolina Railroad, for instance, insisted that among the benefits of extending the company's tracks to the Cooper River wharves would be a reduction in the city's latently rebellious slave workforce. "In deminishing [*sic*] the necessity for Draymen, Cartmen, Porters, Stevedores & all that class of underlaborers, who are chiefly comprised of the most intelligent and able bodied of the Negroes and who are in command of time, opportunities and horses for mischief, and turning them to more useful employment and less dangerous associations," the 1845 report contended, "something will be attained worth all consideration." As long as the rail lines remained remote from the waterfront, the need for such risky laborers would continue to climb along with cotton exports. "The History of 1822, should not be forgotten," the ill-fated proposal exhorted.[53]

But ultimately is was the Great Famine in Ireland and social and political unrest in Germany that finally precipitated what foreboding essays, speeches, and reports could not: the "whitening" of Charleston's waterfront workforce. Between 1830 and 1860 nearly 5 million foreign immigrants poured into the United

States, most of whom originated from Western and Central Europe and especially Ireland and Germany. A great majority of these white foreigners landed in the North, and finding work and relatives in large port cities like New York, Boston, and Philadelphia, most remained north of the Mason-Dixon Line and thus avoided labor competition with black slaves.[54]

But immigrants did make their way to southern cities, including Charleston, in search of employment and opportunities for upward socioeconomic mobility. Irishman Thomas Carrol, for example, arrived in New York City as an eight-year-old child in September 1847 and by 1860 was working on Charleston's waterfront as a skilled stevedore. The *Charleston Mercury* referred to Carrol in 1891 as "a well known stevedore," and he still lived in the city in 1900 at the age of sixty-two.[55] John Torrent was born in Spain in 1804, but by the mid-1830s was in Maryland. Before long Torrent and his family made their way to Charleston, where John was employed as a rigger in 1840. Eventually partnering with his two eldest sons, the Spaniard operated a rigging and stevedoring business throughout the 1840s and 1850s. By 1860, fifty-six-year-old John Torrent owned $4,500 in real estate and $2,500 in personal property, including several horses for hoisting cargo and rigging vessels and a male slave who likely was employed on the docks.[56] And William Doran—born in Ireland in 1809 or 1810 but residing in South Carolina by 1849—also was working as a rigger in 1855 and then as a stevedore by 1857. Despite losing an arm during the Union bombardment of Charleston, Doran continued to work as a professional stevedore after the Civil War until his death in 1880.[57] In all, federal census schedules tallied 2,359 Irish immigrants living in Charleston in 1850, comprising 5.5 percent of the city's total population and 11.8 percent of all white inhabitants. By 1860 there were 3,263 Irish-born Charlestonians, 8 percent of the city's residents and 14 percent of whites.[58] In addition, 1,901 Germans—many of whom were skilled tradesmen or professionals—populated the city in 1860.[59] And a local census conducted in 1861 found that 3,662 Irishmen, 2,437 Germans, and 1,401 immigrants from all other countries resided in the city.[60]

Such figures may be low, however, given the continuous relocation of workers and the timing of various population counts. Though some newcomers—such as Carrol, Torrent, and Doran—settled in Charleston permanently, many others migrated seasonally between northern and southern port cities. Thomas Pinckney proposed in 1822 that, in addition to recruiting Irish and other foreign laborers to immigrate to Charleston, itinerant workers already on the continent could be persuaded to remain in the city indefinitely. For years Charlestonians had witnessed "every autumn . . . the importation of a considerable number of industrious mechanics and fishermen from the Northern and Eastern States." As with prospective immigrants, if the humiliation of being "placed so nearly on a level with the slave" could be removed along with the city's bondsmen, Pinckney argued that these transient white laborers could be convinced to end their "present practice of returning home in the summer" and settle in Charleston year-round.[61]

Pinckney's observation that workers typically traveled southward in the fall and returned to the North in the summer was accurate. When Robert Russell visited Charleston in January 1855, the Englishman remarked, "The greater part of the business being transacted in winter . . . A large influx of merchants and labourers takes place in winter, but they again depart during the hot season."[62] Scholars have offered a number of plausible explanations for this seasonal pattern of migration, including that immigrant laborers left frigid New York City or other northern ports due to a dearth of employment opportunities in the late fall and winter, and departed Charleston before the arrival of the summer heat and the onset of the annual threat of diseases such as malaria and especially yellow fever.[63] Irish immigrants living in the North also were recruited to come south to toil at tasks considered too dangerous for valuable slaves, such as the construction of roads, canals, railroads, and large buildings. After the completion of these projects, workers either secured another job or returned northward.[64]

Rarely mentioned, however, is that many of these transient Irish and other immigrants came to Charleston specifically to work on the city's waterfront.[65] Again, the majority of native white southerners eschewed menial waterfront employment. But whether by choice or necessity, many white immigrants found such work to be acceptable. Since the preponderance of newcomers, and especially the Irish, qualified only as lowly paid day laborers performing the most grueling, unhealthy, and perilous tasks, most regarded unskilled or semiskilled jobs such as loading and unloading ships on the docks or draying and carting goods to be relatively desirable.[66]

Because commercial shipping was seasonal, so was dock work. The port was, of course, open for business year-round, but demand for waterfront and transportation labor waned in the late spring and summer months. Therefore, stevedores, wharf hands, porters, draymen, and other waterfront laborers in Charleston could rely upon steady work only about seven months of each year. For those slaves, free blacks, and whites who lived and labored in Charleston permanently, the remaining five months typically were split between the docks and working other jobs.[67] Some Irish draymen and carters—and even master stevedore William Doran—bid to become city scavengers or street contractors, whereas other workers would join fire companies or moonlighted as city guardsmen or night watchmen.[68]

Many immigrant laborers, on the other hand, departed Charleston at the close of the shipping season and set out in search of employment on the thawing docks of northern port cities, only to return to the South looking for work in the fall. Irish immigrants and other whites who worked as timber stowers in Quebec City, for example, migrated southward each year when the St. Lawrence River froze over to labor as cotton stevedores on the waterfronts of New Orleans, Savannah, Mobile, and Pensacola. Some transients were deep-water sailors, mainly Irishmen and Englishmen, who seized short-term opportunities for more advantageous employment as they traversed the Atlantic World. As maritime folklorist Stan Hugill described it, "as soon as the packet moored in New York or Boston, many of them evolved a regular pattern of jumping the ship and heading south as fast as their legs or a coast-wise vessel would take them. Others would leave their packets in order to dodge the hauling of frozen ropes and the wading waist deep in icy water at the lee fore brace during the W.N.A. (Winter North Atlantic), preferring the warmer climes of Louisiana until the spring came." After stowing cotton alongside southern blacks for several months, these white mariners returned to sea aboard cotton-laden vessels bound for European ports.[69]

This seasonal circuit of dockworkers included Charleston as well. With the establishment of more regular and reliable coastal packet service between Charleston and New York in 1822, the steady flow of seasonal laborers became a torrent.[70] Created to transport cotton and other goods between the two Atlantic ports, the packet lines also initiated an active passenger service. In addition to relatively affluent cabin travelers, these vessels offered steerage passage, enabling thousands of transient white workers—most of whom were poor and unskilled Irish immigrants—to travel back and forth between New York and Charleston in search of employment.[71] One study estimated that the Charleston–New York vessels accommodated 10,900 to 14,800 one-way travelers in 1824 and 26,000 to 32,500 one-way trips in 1836.[72] In the years just before the Civil War, the New York and Charleston Steamship Line charged seven or eight dollars for one-way steerage tickets, over a week's wages for a day laborer but about half the price of cabin fares.[73] Though not cheap, this packet service proved convenient and sometimes lifesaving to Charleston's itinerant dockhands. In July 1858, for instance, George A. Gordon wrote to his future wife Krilla that the sudden arrival of yellow fever in the city "made a stampede of the Irish population and crowded the steerage of the *Columbia*," a steamship that plied regularly between Charleston and New York.[74]

Data from 1845, 1849, and 1855 verify that the greatest influx of steerage passengers to Charleston took place during the fall and winter months, the port's commercial peak and more salubrious seasons. The heaviest flow of steerage passengers back to New York occurred between March and August, as maritime commerce and the resultant demand for waterfront labor dwindled, and the hazards of heat and health swelled. More specifically, 400 steerage passengers arrived in Charleston between May and August 1855, but over 1,000 passengers left the city and returned to New York during those same months. But between September and December 1855, as cotton bales and barrels of rice were piled up on

Charleston's wharves and an increasing number of vessels entered the harbor, over 1,700 passengers traveled from New York to Charleston in steerage whereas only 400 made the northward trek, a net inflow of 1,300 workers.[75]

As a result, the laboring population of Charleston fluctuated greatly during the year, ebbing and flowing with the seasons of maritime commerce. But this annual flux of thousands of working-class immigrants into and out of Charleston via the northern packet lines often did not produce a significant net increase in the city's permanent white laboring population. Throughout 1855, for example, approximately 2,800 steerage passengers traveled to Charleston, but about 2,700 went to New York. The number of white laborers—and particularly waterfront workers—clearly surged in the fall and winter. But since census and city directory data often were collected during the summer months, many of these seasonal workers were not in the city at the time and thus were not included in these counts. The 1860 U.S. Census, for instance, was conducted in Charleston between June 1 and August 2, the nadir of the southern shipping season and a time of year when the vast majority of transient white laborers were not present in the city. If the population figures instead had been generated in January and February, hundreds more white dockworkers would have been recorded.[76]

Whether white immigrants came to Charleston to work and settle permanently or for seasonal labor, they inevitably came into competition with the city's free blacks and slaves for waterfront and transportation work. And it was indeed on the docks and drays that these newcomers successfully challenged black workers.[77] Considered unskilled common labor, most of Charleston's free dockworkers were enumerated among all of the other "laborers" on the 1850 and 1860 U.S. Census schedules.[78] Tabulating their actual numbers with any degree of precision therefore is impossible.[79] The calendric fluctuation of the city's population also renders the use of census data imperfect. In spite of these challenges, census takers did specifically list free draymen, carters, and porters on their rolls.[80] Also included was the emergent waterfront occupation of superintending stevedores;

Free Waterfront Workers in Charleston, 1850 and 1860

	1850			1860		
	Total	Whites	Free Blacks	Total	Whites	Free Blacks
Stevedores	13	7 (54%)	6 (46%)	19	18 (95%)	1 (5%)
Porters	19	5 (26%)	14 (74%)	75	52 (69%)	23 (31%)
Draymen	75	28 (37%)	47 (63%)	147	122 (83%)	25 (17%)
Carters	12	4 (33%)	8 (67%)	34	23 (68%)	11 (32%)
Total	119	44 (37%)	75 (63%)	275	215 (78%)	60 (22%)

Source: 1850 U.S. Census and 1860 U.S. Census.

and between 1850 and 1860 a relatively small white cohort of these professional-ized contractors ravaged their free black competitors. The federal census revealed that six free black stevedores worked on Charleston's waterfront in 1850 along with seven whites, five of whom were Irish immigrants.[81] But by 1860 whites had shattered this nearly equal distribution of stevedoring jobs among free workers, claiming eighteen out of nineteen of the positions listed, including seven Irishmen, the most of any ethnic group.[82]

The 1850s were the key years of transition for other waterfront occupations as well. In 1850 the census listed 75 free draymen in Charleston, 47 of whom were free blacks and 28 were whites. Of the 12 carters recorded, 8 were free blacks and 4 were whites. In the same year 19 porters were listed, with 14 free blacks and only 5 whites. By 1860 a dramatic shift had occurred. In that year's census 147 individuals were listed as draymen, but with only 25 reported as free black and 122 as white. Moreover, among the 34 carters listed in the city in 1860, 23 now were whites and only 11 were free blacks. Of the 75 porters, whites claimed 52 and free blacks 23 of these positions. In short, by 1860 white immigrants—and particularly the Irish—had established a dominant presence among free workers on Charleston's wharves, occupying nearly 80 percent of the recorded positions. And some of these newcomers were not content with solely taking over free blacks' jobs. James M. Johnson, a tailor and free person of color, wrote to his brother-in-law Henry Ellison in August 1860 that he had observed an Irish carter inquiring about free black homes on Coming Street.[83]

The 1856 city directory provided a snapshot of Charleston's waterfront work-force in the midst of this racial and ethnic transformation. In that year, 12 white stevedores were counted, along with 44 white draymen, 18 carters, and 32 porters. Several white stevedores who newly would appear in the 1860 U.S. Census, such as future Longshoremen's Protective Union Association member George B. Stoddard and William Watson, had established themselves in the business.[84] Irish draymen such as James Corcoran and Thomas Green had made their journeys to Charleston and had found employment in this traditionally black occupation, as did fellow Irishman Miles Moran, who began work as a porter as early as 1855.[85] Among free blacks, on the other hand, only 2 stevedores, 13 draymen, 3 carters, and 6 porters were found to be laboring in the city in 1856. Already gone from the wharves were all 6 of the free black stevedores who had appeared in the 1850 U.S. Census.

The sole free black stevedore listed on the city's 1860 census rolls was a fifty-four-year-old native South Carolinian named Joseph Edmonston. But other sources captured the lingering presence of additional such workers, as in March 1858 when the *Columbus Times & Sentinel* (Georgia) published the following announcement: "Large Cargo—The ship *Agamemnon* was cleared at Charleston Custom House on the 16th inst., for St. Petersburg, having on board a cargo of

2,982 square bales cotton, containing 1,286,999 pounds. This exceeds the heaviest cargo ever carried in the same ship from New Orleans, to the extent of 177,000 pounds. Her stevedore was Samuel Pervis, a colored man." A reader of Savannah's *Daily Morning News,* which reprinted this item on March 23, wrote to the paper's editors that the episode demonstrated "what is not generally known to shipowners, that in Savannah and Charleston we can put more pounds of cotton into a ship, because we have the best cotton presses in the United States, and our stevedores do ample justice to their work." The Savannahian then cited his own examples in support of the argument that the stevedores along the south Atlantic coast routinely stowed vessels more professionally and effectively than those in New Orleans or Mobile. Though few in number, skilled free black men like Samuel Pervis doggedly and ably competed for work with Charleston's white stevedores until the Civil War.[86]

Meanwhile, just as the Irish and other white immigrants displaced many free black stevedores, draymen, carters, and porters, they also made inroads against Charleston's slaves. Documenting, let along tabulating, enslaved black rivals is an extremely difficult task, however. Evidence about individual waterfront slaves, such as the Vanderhorsts' Will and Dublin, John Andrew Jackson, or Robert Smalls, is invaluable to scholars; but U.S. Census records and city directories excluded the names and occupations of slaves, inhibiting the tracking over time of those who toiled on the wharves. Data from slave badge production and sales most definitively suggested that between 1,000 and 1,600 of Charleston's hired-out slaves worked on the waterfront as porters, draymen, carters, and day laborers during the late antebellum years.[87]

But just as contemporaries thoroughly documented enslaved blacks' dominance of the pre-1840s waterfront, they subsequently detected the shifting racial composition of the port's labor force as well. When northern author and future Union Army officer and Freedmen's Bureau agent John W. DeForest arrived in Charleston in 1855, for instance, he was struck by what he observed upon reaching the wharf. "[T]he crowd of porters & coachmen that met us on the dock presented not above half a dozen black faces," DeForest wrote to his brother. "Instead, I saw the familiar Irish & German visages whom I could have met on a dock at Boston or New York." After DeForest discussed his experience on the wharves with Charlestonians, he explained that the racial makeup of the city's workforce "was different years ago . . . and it is only lately that the whites have begun to crowd the blacks out of the more responsible lower employments."[88]

Others recorded similar observations. As early as 1840 the commissioners of Charleston's alms house reported that "the labouring classes in our City are daily changing, the white labourer is gradually taking the place of the Slave." These officials were so concerned about the rising numbers of poor white working people who were turning to the alms house for shelter and sustenance, in fact, they urged that land owned by the institution not be sold to the Charleston Literary and Philosophical Society in case an expansion of the alms house became necessary.[89] The authors of the city's 1848 census, John L. Dawson and Henry W. DeSaussure, acknowledged that the number of slaves and free blacks indeed had decreased. They reported that, whereas between 1840 and 1848 the white population of Charleston had increased by 8.9 percent, the percentage of blacks—both free and enslaved—had dropped by nearly 25 percent, including almost three thousand slaves who had "been removed from the city and its neighborhoods." "It is a question of interest, and one of some importance to the city," wrote Dawson and DeSaussure, "as to the cause of this rapid decrease of her slave population." Some Charlestonians thought this decline "a mere change of domicile," that is, due to the relocation of slaves and free blacks from the city proper to the "Neck" north of Boundary Street. But others believed that this was "a bona fide decrease," the slaves having been "driven away by free labor introduced from abroad."[90]

Contemporary images also captured the enlarged presence of white workers in waterfront occupations. When Englishman Eyre Crowe sketched the scene inside the lobby of the Charleston Hotel on March 22, 1853, amid the crowd of well-dressed gentlemen smoking, reading, and conversing, the artist portrayed at least two white workingmen—either porters or draymen who met arriving travelers like John W. DeForest on the docks—carrying luggage and cases into the hotel (see figure 9).[91] Advertisements for Walker, Evans & Co. during the late 1850s frequently included an image of a white drayman transferring wooden crates between his vehicle and the printers' building at 3 Broad Street near East Bay Street (see figure 15). And a Civil War–era South Carolina Railroad fare ticket similarly depicted three white workers laboriously heaving bundles onto a dray at either the company's depot or a wharfside warehouse (see figure 17).[92]

This recomposition of the labor force was not unique to Charleston. In fact, Irish, German, and other white immigrants triumphed over many black competitors in port cities throughout the late antebellum South.[93] An observer in Baltimore, for example, commented as early as 1835 that, even though there were 20,000 free blacks and 3,000 to 4,000 slaves residing in the city, "The Irish and other foreigners are, to a considerable extent, taking the place of colored laborers, and of domestic servants." As one Marylander put it in 1851, "The white man stands in the black man's shoes, or else is fast getting into them."[94] When Charles Lyell visited New Orleans in 1846, he heard that "the white race has been superseding the negroes." He also learned that ten years before, "all the draymen of New Orleans, a numerous class, and the cabmen, were colored. Now, they are nearly all white," and mostly Irish immigrants. In the early 1850s, Frederick Law Olmsted too observed, "White working men were rapidly displacing the slaves in all sorts of work," and had "very much gained the field of labor in New Orleans to themselves."[95] From the Chesapeake to the Mississippi River, white immigrants and especially Irishmen rivaled blacks on the South's docks and drays.[96]

Less clear to antebellum onlookers, however, was whether white workers in Charleston and elsewhere forcibly dislodged slaves from their relatively advantageous waterfront jobs or opportunely filled these bondsmen's vacated positions. Whereas some observers were convinced that slaves were being "crowd[ed] out," "driven away," or "displac[ed]," others described a far more passive process of Irishmen "taking the place" of those blacks already "removed from the city." The fire-eater editor of the *Charleston Mercury*, Leonidas W. Spratt, displayed this interpretive ambiguity when he asserted in February 1861, "Within ten years past as many as ten thousand slaves have been drawn away from Charleston by the attractive prices of the West, and laborers from abroad have come to take their places." These Irish and other foreign workers who were flowing into Charleston, Spratt then contended, "have every disposition to work above the slave, and if there were opportunity would be glad to do so; but without such opportunity they come to competition with him; [and] they are necessarily resistive to the contact. Already there is the disposition to exclude [slaves]; from the trades, from public works, from drays, and the tables of hotels, [slaves are] even now excluded to a great extent." If the African slave trade was not reopened to replenish the slave population in Charleston, the secessionist editor insisted, then "pauper labor from abroad" as well as unemployed immigrants from the North would continue to pour into the city and supplant slaves.[97]

Spratt may have been correct in his observation that roughly 10,000 slaves had been sold or removed from Charleston to work on lucrative cotton plantations, especially in the new Gulf Coast states. The South Carolina port indeed experienced a decrease in its slave population amid the influx of Irish inhabitants during the 1850s. But since slaves also entered Charleston, the city endured a net loss of only 5,623 slaves between 1850 and 1860. During the same decade, the number of Irish immigrants residing in Charleston increased from 2,359 in 1850 to 3,263 in 1860, a net gain of 904. Scholars long have grappled with the causes of such workforce transformations, and why some southern cities including Charleston suffered sharp decreases in their slave populations during the 1850s. Historian Richard Wade argued, for instance, that this drawdown was the endgame for a master class repeatedly unable to control enslaved workers within an urban environment utterly incompatible with the institution of human bondage. But economist Claudia Dale Goldin disagreed, countering that the redistribution of the slave population from cities into the southern countryside was due to a rising demand for bound labor on rural plantations as slave and especially cotton prices rose.[98] But just as waterfront workers—black and white, enslaved and free—were largely impervious to Charleston's commercial decline relative to other southern ports, the heightened demand for draymen, dockhands, and stevedores to handle the mounting exports of cotton shielded many seaboard slaves from being "sold down the river" along with other black Charlestonians. One might argue that the need for wharf labor during the 1850s was so robust, in fact, that employers required both enslaved blacks and Irish immigrants to keep trade flowing efficiently.[99] Without strong labor market demand and the associated wage-earning opportunities, it is far more enigmatic why free and white workers would have departed northern docks to compete and toil shoulder to shoulder with enslaved southern blacks.

In any event, some white Charlestonians welcomed the gradual shift to white labor and any concurrent decline in the city's still considerable black population. But L. W. Spratt bemoaned that these whites laborers "will question the right of masters to employ their slaves in any works that they may wish for," thus endangering both slaveowners' incomes and authority. After all, as increasing numbers of white workingmen settled in the city, they inexorably "will invoke the aid of legislation; they will use the elective franchise to that end; [and] they may acquire the power to determine municipal elections." If this were to occur, Spratt was concerned that even Charleston—the bastion of states' rights and "at the very heart of slavery"—could morph into "a fortress of democratic power against" the South's peculiar institution. What's more, a "contest for existence may be waged" between free and slave labor, in which "one race must increase as the other is diminished." Fearing that enslaved blacks ultimately would lose this battle, L. W. Spratt assailed Irish and other white immigrants for threatening slave masters' hegemony and the institution of slavery itself.[100]

Spratt had good reason to be leery of the white workingmen's ascending political might. An amendment to South Carolina's constitution ratified in 1810 removed property requirements for voting and initiated universal white male suffrage in the state for those over twenty-one years of age. But the upsurge during the 1840s and 1850s of the enfranchised white proletariat, ostensibly tainted with foreign and northern-inspired labor activism and abolitionism, distressed prominent Charlestonians other than L. W. Spratt. Given the choice, State Representative Christopher Memminger and City Postmaster Alfred Huger opted for free black workers rather than, as Huger put it in 1858, "the insolence and profligacy that is poured out upon us by every ship that comes here, either from Ireland or the North." Free people of color, at least, had "no votes" and thus were incapable of "inflicting injury upon the Public by the 'general suffrage law.'"[101]

But Charleston's Irish indeed had the franchise, and they wasted little time employing it to great effect. In the face of threats from the nativist Know-Nothing Party, Irish immigrants helped get College of Charleston professor and reformer William Porcher Miles elected to the mayoralty in 1855. Disgruntled partisans of the xenophobic and anti-Catholic Know-Nothings, in fact, maintained that three hundred of the ballots for Miles, who won by only four hundred votes, were cast illegitimately by the city's most recent newcomers. After Miles overhauled Charleston's police force, with Irishmen largely filling the rank and file, the mayor's opponents derided municipal policemen as "Paddy Miles's Bulldogs." When Miles was elected to the U.S. House of Representatives in 1856, immigrant laborers threw their support behind lawyer Charles Macbeth, who one backer hailed as knowing "no distinction of persons" and who served as the city's mayor from 1857 until the end of the Civil War. For much of the 1850s, then, white workingmen indeed wielded a measure of influence over the mayor's office as well as several sympathetic members of the City Council.[102]

The ballot was not immigrants' only weapon in their "contest for existence" with black laborers, however. Proslavery Charlestonian William Henry Trescot contended, after all, that "Free labor hates slave labor"; Olmsted, an antislavery New Englander, similarly observed among immigrant laborers in South Carolina a "hatred of the negro" and disinclination to compete with slaves.[103] Yet one historian determined that, unlike on northern docks, "racial competition for waterfront employment in the antebellum era rarely erupted into large-scale racial violence, in New Orleans or elsewhere." Another concluded that this "absence of racial conflict is surprising considering the racist foundations upon which slavery rested," citing the lack of reported violence between Irish and enslaved dockworkers, deck hands, and canal diggers who often worked side by side in the South.[104] Though perhaps understating the matter, both scholars conceded that occasional acts of racial violence related to labor competition indeed occurred on antebellum southern waterfronts. Irish draymen in New Orleans, for example, hurled paving stones at black rivals who dared to drive through areas of the city deemed the Irish workers' terrain.[105]

At times Charleston's Irish immigrants, restive and frustrated with the contentious struggle for employment, also turned violent and vicious. One local judge declared in 1855, "it is but too true, that a great proportion of those we receive in Charleston from Ireland, manifest a proclivity to turbulence. I am afraid there is an inclination to make war upon the Negro." The judge recalled an incident from a few years before when "one of the only two Irishmen who drove drays in this city . . . was tried . . . for knocking out the eye of a slave, his competitor."[106] Cooper Jacob Schirmer noted this or a very similar case in August 1846, writing in his diary that a slave drayman named Sam—who was owned by Southern Wharf merchant A. O. Andrews—"got a severe beating from an Irish drayman."[107] More than a decade later Schirmer reported "a row" that broke out near a boat "between some young men from town and the Irish, when Scott the carter was considerably cut up."[108] Nor were these isolated incidents. So acute was the problem of violence against the city's bondsmen, Charleston's Grand Jury—led by the aptly named dry goods merchant and slaveowner James S. Bowie—complained in 1854, "The unlawful beating and stabbing and otherwise maiming of slaves, is increasing and becoming a very serious evil." Not only revolting to human nature and disruptive of civic peace but also injurious to slaveowners' valuable human property, the grand jurors asked state legislators to implement more severe penalties and punishments for offenders.[109]

The fact that, unlike other dockworkers, the wage rates of black and white draymen and carters were prescribed equally since the mid-eighteenth century helps explain the ferocity of their struggle. Finding it difficult to make ends meet, white draymen petitioned the City Council in 1854 requesting an increase in the established transport rates. The Committee on Licenses rejected the petitioners, however, arguing that the costs of provisions and living had not risen since the fares were updated in 1837. The councilmen further retorted, "if draying is not at present as remunerating as formerly, it is owing rather to the keenness of competition than the rates established by law." Aside from snatching up many jobs, slaves often charged customers less for hauling goods than the maximum allowance, thus undercutting white rivals. But the reason white draymen and carters were so successful in displacing blacks was due to the minimal racial differentiation in wages, thus freeing employers to economically hire whites. Boyce & Co.'s Wharf factors Carson & Sons, for instance, selected to patronize aforementioned Irish drayman James Corcoran to convey goods to and from the waterfront in the mid-1850s. And in March 1857 factors Oswell Reeder and John B. DeSaussure described their head drayman as "a white man, quite inteligent [*sic*]" and reliable.[110]

Though not all instances of physical confrontation can be attributed to such vigorous employment competition, Charleston's antebellum court records were rife with cases of white waterfront workers perpetrating violence against slaves. In late October 1856, for example, stevedore G. B. Stoddard was indicted for assault and battery. Irish stevedore Thomas Nolan also was charged with assault and battery in November 1856 and sentenced to a one-month imprisonment and a hundred-dollar fine.[111] Some Irish workers were brought before the court for beating slaves. Laborer Morris Roach was indicted for attacking a slave in January 1859.[112] Drayman Martin Murphy was convicted for beating a bondsman owned by commission merchant Charles L. Trenholm in October 1859 and fined twenty dollars. On the same day the grand jury indicted Murphy, it elected not to endorse a bill of indictment for the same offense against Patrick Carroll. This thirty-two-year-old Irish drayman did not remain out of jail for long, however. He was charged with murder in April 1860, convicted of the lesser charge of manslaughter, and sentenced to a twelve-month imprisonment and a hefty five-hundred-dollar fine. Patrick Carroll was joined in the city jail by three other Irish draymen. James Smith was serving a sentence for murder, and Michael Lalby and Patrick Holleran were being held for assault, an offense that also landed five Irish laborers behind bars, some of whom surely worked on Charleston's waterfront.[113]

Rather than openly assaulting, beating, or killing a rival, the dangerous nature of waterfront work presented copious opportunities to intimidate or eliminate a competitor. Take for instance the case of Harry Simmons, a black stevedore who died in March 1847 from "an injury received by the falling of a bale of cotton on him."[114] With white stevedores and dockhands vying for Simmons's job, it is conceivable that they intentionally dropped this 400- to 500-pound cotton bale onto their unsuspecting rival in the hold below. But whites too had to beware a similar fate. On January 25, 1860, David Nagle—an eighteen-year-old Irishman who had arrived from New York three years before and was employed in Charleston by white stevedore John Torrent—"was knocked into the hold . . . by a bale of Cotton, while it was being hoisted from the wharf, and fell a distance of about 10 feet, injuring him so seriously that he died." The *Charleston Tri-Weekly Courier* concluded, "This occurrence was the result of [Nagle's] own imprudence"; but like a house cook covertly poisoning one's master, slave wharf hands employed occasions of "accidental" violence to preserve coveted access to wage labor and avoid removal from the relatively autonomous and advantageous urban and littoral environment.[115]

Charleston's white and black waterfront workers shared other forms of labor misconduct and protest, whether directed at competitors, employers, or the city's aristocratic slaveowners. In the rush to transport cotton and other commercial goods hither and thither, white draymen also drove recklessly and terrorized pedestrians. "Great indignation was manifested yesterday by the bystanders, at the conduct of a white drayman," the *Charleston Mercury* reported in February 1858, "who threw down an elderly lady at the corner of Broad and East Bay streets." Not bothering to stop, neither the driver nor the dray number was identified. Such perpetrations among whites were so common that in 1855 William Henry Trescot touted in verse the policing function of the municipal Mayor's Court:

> To check the wicked and sustain the weak
> To guide the erring with a saintly grace
> To make the Irish Hack-men very meek
> And stop the "runner" in his reckless pace.[116]

Given opportunities to earn extra money in a competitive and tightly regulated labor environment, Irish and other white draymen—like the slaves who swindled Thomas Napier in 1857—also sometimes overcharged unwary customers. A drayman named James Morgan, listed in the 1860 U.S. Census as an Irish laborer, was arrested for extortion in September 1859. Upon the arrival of the New York packet ship *Columbia,* Morgan loaded the luggage of a Frenchman onto his dray and promised to transport the visitor and his bags for 25 cents. But finding the route longer than expected and disregarding that drayage rates were fixed and capped, the white drayman asked his passenger for another quarter. According to the *Charleston Mercury,* "The Frenchman assented, which so encouraged Morgan that the trip was prolonged indefinitely. The fee had reached the size of a dollar, when the drayman imprudently driving past the Guard House, was arrested and locked up for examination." And during the devastating fire of December 1861, Charlestonians extolled the actions of a free black drayman named Richard Dereef, who transported for free several loads consisting of the belongings of a destitute white woman. Whereas there had been "no single case of attempted extortion by a colored drayman or driver," a newspaper correspondent observed, "White men demanded $50 a load." Those who preferred disenfranchised free blacks to immigrant whites surely took satisfaction in the latter's depiction in such a negative and predatory light.[117]

Notwithstanding fairly regular acts of work-related delinquency and violence, and the undeniable dislocation of many slaves and free blacks from the city's docks and drays, Irish and other white immigrants certainly were not able to expel all black Charlestonians from their jobs. As a result, during the last of the antebellum years, emboldened white waterfront workers brought their protracted battle against black labor competition to a head with both public supplications and official petitions to state and municipal authorities. Through such legitimate and respectable expressions, not to mention participation in the democratic electoral and legislative processes that so distressed L. W. Spratt, immigrant workingmen in particular demonstrated their Americanness while simultaneously claiming their rights as white men in the slave South.

At a "large and enthusiastic meeting" of Charleston's white mechanics and workingmen on the evening of October 8, 1858, for instance, it unanimously was agreed "that a baneful evil exists in our City and State at large, to wit: the hiring by slaves of their own time." The ensuing petition to the state legislature contended that this enduring and pernicious practice harmed not only white workers, but also the state and its institutions and citizens, slaveowners, and the "well-being and usefulness of the slave himself." Labeling existing slave hiring laws as "a dead letter," the workingmen called for the indictment of both the employer and the owner of any slave hiring out his or her own time and "the more rigid enforcement" of legislative statutes.[118] This petition was signed by 163 white laborers and tradesmen, including master stevedores William Watson and John Symons, the latter who paradoxically—some might say hypocritically— hired slave Robert Smalls for a number of years in the 1850s.[119] The officers of both the Charleston Mechanic Society and the South Carolina Mechanics Association submitted similar petitions to the South Carolina General Assembly in November 1858, suggesting that the city's white workingmen were launching a coordinated assault against black competitors.[120]

State legislative leaders instructed the Committee on Colored Population to consider all of these grievances conjointly, and on December 7, 1858, the members reported their findings.[121] Though acknowledging that existing laws against slaves hiring their own time were unenforced, defective, and in need of reform, the committee also contended that white Charlestonians were irreversibly committed—addicted, really—to slave labor, especially for particular jobs.[122] Despite the influx of able and willing immigrant workers, "The domestic servants, most of the common laborers and porters, draymen, wagoners, cartmen, and on the seaboard, the stevedores, are mostly negroes," the report declared. "We are accustomed to black labor, and it would create a revolution to drive it away." If laws against slave hiring were enforced or strengthened and masters made to personally contract every job, it would become impossible for slaves to be employed as waterfront and transportation workers. "The subject, therefore, is full of difficulty," the legislators argued amid a backdrop of escalating abolitionist attacks and southern nationalism, "and, until you can change the direction of the public prejudice, prepossession and habit, you can never enforce a law which conflicts with them." Charlestonians were so "habituated to slave labor" to unload and load ships and transport goods to and from the wharves, in fact, the report concluded that "there must inevitably be an exception to the rule which prohibits the slave working out, as in the case of licensed draymen, carters, wagoners, stevedores, porters, &c." These were, of course, the bulk of the very occupations for which white immigrants sought employment and competed with wealth-generating hired-out slaves in late antebellum Charleston.[123]

But these employment positions also were those that most troubled and frustrated the city's security hawks over the years. Though rejecting the white petitioners on the grounds of black slaves' irreplaceable necessity, efficiency, and convenience, the committee—itself split between the diametrically opposed exigencies of preservation and prosperity—simultaneously lamented "the breaking down [of] the relation between master and slave—the removal of the slave from the master's discipline and control, and the assumption of freedom and independence, on the part of the slave, the idleness, disorder and crime which are consequential, and the necessity thereby created for additional police regulations to keep them in subjection and order, and the trouble and expense which they involve." For state and municipal authorities long immersed in fixing hiring locations, capping wages, censuring work songs, monitoring movements, curtailing communications with northern and foreign seamen, inspecting vessels for absconded stowaways, and combating theft and pilferage, far more alarming than the racial contest for employment was this ongoing struggle to master and harness bondsmen's labor and customs—a tug-of-war many slaves were winning. But rather than again clamping down or throwing seaboard labor to free whites as Charlestonians like Thomas Pinckney and Edward Laurens had advocated, the committee schizophrenically proposed a bill to render de jure the de facto exemption of enslaved waterfront workers from slave hiring laws.[124]

With the collective power of the franchise in their possession and their ranks swelling with a steady stream of newcomers, Charleston's white workingmen were gaining access to and reshaping the agendas of local and state institutions.[125] An increasing number of successful immigrants also were joining more established Irish and German waterfront employers like James Adger, Charles A. Magwood, William Kunhardt, and Jacob Schirmer, who perhaps hired some of their fellow white emigrants. But despite having displaced substantial numbers of black workers, most of the port's white draymen, carters, porters, and common laborers were unable to overcome the entrenched interests of wage-craving masters or alter employers' longstanding dependency upon and inclination toward hiring slaves. Much like their enslaved competitors, then, these white waterfront workers were ensnarled amid the wrangling between unnerved security scolds and unflinching commercial boosters.

But the city's burgeoning contingent of highly skilled and articulate white stevedores was alarmed and offended by the committee's suggested legislation, and they soon demanded the exclusive right to stevedoring in Charleston. In early December 1859 the South Carolina House and Senate considered a petition solely from the white stevedores "praying legislation in the employment of slaves as stevedores."[126] The stevedores who signed this petition had diverse origins: Massachusettean G. B. Stoddard, Englishman John Symons, Irishman William Doran, Mainer Daniel Lapham, Canadian William Watson, Spaniard John Torrent, Marylander Joseph Torrent, and South Carolinians John Torrent Jr. and Adolphus W. Lacoste. To national and sectional distinctions could be added dissimilarities of ethnicity, culture, creed, accent, age, and socioeconomic trajectory. But besides their profession, what these men had in common was their status as free and white workers in a slave society and on a southern waterfront that traditionally had been the milieu of black slaves.

The white stevedores began their petition by asking to be placed "on equality with our fellow Citizens the *Mechanics,* and not to Class us with Slaves, as the Bill now before you *reads.*" To demonstrate that they were not mere wharf hands or transient day laborers but rather the trained supervisors of such common workers, the stevedores pointed out that they had "upwards of $40,000 invested in the business on which they have to pay taxes, [and] they have to perform all the duties that the City or State may require of them," such as jury, militia, or fire duty. And therefore, like their fellow skilled workingmen the mechanics and artisans, these white stevedores demanded respect and the protection of their vital jobs. The bill under the consideration of the General Assembly, however, grouped the stevedores with the unskilled and stated that urban slaves working "as Stevedores . . . shal [*sic*] not be includid [*sic*] within the inhibition of the act" against slaves from hiring their own time.[127]

But then the petition turned from an appeal for justice to one of fear. Ship captains long had been hiring slave stevedores and thus undermining the state's Negro Seamen Acts by enabling seditious communications between these bondsmen and northern and foreign free black mariners. Moreover, by employing slave stevedores, who in turn hired gangs of enslaved screwmen and wharf hands, blacks were able to assemble in scores and far from any white oversight. The white stevedores warned that, though it was illegal for Charleston's black slaves to gather unsupervised in such large groups, they were doing so while stowing vessels.[128] The implication was that within the depths of ships' holds at the city's own wharves, and with the assistance of visiting free black sailors and abolitionists, slaves surreptitiously were plotting their next insurrection and massacre of Charleston's white population. If the responsible and reliable white stevedores instead were exclusively hired to contract work gangs and supervise the stowing and unlading of vessels—that is, to become even more firmly anchored within the security and control apparatus so long disdained and foiled by black and white common dockworkers alike—no such secretive and potentially catastrophic scheming would be possible. Unmentioned, as usual, were enslaved workers' interactions with white mariners like Edward Smith or the steward who aided John Andrew Jackson's escape to Boston.

In closing, these "Master Stevedores" moreover emphasized that "the object of this Petition is not to drive away Slave Labour, but to prevent them from becoming Contractors." They were not abolitionists—or even revolutionaries like Pinckney or Laurens—seeking to replace black dockworkers with whites. In fact, "we are desireous [*sic*] to give the slaves the preference [*sic*] as Labourers on all Ocasions [*sic*]," the petitioners insisted.[129] Though the stevedores often had joined with other white workingmen to protest slave hiring, these efforts having been repeatedly stymied by state officials, they now sought to shield their own positions on the wharves from black rivals. But in doing so, the stevedores further turned their backs on less skilled, propertied, and articulate fellow whites who too faced robust labor competition on the city's docks from enslaved blacks.[130]

Despite these pleas, the Committee on Commerce, Manufacturers, and the Mechanic Arts declared its unanimous opinion that "it is inexpedient to legislate on the subject" and recommended that the white stevedores' petition be rejected.[131] The legislature also never adopted the bill proposed by the Committee on Colored Population seeking to officially exempt enslaved waterfront workers from hiring laws. Nonetheless, everyday practice continued to absolve from punishment the masters, employers, and hundreds of slaves who hired themselves out on Charleston's docks and drays. Clearly white waterfront workers—skilled or unskilled—were not going to gain protection from legislators in Columbia. Abandoning appeals for statewide laws that endeavored to mini-mize slave competition for white workingmen throughout South Carolina, the stevedores turned for local relief to the Charleston City Council.

In January 1860 the City Council considered yet another bill to prohibit slaves from hiring their own time, labor, or service.[132] Almost immediately the city's influential slaveholders and businessmen—some of whom also served as councilmen—attacked the proposed ordinance, claiming that it would injure the city's commercial economy by driving away much-needed slave labor and trade. "The bill offered in relation to slaves hiring out their own time, would, if it became an ordinance, extend and aggravate the disabilities to which vessels are subject which visit our port," argued one opponent in the pages of the *Charleston Evening News*. Then embracing the stance of the state Committee on Colored Population in 1858, "Why not except from the operation of the ordinance that class of laborers which are essentially necessary to load vessels, and without which dispatch could not be obtained?" Ignoring that dozens of professional white ste-vedores and hundreds of white day laborers and wharf hands were available for hire on the city's waterfront, this defender of prevailing slave-hiring practices contended, "The difficulty of obtaining stevedores and other laborers, through the rigid application of such an ordinance, would have the obvious tendency to give a preference over Charleston to [other] Southern ports, thus discriminating against ourselves."[133] Though the demand for dock laborers was on the rise as mountains of cotton continued to pile up on the wharves, the port's declension-minded commercial class did not wish to add to an already lengthy list of com-petitive disadvantages ranging from Negro Seamen Acts and ship-inspection laws to a reputation for sectional extremism and railroad terminals disconnected from the waterfront.

Still smarting from their defeat one month earlier, the stevedores responded to this assessment in a letter to the editors of the *Charleston Courier* on January 30, 1860. Clearly irritated, they claimed that the writer of these statements knew little if anything about the state of stevedoring in Charleston. Ship captains and merchants already were suffering under the "present system of granting a licen-tious freedom to slaves," who were acting as free white men and "will work only where and for whom they please, and only so long as it suits them"—a remark-able assertion given the century-long effort to squash these very practices. "The white stevedores of Charleston," on the other hand, "are responsible men, men of family, and have from thirty to forty thousand dollars invested in the city; and most of them have a home of their own, and all are tax-payers, and are identified with South Carolina in every sense of the word."[134] Of the eighteen white steve-dores listed in the 1860 U.S. Census, at least fourteen indeed were married and nine had children living with them in the city.[135] And an array of extant sources substantiated claims to real and personal property holdings, tax payments, and jury and fire service. But like the signers of the aforementioned white mechanics' petitions, most stevedores were not slaveholders, with only Irishman William Doran and Spaniard John Torrent owning bondsmen between 1858 and 1864.[136] Furthermore, only three of the eighteen in the 1860 Census—South Carolinians Samuel Barr and John Torrent Jr., and Marylander Joseph Torrent—were native-born southerners. Most white stevedores, like the vast majority of lesser skilled and well-off white waterfront workers, did not generate income by hiring out personal slaves and thus had nothing to lose and everything to gain financially and professionally by eradicating slave competitors. In that sense, municipal and state authorities—many of whom were slaveowners with bondsmen hiring out in the city and earning wages for their masters—could question the stevedores' loyalty to South Carolina, the South, and the institution of slavery.[137] Well aware of these obstacles, not to mention their ethnic, religious, and linguistic "otherness," the stevedores stressed, "They have faced your yellow fever, and are found in your banks, your jury box, or at the brakes [of fire engines] whenever required of them. And these are the citizens to be proscribed. Have they not paid their taxes and done all the duties required of them? If so are they not as good citizens as any other class in the city? and they ask the same protection."[138]

Having presented their case for allegiance and reliability, the stevedores reiterated that, just because most of them did not own slaves, they did not seek to banish common slave workers from Charleston's waterfront. Instead they again proposed that, if the white stevedores were granted the exclusive right to act as contractors and supervisors, "The owners of slaves hiring their own time can hire them to the white stevedores at the same price they pay, and perhaps more." These skilled white stevedores, in other words, did not oppose the employment of common slave dockhands on the city's waterfront, so long as the bondsmen were not allowed to work as stevedores and were hired out directly by their masters rather than hiring their own time. Then pointedly addressing their critics, they asked, "Where, then, is any injury to come to the shipping? Will [slaves] not be employed at the same work and the same facilities afforded as at present, and more?" The stevedores concluded their public letter by imploring the City Council to protect them, rather than their slave competitors. But if it was the goal of local authorities "to drive away from Charleston those [white] stevedores, some of whom have been living here for upwards of twenty years, it is time that the stevedores should be aware of the fact."[139]

At the end of February 1860, a special committee of the City Council assigned the task of considering the proposed ordinance against slaves hiring their own time agreed with its counterpart in Columbia that it was "both inexpedient and improper" to adopt such a rule. Sidestepping the stevedores' entreaties for the exclusion of rival slave contractors, the crux again was the inconvenience to employers and slaveowners alike if forced to personally arrange every job. "In all large cities," the committee report explained, "the successful prosecution of trade and commerce requires a great number of laborers by the day or by the hour, and during the business season. They are generally employed, and are constantly changing their employers. At times almost every one engaged in business, are [*sic*] obliged to employ this kind of labor; but, very few require it permanently." In short, the economic health and uninterrupted function of the port necessitated that slaves be permitted not solely to hire out, but to hire out their own time without the direct involvement of their masters. The committee members, all three of whom were slaveholders, predicted that if laws banning slaves from gaining employment in this manner were passed or enforced, then "The stevedores, barbers, chimney sweeps, woodsawyers, and laborers who are slaves, would be stopped and the business thrown into other hands."[140] This assertion must have flabbergasted the city's white stevedores and other waterfront workers, since the appropriation of slaves' jobs was the very aim of their many appeals over the years.

Despite emerging as a distinct and vital profession and rising to socioeconomic and occupational respectability, Charleston's cadre of white stevedores ultimately failed to gain official protection from enslaved competitors in a port long dominated by black waterfront laborers. In the final months before the Civil War the stevedores necessarily joined with other trained white artisans to alternatively target—as Edward Laurens had proposed nearly three decades earlier—their more finite but assailable free black rivals.[141] This undertaking, however, vividly accentuated white waterfront workers' class, skill, and occupational tensions and divisions. A petition to state legislators from December 1860, for example, protested "That it is a prevailing and common practice in the City of Charleston for free negroes and persons of color to carry on and conduct mechanical and other pursuits as contractors and masters."[142] The petitioners contended that the skilled white workingman such as the stevedore "who understands, and is capable of conducting his business *must* be endowed with intellectual powers above what are necessary for mere manual labor." After all, "every other pursuit, except such as your petitioners are engaged in, where skill and intelligence are required, above what is necessary to the mere laborers, is carefully protected by stringent enactments of law against the intrusion of the colored and slave races." The Charleston City Council, in fact, had complained to the General Assembly in the 1820s about the use of free blacks and slaves as clerks, salesmen, or "any engagements which require the exercise of greater intelligence and improvement," since such situations were "inconsistent with their Condition."[143] By the early 1860s the city's white wharfingers, clerks, shopkeepers, lawyers, and doctors all were shielded by law from black competition.[144] Jacob Schirmer reported in November 1853, for instance, that a commission merchant on Atlantic Wharf was "tried this week for employing a coloured clerk and found guilty."[145] The vocations of mechanics and stevedores, however, were not similarly protected, and the "unjust and unfair" laws that permitted this "degrading distinction" were "serious public evils." The "mere" menials who comprised the preponderance of whites seeking employment on Charleston's seaboard, of course, were protected neither by law nor by their more highly skilled and compensated fellow whites.[146]

Also in December 1860, James M. Eason—a Charleston machinist and foundry operator, and advocate for white workingmen on the legislature's Committee on Colored Population—introduced a bill in the General Assembly that similarly sought to prevent free blacks from achieving master status in their occupations and thus relegate them to menial labor. The proposal specifically barred free blacks from "carrying on any mechanical business on their own account," or from "entering into contracts for any mechanical pursuits," such as agreements between master stevedores and ship captains. Like the architects of the Negro Seamen Acts or those slaveowners pondering whether to hire out their valuable bondsmen amid the seductive and corruptive urban environment, Eason feared that "in allowing Free Negroes to carry on the Mechanical trades as Masters, there is a very great tendency to infuse into our slaves coming into contact with them a spirit of dissatisfaction and insubordination—and fasten on his mind the fact that it is only for him to obtain his freedom—to be placed as an equal in carrying on any Mechanical trade with the white man." Then taking a page from the white stevedores' playbook, the bill's author contended that the aim was not to block free blacks from the trades, "but to prevent him from assuming the standard of a Master, and consequently degrading the Free white man, who occupies that position."[147]

Though Eason's proposal never received a vote in the legislature, further enactments circumscribing the employment of free black Charlestonians proved unnecessary. In what historians Michael Johnson and James Roark described as a late "antebellum *Krystalnacht*," many of the city's free persons of color—including some of the few remaining skilled stevedores—fled the port in late 1860 and early 1861. Under pressure from white workingmen on the one hand and proslavery secessionists on the other, municipal authorities including Mayor Macbeth besieged free blacks' liberty by newly requiring free people of color to purchase and wear badges and threatening violators with enslavement. The announcement of this policy in the *Charleston Courier* on August 9, 1860, sparked a panic among the city's free blacks and subsequently prompted hundreds to leave Charleston for northern cities such as Philadelphia and New York. As many as a thousand free black Charlestonians—including three hundred adult males—participated in this "Colored Exodus from South Carolina," which was comprised mostly of those "bred to industrial calling" and included skilled tradesmen such as tailors, carpenters, shoemakers, barbers, blacksmiths, shipbuilders, and stevedores. The *Philadelphia Press* and *The Liberator,* in fact, reported how one free black man arrived in Philadelphia with his porter badge.[148]

Exactly one week prior to the commencement of this crackdown, federal workers in Charleston completed data collection for the 1860 U.S. Census. What they found was remarkable: for the first time its 190-year history, Charleston was a white-majority city. And yet the port was far from safe for white workingmen. Even as both free and enslaved black competitors departed Charleston by the hundreds, slaveowners doubled down on defending their peculiar institution and labor habitudes from internal and external threats alike. Though constraining the troublesome labor customs of the still substantial and concentrated urban slave population remained a priority, insulating those bondsmen from the scourge of free black seducers and abolitionist infiltrators took precedence as secession and civil war loomed. Antebellum Charleston increasingly had become a closed city, and in late 1860 the security hawks and fire-eaters finally reigned supreme over more moderate commercial and political pragmatists.

But what no faction of Charlestonians could vanquish prior to the Civil War was the menace of epidemic disease. Beyond the command of a controlling master class, trade vessels delivered pests to the city's wharves far more disruptive than enfranchised white newcomers or insurrectionary pamphlets. The impact of imported contagions on the market and competition for waterfront labor was especially momentous. To the surfeit of considerations facing seaboard employers, such as race, status, aptitude, class, ethnicity, language, and religion, was added a worker's comparative susceptibility to local diseases, or "acclimation."[149] After all, unlike panicked Irish transients swarming aboard northern-bound packets to escape death at the hands of "strangers' fever," Charleston's white stevedores reminded municipal authorities and fellow inhabitants that they had stayed and repeatedly "faced your yellow fever." They were permanent and seasoned members of the community, time-earned attributes that this small but skilled cohort of waterfront workers insisted ought to be rewarded with some measure of gratitude, respect, and occupational protection.

Chapter Five

"The unacclimated stranger should be positively prohibited"

Comparative Disease Susceptibility and Waterfront Labor Competition

For both black and white workers struggling mightily and sometimes violently against one another for employment along Charleston's antebellum waterfront, the specter of epidemic diseases rivaled the threat of even their most hostile labor competitors. Cholera's disproportionate impact upon black Charlestonians quickly established the malady's reputation as another "Negro disease," to the morbid advantage of white job seekers.[1] But to the benefit of blacks striving to retain the many relative perks of urban waterfront employment, yellow fever overwhelmingly targeted recently arrived and "unacclimated" white immigrants. With the etiologies and epidemiologies of these diseases yet undiscovered, local medical authorities and municipal officials failed to agree whether sanitation measures or a strict maritime quarantine would most effectively secure the well-being and lives of the city's inhabitants. Rendered collateral damage in a perennial feud between the rival interests of human health and commercial wealth were Charleston's dockworkers. Paternalistic white slaveowners and employers—the very elements of the master class who maneuvered to preserve the expediencies and profits of the slave-hiring system against the onslaught and protests of white immigrant workingmen—could do little to shield their urban hirelings from cholera's deadly grasp.[2] Nor could elected officials who endeavored to court and reward the votes of white immigrant laborers unilaterally defend these constituents from the scourge of yellow fever. Not merely passive observers, however, black and white waterfront workers boldly navigated the narrow path between making ends meet and surviving to toil another day.

Scholars long have considered the intersection of comparative disease susceptibility and race to elucidate slaveowners' preference for black plantation laborers in the South Carolina lowcountry and beyond.[3] The nearly exclusive use of enslaved blacks on southern plantations firmly was established during the early eighteenth century, when colonial Charles Town was British North America's only walled city. But the influx of unskilled white immigrants during the mid-nineteenth century reignited a debate over disease and race throughout the urban South. By defiantly challenging blacks' dominance of Charleston's waterfront workforce, these newcomers also fundamentally altered the city's epidemiological defensive wall that for a century and a half had been comprised of laborers more or less immune to imported yellow fever. Beyond employing epidemic diseases to complicate existing interpretations of labor competition and how and why the racial and ethnic makeup of the Old South's urban workforce changed over time, what follows is furthermore a prism through which to more fully illuminate and reflect upon many of this book's major themes: struggles for control between masters and slaves, employers and employees, governors and governed; relations and contentions among workers, both enslaved and free, black and white, native and immigrant; waterfront workers' indispensable role in the uninterrupted flow of commerce, even as authorities subordinated these laborers' liberties, livelihoods, and welfare to the pursuit of the port's relative economic recovery, prosperity, and security; and especially agency amid circumscription and oppression, whether manifested by flight from bondage and pestilence, a temporary work stoppage to demand higher wages, or the perseverance and recalcitrance of those whose presence along the waterfront was deemed deleterious to the public health.

First appearing in the United States in 1832, cholera is an infectious bacterial disease rapidly spread by contaminated water or food. Originating on the Indian subcontinent in 1817 and extending by 1823 to Southeast Asia, China, the Middle East, northern Africa, and the Mediterranean, the first cholera pandemic claimed hundreds of thousands of lives and seized the attention of government officials and medical authorities across the globe.[4] A petition to the South Carolina legislature in 1827 detailed how Charleston's leaders sought to thwart the disease's invasion by land and sea through both rigorous public health efforts and maritime quarantine. Feeling "constantly and alarmingly exposed to the introduction of that dreadful pestilence the Malignant Cholera," the City Council ordered the inspection, cleaning, and purification of insalubrious public streets and private residences, the filling of low lots, and the removal of stagnant water and various "nuisances." To "guard the City & the adjacent Islands against its introduction by water," municipal authorities directed that all vessels arriving in Charleston

Harbor from places stricken with cholera be quarantined for forty days and that communication with persons on these detained vessels be prohibited without "the express permission of the Port Physician or the Intendant of the City."[5] The councilmen also established and staffed a cholera hospital, and purchased land and buildings for a new lazaretto on Morris Island near the entrance to Charleston Harbor (see figures 18 and 19).

Five years passed before Charleston's proactive preparedness was put to the test. Reports of cholera ravaging both New York City and New Orleans during the summer of 1832—epidemics that eventually killed thousands of inhabitants —triggered the enforcement of the city's quarantine regulations and renewed Charlestonians' diligent adherence to local sanitation procedures.[6] In late June, for instance, the council authorized two additional scavenger carts for the removal of rubbish and other nuisances.[7] "All precautions are now making in our City to allay the disease, if it should visit us," wrote cooper Jacob Schirmer on August 1, 1832, adding, "But May God in his Mercy withhold it."[8]

When on November 1 the brig *Amelia* wrecked off Folly Island on its way from New York to New Orleans with "malignant cholera on board," Charlestonians sprung into action. Members of the City Guard were deployed to secure the island, the vessel and its cargo were burned, and both the guardsmen and volunteer citizens patrolled the Cooper River wharves to prevent quarantined crewmen, passengers, or island residents from entering the city.[9] Owing to a combination of sensible actions and good fortune, Charleston escaped in 1832 with only a few cases of cholera among its inhabitants.[10] But the *Amelia* episode ought to have furnished a lesson on the disease's capacity to swiftly strike down black dockworkers along the water's edge. When news of the shipwreck reached Charleston the first week of November, the vessel's consignee contracted with a Mr. Charles Jarvis to salvage the valuable cargo. With wharves and warehouses filling with cotton and the waterfront's porter stands teeming with enslaved dockhands, Jarvis hired thirteen wreckers to accompany him to Folly Island. "In forty-eight hours after they commenced their work," reported Judge A. P. Butler, "five or six of the wreckers died of cholera."[11] As many as eight—constituting over 60 percent—of the laborers who engaged in this dangerous and unhealthy work and interacted with the *Amelia*'s passengers and crew eventually perished.[12]

Most white Charlestonians nevertheless remained ignorant of the grave threat cholera posed to slaves. Whereas blacks enjoyed a veritable protection from yellow fever and malaria, innate racial characteristics offered no such defense against cholera.[13] Denouncing the popular notion that blacks were immune to the disease, the *Charleston Courier* had warned in early August 1832 that the failure to recognize this fact "might lead to disastrous results."[14] Subsequent encounters with cholera rendered the *Courier*'s exhortation prophetic; in a reversal of public opinion, southerners soon considered the disease "a peculiarly black affliction."[15]

When cholera struck rural plantations in 1833 and 1834, South Carolinians gradually developed a keener sense of the risk. Writing in Charleston in mid-September 1834, James L. Petigru reported that the malady already had slaughtered 250 slaves along the Savannah River. "As yet it is confined to the negroes," Petigru observed, "as if, like the yaws, it was an African disease."[16] With the port tightly quarantined, Charleston again dodged disaster.[17] But the city's luck, and especially that of its black slaves, ran out in 1836.

With no maritime quarantine in place and city authorities asleep at the switch, a vessel with infected persons aboard docked unencumbered at Charleston's wharves.[18] The disease soon commenced its deadly work, disproportionately targeting black inhabitants. On August 20, 1836, Jacob Schirmer noted in his diary, "during the last week several very sudden deaths among the Blacks, said to be cholera."[19] Having estimated that three hundred people already had died in the ill-prepared city, William Mazyck Porcher wrote to a friend in New York in mid-September, "You may suppose that there was & is a considerable panic here—this is not the case; I never saw people take anything so cooly [*sic*] in my life & never did I suppose that I could live in [the] city when the cholera was prevailing & care so little about it—It has killed so few white persons that they are not afraid of it on their account, but are distressed about their servants. There have been some melancholy deaths among the Negroes—some of them have been carried off in a very short time."[20] Black Charlestonians indeed had good reason not to share white residents' calm disposition toward the disease. Schirmer reported the "very alarming" news that, during just one week in late September and early October, cholera had killed eighty blacks living within the city limits south of Boundary Street.[21]

Modern epidemiologists insist that cholera is colorblind and that blacks do not possess an innate racial predisposition to the disease. Contemporary Charlestonians recognized that whites too were subject to illness. In early September 1836, Richard Bacot observed that cholera victims were "either negroes or dutchmen & low people" and that only two respectable whites—both old ladies—had died.[22] Reverend John Bachman concurred, remarking, "The disease is confined principally to our domestics, and the irregular among the whites."[23] Only the disreputable whites, the "irregular," needed to worry; "respectable," wealthy white residents—men like Petigru, Schirmer, Porcher, Bacot, and Bachman—remained cool and collected as their social and racial "inferiors" suffered. We know now that environmental and socioeconomic factors such as access to fresh and clean food and water dictated susceptibility to cholera. Dockworkers who handled and consumed contaminated produce and seafood landed and marketed on the docks ran an increased risk of infection.[24] But in the eyes of the master class, victims shouldered the blame for their own innate racial, ethnic, and character flaws. Though some of the ascribed causes of cholera—poverty, overcrowding, poor diet, and filth—were in fact indirectly culpable, also faulted were vices such as immorality, impiety, imprudence, ignorance, idleness, and intemperance.[25] City guardsman Moses Levy, who participated in the burning of the *Amelia* and its cargo on Folly Island in 1832, testified that the several salvors who contracted and died from the disease "were very intemperate." They "would dip up spirits out of the sand after it had been poured out of casks and barrels."[26] Richard Bacot blamed blacks and whites stricken with cholera in 1836 for their carelessness with food; William Porcher emphasized their "dissipated" behavior and "bad habits."[27]

Black slaves and impoverished whites living and laboring in the city's unsanitary waterfront neighborhoods technically may have been equally vulnerable to infection. But the 1836 epidemic solidified antebellum southerners' by then widely shared conviction that cholera was predominantly a "Negro disease," and perception was reality.[28] Of the 408 persons who fell victim to cholera in Charleston between late August and early November 1836, after all, 339 or 83 percent were black and only 69, or 17 percent, were white.[29] "The most striking characteristic of cholera, however," the Charleston-based *Southern Literary Journal and Monthly Magazine* logically concluded in 1837, "was the *peculiar liability of* NEGROES, and other persons of color, to its attacks, while the WHITE POPULATION, whether strangers or natives, were comparatively exempt."[30] Among the deceased blacks hitherto employed on the city's waterfront were two thirty-four-year-old slaves, Adam and David, belonging to wharf owner Joseph Prevost; cooper David B. Lafar's eighteen-year-old bondsman Jack; an unnamed thirty-five-year-old slave owned by wharfinger Newman Kershaw; and Jim and Cato, young slaves attached to the estate of the wharf-owning Fitzsimons family.[31]

Endeavoring to protect residents and improve cleanliness and salubrity, city authorities passed ordinances both during and in the years that followed the 1836 epidemic establishing or expanding the duties of the superintendents of streets, Board of Health, and Board of Inspection.[32] In September 1836 municipal officials even enacted strict regulations on the marketing of foods such as fish, fruits, and vegetables, especially during an outbreak of the "Malignant Cholera."[33] But alarmed by the heavy hand with which the disease struck down so many of Charleston's enslaved blacks, slaveowners anxiously contemplated the best means to further protect their valuable bondsmen.[34] Those toiling on rural plantations, some argued, ought to be withdrawn immediately from sickly neighborhoods. "The removal of negroes is easily effected, and exposes them to no risk whatever," contended the *Southern Literary Journal*.[35] Far more challenging, however, was securing the thousands of hired-out slaves living and working in urban Charleston, including hundreds along the city's vital waterfront. That the wholesale removal of the port's principal labor force was logistically impossible and invited commercial disaster was understood.[36] Some individual masters fled the city with their slaves; others moved their hired-out bondsmen to safer climes until the epidemic passed. But with no chariot let down to save the thousands remaining in the port during the late summer and early fall of 1836, many black Charlestonians took action for their own self-preservation.[37]

The most obvious, yet no less bold, recourse was to run away. Seizing a dual opportunity for freedom and survival, an elderly dockhand named March belonging to recently deceased wharf owner Simon Magwood absconded amid the maelstrom of the epidemic in October 1836.[38] Around the same time "a fugitive negro boy" named Bill was discovered stowed away aboard the New York–bound steam packet *Columbia,* the same vessel that delivered antislavery pamphlets to Charleston the previous summer.[39] The flight of scores of such workers soon created an impediment to the smooth flow of commercial goods into and out of the port. By early November, as dozens of vessels filled the wharves and the waterfront sprung into full gear, ship master Charles Hunt—described in the *Charleston Courier* as "a gentleman well known to the mercantile community, as an experienced seaman, and accomplished gentleman"—wrote to Boston merchant Thomas Lamb that cholera "has frightened [many of the city's slaves] from here."[40] The practical effect of this mass exhibition of slave agency was—perhaps for the first and only time in Charleston's long commercial history—a shortage of dockworkers. Because "Negro's [*sic*] are very scarce," Hunt reported to Lamb, "we move along slow in loading." Having been in port for three weeks but with a mere 1,200 bales of cotton aboard his Le Havre-bound vessel, the frustrated captain grumbled that "if we had ever so much cotton, it would be impossible to store it." Hunt elucidated that he only had been able to assemble two work gangs to stow the cargo, and that many other vessels had to be loaded by their crews rather than Charleston's black dockworkers as was customary.[41]

On November 4, just the day before Captain Hunt penned his letter to Boston, the Medical Committee of the Board of Health publicly congratulated Charlestonians for weathering "a long and extensive prevalence of Cholera among us," and assured inhabitants "that there is no cause for the interruption of commerce."[42] Municipal officials failed, however, to recognize that among those most severely affected by the recent epidemic were the black slaves who in the mid-1830s still dominated the commercial waterfront's workforce. With demand for dock labor mounting daily—work that the vast majority of native whites regarded as demeaning—the port possessed no substantial alternative labor force to replace the multitude of dead and absent bondsmen. Even the droves of itinerant laborers seasonally migrating southward were unlikely to opt for the only major Atlantic or Gulf port suffering under cholera during the autumn of 1836.[43] The belated institution of a maritime quarantine was another potential deterrent to transient workers.[44] Being nearly a decade prior to the influx of the famished Irish, wharf owners and managers thus had little choice but to solicit local masters for yet more enslaved dockhands. Beginning in late October and early November, Hamilton & Co.'s Wharf advertised to hire "three or four well grown BOYS" and "eight or ten able bodied LABORERS," all of whom were promised liberal wages for their indispensable work on the docks. Commercial Wharves likewise sought six laborers to relieve the vexations of merchants, factors, consignees, and ship captains like Charles Hunt desperately in need of slaves to discharge and stow their vessels.[45]

Charleston's bout with cholera in 1836 was the deadliest epidemic of any disease in the city's history to that date, unsettling masters, employers, and slaves for the duration of the antebellum period.[46] Though an estimated 10,000 southern slaves perished during a widespread outbreak in 1849, Charleston was exempted.[47] But in October 1852, plantation boat hands delivering rice to Savannah's mills contracted the disease, attributed at the time to sick persons aboard a New York vessel docked at the Georgia port's wharves.[48] The first cholera victim in Charleston died in early December, after arriving already ill on a steamboat from Savannah.[49] Over the next two months there was "an extensive diffusion of the germs of the disease," which "occurred in almost every part of the town."[50] Though the western portion of the city was hardest hit—including half a dozen deceased workers at Bennett's and Lucas's rice mills along the Ashley River—there also were eight deaths on Chalmers Street near the Cooper River wharves. Among other waterfront victims were a twenty-six-year-old slave named Henry living in "a confined, dirty location, near East Bay street," a ship captain at Southern Wharf, and the fireman aboard the steamer *Etiwan*.[51]

When the epidemic ended in early February 1853, local medical authorities counted eighty-five victims. Federal census takers had tallied 2,359 Irish and hundreds of German and other white working-class immigrants in Charleston in 1850, with many residing in unhealthy, mixed-race waterfront neighborhoods. Yet remarkably few of these foreign newcomers were among the deceased during the winter of 1852–53. Nearly 65 percent of the cholera fatalities, 55 in number, were black Charlestonians.[52] It should come as little surprise, then, that slaves continued to labor under the stigma of innate racial susceptibility to the ever-threatening disease until the Civil War.[53] To the benefit of the hundreds of Irishmen settling in Charleston during the 1850s and struggling against black bondsmen for waterfront employment, even the rumor of cholera's deadly presence scattered fearful slaves and prompted masters to remove their valuable property from the city.

But by the late antebellum period blacks were not the only waterfront workers coping with the perpetual threat of epidemic illness. In January 1853—as cholera plagued the port's slaves—the South Carolina–based and proslavery *Southern Quarterly Review* decried that poor white immigrants were "gradually usurping the places of blacks" in Charleston. Pushing aside "the submissive, acclimated, non-voting Negro" was "the turbulent, feverish, naturalized foreigner," who not only arrived "with habits adapted to far different climates," but also "constitutions prone to every febrile disease."[54] Though white immigrants supplanted many free blacks and slaves on the city's docks and drays in the years before the Civil War, the annual threat of yellow fever—stretching nearly six months, from late May through early November—prevented blacks from losing even more waterfront jobs. Already stigmatized for performing "nigger work" in the slave South, immigrant laborers were further branded as "unacclimated" to lowcountry diseases and thus responsible for Charleston's increasingly common and virulent encounters with "strangers' fever."[55] As hundreds of Irishmen and Germans continued to flood the city's unskilled and semiskilled labor markets during the 1850s, that decade's deadly yellow fever epidemics prompted public statements and municipal decrees voicing preference for and even requiring "seasoned" or "acclimated" black waterfront workers over their "feverish" immigrant competitors. But despite the inherent dangers of altering the state of the community's health, many truculent white newcomers fought back.

During the mid-nineteenth century, medical theories were infused with contemporary notions of race, class, ethnicity, and nativity. More than a century and a half of ensuing historical and scientific inquiry into yellow fever has verified some past beliefs and refuted others. These theories, though often fallacious, shaped policies that had significant repercussions for the labor history of Charleston's antebellum docks. Remaining ever cognizant of subsequent medical discoveries and modern epidemiological realities, scholars nevertheless ought to take seriously the antiquated and frequently mistaken views of eras past.[56] Of chief importance is an understanding of what antebellum Americans termed "acclimation," or the process of adapting and becoming accustomed to the Carolina lowcountry's climate and disease environment.[57] It was widely believed, for instance, that if a native Charlestonian maintained uninterrupted residence in the city until maturity, he or she was thereafter "acclimated" or virtually immune to local diseases, including yellow fever. It's now known, according to *The Cambridge World History of Human Disease,* that the preponderance of a population "in areas frequently visited by yellow fever can become more or less quietly immune as children experience the illness as just one more in a train of childhood ailments."[58] Neither a foolproof nor an all-inclusive process, however, this conventional wisdom was challenged by several of Charleston's antebellum doctors.[59]

Among whites, meanwhile, doctors correctly warned that rural folk from the interior, northerners, and especially recently arrived foreign immigrants were particularly vulnerable.[60] "Our Stranger's Fever is most emphatically well named from its inhospitable tendency to assail . . . the newly arrived stranger," wrote Charleston physician Samuel Henry Dickson in January 1840. The editors of the *Charleston Medical Journal and Review* asserted in November 1856, "The Irish Celts, and the lower classes from Southern Europe, are most susceptible to the disease, and succumb most readily to its deleterious influence."[61] "Unacclimated" working-class immigrants, such as Irish dockworkers who labored and lived along the waterfront, were thought to be especially vulnerable to their new surroundings. Mayor Henry L. Pinckney, reporting on the relief of the sick poor during the 1838 yellow fever epidemic, claimed that the disease "was confined to those who were not only not accustomed to our climate, but whose constant exposure to the sun, aided by hard labor and dissipated habits, had emphatically prepared them to become its victims." As with cholera, the immoralities of working people were thought partly to blame for their struggles with yellow fever.[62]

Many medical doctors maintained, however, that if an unacclimated person—including a foreign immigrant—was stricken with yellow fever but recovered from the attack, then "the individual having it is not liable to another attack." Others held that newcomers who resided in Charleston for a number of years could develop acclimation.[63] The antibodies remaining in the blood of a surviving victim does, in fact, provide a lifelong immunity against reinfection from the virus.[64] These theories too nevertheless had their contemporary detractors, and some physicians warned their colleagues that a misdiagnosis of yellow fever during a previous epidemic could lure some into a false sense of security.[65] There also was a lack of concurrence regarding how long it took an immigrant to gain acclimation. Some physicians thought only a couple of summers in the city sufficient. Dr. William Hume described the "remarkable" case of a Spaniard who had been a resident of Charleston for three years but nonetheless became ill during the 1854 fever. Dr. John L. Dawson reported that in August 1856, Elizabeth Graham, "from Ireland, four years in Charleston," died with black vomit, regarded as the truest indicator and "most dreaded symptom" of yellow fever.[66]

Whether native or immigrant, young or old, working class or elite, genuine infection alone conferred complete immunity to yellow fever. But medical authorities agreed—and modern science has confirmed—that Charleston's black residents, both enslaved and free, were decidedly less susceptible to the disease than whites. Though current scholars continue to debate whether African blood afforded blacks an innate or acquired resistance to yellow fever, the results were the same.[67] During one of Charleston's earliest encounters with yellow fever, in 1699, Reverend Hugh Adams recorded that 162 whites and only 1 black resident died during the epidemic.[68] Dr. Henry B. Horlbeck offered the following statistical evidence from the city's antebellum yellow fever epidemics:

Yellow Fever Deaths in Charleston, 1819–1852

Year	Total Deaths	White Deaths	Black Deaths
1819	172	167	5
1838	354	350	4
1839	134	133	1
1849	124	123	1
1852	310	309	1

Source: Horlbeck, "Maritime Sanitation," 9.

"In the above list . . . ," commented Horlbeck, "the great exemption from the disease among the black race is evident."[69] Blacks accordingly were regarded as "acclimated" and thus essentially immune to yellow fever, whereas white immigrants were presumed "unacclimated" and vulnerable to contracting and spreading the disease. It was in the context of such convictions that Charleston's municipal leaders—some being physicians—debated the origins of yellow fever and how best to prevent the disease in the city. At stake in this argument was an edge in the ethnic and racial struggle for control of the waterfront workforce. Locked in fierce competition for labor on the docks, blacks reaped the reward of relative resistance to yellow fever, even as the mere presence of their febrile white rivals was identified as the Achilles heel in the city's defenses against the disease.

In 1800 Charleston physician and historian David Ramsay wrote to a doctor in New York, "The disputes about the origin of yellow-fever which have agitated the Northern States have never existed in Charleston. There is but one opinion among the physicians and inhabitants, and that is, that the disease was neither imported nor contagious."[70] Nearly forty years later this harmony was so well intact that when Dr. Benjamin B. Strobel concluded that yellow fever was imported in 1839 from the West Indies, he found that Charleston's physicians were in almost unanimous and "decided opposition to such a conclusion." Though his claims had become "a subject of ridicule and laughter" among the city's doctors, Strobel—who served as the physician of the Charleston Marine Hospital during the 1839 yellow fever epidemic—nevertheless published his findings in 1840. Ramsay's consensus had been shattered, and during the next two decades Charleston's most learned and influential physicians and leaders clashed over whether yellow fever was domestic or foreign in origin.[71]

In this "origins debate" the preponderance of the city's mid-nineteenth-century medical professionals—influenced by the teachings of Ramsay and especially the Philadelphia physician Benjamin Rush—subscribed to the erroneous theory that yellow fever arose in Charleston from a variety of local sources.[72] These "localists" insisted that yellow fever was caused by "meteorological phenomena" and was "Produced by a vaporous poison, engendered in the soil, out of the decomposition of the animal and vegetable matter, aided by heat and moisture, and precipitated on the subject."[73] Others including Thomas Y. Simons—who was both the port physician and chairman of the city's Board of Health—similarly blamed dock mud mixed with decomposed vegetables and other offensive materials swept in by the tides, which released a venomous vapor when disturbed.[74] Another explanation hypothesized that "the germs of the disease exist everywhere in the soil of our city, ready to spring up under the favorable influence of our usual summer temperatures, whenever the earth is upturned during the season, surely to grow, ripen, and yield the harvest of death."[75] Other commonly espoused local causes paralleled those of cholera: stagnant water and low lots, the dumping of offal in the streets, and crowded and filthy dwellings and neighborhoods. Localists even imaginatively suggested that one of the "active agents of the disease" was the excitement of municipal elections. Irish and German immigrants were particularly vulnerable to this cause since competing political factions were always vigorously pursuing their votes. Following the calamitous yellow fever epidemic of 1852, credulous city and state lawmakers moved Charleston's local elections from early September to early November.[76]

Rejecting local explanations, a few Charleston doctors rightly focused on external sources of yellow fever. Back in 1753 Dr. John Lining observed, "This fever does not seem to take its origin from any particular constitution of the weather," but that each time the disease had broken out in Charleston "it was easily traced to some persons who had lately arrived from some of the West Indian islands, where it was epidemical." Almost exactly one hundred years later, Dr. William Hume—a city alderman and professor of experimental science at the Citadel, the state military academy in Charleston—joined B. B. Strobel to argue that the disease did not originate in the soil or climate of the city; instead commercial trade with foreign vessels was to blame for the introduction of the disease.[77] Medical authorities later confirmed this importation theory: yellow fever was not endemic, or native, to the Carolina lowcountry; it was delivered from elsewhere, usually the West Indies.[78]

It also was not yet understood that female *Aedes aegypti* mosquitoes—which live and breed in stagnant water and thus pervaded Charleston's waterfront, and feed on human blood—were the vectors responsible for transmitting the yellow fever virus from infected visitors at the wharves to susceptible Charlestonians.[79] Without the benefit of this knowledge, "importationists" mistakenly claimed that inanimate objects like cargo or a vessel itself could become contaminated while lying in a port such as Havana where yellow fever was prevailing. Adherents of this view contended that, upon arrival in Charleston, the disease could then be passed to unacclimated individuals who came into contact with the "foul air" of the vessel and imparted to those who handled the "infected" cargo. Importationists wrongly believed, in short, that yellow fever was a contagious disease spread by direct contact rather than by a vector such as a mosquito.[80]

Meanwhile, this premodern and pseudoscientific squabble between localists and importationists led to profoundly different preventive policies. Localists urged municipal and state leaders to improve the public health of the city.[81] Aiming to reduce mortality from cholera, yellow fever, and other epidemic diseases, the Charleston City Council enacted numerous sanitation measures during the early nineteenth century. The council, for instance, outlawed the casting of human bodies into local rivers and marshes in 1805, forbade in 1839 the throwing of dock mud or any other substance "of an offensive character" onto the wharves between May 1 and November 1, and required the removal of offal or any other "dangerous nuisance . . . by which the air shall or may be impregnated with foul and noxious effluvia" in 1806 and 1836.[82] Also in 1836, under the leadership of Mayor Robert Y. Hayne, a "general system of internal medical police" was implemented and focused on improving drainage and eliminating stagnant water and low lots.[83]

Importationists acknowledged that such actions likely would inhibit the propagation of yellow fever after the disease was introduced into Charleston by a foreign vessel. But they prudently insisted that maritime quarantine regulations offered the best defense against its introduction.[84] In 1840—after yellow fever had struck down 354 individuals in 1838 and 134 in 1839—Dr. B. B. Strobel reported that between May 1 and July 30, 1839, at least thirty-six vessels arrived in Charleston from infected West Indies ports. Of those ships, twenty-three were not subjected to any quarantine and were allowed to come directly to the wharves. And of the thirteen that were detained, the length of quarantine ranged from five days to only a few hours, with one day the most common period of detention before docking in the city. Though the vessels subjected to quarantine were relatively few, their potential impact upon the city's health and prosperity was disproportionately devastating. Dr. Strobel thus concluded, "We have tried the plans of those who contend for the local origin of the disease for more than 100 years ineffectually. Let us make now the experiment suggested by an opposite theory—a rigid and efficient quarantine."[85]

In the wake of the yellow fever epidemic of 1839, the Charleston City Council passed "An Ordinance to Provide and Establish Quarantine Rules and Regulations for the Port and Harbor of Charleston," which was ratified on June 29, 1840. According to this law, all vessels arriving "from any place where infectious or malignant maladies usually prevail" were to report to the quarantine ground—located two miles from the city near Fort Johnson—and remain there at least five days (see figures 18 and 19). Vessels with sick persons on board at the time of arrival in Charleston, regardless of the vessels' port of departure, were quarantined for at least twenty days. The ordinance further stipulated that, if the mayor or the port physician deemed it necessary or expedient, all "infected" cargo was to be removed at the quarantine ground, after which the vessel was to be cleaned and purified. Also, no one was allowed to board or communicate with a quarantined vessel without the special permission of the mayor or port physician. This official authorization applied to laborers hired to discharge "infected" cargo or to clean and purify vessels at quarantine. An earlier state quarantine act, in fact, expressly included those persons "handling such infected cargo" as necessitating this special consent. Finally, after serving their quarantines and with the permission of the port physician, these vessels could come to the city.[86]

The 1840 ordinance remained on the books as Charleston's quarantine rules and regulations for fifteen years. In the opinion of importationist William Hume —the most outspoken advocate of quarantine measures in late antebellum Charleston—it was "sufficiently comprehensive to embrace all the necessary details when directed to be rigidly enforced." But with the majority of the city's physicians and municipal leaders still adhering to a belief in local causes of yellow fever, Dr. Hume suggested in March 1854 that the laws were being "loosely and carelessly carried out" due to a "neglect of duty in our officers." Localist Thomas Y. Simons—who as port physician ironically was the chief enforcer of the city's quarantine—admitted that the quarantine regulations, much like slave-hiring measures, were not being executed to the letter of the law under pressure from influential mercantile interests and with the acquiescence of the City Council.[87] Recommending that municipal officials enforce the 1840 ordinance, William Hume further sought to extend and strengthen the quarantine laws. To keep "infected" vessels from unhealthy ports away from the city's waterfront and susceptible inhabitants, Dr. Hume suggested that such vessels be discharged using lighters at the quarantine ground rather than at Charleston's wharves. The purportedly tainted cargo could be purified and transported to their consignees in the city. The emptied holds then would be thoroughly ventilated and cleansed at the quarantine before the vessels were permitted to enter the docks to load export cargo. Hume emphasized, misguidedly, that it was vital that the quarantined vessels' holds be purified before coming up to the city. Otherwise upon their "arrival at the wharf, and the hatches removed, the infection is diffused" among "the mass of clean vessels, and . . . the usual congregations of seamen and other foreigners."[88]

William Hume insisted that this latter means of dissemination occurred regularly but usually went unnoticed. In 1849, for instance, three vessels—the *Numa,* the *Isabel,* and the *Merchant*—arrived from Havana between July 18 and August 25 with none having sickness on board at the time of arrival. Contrary to law but in accordance with prevailing practice, all three ships were allowed to come up to the city and dock at Union Wharves without performing quarantine (see figures 7, 13, and 21). But on August 6 a seaman from the *Numa* took ill and died at the Marine Hospital with black vomit, and on August 7 the engineer of the *Isabel* sickened. Meanwhile, two vessels—the *Queen Victoria* and the *Huron*—arrived from British ports where yellow fever was neither endemic nor prevailing and legally moored at the wharves north and south of Union Wharves respectively, so that "the pure and the impure vessels were all in the vicinity of each other." By the end of August the captains of both British vessels had been sick with yellow fever and one had died. Five sailors from the *Queen Victoria* were stricken, but all recovered.[89]

Charleston's more vulnerable residents also were affected. Mr. Sahlman, a twenty-four-year-old German who resided at the corner of East Bay and Elliott streets, regularly boarded the West Indies vessels tied up at Union Wharves to purchase cigars. On August 26, the day after one of these visits, Sahlman became ill and on September 2 he died of yellow fever.[90] Then in August 1852, three vessels from the West Indies similarly were allowed to come up to the city without being cleansed at quarantine and unload their cargoes at Atlantic Wharf, and two others at Accommodation Wharf. The *Clara S. Bell* docked among these West Indies vessels at Brown's Wharf, where Mrs. Cole—a forty-one-year-old passenger from Boston—died during the week of August 15 from yellow fever. About two weeks later, an eight-year-old "little Irish girl" named Mary Ryan, "who was in the habit of frequenting the wharves to pick chips," died of yellow fever at her house on Philadelphia Street not far from the waterfront.[91]

Such incidents prompted William Hume to pen an updated quarantine bill, which received its first reading at the City Council meeting on February 14, 1854.[92] Hume publicly implored his fellow aldermen to take action to keep potentially lethal vessels, cargo, and persons away from the wharves altogether, thus elevating concerns for human health over commercial wealth. "Exclude the foreign element from our port, or extinguish it in the habour," he pleaded, "but never let it reach our wharves."[93] The bill newly proposed that all vessels arriving between May 31 and October 1 from ports where yellow fever existed at the time of departure, or having sickness on board during the voyage to Charleston, would be quarantined for no fewer than thirty days after arrival and at least twenty days after the discharge of all cargo. Hume explained that prevailing practice had permitted those West Indies vessels with healthy crews to bypass the quarantine ground and immediately dock at the wharves. But due to the periodic outbreaks of fever in the city, prudence "would urge us to close this possible mode of entrance, which the present bill most earnestly provides for."[94]

Like many diseases, yellow fever has an incubation or latency period—the time elapsed between exposure to the virus and the onset of symptoms—of three to six days.[95] Outwardly healthy persons infected with yellow fever therefore sometimes arrived in Charleston prior to the manifestation of the disease. Hume accordingly maintained that, while vessels were being discharged and purified at the quarantine ground, "the period of incubation of the fever is advancing, and it is probable that these delays will equal the time necessary to decide whether the disease will or will not be developed in the crew." Another rationale for such restrictive measures was as follows: "The detention of a vessel for 30 days, is a penalty to enforce the discharge of cargo and undergo a purification, while the 20 days detention after discharge of cargo is to encourage or enforce the re-loading at the quarantine ground," rather than at the city's wharves. The bill indeed permitted quarantined vessels—after being thoroughly cleaned and purified, and if no sickness was prevailing on board—to load cargo at the quarantine ground using lighters, thereby enabling such ships to return to sea before the expiration of their detentions. And so, with the cases of Mr. Sahlman, Mrs. Cole, and Mary Ryan in 1849 and 1852 still fresh in his mind—not to mention the rising tide of newcomers toiling on the city's waterfront—Hume concluded, "There is certainly more safety in the absence of doubtful vessels from the wharves, than in their presence."[96]

Despite the endorsement of dozens of physicians and approximately two hundred merchants not engaged in the West Indies trade, opponents wasted no time in attacking the pending ordinance.[97] David Ramsay had observed in 1790 that in Charleston and the surrounding lowcountry, "Health and wealth seem to be at variance." In 1840 Dr. B. B. Strobel similarly observed, "It is the object and interest of all commercial communities, to establish, if possible, the noncontagious character of all diseases; and for the very plain reason, that the restrictions necessary to prevent the extension of such diseases, are calculated to interrupt free intercourse between commercial cities."[98] In the late spring of 1854, amid angst over the port's relative economic decline, the interests of commercial wealth again overcame those of community health. On May 29 the Chamber of Commerce—dominated by West Indies merchants opposed to tough quarantine measures—passed resolutions unanimously declaring the legislation "unnecessarily rigid" and "calculated to prostrate a large and valuable trade with Southern ports." The Chamber's representatives specifically argued that the thirty-day quarantine was "useless" and that the discharge of cargo was "ruinous in expense." The latter point was not unfounded, since transferring cargo between oceangoing vessels and lighters in open water was, in fact, more difficult and costly than discharging and loading goods at the wharves. Then in a memorial to the City Council—in the midst of debating the ratification of the ordinance after its passage on May 23—merchants involved in the West Indies trade proposed deleting the clause calling for the "indiscriminate" detention of vessels for twenty days after their cargo was discharged at the quarantine ground, even when there was no illness on board. They instead suggested leaving the duration of the confinement to the discretion of the mayor and port physician.[99]

With opposition to his bill mounting, William Hume reluctantly offered to reduce the detention of quarantined vessels after discharge of cargo from twenty to ten days. He then urged that the City Council act quickly to ratify the ordinance, since "as time wears on, the disease may arrive before we are ready to [impose] any impediment to its entrance into our city."[100] But reminiscent of the remonstrances that pressured city leaders into lax enforcement of the quarantine rules and regulations in 1840, on June 6 the localist-dominated City Council voted eleven to five to "indefinitely postpone" the final approval of Hume's bill.[101] During the next council meeting on June 13, 1854, the port physician—who persisted in his own pro-commerce, localist views—suggested the propriety of putting into effect the existing summer quarantine measures until the adoption of a new ordinance.[102]

On June 25, 1854, the British bark *Aquatic* departed Matanzas, Cuba, with a cargo of molasses bound for Cork, Ireland. On July 3 a member of the ship's crew died of yellow fever, and the next day a second died and two more seamen took ill. Meanwhile, the vessel sprung a leak and with "the remainder of the crew being more or less disabled," the captain was forced to run the vessel ashore north of Georgetown, South Carolina. The steamer *Nina,* under the command of a Captain Magee, left Charleston and went to the *Aquatic*'s assistance, and when Magee arrived the bark had eight feet of water in its hold. After pumping out the water and discharging some of the cargo to prevent the vessel from sinking, the *Nina* towed the *Aquatic* to Charleston with a steam engine pumping water out of the hold the entire way. On July 13, "in a sinking condition" and "with her hold in a very foul state," the *Aquatic* arrived and dropped anchor at Charleston's quarantine ground, where only its fore and aft cabins were cleansed and disinfected. None of the remaining members of the vessel's crew were ill, but all were sent to the Lazaretto—the quarantine hospital located nine miles from the city on Morris Island—"so as to see if sickness would occur, which did not." With the steam engine pump still running continuously to keep the *Aquatic* afloat and with no lighters available to unload the cargo, the port physician was faced with the decision of "whether she should sink or be brought to the city." Thomas Y. Simons chose the latter, and with its hold still filthy and "containing molasses in a state of fermentation, bilge-water, &c.," the *Aquatic* was released from quarantine and came up to North Commercial Wharf where it laid for two days. Then on July 16, the vessel was towed to Union Wharves to be pumped out, discharged, and cleansed.[103]

Having taken a substantial public health risk by allowing the *Aquatic* to come up to the city's central wharves in such an unsanitary condition, Dr. Simons stressed, "As regards the men to work on board the Aquatic, I had made it an especial condition with Captain Magee and the Stevedore, that blacks should be employed in discharging the cargo, which was done." Or so he thought. When on July 21 the stevedore commenced unloading the *Aquatic*'s remaining cargo—approximately nine hundred hogsheads of molasses—he was reported to have "prudently determined to employ acclimated negroes in the hold, while his Irish hands laboured on deck, and on the wharf." Though a truly judicious arrangement would have excluded susceptible Irish workers entirely, the stevedore calculated that barring the unacclimated Irishmen from the ship's hold was sufficient.[104]

One typically might expect the expendable Irish hirelings to have been assigned the more difficult, dangerous, and unhealthy work in the *Aquatic*'s hold, while the valuable chattel labored on the deck and wharf. When in Claiborne, Alabama, in the early 1850s, Frederick Law Olmsted observed enslaved workers releasing cotton bales "with fearful velocity" down a slideway from a 150-foot bluff above the Alabama River to awaiting Irishmen on a steamboat's deck below. When the northern traveler queried about this "reckless" procedure and the rationale for the racially segregated labor gangs, the mate candidly replied, "The niggers are worth too much to be risked here; if the Paddies are knocked overboard, or get their backs broke, nobody loses anything!"[105]

Some Charlestonians agreed wholeheartedly with these sentiments, tingeing their reactions to yellow fever's stalking of vulnerable immigrants. William Hume lamented in March 1854 that "there is among our merchants a moral principle paramount to the love of gain," adding, "Of death and desolation we need not argue, for habit has rendered us callous to such considerations; and the exemption which the native enjoys, may make him careless of the suffering of others." Following the 1854 epidemic, Hume suggested that greed was influencing hiring decisions and alleged, "the decree has gone forth that some must die that others may be enriched."[106] The Irish and Germans, despite their rising numbers, no doubt fell under the category of "others" in 1850s Charleston, and for some an immigrant worker struck down by yellow fever could be quickly replaced by another Irishman or German and was much less costly than the loss of high-priced slave property.

But the specter of epidemic disease lurking at Charleston's doorstep in July 1854 altered significantly any such prevailing employment arrangements. Faced with precarious and unusual circumstances, the stevedore reversed convention and deployed valuable but acclimated black slaves as the city's first line of defense within the vessel's dank and noxious hold. The white immigrants tasked with toiling amid the supposed salubrity of the *Aquatic*'s deck and adjacent wharf did not passively accept the real perils to their welfare and lives, however. A few hours into the unloading of the vessel, the Irish dockhands noticed that the customhouse officer, who ordinarily would have been carrying out his duty aboard the ship, was instead sitting on the wharf. When these white laborers asked him for an explanation, he replied that "the vessel had had yellow fever on board, and that he would rather remain where he was." Neither this white official's native-born status nor long-term city residence steeled his spine against the presence of a vessel tainted with yellow fever docked at the Cooper River wharves. The Irishmen having begun work on the *Aquatic* without being informed of the vessel's allegedly poisonous atmosphere, one of the gang retorted, "And, by jabbers, is it yellow fever that's aboard this vessel, and divil a turn more will we give the windlass." Vying to retain control over their labor and very lives, the Irish wharf hands immediately went on strike until they were able to renegotiate their wages to account for the added peril inherent in such unhealthy and potentially fatal work.[107]

Given Charleston's nearly nonexistent history of either work stoppages or collective action among common laborers under the strict controls and anti-proletariat influence of the institution of slavery, these striking Irishmen exhibited remarkable agency and intrepidity. Were they predominantly transient workers who unwittingly yet successfully introduced the tactics of unionized northern docks? Why did the stevedore—who hired, supervised, and paid these wharf hands—engage in compromise rather than fire the troublesome and replaceable workers? Was the contracting stevedore a fellow Irishman who insisted on their employment and retention despite a disruptive and potentially embarrassing work delay and demand for higher wages? The historical record generated far more questions than definitive answers. This Irish gang's brazen indifference to dismissal nevertheless suggested a relative dearth of enslaved common dockworkers in the city. Whether removed to rural plantations to capitalize on higher cotton prices, driven from Charleston by withering labor competition, or still on the lam in the wake of the city's 1852–53 cholera outbreak, a declining number of black slaves were available for immediate hire in July 1854. As to why these immigrants struck rather than quit, bear in mind that the threat of yellow fever was just another of the copious dangers of waterfront labor. "Unacclimated" as they were, the Irishmen who worked aboard vessels such as the *Aquatic* had little choice but to risk contracting the disease if they hoped to make ends meet.[108]

On August 4, after the last hogshead of molasses had been unloaded by the joint efforts of the segregated Irish and black dockworkers, the unnamed stevedore, accompanied by a Mr. Garvey and a Mr. McNeal, descended into the *Aquatic*'s rancid and damp hold, which they washed out with a fire hose. Eight days later Mr. Garvey became ill, and within forty-eight hours he was dead. Subsequent reports revealed that Garvey was a twenty-six-year-old Irish stevedore who resided at 20 Pinckney Street. He had been "employed in pumping out and disinfecting the bark Aquatic during the greater part of which time he worked in the hold," where "heated by work he was wet by rain." The city register, who kept a record of all marriages, births, and deaths, reported that, on August 12, Garvey "had been at work on board of the Aquatic, and residing in Pinckney-street, sickened with fever and died on the 14th without throwing up black vomit." Dr. Simons seized on the fact that Garvey "had no black vomit," and that he was originally determined to have died from "Congestion of the Brain." But Simons admitted that "afterwards the physician said it was yellow fever," and death records affirmed the disease as the cause of Garvey's death. As for Mr. McNeal, described as "an Irishman employed with Mr. Garvey in the hold of the Aquatic," he also fell ill with yellow fever, but recovered.[109]

Dr. Daniel J. Cain, who was the physician of the Marine Hospital during the 1854 epidemic, reported that Garvey and McNeal "were the only men who were employed *in the hold of the vessel*," presumably, that is, besides the unnamed stevedore and black slaves. Fifteen others—the Irishmen who had struck for higher wages—were said to have been employed on the deck of the *Aquatic* during its unloading, but did not enter the hold.[110] The port physician—vexed that Captain Magee and the stevedore had failed to employ only blacks, and omitting that Garvey, McNeal, and the white work gangs were Irish immigrants—claimed that these "15 were not sick at all."[111] In fact, two of these men died, whereas, according to William Hume, "the rest still live ready to unload another yellow fever vessel at the same wages."[112] Only Mr. McNeal, who had sickened and recovered, possessed the antibodies that newly afforded him immunity to yellow fever. Yet Hume dubiously asserted that the thirteen surviving Irish workers "had resided here many years, and may now be considered acclimated to the infected hold of a vessel."[113] Though these Irish wharf hands were unacclimated when hired in July 1854, having toiled on the *Aquatic* they mistakenly were recognized as among the immune who thereafter could work safely on the Cooper River waterfront, including during future yellow fever epidemics.

Among those purported newly acclimated Irish dockhands who had worked on the deck of the *Aquatic* was a Mr. Gorman. Though Gorman did not sicken with yellow fever, Dr. Cain hypothesized—wrongly and impossibly—that "it was communicated to his wife by the fomites of his clothes," rather than *Aedes aegypti* mosquitoes.[114] Mrs. Gorman, who was twenty-five years old in 1854 and described both as "an Irishwoman" and the "wife of an Irishman," resided on Calhoun Street near Elizabeth and Anson streets with her husband and two-year-old daughter Mary. Mrs. Gorman came down with yellow fever on August 15, and lay sick in her house for two days before calling a physician. Despite the best efforts of the doctor and several visiting friends, having thrown up black vomit she died on August 18. Not only did Mr. Gorman lose his wife, his daughter Mary—who shared a bed with her sick mother—died five days later also with black vomit. William Hume mused that, although Mr. Gorman came to Charleston at the same time as his family, he "passed the whole summer in the same house in perfect health." Death records showed that Mary Gorman was born in New Jersey, and being two years old when she died in August 1854, Mr. Gorman could not have resided in Charleston for more than two years. And in fact, in an essay appearing in the *Charleston Medical Journal and Review* in March 1858, Hume revealed that the Gormans arrived in Charleston in January 1854, only seven months before Mrs. Gorman and Mary Gorman took ill and died. This evidence refuted Hume's claim that the white workers who had labored on the *Aquatic* had lived in Charleston for "many years," and corroborated that unacclimated Irishmen—rather than their effectively immune black competitors—were hired to work on ostensibly contaminated vessels on Charleston's waterfront during the summer of 1854.[115]

Before the 1854 epidemic, Hume recognized that unacclimated dockworkers were potentially a major chink in the city's quarantine armor, and warned that laborers who discharged "infected" cargo could become ill and spread yellow fever throughout the city. Though Thomas Y. Simons unequivocally dismissed Hume's claims—stating that such a "circumstance has not occurred in my experience of thirty years"—the 1854 epidemic demonstrated that Dr. Hume was not too far off the mark.[116] Again, ubiquitous mosquitoes along the Cooper River waterfront rather than "impure" cargo and vessels served as the true vectors of death, transmitting yellow fever from infected persons to those who were healthy but susceptible. Hence the presence of scores and perhaps hundreds of unacclimated Irish and other immigrant dockworkers such as Garvey, McNeal, and Gorman assuredly put the city at greater risk and played a major role in the widespread propagation of the disease in 1854.

After all, Garvey and McNeal were the second and third Charleston residents to sicken with yellow fever in 1854, and by all accounts Garvey was the city's first inhabitant to die in that year's epidemic. And, indeed, some implicated these Irishmen for the proliferation of the fever from the waterfront to the rest of the city. William Hume, for instance, implied that Mr. Garvey was to blame for spreading the disease to his home and infecting Pinckney Street. Death records revealed that a twenty-five-year-old German named Mr. Livingston, who lived on the street, died of yellow fever on September 2. John Slattery, a forty-seven-year-old Irishman and also a resident of Pinckney Street, was taken by the disease on September 21.[117] Meanwhile, medical authorities blamed Mrs. Gorman for propagating the disease throughout her neighborhood on and near Calhoun Street. "Mrs. Gorham's [*sic*] case seemed to be the centre of radiation of the fever in that locality," wrote Dr. Cain in his history of the 1854 epidemic. Dr. Hume argued that three individuals from various areas of the city became ill after visiting Mrs. Gorman, and that shortly after she died "several cases occurred in the immediate vicinity, gradually enlarging the circle so as to involve the four streets bounding the square." On Calhoun Street alone, between Elizabeth and Meeting streets near the Gorman's residence, thirteen people were said to have died from yellow fever in 1854.[118]

And so, as in 1849 and 1852, ineffective quarantine measures in 1854 left unacclimated residents working on or living near the waterfront exposed to the deadly scourge of yellow fever.[119] As Dr. Cain observed, "It occurs first among the shipping, and then spreads" through the entire city and mainly "among the unacclimated foreign population, chiefly the Irish and Germans." With nearly twenty yellow fever deaths in Charleston since the *Aquatic*'s arrival in mid-July, master cooper Jacob Schirmer penned the following diary entry on August 23, 1854: "Yellow fever—for some days rumor has been about, that this disease is amongst us, and no doubt several cases were in the Hospital from Ashley River and Frazer's Wharf, but to day the [Charleston] Courier announces the fact, and gives the names of the cases, but I fear it is worse than represented and the Doctors say it is spreading." In September 1854 the editors of the *Charleston Medical Journal and Review* belatedly announced, "It is with great regret that we record the prevalence, in this city, of the Yellow Fever," and added, "This summer the destroyer has laid his heavy hand upon . . . Charleston."[120]

Indeed it had. Dr. Samuel Henry Dickson reported that the number of sick was estimated at 20,000 or more, prompting him to remark, "In 1854 the number of persons attacked by Fever in the city was wholly beyond precedent." Dr. Cain labeled the outbreak a "Pandemic." By the end of September the number of yellow fever deaths already far exceeded the city's previous record death toll of 354 during the 1838 epidemic. By late autumn, when frost killed off the disease-carrying mosquitoes, 627 were dead. Of these, 612 were white, and 256—over 40 percent of the victims—were natives of the Emerald Isle. The Germans were a distant second with 131 dead.[121] With escalating numbers of susceptible immigrants employed on the waterfront, Charleston's deaths tolls from yellow fever soared during the 1850s. Gradually recognizing this connection, local authorities and residents soon championed restrictive employment policies with significant consequences for those competing for labor on the city's late antebellum docks and drays.

In the aftermath of this devastating epidemic, William Hume excoriated those who placed profits over people, localists for their obstinate devotion to "internal medical police" alone, and the port physician. Labeling existing laws as defective and renewing calls for more stringent and judicious quarantine regulations, Hume again recommended "The exclusion of infected, or presumed infected vessels from our wharves," which would—if enforced—be "common justice" to foreign seamen and unacclimated Charlestonians.[122] Alarmed by the previously unfathomable loss of life and pressed by "considerable excitement on the subject," the Charleston City Council passed and ratified a new quarantine ordinance in April 1855. These rules proved to be nearly identical to William Hume's failed 1854 bill. Vessels arriving between May 31 and October 1 from ports prevailing with yellow fever at the time of departure, or having fever on board during the voyage to Charleston, were to be detained for at least thirty days after arrival and at least twenty days after all cargo was unloaded. This ordinance aimed at preventing unhealthy vessels from coming up to the city's wharves, which were swarming with "pure" vessels as well as unacclimated and thus highly susceptible immigrant dockworkers and foreign seamen. After discharging their cargo and having their vessels "thoroughly cleaned and purified" at the quarantine ground, captains were encouraged to load freight using lighters and go back to sea without serving the full duration of their quarantine and without ever coming up to the city.[123]

In the past, city authorities—most of whom were localists who doubted the efficacy of quarantine measures and espoused pro-business policies—had not enforced even the flawed quarantine rules and regulations. But William Hume and the importationists had reason to anticipate the support of Charleston's new mayor, William Porcher Miles, who was elected in 1855 with the strong backing of Irish immigrants. Obliged to better protect his Hibernian constituents laboring on or residing near the waterfront, Mayor Miles advised the City Council to "Keep vessels arriving in our harbor from infected ports at a safe distance from our docks, and prevent their cargoes, charged with the seeds of death, from being at once landed on our crowded wharves teeming with an unacclimated laboring population, peculiarly susceptible to disease." Aside from exposing Miles and his reformist successor Charles Macbeth to charges of unreasonable hostility and obstruction to the city's vital maritime trade, such a position ironically may have caused more harm than good for the mayor's newly arrived white working-class supporters.[124] By conceding that these waterfront immigrants were "unacclimated" and "susceptible" to yellow fever—and thus joining in their stigmatization as "others" who were responsible for inaugurating and then disseminating increasingly devastating epidemics throughout the city—critics of commercial avarice and callousness and proponents of greater community and worker protections such as Miles and Hume actually made it more difficult for Irish and other immigrants to secure labor on Charleston's docks and drays. Also paradoxical, foreigners in dire need of employment and boosters in pursuit of unhindered commercial revival and greatness—many of whom were nativists—found some common ground in opposing the very quarantine designed in part to safeguard the city's abundant "strangers." Struggling to make ends meet and to control their labor and lives, these workers ultimately could not rely upon well-intentioned political patrons for indemnity against either unfavorable public opinion and policy or black labor competition.

Yellow fever did not strike Charleston during the summer of 1855. But on July 8, 1856, after a six-day voyage from Havana, the brig *St. Andrews* appeared off the bar of Charleston Harbor with a healthy captain and crew. Under the old quarantine practices, this vessel would have been allowed to proceed to the city's wharves.[125] But under the new April 1855 regulations, because it had arrived directly from Havana after May 31 and because two seamen aboard had died of yellow fever while in the Cuban port, the *St. Andrews* reported to the quarantine ground. On July 15, workers discharged the vessel's shipment of sugar using lighters, and delivered the cargo to Brown's Wharf. Having no additional cases of yellow fever while in Charleston, the *St. Andrews* then was loaded with export cargo again using lighters at the quarantine ground, and it sailed out of the harbor having never docked at the city's wharves.[126] The quarantine laws, it seemed, were working.

But then on July 26, John Abbott became ill at his residence on King Street near Broad Street. The attending physician asked City Register Dr. J. L. Dawson to visit Abbott, and agreeing that the case was yellow fever, Dawson advised Mayor Miles to remove the sick man to the Lazaretto. Early the next morning Abbott was sent from the city to the Lazaretto, where he recovered. John Abbott was a twenty-three-year-old Irishman who had arrived in Charleston in February 1854, and had remained healthy during the 1854 epidemic while working as a servant at the Mills House hotel on Meeting Street. Not previously having had yellow fever, and only having been in Charleston for a little over two years, most contemporary physicians would have deemed this recently arrived immigrant unacclimated. Nonetheless, during the week leading up to his sickness Abbott had been employed loading the *St. Andrews* at the quarantine ground. According to the city's Committee on Health and Drainage—consisting of Dr. William T. Wragg, William Hume, and white workingmen's advocate James M. Eason, and reporting "on the Origin and Diffusion of Yellow Fever in Charleston in the Autumn of 1856"—Abbott's case "may be fairly traceable to the infected vessel."[127]

Michael Denning was less fortunate than John Abbott. Denning, an Irishman who had likely only recently arrived in Charleston, got sick with fever on July 31 and was sent from his residence on East Bay Street near Pinckney Street to Roper Hospital in the city. There it was ascertained that Denning had been employed loading the bark *Industria* at the quarantine ground. The *Industria* had arrived from Havana on July 13 with a load of wine and lead, twenty crewmen, and an unspecified number of passengers, and was detained at quarantine. The next day a sick passenger was sent to the Lazaretto where he died on July 17. On July 16, three men were sent from the vessel to the Lazaretto but recovered, but two others were sent on July 23, and both subsequently died. Early in August lighters landed the *Industria's* cargo at Union Wharves, and soon thereafter lighters from South Dry Dock Wharf loaded the vessel at the quarantine ground. The *Industria*, like the *St. Andrews*, went to sea without ever docking in the city. But once Mayor Miles was informed that Denning had been working on the *Industria*, he ordered the Irishman to be transferred from Roper Hospital to the

Lazaretto on August 6. Having thrown up black vomit, Michael Denning died the next day.[128]

William Hume fallaciously maintained that the *Industria* was an infected vessel, and that though Denning had no contact with any of the sick persons on board, "it is apparent that [he] took his disease on board of the vessel after the sick crew had been removed." The Committee on Health and Drainage agreed, concluding that, even though Denning lived on East Bay Street not far from Palmetto Wharf, like Abbott he "most probably got his illness in the vessel."[129] In other words, even though the new quarantine rules had kept the *St. Andrews* and *Industria* away from the thronged docks, they had failed to keep vulnerable immigrants such as Irishmen John Abbott and Michael Denning away from these West Indies vessels, their captains, crews, passengers, and cargoes, all thought to be shrouded with "seeds of death." Like those toiling aboard the *Aquatic* in 1854, these Irish laborers were compelled to run the gauntlet between unemployment, poverty, and starvation on one side and illness, physical suffering, and death on the other. Aware of the health risks associated with working amid "infected" and quarantined vessels, Abbott, Denning, and scores of other newcomers—as we soon shall see—defied the prohibitions of local authorities in the effort to avoid both the alms house and the Lazaretto.

As with Mr. Garvey and Mr. McNeal in 1854, Irish waterfront workers were the first Charleston residents to sicken with yellow fever in 1856, and Denning was the first to die from the disease.[130] Furthermore, like his fellow Hibernians Mr. Garvey and Mrs. Gorman, the deceased Denning was blamed for spreading the illness to and throughout his neighborhood. The Committee on Health and Drainage reported that "other cases occurred near [his residence] afterwards which by some are attributed" to Denning. Hume theorized that, when Denning was taken from his house on East Bay Street to Roper Hospital, "he left behind him the influence of his disease." Denning's fever reportedly spread when it struck Mr. and Mrs. Douglas who dwelled with Denning, and Ann and Bridget Burns who lived in an adjacent house. Ann was a seventeen-year-old Irish girl who died with black vomit on August 21. In total, the 1856 yellow fever epidemic claimed 212 lives, of whom only 9 were black and 203—mostly foreign-born immigrants—were white.[131]

Notwithstanding the new and more stringent quarantine ordinance, in a fresh public debate some turned to an old problem to explain the 1856 yellow fever epidemic. In a letter to the editors of the *Charleston Mercury* on August 13, 1856, "A Citizen" contended that "the lax and imperfect manner in which our quarantine laws have been administered" was to blame. This anonymous Charlestonian detailed how, with the docks still swarming with unacclimated workers, vessels from unhealthy Cuban ports other than the *St. Andrews* and *Industria* had not properly been detained according to law.[132] In mid-July the City Council had ordered all vessels from the West Indies to unload and load at the quarantine ground, thus forcing the localist port physician to more scrupulously execute the quarantine laws.[133]

"A Citizen" furthermore alleged that the officers and crew members of quarantined vessels regularly had been "permitted to visit the city immediately after their arrival at quarantine."[134] The 1855 ordinance prohibited all persons arriving in detained vessels from leaving quarantine until twelve days after sailing from the port of departure, fifteen days after the last case of fever on board, and eight days after arrival at Charleston's quarantine ground, unless discharged sooner with a certificate of acclimation from the port physician.[135] Thomas Y. Simons confirmed on August 18, "In accordance with the Ordinance, no persons are permitted to come from any vessels at Quarantine, unless the Port Physician is satisfied that they are acclimated."[136] "A Citizen" snapped back that the bark *Balear* arrived on June 27 from Havana, where yellow fever had been prevailing. The very next day and on subsequent days Captain Sagrista and his mate Jose Fiol were allowed to come up to the city, where they were entertained by respectable families, attended church, "and mingled freely with our people." Mr. Fiol returned to the quarantined *Balear* on a Sunday evening; by Monday morning he was sick with yellow fever, and a week later he was dead.[137] Dr. Simons's method of assessing acclimation, entailing little more than taking individuals at their word, obviously was unsound.

Similarly, the Committee on Health and Drainage described the case of the schooner *George Harris,* which arrived from Baltimore on July 21 without any sickness on board, and therefore was allowed to dock legally at Central Wharf. A thirty-four-year-old sailor from Delaware named Stephen Pellighon serving on the *George Harris* "had felt great alarm" that the captains and crew members of quarantined vessels regularly landed at Central Wharf. Pellighon even "was heard to say that there was no use in keeping the vessels at Quarantine if the men were allowed to come up" to the city. On August 3 Pellighon fell ill with yellow fever and died at the Marine Hospital, a death in all likelihood enabled by the very flaw in the quarantine policy that drew his concern.[138]

When the *Amelia* shipwrecked off Folly Island nearly a quarter-century earlier, city guardsmen and local residents joined to ensure that none aboard the quarantined vessel set foot upon Charleston's wharves. Because the wreckers contracted to salvage the *Amelia's* supposedly cholera-ridden cargo did so "at the hazard of the public health," municipal officials "wisely, and legally" forbade them from entering the city. One local judge pondered the consequences had anyone "brought infected goods into town, or had come into town themselves, at the risk of spreading the infection" during that 1832 affair.[139] Then in 1840 Dr. Robert Lebby divulged instances of harbor workers—often foreign or northern-born—transmitting yellow fever to the city during the 1830s.[140] So why, many Charlestonians began to ask publicly during the 1850s, were lightermen such as Abbott and Denning still allowed to continuously pass between the quarantine ground where they toiled amid infection and the city where they lived, thus endangering the entire community? "A Citizen" protested that workers employed in lightering cargo to and from vessels at quarantine were "allowed free intercourse with the city," and were "permitted to visit the city at their pleasure, and mingle indiscriminately with the acclimated and unacclimated portions of our community."[141] Dr. Dickson too observed that a large number of "foul vessels" had anchored in the Cooper River not far from the wharves, and "kept up a continual intercourse by captains and consignees and their boats' crews, lighters, and lightermen—the latter furnishing . . . two of the earliest subjects" of the epidemic (that is, Abbott and Denning).[142] And the 1856 Committee on Health and Drainage confirmed, "The lighters employed in this business usually returned to the wharf after their trips to Quarantine," and noted the frequency which small boats had docked at the city's Cooper River wharves "with hands returning from working in the vessels at Quarantine."[143]

As early as March 1854, William Hume had foreseen the danger of lightermen transferring cargo from vessels at quarantine directly to the eastern wharves, and had called for the City Council to examine and perhaps replicate New York's quarantine system. New York City required a group of stevedores and dockworkers to be hired to labor exclusively at an enclosed quarantine station located at a safe distance from the city, and then prohibited these workers from leaving the station and entering the city. Although the Charleston City Council formed a committee in January 1854 to look into such modifications, like the previous laws, the April 1855 quarantine ordinance stated, "All persons arriving in, or going on board of vessels brought to quarantine, shall be liable to be removed to such place as Council may appoint." But municipal authorities never designated such a location for the port's lightermen.[144] In July 1858, in fact, it still was "customary" for those "who have been engaged in lightering vessels infected with fever, to return to the city after their work has been finished." Concerned that harbor laborers were broadcasting "the seeds of the disease" within the city, Alderman James H. Taylor called upon his fellow councilmen to again consider prohibiting these workers "from landing or entering within the limits of the city, except so far as may be necessary to discharge their respective cargos, at the point designated by the Council." Declining to act, Taylor's colleagues tabled his resolution indefinitely.[145]

Dr. Hume also had made strong recommendations to the City Council in March 1854 about who should and who should not be permitted to work on cargo lighters. "The acclimation of our [native] citizens to the infection of yellow fever presents a great advantage in the process of transhipment [*sic*]," Hume argued, "for they can pass from the vessels to the city without danger of taking the disease and transferring it to the city, while a foreigner would receive it in the vessel, bring it up in apparent health, and in a few days be the means of counteracting all previous efforts, by its development and subsequent extension." William Hume had predicted exactly what was thought to have happened in 1856: susceptible immigrants including John Abbott and Michael Denning had been hired illegally to work on lighters at the quarantine ground, became infected while toiling on detained vessels, and then transferred the disease to the city where it was spread throughout the community. Hume therefore went on to explicitly advise—much to the delight of slaveowners with bondsmen for hire—that "Great caution should be exercised in the selection of the transferring crews and labourers; negroes are decidedly to be preferred, and the unacclimated stranger should be positively prohibited from joining the party."[146] In short, if the 1854 epidemic suggested the impropriety of employing unacclimated stevedores and dockhands on the Cooper River wharves during fever season, it also was unwise to allow unacclimated men to work on cargo lighters and at the quarantine ground.

In fact, city authorities had regulated the acclimation of such workers after the passage of the April 1855 quarantine ordinance but before the 1856 epidemic.[147] At a City Council meeting on May 15, 1855, Alderman Hume offered the following preamble to a resolution successfully establishing acclimation restrictions: "Whereas, It has been well observed that long residence in the City of Charleston, or the actual having and recovering from Yellow Fever, affords ample protection against the same, and that personal communication between the city and infected vessels, or vessels presumed to be infected, is indispensable to the due executions of the Quarantine Ordinance; and whereas the Quarantine Bill provides that in certain circumstances, certificates of acclimation may be granted by the Port Physician." The resolution then stated that persons could prove their acclimation and thus obtain a certificate by presenting a "competent witness," obtaining documentation from an attending physician, or by any other means the port physician deemed "satisfactory and conclusive." As for workers hoping to gain employment on cargo lighters and aboard quarantined vessels, only those with certificates of acclimation were permitted to "be employed about, or allowed to board, any vessel performing Quarantine, and afterwards return to the city."[148] Some immigrants elected to seek other work rather than defy this public policy or jump through the hoops necessary to document genuine claims to acclimation. But in the hard-fought quest for survival and a measure of control over their laboring lives, numerous others manipulated these imprecise and pliable requirements to illegally acquire a certificate or elude the system altogether.

With the City Council's authority, the port physician began to issue certificates or permits to those working on cargo lighters. Dr. Thomas Y. Simons publicly asserted on August 18, 1856, "The officers and crews of the lighters are required to be acclimated. Now, no permit has ever been given before the Port Physician has been fully satisfied that they were acclimated." But how, if the port physician rigidly enforced the May 1855 resolution requiring lightermen to prove their acclimation, were Irishmen John Abbott and Michael Denning authorized to work aboard quarantined vessels and to move freely between the quarantine ground where they likely contracted yellow fever, and the city where—as with Garvey and the Gormans in 1854—Denning was accused of propagating the disease? Simons contended that, "of the great number of vessels to which the lighters have gone, either to discharge cargoes or load at Quarantine, only two cases of sickness occurred." One of these cases—evidently Michael Denning—was sent to Roper Hospital with a "suspicious case of fever." There the man confessed to the port physician "that he had no permit, but that Capt. MILLS had obtained the permit, with [Mills] and three negros [*sic*] as his crew, and no white man, to carry to Quarantine." In other words, Mills claimed that his crew would be comprised of acclimated blacks only, but nonetheless hired the unacclimated Irishman Denning to work on his quarantine lighter. Captain Mills acknowledged his guilt, and Simons took away his permit, thus depriving Mills of any future command of a quarantine lighter.[149]

Thomas Y. Simons also detailed the case of John Abbott, "a decent young man, who had been here several years, and in the fever of 1854," and had been working "on board of a vessel carrying a cargo to the brig St. Andrew [*sic*], with a black crew." When Abbott became ill he was sent to the Lazaretto; but convinced that the man's condition was due to prolonged exposure to the sun and not yellow fever, Simons ordered Abbott to be treated at the "Doctor's House" of the Lazaretto. The Irishman soon recovered from his illness, but Simons—who never fully took responsibility for the improper issuance of acclimation certificates—declared that, "After this circumstance, no new permits were given to white men to go on board of lighters."[150] Then in a letter appearing in the *Charleston Mercury* on August 20, 1856, "CHARLESTON" affirmed that "Rigid regulations should be applied to vessels engaged in lightering cargos, that none should be employed on board but persons who can bring clear proof of their being acclimated."[151] In short, the rising public sentiment held that no Irish or other white immigrants need apply for lightering work in Charleston.

Not only did the port physician stop issuing lightering permits to white workers, but employers—even those who had wanted to hire white stevedores and laborers—felt mounting pressure to hire only acclimated blacks to safeguard the city's health. Five of Charleston's leading West Indies commission merchants, for example, were obliged to publicly divulge and defend their employment practices:

> In regard to the stevedores the following is offered:
>
> Charleston, 13th August, 1856.
>
> We hereby certify that we have had none but black stevedores to load our vessels at Quarantine or discharge. P. A. AVEILHE
>
> > MORDECAI & CO.
> >
> > HALL & CO.
> >
> > CAY, MONTANER & CO.
> >
> > STREET BROTHERS.
>
> NOTE.—The above statement holds good, with the exception, in our case, that the steamer Isabel had white acclimated persons to load and discharge early in the season, but not on the last trip.
>
> MORDECAI & CO.[152]

During the 1854 epidemic, Simons had attempted to ensure that Captain Magee and the stevedore employed only blacks—who were assumed to be acclimated and indeed were far less susceptible to yellow fever—to unload the *Aquatic.* Also in 1854, William Hume reported that the loading of two Spanish polacres, the *Concha* and the *Columbus,* "was performed by acclimated negroes," a fact deemed to have averted the further propagation of the disease from these vessels into the community.[153] Increasingly, then, despite blacks' vulnerability to both cholera and robust labor competition, Irish and other unacclimated white workers in Charleston were at a severe disadvantage in the contest for lightering and waterfront work during the lengthy fever season.

Even those white master stevedores who claimed acclimation from their long residence in the city now faced the added impediment of their dubious immunity. When entreating state and local lawmakers for protection from enslaved competitors, these skilled contractors felt obliged to ask, "in whom can the stranger Captain place the most reliance when he has to fly from the epidemic, to take care of his ship or when the hurricane and epidemic both prevail, as is often the case?"[154] Concerned on the one hand about sedition, secretion, and theft among slaves, and pressured on the other both by powerful slave-hiring interests and growing consternation over the employment of "febrile" whites, waterfront employers' response was far from clear.

White immigrant draymen also were unable to escape the impediment of their unacclimated status. Prompted by the outbreak of yellow fever during the summer of 1856, the City Council appointed a special committee to examine the quarantine system and suggest improvements. In April 1857 the committee published its findings, written by William Hume, and recommended that a wharf and warehouses on the city's western Ashley River waterfront—an area where far fewer immigrants resided—be acquired for the landing and storage of "infected" cargo lightered from the quarantine ground. Then, based on the principle that "where there is no unacclimated population, there will be no yellow fever," the committee suggested "That these cargos shall remain in these stores until wanted for immediate consumption, when they shall be delivered to acclimated negro draymen, to be conveyed on drays to their proper destination." The report also called for draymen to be "known," further minimizing the likelihood that recently arrived immigrant draymen, or even country slaves, would be hired to transport this cargo.[155]

Despite the protests of Irish and German draymen and the political discomfiture of a mayor elected with the votes of immigrant waterfront and transportation workers, Hume reiterated that the key to thwarting the spread of the "poison" into the rest of the city was that "the draymen should be acclimated negros [*sic*]."[156] At least in this case, then, acclimation alone was not sufficient; though regarded as not entirely white in the eyes of some native white southerners, immigrant and especially Irish draymen—even those who were considered safely seasoned— were barred by their whiteness from handling this reputedly hazardous cargo. But also excluded were native-born white transportation workers, who though few in number were regarded as acclimated. And unlike local free black draymen, these Charlestonians possessed the ballot. Establishing this latest waterfront labor regulation along strict racial lines, however, enabled employers—much as with porter stands and slave badges—to more easily and quickly determine who was and who was not acclimated and therefore legally eligible to transport cargo brought from the quarantine ground. Persuaded by Hume's remonstrations and choosing to protect the entire city at the risk of alienating Irish and other enfranchised white workingmen, the City Council and Mayor Miles adopted the committee's recommendations word for word on May 12, 1857.[157]

But Irish and German draymen were not solely denied employment in transporting the goods of quarantined vessels from this western wharf; they also were prohibited from hauling potentially tainted cargo arriving at the eastern wharves. At the City Council meeting on June 23, 1857, commission merchants Hall & Co. petitioned for the cargo of the quarantined vessel *Eben Atkins* to be brought to the city in lighters and landed at Union Wharves. At a special meeting held three days later, municipal authorities granted this request, provided that the cargo "be conveyed to the store by negro or acclimated draymen." The cargo of the quarantined brig *Somers* had been discharged and transported in the same manner just days earlier.[158]

Having set this precedent, the council received a steady stream of petitions during subsequent summer sessions requesting similar exemptions from the quarantine laws. Take early August 1857, when Henry Cobia and Co. asked the council's permission for the bark *Uncle Sam* to leave the quarantine ground and load cargo at the city's eastern Cooper River wharves; or the June 1858 appeal from the consignees of the brig *Eliza* and polacre *Concha*—the same ship implicated in the 1854 epidemic—to likewise bring these vessels to the docks.[159] Rejecting these latter requests, however, a majority of the council members firmly upheld the quarantine regulations. July 1858 witnessed an unsuccessful attempt from the agents and consignees of the schooner *Hannah Martin* to lighter the vessel's cargo to Brown and Co.'s Wharf, aimed to "save your petitioners from vast trouble and expense." The merchants were instructed to land the cargo at the city's designated western wharves in accordance with the quarantine ordinance passed in May 1857. But then in late August, city officials again made an exception and authorized the brig *Heyward*—like the exempted *Eben Atkins* and *Somers* one year before—"to land her cargo by lighters at Vanderhorst's wharf."[160] The compulsory hiring of acclimated black draymen in such circumstances presumably remained in effect.

Employment opportunities for white immigrants dwindled further as the number of quarantined vessels swelled. In 1856, Dr. Dickson noted "the continuous squadron of foul vessels, sometimes amounting to nearly a score in number" at the quarantine ground. New Port Physician William C. Ravenel—who the governor appointed after the death of Thomas Y. Simons in June 1857—reported that between May 1 and October 1, 1857, 78 vessels arrived at quarantine, 36 of which were detained and required lighters to discharge and load cargo. And during the six months between May 1 and October 31, 1858, 103 vessels arrived at quarantine, 65 of which were detained.[161] This increasing number of vessels required black acclimated laborers to unload and load cargo at the quarantine ground, convey the freight to and from the wharves, and transport these goods throughout the city. The result was far fewer jobs for unacclimated workers during the yellow fever season.

With dock work already relatively scarce in the summer months, some white immigrants had to give up waterfront labor and turn to other sources of income in the struggle to make ends meet. Off-season and supplemental employment included working as common laborers, street scavengers, firemen, private watchmen, or city guardsmen. During the devastating epidemic of 1858—the deadliest in the city's history, claiming 716 lives—the first case of yellow fever was John Abbott, "a policeman . . . taken sick on his post in Market, near East Bay street, at 1 o'clock, A.M., of the 10th July." The committee assigned the task of reporting on the origin and diffusion of yellow fever in 1858 reminded the City Council of the incredible happenstance that "John Abbott had yellow fever in 1856, was the first case that year, traceable to the brig St. Andrew [*sic*], at quarantine, on board of which he had been employed."[162] Unable to find work on the city's docks or lighters after his much-publicized and disputed case in 1856, and given the prescribed demand for immune blacks, Abbott was forced to change jobs. The fever nevertheless attacked John Abbott in 1858 just steps from the waterfront. Regardless of occupation, it was perilous for white immigrants to venture too close to the wharves during the sickly period. Residing in the city for over four years, passing through the 1854 epidemic unscathed, and recovering from what proved to be a misdiagnosis of the disease in 1856 clearly did not provide the still-unacclimated Abbott sufficient protection. After throwing up black vomit for days, twenty-five-year-old Irishman John Abbott died at his residence on Tradd Street on July 17, 1858.[163]

But countless other unacclimated white immigrants—notwithstanding mounting obstacles, and with rent to pay and mouths to feed—resisted efforts to dictate their labor and lives, and successfully found work on lighters and on the city's docks and drays during the fever season. John Abbott and Michael Denning, after all, had managed to cheat the system and evade the rules in 1856, much in the way Charleston's waterfront laborers had for decades habitually opposed the circumscription of their hiring, payment, and work processes. And though immigrants were not officially barred from working on or handling the goods of non-quarantined vessels, city death records revealed that scores were employed on the Cooper River waterfront during the summers before the Civil War despite public trepidation and antagonism to their presence. Twenty-nine-year-old Irishman John McElroy, for example, died on board the ship *Southern* from the "effects of heat" in July 1856; thirty-five-year-old Irishman Matthew Stevens drowned near the *Southern* in August 1857; twenty-two-year-old Irishman Michael Lanneau died of yellow fever on South Atlantic Wharf in November 1857; twenty-nine-year-old Irishman Thomas O'Brien died of yellow fever on Gadsden's Wharf in August 1858; forty-five-year-old Irishman Michael Quinn drowned at Gadsden's Wharf in September 1858; thirty-year-old Irishman John Fisher died from sun stroke while on board a ship in July 1859; and thirty-two-year-old German J. A. Fleischmann died after an accident on Boyce's Wharf in June 1864.[164] A few such deceased immigrants admittedly were not waterfront workers, whereas others were considered acclimated and thus no threat to community health. But despite what ought to have been the lessons of the 1854 and 1856 epidemics, rising public fear and sentiment against the employment of unacclimated immigrants, and official resolutions requiring the use of immunologically advantaged blacks for particular jobs while the quarantine was in effect, white immigrants tenaciously persisted to seek and find waterfront work during and after the summer of 1856.

Irish and other white immigrants in the South clearly had far different experiences from those in northern cities. And they had an impact on Charleston and southern history that went far beyond their labor contributions to the city's and region's vital export economy. The influx of unacclimated immigrant workers to

American ports liable to yellow fever put these cities at considerably greater risk for the introduction and widespread propagation of the potentially devastating disease. Prior to the arrival of thousands of new white immigrants in Charleston, yellow fever epidemics as deadly as that in 1856 were rare and those as ruinous as in 1854 and 1858 unimaginable. Throughout the 1820s, 1830s, and 1840s there were only four years in which yellow fever claimed more than 100 lives in the city, and in most years the disease either did not strike or claimed only a few. The lethality of the 1838 yellow fever epidemic—the deadliest in Charleston to that time with 354 victims—was attributed to the destructive fire of April 1838 that both exposed countless drains and cisterns and attracted scores of susceptible transient workers to rebuild the "burnt district" adjacent to the Cooper River waterfront.[165] Thomas Y. Simons insisted that yellow fever did not spread to laborers who were unloading and loading "foul" vessels at the city's wharves during the 1838 and 1839 epidemics.[166] But in these years, those who were discharging and loading West Indies ships and mingling with sick captains, mates, and crew members were almost exclusively acclimated black slaves—who though disproportionately vulnerable to the region's cholera epidemics, were virtually immune to yellow fever. Instructive was Dr. Robert Lebby's investigation into the origins of the 1839 epidemic, during which he canvassed the whereabouts, contacts, health, nativity, and acclimation of the port's lighter officers and crews. Captain Parker, a New Englander who had resided in the city since 1831, avowed that his "Crew was composed of Blacks belonging to Charleston." The lighter's two mates were white, one of whom recovered after contracting the illness whereas the other only joined the vessel in early November. Born in Maine but inhabiting the lowcountry for nineteen years, Captain Daniel Wells too reported that his crew was comprised of four blacks who "were all hired from persons in Charleston." The steamer's English engineer had been in the city for two years and its Irish mate for only one, but all remained healthy throughout the epidemic.[167]

After the immigration of substantial numbers of working-class Irishmen beginning in the mid-1840s, however, Charleston suffered its second most lethal yellow fever epidemic in 1852 when 310 people died, and three of the four deadliest yellow fever epidemics in the city's history during the 1850s.[168] The higher death tolls of that last antebellum decade were in large part due to the greater presence of immigrant "strangers" in the city—"the receivers and the conductors of pestilence."[169] As one Charlestonian put it in the midst of the 1854 epidemic, the "besotted Irish" were to blame for "keep[ing] the fever up by giving it constant fuel."[170] Charleston had lost its defensive wall of acclimated black workers along the waterfront. In the past the vast majority of stevedores and wharf hands who had mingled with foreign sailors in ships' holds, on the docks and in warehouses, and in the city's filthiest taverns and back alleys were black men more or less resistant to yellow fever, mitigating the propagation of the imported disease into the heart of the city. But despite efforts to prevent susceptible white immigrants from handling "infected" cargo or exposure to the "poisonous" atmosphere of West Indies vessels, once scores of unacclimated Irishmen and Germans doggedly gained work alongside acclimated black slaves on Charleston's mosquito-infested waterfront and at the quarantine ground, the city's human health shield was easily penetrated.

The catastrophic 1858 yellow fever epidemic was the last in Charleston's antebellum history. The disease did not infiltrate the city during the even more destructive Civil War. By stifling the West Indies trade, the Union Navy's blockade of Charleston Harbor and the South Carolina coast, ironically and inadvertently, reestablished the port's protective barrier against imported diseases. With the resumption of foreign commerce after the war, the city endured several final bouts with yellow fever during Reconstruction before epidemiological discoveries and mosquito control and eradication efforts ended the threat in the Carolina lowcountry.[171] Transcending the transformative chasm of the Civil War and continuing into the postbellum era and beyond, however, was the contest between waterfront workers struggling to scrape by and the employers, merchants, and authorities who long sought to exploit and control their vital labor.

Postscript

The election of Abraham Lincoln to the presidency in November 1860 set off a series of events that culminated in the Civil War, the abolition of slavery, and the devastation of Charleston's Cooper River waterfront. South Carolina's secession on December 20 quickly bred much financial and commercial instability and uncertainty in the port city. During what normally was the peak of Charleston's shipping season, a correspondent for the *New York Tribune* wrote on January 4, 1861, "There is almost a total suspension of business . . . there is no collection of debts, credit is collapsed, property is without sale or value; the avenues of trade are closed up; and the prospect is darkening every hour." Making matters worse on February 18, the nascent Confederate Congress passed an onerous 24 percent tariff on northern imports. Exempted from this punitive tax, however, was any merchandise purchased before February 28 and shipped southward prior to March 1, thus triggering frenzied commercial activity in northern and southern ports alike. In New York, for instance, newspapers reported on the "furore" and "Busy Scenes" that accompanied this "Sudden and Immense Shipment of Goods for the South." To accommodate all of the cargo necessitating swift transport, northern shippers were obliged "to employ all the vessels of every class bound for ports of the Southern republic," as well as an army of dockworkers. "Stevedores, longshoremen and dock hands have been in constant demand with plenty of employment for them," announced the *New York Herald* on March 1, 1861. Pressed for time and working day and night, laborers finished unloading vessels using one gangplank or hoisting horse, while simultaneously loading the ship with another. The holds and decks of steamers and packets were filled until cargo had to be turned away.[1]

Greeting these southbound vessels when they reached Charleston were merchants, factors, wharfingers, and especially dock laborers in desperate need of work and wages. Observing what proved to be a lively last hurrah for the city's antebellum waterfront and its workforce, a reporter for the *Philadelphia Inquirer* nevertheless rendered a dire and unsympathetic prediction: "In less than a week the New York line of steamers will probably be laid up, the wharves will be deserted, and hundreds of stevedores and laborers will be without employment, and minus food. Truly these violent fanatics will have, within the next six months, to answer for such scenes of distress and misery as even the densely populated cities of the North are total strangers to; for, while all means of employment are daily, and in rapid succession, gliding from the reach of the poor, the imposition of the illegal and treasonable Tariff will raise all kinds of provisions to at least one-fourth more than their highest market price during the past year."[2]

Unfortunately for many Charlestonians, this northern journalist was not far off the mark. A self-imposed embargo of southern cotton exports—intended to create a "cotton famine" in Europe and force England and France to recognize the Confederacy—proved a failure while stifling the flow of the commodity from the hinterlands to Charleston's docks. After Confederate forces fired on Fort Sumter in Charleston Harbor on April 12, 1861, President Lincoln furthermore ordered the blockade of southern ports. By the end of April, Jacob Schirmer noted the rising prices of basic staples such as butter and bacon, already in short supply. "Business of every Kind [is] almost perfectly paralyzed," wrote the master cooper on April 27, 1861.[3]

Blockade running became a considerable and potentially lucrative venture in wartime Charleston. Though vessels successfully evading the Union Navy required unloading and loading, they were too few in number to employ more than a handful of dockworkers at any given time. Waterfront traffic was so anemic, in fact, that many of the port's custom-house officers were discharged at the end of June 1861. Schirmer explained that there was simply "no Work for them to do."[4] English hardware manufacturer and merchant William C. Corsan traveled to the United States in late 1862 to evaluate his waning consumer market in the American South. When in Charleston he commented upon the sluggishness of the city's commercial districts. Conceding that the blockade runners employed a number of porters, draymen, and other laborers, Corsan also observed that Meeting, King, Hayne, and East Bay streets, "bustling places in times of peace—were now little more than rows of closed stores, and looked very much as if a perpetual Sunday or holiday prevailed." The Englishman concluded, "In a commercial sense Charleston is, for the present, out of business."[5]

With the transshipment of trade goods grinding to a halt, the demand for waterfront laborers diminished precipitously. Along with the paucity of employment opportunities, secession, armed conflict, and the blockade all dammed up the influx of immigrants and seasonal transients who for decades had found winter-time work on southern docks. Contemporaneous to the enslavement crisis that chased hundreds of free black workingmen and mechanics from Charleston in late 1860 and early 1861, municipal authorities wary of northern abolitionist spies had begun turning away these itinerant white laborers in the weeks following Lincoln's election.[6] As for those newcomers who permanently had settled in the lowcountry before the war, some entered the Confederate Army. Take stevedore John Conroy, who was a first corporal in the Charleston Battalion of the Irish Volunteers. Joining Conroy in military service were dozens of Irish porters and draymen.[7] Other white waterfront workers remained in the beleaguered port at-tempting, though often failing, to make ends meet. A report to the South Carolina General Assembly in 1862, for instance, detailed the substantial number of Irish-men still receiving relief from Charleston's alms house in the midst of the war.[8]

Enslaved dockhands, meanwhile, often were put to work constructing the city's military defenses. Wharf owner Otis Mills, though born in Massachusetts, was an ardent secessionist and supporter of the Confederacy. When Mills died years after the Civil War, his obituary recounted how "In 1862, when Charleston was threatened, he turned out his wharf hands and with them went out of the city to the fortifications, and although in feeble health, remained with them and superintended their work upon the entrenchments."[9] Likewise, a sizable number of slaves owned by the South Carolina Railroad, as well as white laborers in the company's employ, occasionally were sent to the Sea Islands to work on forti-fications.[10] But with Union forces occupying much of the South Carolina and Georgia coasts by late 1861, and with the blockading fleet located just miles from Charleston's wharves, some slaves continued to claim the benefits of the urban and littoral environment and seek freedom via the Maritime Railroad. Shortly after the commencement of the blockade, two bondsmen "attempted to go off in the British Ship A & A," but were discovered and returned to Charleston.[11] On April 28, 1862, Jacob Schirmer commented how the night before "some 8 negroes run [sic] away with one of Genl Ripley's boats and gone [sic] out to the Fleet."[12] Still more daring, on the night of May 13, 1862, erstwhile dockhand and stevedore Robert Smalls famously guided the steamship *Planter,* with his family and several other slaves on board, out of Charleston Harbor and delivered the vessel to the Union Navy.[13]

For those relatively few laborers—whether black or white, enslaved or free, native or immigrant—who continued to toil along the water's edge during the conflict, to the many hazards of the work was added the Union bombardment of the city that lasted from August 1863 until February 1865. The boiler of the steamship *Hibben,* for example, was struck with a shell while being discharged at the wharf of Fort Sumter on August 12, 1863, wounding eleven on board. Among the casualties were nine black laborers who were scalded horrendously, some fatally.[14] Nor were wharf hands safe after the close of the workday. The daughter of a former slave and free black man named Forest Gibbs, who labored on the docks both before and during the Civil War, recalled how "Her father had returned home one afternoon and was resting from a hard days [*sic*] work, when a shell crashed through the walls of their little home on Tradd street, and passed immediately over him as he lay on his cot." Though the house was destroyed, Gibbs and his family escaped unharmed.[15] Irish stevedore William Doran was not so lucky. Though it is unclear whether Doran worked on the waterfront amid the hostilities, he ran a boardinghouse for refugees at his thick-walled residence on Bedon's Alley in the southern portion of the city and well within range of the federal guns. According to Doran family lore, "on one occasion during the bombardment he was reaching for a match on the dining room mantel to light someone's pipe when a cannon ball took off his arm. For years afterwards, he was teased: 'Generous old William Doran, ask for a light and he gives his arm.'"[16] One young slave impressed into Confederate service in Charleston, Sam Aleckson, dryly conjectured that "it would have been rather unpleasant to be standing on a wharf and have a shell come whistling by taking one's head off."[17]

Lasting 567 days, the Union siege demolished the Cooper River wharves, some of which remained in disrepair and useless to maritime commerce for years after the war.[18] Noting the frequent conflagrations that contributed to the waterfront's destruction, Jacob Schirmer wrote on September 18, 1864, "Another fire broke out . . . all no doubt caused by Shells as the Enemy is now shelling the city furiously." Even before the termination of the bombardment, Schirmer thought the lower part of the city "heartrending," adding, "it has almost become a Wilderness of weeds."[19] At war's end, mere wreckage remained (see figure 20). "What desolation," lamented wharf owner Elias Vanderhorst's wife, Ann, during a brief wartime visit to the city. "Alas' Poverty seems closing fast upon us. The structure of an ancient family gradually tumbling down & there is nothing to stay the impending injury."[20]

But when the shelling stopped and the dust settled, more than waterfront warehouses and wealth had been toppled. Also smoldering in the ruins was the institution of slavery and the port's antebellum labor system. Constructed primarily of enslaved blacks since the city's founding in the late seventeenth century, a new order of labor relations arose in the immediate aftermath of emancipation and the Civil War. Much about the work and its many dangers and difficulties persisted. But in place of mostly subtle or latent defiance against exploitative and controlling slaveowners, employers, and local and state officials, a formal and formidable association of essential waterfront workingmen that was centuries in the making manifested from its antebellum roots. Dominated by former slaves, members of the emerging Longshoremen's Protective Union Association took direct and bold action as early as January 1867 to better their labor conditions and lives.[21] Though this union was open to whites, the unshackling of over 400,000 slaves in South Carolina and nearly 4 million blacks nationwide largely stemmed the tide of white immigrants able and willing to conduct "nigger work" on Charleston's docks. Even some of the port's most firmly entrenched prewar stevedores ceased competing for wharf labor in the postbellum environment. Spanish stevedore and slaveholder John Torrent, for example, abandoned his twenty-year business in Charleston during the 1860s and took up farming in Richmond County, Georgia.[22] Others stayed, however, and resumed their roles in the waterfront's abiding and abundant struggles. Despite losing an arm as well as his slaves, Irishman William Doran and his eldest son James carried on in the stevedoring trade through the end of the nineteenth century.[23] Fellow Irish stevedore Thomas Carrol and his son similarly braved the seismic shifts of the New South.[24] And perhaps with nowhere else to turn for occupational protection and socioeconomic preservation, the leader of the white master stevedores' antebellum efforts to dislodge their black rivals, Massachusetts native George B. Stoddard, sent aftershocks across the port's convulsed landscape by joining both the freedmen-filled longshoremen's union and the "Black Republicans."[25] But irrespective of one's race, politics, previous status, or task, all of the burgeoning class of workers hoping to earn a living along Charleston's reconstructed waterfront embarked upon a well-worn and tortuous path of conflict and conciliation, resistance and accommodation, tragedy and triumph.

Abbreviations

ARC   Avery Research Center for African American History and Culture, College of Charleston, Charleston, South Carolina

CCPL   Charleston County Public Library, Charleston, South Carolina

CLS   Charleston Library Society, Charleston, South Carolina

CRCMS   Collections Research Center, Mystic Seaport, Mystic, Connecticut

MHS   Massachusetts Historical Society, Boston, Massachusetts

NAA   National Archives at Atlanta, Morrow, Georgia

RL   David M. Rubenstein Rare Book and Manuscript Library, Duke University, Durham, North Carolina

SCDAH   South Carolina Department of Archives and History, Columbia, South Carolina

SCHS   South Carolina Historical Society, Charleston, South Carolina

SCL   South Caroliniana Library, University of South Carolina, Columbia, South Carolina

SHC   Southern Historical Collection, Louis Round Wilson Special Collections Library, University of North Carolina at Chapel Hill, Chapel Hill, North Carolina

Notes

Introduction

1. U.S. Census; Gazlay, *Charleston City Directory . . . for 1855;* Purse, *Charleston City Directory . . . for 1856;* 1860 U.S. Census; Powers, *Black Charlestonians,* 130; *Charleston Daily Republican* and *Charleston Daily News,* qtd. in Powers, *Black Charlestonians,* 130.

2. Powers, *Black Charlestonians,* 127–29; *Charleston News and Courier,* January 26, 1875, qtd. in Powers, *Black Charlestonians,* 128; Spero and Harris, *Black Worker,* 182–83; *Charleston Daily News,* qtd. in Spero and Harris, *Black Worker,* 183.

3. Powers, *Black Charlestonians,* 127–35.

4. For examples of recent revolutionary era studies, see Gilje, *Liberty on the Waterfront,* and Carp, *Rebels Rising.* Drawn by the violence and struggles surrounding late-nineteenth and twentieth-century labor unionization, scholars of Charleston's waterfront—and other southern waterfronts—have emphasized the post–Civil War era. See, for instance, Hine, "Black Organized Labor"; Poliakoff, "Charleston's Longshoremen"; Arnesen, *Waterfront Workers of New Orleans;* Rosenberg, *New Orleans Dockworkers;* Hirsch, "On the Waterfront"; Northrup, "New Orleans Longshoremen"; and Farrington, "Biracial Unions."

5. See Erem and Durrenberger, *On the Global Waterfront,* and Fletcher and Gapasin, *Solidarity Divided.* Also see *The State* (Columbia), August 20 and 27, 1897.

6. Though scholars often have acknowledged the extensive and central role waterfront workers—and especially slaves—played in southern maritime commerce, most have neglected to provide details regarding these laborers and their work. See, for example, Wood, *Black Majority,* 208, 228, 230; Olwell, *Masters, Slaves, and Subjects,* 164; Powers, *Black Charlestonians,* 11; Starobin, *Industrial Slavery,* 9, 30; and Schweninger, "Slave Independence," 113.

7. According to historian George C. Rogers Jr., Charleston's "golden age of commerce" stretched from the 1730s until roughly the 1820s. Maritime scholar P. C. Coker argued that the city's commercial golden years more accurately stretched from 1795 until 1819 (Rogers, *Charleston,* 3; Coker, *Charleston's Maritime Heritage,* 171–72, 35). Also see Coclanis, *Shadow of a Dream,* and Pease and Pease, *Web of Progress.* Cotton prices plummeted from roughly 30 cents per pound in 1818 to about 12 cents in 1823. During the 1840s and 1850s prices were lower still, averaging only 10 cents per pound. But a

significant increase in cotton production, sales, and exports often made up for these depressed prices (Edgar, *South Carolina*, 273–74).

8. Edgar, *South Carolina*, 275.

9. Coker, *Charleston's Maritime Heritage*, 174, 176–78.

10. Edgar, *South Carolina*, 154, 269, 271, 274–75, 287; Coclanis, *Shadow of a Dream*, 255, note 122. Also see Tuten, *Lowcountry Time and Tide*, 26, table 1.3, and 43, table 2.1.

11. See Taylor, *Transportation Revolution*, and Sellers, *Market Revolution*.

12. Van Deusen, *Economic Bases*, 333, appendix C. Also see Collins, "Charleston and the Railroads," 100, table 5; Dawson and DeSaussure, *Census of the City of Charleston . . . 1848*, 90–102; Coclanis, *Shadow of a Dream*, 82, table 3.13; and Chaplin, *Anxious Pursuit*, 260.

13. See, for instance, Stuart, *Three Years* 2: 98; Stirling, *Letters*, 250; and Abbott, *South and North*, 182.

14. Vanderhorst Wharf Business Papers, folders 9, 10, SCHS.

15. See Arnesen, *Waterfront Workers of New Orleans*, 24, 38, 176.

16. Charleston Chamber of Commerce, "Report of a Special Committee," 18–19.

17. See, for instance, Rockman, *Scraping By*; Buchanan, *Black Life on the Mississippi*; and Cecelski, *Waterman's Song*.

Chapter One: "Using violent exercise in warm weather"

1. Thomas J. Tobias Papers, "Wharves and Warehouses" folder, SCHS; Fraser, *Charleston! Charleston!*, 63. Some accounts from the 1730s reported that as many as 100 ships were in the port at one time during the fall months (Coker, *Charleston's Maritime Heritage*, 37–38). In 1748 nearly 200 vessels sailed out of Charleston Harbor loaded with exports, including 68 ships bound for Europe, 87 for the West Indies, and 37 for northern ports (Eaton, *History of the Old South*, 47; Pease and Pease, *Web of Progress*, 10).

2. Traveler Carl David Arfwedson remarked in 1832 that Charleston's "advantageous situation" placed it "in the rank of the most considerable city [*sic*] for commerce . . . which I firmly believe it will continue to occupy for a long period" (*United States* 1: 379). Also see Buckingham, *Slave States* 1: 46. The construction of Gadsden's Wharf began in 1767, and it was advertised as open for business in March 1773. Wharves also were built along the Ashley River beginning in the 1770s, including William Gibbes's 800-foot-long dock. See Thomas J. Tobias Papers, "Wharves and Warehouses" folder, SCHS; Reynolds, "Fort Sumter National Monument 'Dockside II Study,'" 3, SCHS; Coker, *Charleston's Maritime Heritage*, 42, 45; Joseph et al., "Vendue/Prioleau Project," 3–8; and Zierden and Reitz, "Excavations on Charleston's Waterfront," 1–2, 7–22.

3. Michaux, *Travels to the West*, 122; Buckingham, *Slave States* 1: 53; Mackay, *Life and Liberty*, 195; Hall, *Travels in North America* 2: 190–91; Letters of an American Traveler, 9, SCL.

4. Charles Barron to John Barron, November 11, 1839, Charles Barron Letters, SCL.

5. Mackay, *Life and Liberty*, 195; also see Mackay, *Western World* 2: 175.

6. Arfwedson, *United States* 1: 381. Englishman John Henry Vessey similarly observed in April 1859, "Cotton is the great article of export from Charleston. All the

wharves are filled with it, and I suppose that this is not the most busy season of the year" (*Mr. Vessey of England,* 62).

7. Letters of an American Traveler, 85, SCHS. Also see Ogilby, "British Counsel Report," nos. 14 and 15, SCL; Mackay, *Western World* 2: 184–85; Dowling, *Dowling's Charleston Directory . . . for 1837 and 1838,* preface, i–ii; and Gazlay, *Charleston City Directory . . . for 1855,* 119.

8. The city's wharf owners argued that there was storage for only 55,000 bales. See City Council Minutes, February 15, 1847, *Southern Patriot* (Charleston), February 16, 1847; and City Council Minutes, March 5, 1847, *Southern Patriot,* March 6, 1847; Reeder and DeSaussure to A. H. Boykin, March 17, 1856, Boykin Family Papers, SHC.

9. Thornbury, *Criss-Cross Journeys* 1: 278–79; Russell, *North America,* 162; Michaux, *Travels to the West,* 122; Olmsted, *Journey,* 511; Milligan, *Charleston Directory* (1790), 52, 55; Milligan, *Charleston Directory* (1794), 44–48; Nelson, *Nelson's Charleston Directory . . . 1801,* 46–47, 3–13; Negrin, *Negrin's Directory for the Year 1807,* 43–49; Hrabowski, *Directory for the District of Charleston* (1809), 119, 128–33; Folker, *Directory of the City and District of Charleston . . . 1813,* 97–101; Schenck and Turner, *Directory . . . for the City of Charleston . . . 1819,* 38–41; Schenck, *Directory . . . for the City of Charleston* (1822), 25–29; Smith, *Charleston Directory and Register for 1835–6,* 124–28; Dowling, *Dowling's Charleston Directory . . . for 1837 and 1838,* 16–19; and Purse, *Charleston City Directory . . . for 1856,* 238–44.

10. Hall, *Travels in North America* 2: 189–91.

11. Rogers, *Charleston,* 88.

12. The City Council responded with an ordinance in October 1854 prohibiting the mass storage of guano near occupied houses without the knowledge and consent of the inhabitants. See City Council Minutes, June 21, 1854, *Charleston Mercury,* June 23, 1854; and Horsey, *Ordinances of the City of Charleston from the 14th September, 1854, to the 1st December, 1859,* 1. Also see Schirmer Diary, September 30, 1853, SCHS; Steam Ship *Southerner* v. Ship *Harkaway,* December 6, 1854, Admiralty Final Record Books and Minutes of the District Court 5: 316–17, NAA; and *Charleston Courier,* January 19, 1860.

13. See Davidson Diary, April 2, 1853, John Matthew Winslow Davidson Papers, SHC. Maine ship captain James Carr colorfully described the city's Gullah hucksters and their street cries during the summer of 1815 (James Carr Papers, SCL). Basil Hall commented in 1828 on the "broken English and peculiar Creole tone" of two black coopers, which "showed them to be natives of some French West India Island" (*Travels in North America* 2: 191). When the English painter Eyre Crowe was in Charleston in March 1853, he noted that the waterfront afforded opportunities to observe and record the "callings" of black workers (*With Thackeray,* 152). Also see Leiding, "Street Cries"; and Pease and Pease, *Web of Progress,* 7–8. For examples of city ordinances and state acts regarding the sale of goods on the waterfront, see Eckhard, *Digest of Ordinances of the City Council of Charleston From the Year 1783 to Oct. 1844,* 78–80, 137–50, 158–59, 171–72, 255, 406–7.

14. Arfwedson, *United States* 1: 381–82.

15. Henry Burr to Daniel Burr, November 11, 1838, December 7, 1838, Letters of Captain Henry P. Burr, CRCMS.

16. See Dawson and DeSaussure, *Census of the City of Charleston . . . 1848*, 60–71, 90–102; Van Deusen, *Economic Bases*, 333, appendix C; and Collins, "Charleston and the Railroads," 100, table 5.

17. Master cooper Jacob Schirmer's diary illuminated holiday activity, or inactivity, on Charleston's antebellum waterfront. For Christmas, see December 26, 1833; December 31, 1834; December 26, 1845; December 27, 1845; and December 25, 1856. For New Year's Day, see January 1, 1835; January 1, 1841; January 1, 1842; January 1, 1848; January 1, 1850; January 1, 1853; January 1, 1855; January 1, 1856; January 1, 1859; and January 2, 1860. And for Good Friday, see April 20, 1832; March 25, 1842; April 14, 1843; April 2, 1847; April 21, 1848; April 6, 1849; March 29, 1850; April 14, 1854; April 6, 1855; and March 21, 1856. All in Schirmer Diary, SCHS.

18. Russell, *North America*, 162–63. As the Frenchman Michaux put it in October 1801, "commercial activity renders Charleston just as lively as it is dull and melancholy in the summer" (*Travels to the West*, 120). According to visiting ship captain James Carr, "the cotton is usually picked in Octr or Novr—depending some on the season, a rainy cold autumn puts it back, as a warm autumn has the contrary effect—rice is harvested in October, but not considered in shipping order until the following spring—cotton comes in to market from the last of Octr—the greater part of it is in by Christmas— this however depends on its prices—this year [1815–16] the season and price were both favourable—and considerable quantities of the new crop was [*sic*] in market by the 6th of Novr" (James Carr Papers, SCL). Also see John Crawford to Elias Vanderhorst, April 2, 1833; February 9, 1837, Vanderhorst Wharf Business Papers, folders 10, 11, SCHS; Eaton, *History of the Old South*, 406–7; Rosenberg, *New Orleans Dockworkers*, 43; and Pease and Pease, *Web of Progress*, 40–41. For the "Annual Rice Cultivation Cycle," see Tuten, *Lowcountry Time and Tide*, 19, table 1.1.

19. The account books of Charleston's waterfront factors and merchants documented the various charges associated with exporting cotton. Planters who sent their cotton to the city via water commonly paid 50 cents per bale for shipping or freight, and 4 cents per bale for landing or unloading at the wharf. Those who used the railroad, on the other hand, usually paid a dollar per bale for freight and 12 ½ cents per bale for drayage to the wharves. Regardless of how the cotton arrived at the port, wharf owners charged 6 cents per bale for weighing, 8 cents per bale for storage during the first and last weeks, 4 cents per bale during all intervening weeks, and 4 cents per bale loaded onto an outgoing vessel. State authorities, who first regulated wharfage in the 1770s, set these rates in 1807. See John Schulz Account Books, SCL; Anonymous Charleston Merchant Account Book, SCL; Petitions, 1806 #98, 1806 #99, ND #1895, SCDAH; "Memorial of the Wharf-holders of Charleston"; Petition, ND #1587, SCDAH; Milligan, *Charleston Directory* (1794), 43–46; Nelson, *Nelson's Charleston Directory . . . 1801*, 3–11; Negrin, *Negrin's Directory for the Year 1807*, 43–49; Hrabowski, *Directory for the District of Charleston* (1809), 128–33; Folker, *Directory of the City and District of Charleston . . . 1813*, 98–101; Schenk and Turner, *Directory . . . for the City of Charleston . . . 1819*, 38–41; Schenck, *Directory . . . for the City of Charleston* (1822), 26–29; Smith, *Charleston Directory and Register for 1835–6*, 124–28; Dowling, *Dowling's Charleston Directory . . . for 1837 and 1838*, 16–19; and Purse, *Charleston City Directory . . . for 1856*, 238–44. For a description

of slaves aboard various plantation boats delivering cotton to Charleston's wharves, see James Carr Papers, SCL; Collins, "Charleston and the Railroads," 103, table 7; Robertson, "Personal Recollections," SCHS.

20. To better ensure the payment of custom duties, port rules and federal statutes in place during the late eighteenth century stipulated that cargo be discharged in the "open day," and prohibited the landing of imported merchandise "after the setting of the sun and Before the rising of the said Sun." City ordinances passed throughout the first half of the nineteenth century confirmed these diurnal waterfront work hours. An 1810 law, for example, required coal weighers and lumber measurers laboring on the wharves to be available to perform their duties "between sun rising and sun setting." An 1848 measure similarly obliged the coal scales to be kept "ready for use, and at any and all times between the rising and setting of the sun, (Sundays and holidays excepted)." Others employed on the wharves too worked long hours. The harbor master was expected to be at his waterfront office between the rising and setting of the sun. But during the busy commercial season port officials often remained at work much later. Harbor Master Thomas Paine complained to the General Assembly in 1823 that during the winter months he frequently performed his duties on the wharves until 8 or 9 o'clock at night. Henry Clay Robertson, who worked at a cotton factor's office in the late nineteenth and early twentieth centuries, recalled, "Little did I dream of what unreasonable hours I would be keeping during the winter months—10, 11, 12 o'clock and frequently until 2 a.m., 4 a.m. being really the latest I ever did work." Of course, Robertson added that the office often closed at 3 o'clock in the afternoon during the summer. Finally, seamen aboard vessels docked in Charleston often worked long days as well. Those on the New York schooner *Hopewell,* for instance, typically commenced work at 6 o'clock in the morning and did not quit until 6 o'clock in the evening. See Milligan, *Charleston Directory* (1790), 52; U.S. v. 6 bags of coffee, July 7, 1795, Admiralty Final Record Books and Minutes of the District Court 1, NAA; Walker, *Ordinances of the City of Charleston From the 19th of August 1844, to the 14th of September 1854,* 46; Robertson, "Personal Recollections," SCHS; and Logbook of the Schooner *Hopewell,* December 21, 1843–May 20, 1844, CRCMS. Also see Walker, *Ordinances of the City of Charleston From the 19th of August 1844, to the 14th of September 1854,* 73; Eckhard, *Digest of Ordinances of the City Council of Charleston From the Year 1783 to Oct. 1844,* 109; and Petition, 1823 #39, SCDAH.

21. A former slave from Marion, South Carolina, described to a WPA interviewer how plantation horses were used to "work de screw dat press de bale togedder" (Rawick, *American Slave,* vol. 3, part 4, 223; also see vol. 2, part 2, 30–33). Vessey added, "It is a simple process: the covering of the bale, which having been pressed by the machinery on the plantations where it is picked, does not meet by twelve or eighteen inches; after steam pressure this covering considerably overhangs, as you see when the bales arrive in Europe" (*Mr. Vessey of England,* 61). Thornbury explained, "Every bale is to be crushed and squeezed into exactly half its present size, so as to go more compactly into the hold of the swift vessel that will skim over with them to England" (*Criss-Cross Journeys* 1: 214); Nordhoff, *Merchant Vessel,* 39. Also see Chaplin, *Anxious Pursuit,* 301–2.

22. Harleston, who Schulz patronized for much drayage work, appeared as a free black drayman in the 1822 city directory (Schenck, *Directory . . . for the City of Charleston*

[1822]). Receipt Book/Business Ledger, January 13, 1813, 7; Ledger, May 23, 1815; and Account Book, January 8, 1821, 346, May 27, 1822, 451, John Schulz Account Books, SCL.

23. See Cash Book, Charles T. Mitchell Account Books, CLS.

24. Charleston Chamber of Commerce, "Report of a Special Committee," 32.

25. Account Book, May 31, 1819, John Schulz Account Books, SCL; Cash Book, December 1, 1856, October 31, 1859, Charles T. Mitchell Account Books, CLS.

26. Smith was born in 1846 and worked as a cotton exporter in Charleston in the years immediately following the Civil War (*Charlestonian's Recollections,* 138).

27. Crowe, *With Thackeray,* 152, 157.

28. City Council Minutes, March 5, 1847, *Southern Patriot,* March 6, 1847.

29. Factors such as John Schulz, Charles Edmondston, and Charles T. Mitchell typically paid waterfront workers in cash, and then debited the costs from a planter's or shipowner's account, depending on who owned the cotton or other goods at the time they were handled. In this instance, Edmondston paid the laborers $42 and the drayman $5.25. He also shelled out cash to cover bills for such items as the captain's wages, cotton mending, various port fees and services, and a Gadsden's Wharf invoice for landing, wharfage, storage, shipping, and wood. In the end, the owners of the *Alexis* reimbursed Edmondston $894.88 and paid him a 5 percent commission of $44.74 for his services (Edward Hudson Papers, SCL).

30. Logbook of the Ship *Robin Hood,* February 5–March 1, 1833, CRCMS.

31. Robert Pringle to William Cookson and William Welfitt, March 15, 1742, in Edgar, ed., *Letterbook of Robert Pringle* 1: 338. The correspondence of other English merchants confirmed the use of cranes on European docks. See, for example, W. & J. Galloway to Mr. Stuart, October 6, 1840, John Lucas Letters, SCL. Colonial statute qtd. in Joseph et al., "Vendue/Prioleau Project," 4–5.

32. A survey of the port published in the early twentieth century confirmed. "In American ports little use has been made of freight-handling machinery for general cargo, i.e., cranes. In Europe they are universal." According to the report, in Europe "a row of movable half-gantry electric cranes of 3-5 tons lifting capacity straddle the pier-edge tracks and supplement or supplant the ship's tackle in handling freight between ship's hold and car or pier-shed platform. In America the same service is performed by the ship's tackle, often using a 'cargo mast' rail over the roof-edge of the shed, in connection with an electric pier winch. Though the cranes look better, there does not seem to be much difference in efficiency between them and the most approved American system, which the steamship companies here prefer" (Clapp, "Charleston Port Survey," 26).

33. Simon Magwood Papers, SCL.

34. Coker maintained that, even as European ports were utilizing early versions of cranes known as "shears" to unload vessels, wharves in colonial Charles Town "continued to rely largely on block and tackles and the spars of the ships as loading and unloading equipment" (*Charleston's Maritime Heritage,* 39, 41, 45). Vessels' rigging also may have been used to hoist cargo. See the following examples of ships' logs and journals noting seamen at work setting up and tearing down rigging while docked in Charleston:

Logbook of the Schooner *Amazon,* November 7, 1837, CRCMS; Journal of the Schooner *Ganges,* January 6, 1844, CRCMS; and Journal of the Schooner *Nameaug,* June 4, 1856; June 10, 1856, CRCMS.

35. Logbook of the Ship *Robin Hood,* February 4, 1833, CRCMS.

36. Burlin, *Negro Folk-Songs,* 28.

37. *Harper's Weekly,* January 19, 1878. Though this image appeared in 1878 and the vessel depicted is larger than most used before the Civil War, the basic loading techniques were the same as during the antebellum era. With a smaller vessel, however, the distance between the surface of the wharf and that of the ship deck would have been reduced. At low tide workers sometimes had to carry or roll goods down the gangway to the vessel's deck. Gadsden's Wharf, meanwhile, was unique in that it was constructed with a lock-and-gate system to eliminate tidal changes during the unloading and loading of vessels (Coker, *Charleston's Maritime Heritage,* 174, 42, 45; Nordhoff, *Merchant Vessel,* 63–64).

38. *Harper's Weekly,* July 14, 1877.

39. *Charleston Mercury,* May 28, 1856. See Adger's Wharf in "List of the Tax Payers of the City of Charleston for 1859"; Cash Book, February 27, 1858, 46, Charles T. Mitchell Account Books, CLS. Account of the Dutch Bark *Nederland,* February 6, 1860, Charles O. Witte Estate Records, SCHS. Stevedores still were using and hiring horses to hoist goods on Charleston's docks in the late nineteenth and early twentieth centuries. See receipt dated December 28, 1891, in Doran Family Papers, SCHS.

40. Benjamin Willard of Portland, Maine, recounted how stevedores and riggers used a combination of horses and small mobile steam engines on antebellum northern docks as well (*Captain Ben's Book,* 48).

41. Mears and Turnbull, *Charleston Directory* (1859), 51.

42. Ferslew, *Directory of the City of Charleston . . . 1860,* 122. Stevedoring firm James Doran Company paid fifty-five dollars in December 1891 for the rental of an engine to unload a steamship, and on another occasion paid seventy-five dollars for the use of an engine for 7 ½ days (Doran Family Papers, SCHS).

43. Smaller hand screws perhaps used for packing cotton were advertised for sale in Charleston as early as 1813, and retailers of workingmen's tools probably also sold cotton hooks. See John Whiting's ad for "Hand Screws of different sizes," in Folker, *Directory of the City and District of Charleston . . . 1813.* Also see T. L. Bissell's and Lucas & Strohecker's ads for various mechanics' tools in the 1855 and 1859 city directories respectively (Gazlay, *Charleston City Directory . . . for 1855;* Mears and Turnbull, *Charleston Directory* [1859]). Archibald McLeish's 1860 ad also mentioned the repair of jack screws (Ferslew, *Directory of the City of Charleston . . . 1860*).

44. Nordhoff, *Merchant Vessel,* 39–40, 43; Spero and Harris, *Black Worker,* 188.

45. Early twentieth-century ethnomusicologist Natalie Curtis Burlin contended that the "impulse in the Negro to sing at work is inborn" and was "a racial trait common to his African forebears" (*Negro Folk-Songs,* 8). Also see White and White, *Sounds of Slavery;* and Horton and Horton, *In Hope of Liberty,* 156.

46. Burlin, *Negro Folk-Songs,* 28, 31. Another song from the Georgia lowcountry— "Anniebelle"—reportedly was sung not only by stevedores loading lumber, but also by

workers while building railroads, chopping wood, and cutting weeds (Dance, ed., *From My People*, 511–12; also see Parrish, *Slave Songs*, 15, 197–224).

47. Pronounced in two syllables: "ti-yerd."

48. Pronounced with a long o: "ōn" or "*ohn.*"

49. Burlin recorded two additional postbellum verses: "Pay-day here, boys, *hey!* I hear dem say—*hey!*"; and "We'll have money, *hey!* Dis yere day—*hey!*" Burlin noted that the black workers added these modern verses, as well as "fresh extemporaneous verses" (*Negro Folk-Songs*, 29–31).

50. So important was the rhythm of the tune, in fact, it often took precedence over the logic of a song's words, leading some observers to conclude that many slaves' work songs were nonsensical and amusing. See Nordhoff, *Merchant Vessel*, 40–41; Kemble, *Journal*, 128–29; White, *American Negro Folk-Songs*, 251; and Krehbiel, *Afro-American Folksongs*, 48–51.

51. Shantyman and scholar Stan Hugill pointed out, "The word 'cheerily' means 'quickly' and was often used at capstan and halyards when exhorting the men to harder efforts" (*Shanties from the Seven Seas*, 233).

52. It was not uncommon for slave laborers to sing about women. See, for example, White, *American Negro Folk-Songs*, 311–40.

53. James Carr Papers, SCL.

54. Nordhoff, *Merchant Vessel*, 40–43. Also see Erskine, *Twenty Years*, 296–98; Doerflinger, *Songs of the Sailor and Lumberman*, 30, 32–34, 51, 80–81; Frothingham, *Songs of the Sea & Sailors' Chanteys*, 254; and Glass and Singer, *Songs of the Sea*, 56–57. Stan Hugill referred to Mobile Bay as a great "shanty mart" or "meeting-ground of white men's songs and shanties and Negro songs and work-songs." See his *Shanties from the Seven Seas*, 8, 10–11, 15–17, 20–22, 27, 63–65, 72–73, 80, 115–20, 123–26, 155, 179, 184–86, 190–97, 201, 210–11, 231–32, 237, 240, 258, 262, 275, 286, 297–300, 318, 329, 338, 364, 370, 382.

55. Washington, "Preface," *Twenty-four Negro Melodies . . . by S. Coleridge-Taylor*, viii. Also see Krehbiel, *Afro-American Folksongs*, 47.

56. Burlin, *Negro Folk-Songs*, 8. Also see White, *American Negro Folk-Songs*, 251. In addition to the forty-two dollars given to the laborers who unloaded and loaded the *Alexis* in 1823, Charleston factor Charles Edmondston hired and paid forty-five dollars in cash to a man named Archey Condy for leading the other hired hands in the stowing of the vessel. Unclear is whether Condy was black or white, enslaved or free (Edward Hudson Papers, SCL).

57. For Peabody's observations, see Krehbiel, *Afro-American Folksongs*, 47; and White, *American Negro Folk-Songs*, 250.

58. Logbook of the Ship *Robin Hood*, February 27, 1833, CRCMS.

59. *Charleston Courier*, January 30, 1860.

60. Robert Greenhalgh Albion, the dean of American maritime history, noted that, whereas common dock workers only required the muscle needed for moving and hoisting freight, the stevedores who directed them were responsible for the proper stowage of the cargo and required and possessed "a considerable amount of skill" (*Rise of New York Port*, 223).

61. Murphy and Jeffers, *Nautical Routine;* Stevens, *On the Stowage.* Early stevedores also read Glascock, *Naval Service;* and Glascock, *Naval Officer's Manual.*

62. Murphy and Jeffers, *Nautical Routine,* introduction to part 3. This book was advertised as "Being a complete manual of practical reference for merchants, insurance companies, naval officers, masters of vessels, constructors, navigators, stevedores, sailors, &c. &c. . . . This work treats of every important subject touching the nautical profession . . . also, rules for the stowage and management of every species of merchandise" (*Boston Atlas,* June 25, 1849). Irish stevedore William Doran's large and assorted collection of work tools nearly got him into trouble in September 1857, when he was prosecuted for violating a city ordinance prohibiting secondhand shops. Upon further inspection, it was discovered that "the informer was mistaken as to the nature of his business, he being a stevedore, and his storeroom of tools presented the appearance of a junk shop." See City Council Minutes, September 1, 1857, *Charleston Mercury,* September 3, 1857; and City Council Minutes, September 29, 1857, *Charleston Mercury,* October 1, 1857; Horsey, *Ordinances of the City of Charleston from the 14th September, 1854, to the 1st December, 1859,* 40–41.

63. Stevens cautioned, "Where vegetable oil, especially linseed oil, or tar, is spilt on cotton, afterwards subjected to moisture, spontaneous combustion is almost sure to ensue; it is a saying at New Orleans that there is even sufficient oil in one seed when crushed or broken, to ignite a whole cargo." A minor cotton fire on Liverpool's waterfront on August 13, 1860, was thus blamed on Charleston's stevedores. According to the *New York Herald,* "A bale of cotton, ex *Richard III,* from Charleston, was discovered on fire this morning, in the warehouse, supposed from spontaneous combustion as the bail [*sic*] burnt was soaked with oil. On examining the cotton still undischarged from the *Richard III,* two bails [*sic*] were found; on which sweet oil had apparently been spilt, and several strands of rope which had imbibed sweet oil were discovered loose among the bales, which appeared to have been used by stevedores in Charleston to clean the screws, and thrown carelessly amongst the cargo." See Stevens, *On the Stowage,* 50–51; Hugill, *Shanties and Sailors' Songs,* 50; and *New York Herald,* August 27, 1860.

64. See *The Emancipator* (New York), October 18, 1838. If an employer refused to pay a stevedore's wages, the contractor could appeal to an official body such as the Charleston Chamber of Commerce, City Court, Admiralty Court, or harbor master. See Eckhard, *Digest of Ordinances of the City Council of Charleston From the Year 1783 to Oct. 1844,* 106, 328–36. If enslaved stevedores or other dockworkers were denied wage payments, on the other hand, the bondsmen could turn to their masters for assistance. See Jones, *Experience,* 60.

65. Mitchell also fronted money for the captain's wages, bills for clothing, shipping, tonnage, water, pilotage in and out of the harbor, custom-house clearance, pressing and insuring the cotton, and for the services of the harbor master and British consul (Cash Book, 45–46, Charles T. Mitchell Account Books, CLS).

66. Again, Mitchell also covered the shipowner's costs for the captain's wages, riggers, a ship carpenter, butcher, tonnage, water, freight, cotton pressing, and insurance on the cotton while at the presses (Cash Book, 45–49, Charles T. Mitchell Account Books, CLS).

67. Nordhoff, *Merchant Vessel,* 65.

68. See John Torrent & Sons' advertisement between pages 178 and 179 in Purse, *Charleston City Directory . . . for 1856.* Also see William Doran, George Jefferson & Co., G. B. Stoddard, John Symons, and John Torrent in Charleston Tax Records, CLS; and see William Purvis in Charleston Free Black Capitation Tax Book, 1861, CCPL. Torrent and Symons & Co. owned eight horses in 1858, and John Torrent and John Symons owned six and four horses respectively in 1859. See "List of the Tax Payers of the City of Charleston for 1858"; and "List of the Tax Payers of the City of Charleston for 1859."

69. Cash Book, 68–71, Charles T. Mitchell Account Books, CLS. For another example of a discharging stevedore, see Cash Book, 113–16. In addition to discharging stevedores, Captain Henry P. Burr wrote to his father in Connecticut in 1845, "It is customary to have a discharging officer" in Charleston, who evidently was tasked with ensuring that unloaded goods were delivered to their proper consignees in the city. The man whom Burr employed "made out so badly that I discharged him and as he sent many of the goods to wrong places I have had trouble enough to rectify mistakes" (Henry Burr to Daniel Burr, September 4, 1845, Letters of Captain Henry P. Burr, CRCMS).

70. Cash Book, 1851–66, Charles O. Witte Estate Records, SCHS.

71. See, for example, the Admiralty Court case of Woolf Myer Cohn v. Brig *Berentine,* Admiralty Final Record Books and Minutes of the District Court 3: 193–99, NAA. Also see Benjamin Jarvis to Captain Daniel Deshon, February 16, 1796, Daniel Deshon Letters, SCL; Charleston Chamber of Commerce Award Book, case 82, November 8, 1836, SCHS; Anonymous Charleston Merchant Account Book, January 29, 1850, 100, SCL; MacElwee and Church, "Comprehensive Handbook," 17–19; and Clapp, "Charleston Port Survey," 29. Occasionally, locals merchants had to pay the ship captain for demurrage. See Henry C. Keene Letters, September 5 and 25, 1859, CRCMS.

72. Christopher Fitzsimons to Stephen Girard, February 18, 1810, Christopher Fitzsimons Letterbook, SCL; Henry C. Keene to Magon and Clapp, March 14, 1859, March 29, 1859, Henry C. Keene Letters, CRCMS. Also see Coker, *Charleston's Maritime Heritage,* 68.

73. Journal, 238, Charles T. Mitchell Account Books, CLS. Also see *Columbus Times & Sentinel* (Georgia), qtd. in *Daily Morning News* (Savannah), March 23, 1858. In August 1829 one New York newspaper reported, "On Monday the cargo of the French sloop *Mars,* 70 hhds. [hogsheads] molasses, was discharged by a gang of stevedores in sixty-one minutes. They were paid $50. Two hours were allowed, and in case of failure, they were to forfeit their pay" (unspecified New York newspaper qtd. in *New Hampshire Statesman and Concord Register,* August 29, 1829).

74. "Memorial of the Wharf-holders of Charleston"; Petition, ND #1587, SCDAH. Also see Petitions, 1806 #98, 1806 #99, SCDAH. Several images of Charleston's waterfront during the 1870s depicted workers using handcarts (similar to modern-day dollies) to transport large bales of cotton about the wharves. It is unclear when these carts first were introduced, but there is no evidence that laborers used them on the city's antebellum docks. Meanwhile, images also showed dockworkers still manually rolling cotton bales during the 1870s. See *Harper's Weekly,* January 19, 1878 (see figure 23); and *Frank Leslie's Illustrated Newspaper,* November 16, 1878 (see figures 24 and 25).

75. "Rules for the Government of the Charleston Chamber of Commerce," 14.

76. Invoices Outward, Charleston, 29, Charles T. Mitchell Account Books, CLS.

77. City Council Minutes, November 23, 1858, *Charleston Mercury,* November 29, 1858; Rawick, *American Slave,* Supplement, series 1, vol. 9, part 4, 1587.

78. Schirmer Diary, after April 29, 1840, SCHS. Cooler was listed in the 1830–31 city directory as Archibald Cohler, but appeared as Cooler in both Schirmer's diary and the 1837–38 city directory. See Goldsmith, *Directory and Strangers' Guide* (1831); and Dowling, *Dowling's Charleston Directory . . . for 1837 and 1838.*

79. *Charleston Mercury,* March 27, 1856; Charleston Death Records, CCPL. Also see *Charleston Tri-Weekly Courier,* January 28, 1860.

80. Eckhard, *Digest of Ordinances of the City Council of Charleston From the Year 1783 to Oct. 1844,* 52–53.

81. Schirmer Diary, October 28, 1835; December 29, 1838, SCHS; Charleston Death Records, CCPL. Also see City Council Minutes, March 5, 1847, *Southern Patriot,* March 6, 1847.

82. City Council Minutes, July 21, 1840, *Charleston Mercury,* July 24, 1840. Also see City Council Minutes, April 27, 1840, *Charleston Mercury,* April 30, 1840; Dowling, *Dowling's Charleston Directory . . . for 1837 and 1838;* Fay, *Charleston Directory and Strangers' Guide for 1840 and 1841.*

83. City Council Minutes, April 19, 1842, *Southern Patriot,* April 21, 1842. Also see City Council Minutes, January 23, 1843, *Southern Patriot,* January 25, 1843; City Council Minutes, undated, *Charleston Mercury,* August 16, 1843; City Council Minutes, November 21, 1843, *Southern Patriot,* November 22, 1843; and City Council Minutes, June 10, 1844, *Southern Patriot,* June 12, 1844.

84. City Council Minutes, June 10, 1844, *Southern Patriot,* June 12, 1844; City Council Minutes, December 2, 1845, *Southern Patriot,* December 3, 1845; Walker, *Ordinances of the City of Charleston From the 19th of August 1844, to the 14th of September 1854,* 16. For what appears to be an image of a parbuckle, see Coker, *Charleston's Maritime Heritage,* 37.

85. *Charleston Mercury,* January 26, 1856.

86. Schirmer Diary, January 26, 1847, SCHS.

87. Schirmer Diary, March 20, 1847, SCHS.

88. *Charleston Tri-Weekly Courier,* January 17, 1860; Schirmer Diary, May 7, 1855, SCHS. Schirmer noted over a year later that Wragg "recently returned from the north with an artificial foot in the place of his natural foot which he had crushed on 7 May last year" (Schirmer Diary, May 25, 1856, SCHS). An interview with former slave James Johnson revealed, "One of [Johnson's] feet was mashed off and the other badly damaged by handling bales of cotton several years ago" (Rawick, *American Slave,* vol. 3, part 3, 42).

89. See Hospital Register, April 24, 1842; December 27, 1844; January 2, 1846; December 9, 1853; August 29, 1854; October 26, 1855; November 5, 1855; February 9, 1856, Charleston Alms House Records, CCPL. Also see Robert Pringle to Edward and John Mayne and Edward Burn, December 14, 1742, in Edgar, ed., *Letterbook of Robert Pringle* 2: 461; and Marine School Ship *Lodebar* Log Book, December 29, 1862, SCL.

90. Hibernian Society Minutes, December 2, 1845, 351, SCHS. See Sweeney in the 1856, 1859, and 1860 city directories, and in the 1860 U.S. Census (Purse, *Charleston City*

Directory . . . for 1856; Mears and Turnbull, *Charleston Directory* (1859); Ferslew, *Directory of the City of Charleston . . . 1860);* New England Society Records, box 8, March 31 and April 2, 1852, SCHS. Also see Walsh, *Charleston's Sons on Liberty,* 145.

91. Charleston Death Records, CCPL.

92. *Charleston Courier,* January 2, 1832; Schirmer Diary, September 25, 1834; March 18, 1855; August 13, 1859, SCHS.

93. Neilson, *Life and Adventures of Zamba,* 169–70. Schirmer noted the near drowning of a clerk named Keetz Rennekers in August 1843, and the drowning of an Accommodation Wharf clerk named James L. Yates in December 1851 (Schirmer Diary, August 17, 1843; December 21, 1851, SCHS). Also see *Charleston Courier,* January 1, 1829, qtd. in Rowe, *Pages of History,* 17; *Charleston Courier,* March 19, 1835; *The Globe* (Washington, D.C.), October 31, 1835; *Charleston Mercury,* February 15, 1858; and Schirmer Diary, October 19, 1835; July 13, 1847; February 15, 1858; September 5, 1859, SCHS.

94. *The Hornet, or Republican Advocate* (Maryland), October 3, 1810; Motte, *Charleston Directory and Stranger's Guide for the Year 1816.* Also see Hill, *Jottings,* 116–17.

95. *Charleston Courier,* August 17, 1818, qtd. in Rowe, *Pages of History,* 17. Dr. Thomas Y. Simons advised the Charleston City Council in December 1842 that a bathhouse was essential to the health of the city's residents, but that the threat of sharks rendered it too dangerous to bathe in the salt water of the harbor during the summer months (City Council Minutes, December 28, 1842, *Southern Patriot,* December 29, 1842; *Charleston Mercury,* December 30, 1842).

96. See Schirmer Diary, October 5, 1847; August 1, 1849; May 17, 1851; June 8, 1852; June 8, 1853; June 1, 1856, SCHS. In 1765 visiting Philadelphia merchant Pelatiah Webster commented on the abundance of alligators in the lowcountry's bays and rivers (Harrison, ed., "Journal of a Voyage," 13).

97. Henry Burr to Charlotte Burr, July 24, 1845; Henry Burr to Daniel Burr, June 4, 1847, Letters of Captain Henry P. Burr, CRCMS; Schirmer Diary, June 24, 1845, SCHS.

98. See Schirmer Diary, September 17, 1842; May 31, 1844; after August 1850; after July 31, 1851; June 30, 1854; after July 1854; after June 1858; August 8, 1858; September 11, 1861, SCHS.

99. *Charleston Standard,* August 2, 1854, qtd. in *Daily National Intelligencer* (Washington, D.C.), August 7, 1854. Also see the city's death records for hundreds of antebellum cases of residents dying from sunstroke or "coup de soleil."

100. See Schirmer Diary, July 4, 6, 11, and 12, 1860, SCHS. The July 12 entry reported that "the heat of the weather [was] so intense" that twenty firemen were overcome while fighting a blaze on Moreland's Wharf; *Charleston Mercury,* July 6 and 7, 1860, qtd. in *New York Herald,* July 11, 1860; Myers was perhaps Henry Meyers, who was listed as a drayman in Ferslew, *Directory of the City of Charleston . . . 1860.*

101. Christopher Fitzsimons to Gustavus and Hugh Colhoun, February 18, 1803, Christopher Fitzsimons Letterbook, SCL; John Crawford to Elias Vanderhorst, January 31, 1834, Vanderhorst Wharf Business Papers, folder 10, SCHS.

102. For example, see Schirmer Diary, March 16, 1828; February 2, 1843; January 7, 1847; December 16, 1851; January 20, 1852; January 10, 1856; January 24, 1857, SCHS.

103. Schirmer Diary, January 19, 1851; January 1, 1856, SCHS. As this comment suggested, bad weather such as strong winds and heavy rain sometimes prevented waterfront work. See Logbook of the Schooner *Hopewell,* March 15 and 16, 1844, CRCMS; Journal of the Schooner *Ganges,* December 23, 1844, CRCMS; Abstract Logbook of the Bark *Edward,* October 11 and December 24, 1845, CRCMS; Journal of the Schooner *Nameaug,* June 9, 1856, CRCMS; and Henry C. Keene Letters, March 3 and November 1, 1859, CRCMS. Even New England ship captains occasionally noted the unexpected cold they encountered in Charleston. See, for example, James Carr Papers, SCL; and Henry Burr to Daniel Burr, December 7, 1838, Letters of Captain Henry P. Burr, CRCMS.

104. It was not uncommon for vessels moored at the wharves to be struck by lightning, and persons on board occasionally were killed. A twenty-six-year-old slave named Isaac belonging to former governor and rice mill and wharf owner Thomas Bennett was struck by lightning and killed during the summer of 1847. See Charleston Death Records, CCPL; and Schirmer Diary, August 6, 1841; July 27, 1847; May 2, 1848; June 8, 1853; June 8, 1861, SCHS. Schirmer noted that, after a severe storm on May 2, 1848, "the Ground was covered with Hail, some of them measured nine inches in circumference" (Schirmer Diary, May 2, 1848, SCHS). Also see Schirmer Diary, April 12, 1832; June 5, 1836; June 4, 1840; May 9, 1846; August 4, 1850; May 31, 1855; April 1, 1860, SCHS. For items regarding the danger of ship and cotton fires, see City Council Minutes, January 20, 1847, *Southern Patriot,* January 21, 1847; City Council Minutes, September 20, 1859, *Charleston Mercury,* September 22, 1859; and *Charleston Mercury,* June 16, 1859. Also see *New York Herald,* April 8, 1858. Notwithstanding city ordinances passed in 1844 and 1858 to prevent smoking on or near the wharves, the pipes and cigars of stevedores and others who frequented the waterfront sometimes were blamed for sparking cotton fires. See Eckhard, *Digest of Ordinances of the City Council of Charleston From the Year 1783 to Oct. 1844,* 271–72; Horsey, *Ordinances of the City of Charleston from the 14th September, 1854, to the 1st December, 1859,* 64; Robert N. Gourdin to William Porcher Miles, December 9, 1856, William Porcher Miles Papers, SHC; and *Charleston Tri-Weekly Courier,* May 22, 1860. For examples of steamship boilers bursting, see Pinckney, "Report, 1837–1838," 4–5, 46–47, 49; Petition, ND #3512, SCDAH; Schirmer Diary, August 14, 1830; December 22, 1853; March 30, 1854; May 3, 1858, SCHS. Also see *Charleston Courier,* August 5 and 6, 1823, qtd. in *Independence Chronicle & Boston Patriot,* August 16, 1823. For examples of falling walls near the waterfront, see Schirmer Diary, January 28, 1845; July 12, 1853; March 19, 1859, SCHS; *Charleston Patriot,* January 29, 1845, qtd. in *Boston Daily Atlas,* February 4, 1845; and *Charleston Mercury,* undated, qtd. in *Daily Morning News (Savannah),* March 21, 1859. Also see City Council Minutes, May 11, 1846, *Southern Patriot,* May 12, 1846, in which a special committee reported that a building at the corner of East Bay Street and Boyce's Wharf was "in a decayed state" and was "dangerous to the safety of persons employed in its vicinity, or passing to, or from the wharf," and recommended that the structure therefore be taken down "or so secured as not to endanger the lives of the citizens."

105. Eckhard, *Digest of Ordinances of the City Council of Charleston From the Year 1783 to Oct. 1844,* 57–58; City Council Minutes, May 19, 1857, *Charleston Mercury,* May 21, 1857.

106. An 1840 city ordinance prescribed that "no vessel lying at a wharf, or in a dock, shall be smoked for the purpose of destroying rats," and Captain James Carr expressed his aversion to Charleston's "large winged Cockroach, with many other legged & winged insects as well as offensive to the eye as the ear & feeling, among them the musquitoe [*sic*] will come first in rank." See Eckhard, *Digest of Ordinances of the City Council of Charleston From the Year 1783 to Oct. 1844,* 105; and James Carr Papers, SCL.

107. See Strobel, *Essay on the Subject of the Yellow Fever,* 172. Port Physician Thomas Y. Simons informed the governor in 1824 that vessels from northeastern ports often arrived with rotten cabbage or other vegetables, which commonly were thrown onto the wharves to decompose. In July 1844 the brig *Dante* docked at Commercial Wharves after a long voyage. Upon examination the vessel was found to have a leak, which had damaged nearly its entire cargo of corn and oats. A city ordinance from 1806 called for the removal from the city of "all damaged grain, and all putrid substances, by which the air shall or may be impregnated with foul and noxious effluvia." The city register, Dr. A. G. Howard, concluded that the introduction of this decaying cargo into the city "would prove prejudicial to the public health." He therefore recommended that salvageable portions of the cargo be landed at the wharf, but that the damaged and potentially deleterious grain "be discharged from the vessel into the outer edge of the channel, opposite said wharf; and that the vessel be then cleaned and properly ventilated." See Governors' Message, 1824 #1361, SCDAH; Eckhard, *Digest of Ordinances of the City Council of Charleston From the Year 1783 to Oct. 1844,* 257, 265–66; and City Council Minutes, July 30, 1844, *Southern Patriot,* August 1, 1844.

108. When in Charleston on November 11, 1838, seaman Henry P. Burr wrote about how he "picked a [pig's] head from a pile upon the wharf last evening . . . & got the old Cook to boil it for Dinner" (Henry Burr to Daniel Burr, November 11, 1838, Letters of Captain Henry P. Burr, CRCMS). Also see Grand Jury Presentment, Charleston District, May 1824, SCDAH; and City Council Minutes, August 2, 1859, *Charleston Mercury,* August 5, 1859. For examples of complaints about "nuisances" in waterfront docks, see City Council Minutes, June 25, 1840, *Charleston Mercury,* June 27, 1840; City Council Minutes, July 21, 1840, *Charleston Mercury,* July 24, 1840; and City Council Minutes, August 3, 1840, *Charleston Mercury,* August 5, 1840. For city ordinances and state acts regarding the throwing of various offensive materials into the docks or onto the wharves, see Eckhard, *Digest of Ordinances of the City Council of Charleston From the Year 1783 to Oct. 1844,* 106, 113, 129, 305, 394; and Walker, *Ordinances of the City of Charleston From the 19th of August 1844, to the 14th of September 1854,* 17.

109. Grand Jury Presentment, Charleston District, September 1799, in Governors' Message, 1799 #744, SCDAH.

110. One South Carolina judge ruled in 1848, "When the hiring is general, the hirer may employ the [slave] in any way he chooses, 'consistently with his obligation not to employ him in any dangerous work, such as a prudent man would not employ his own negro in'" (Catterall, ed., *Judicial Cases* 2: 409). For cases in which slaves were employed and killed performing dangerous tasks in violation of the hiring contracts, see Catterall, ed., *Judicial Cases* 2: 443, 457.

111. See advertisement in Goldsmith, *Directory and Strangers' Guide* (1831), 185.

Chapter Two: "This very troublesome business"

1. Charles Town was renamed Charleston when the city was incorporated in 1783.

2. Harrison, ed., "Journal of a Voyage," 5; Hessian officer qtd. in Carp, *Rebels Rising*, 164; *The Liberator* (Boston), April 18, 1835; G. T. Fox Journal, November 5, 1834, Pease Papers, ARC; Mackay, *Western World* 2: 183; Tower, *Slavery Unmasked*, 136–37. Others were appalled as well. "It is horrid to see such swarm [*sic*] of negroes as are seen in the streets of Charleston," wrote John Perrier to Boston merchant Thomas Lamb in 1833. Perrier elucidated, "they are nearly all slaves; and I never like to see such beings; besides that, a negroe [*sic*] in the worst state of poverty is a disgusting animal; and thousands of that sort are to be seen here" (Perrier to Thomas Lamb, April 1, 1833, Thomas Lamb Papers, MHS). Also see Jackson Diary, October 19, 1832, SHC.

3. Jackson, *Experience of a Slave*, 25; Blassingame, ed., *Slave Testimony*, 373. A visitor to Charleston in November 1841 observed that a slave stevedore "pays his master a dollar a day & earns from three to five $ per day." By the 1840s the term "stevedore" came to mean a highly skilled stower of cotton rather than a common dockworker, which explains why this slave would have earned such a high daily wage (N. M. Perkins to George W. Anderson, November 25, 1841, author's copy of privately owned letter).

4. Catterall, ed., *Judicial Cases* 2: 369.

5. On the other hand, Charleston factor Charles Kershaw informed widow and planter Charlotte Anne Allston that he had spoken to a Mr. Black about hiring Allston's slave James in the city, but that Black insisted that Allston provide James with clothing and shoes and also pay all doctors' accounts (Charles Kershaw to Charlotte Anne Allston, February 8, 1819, Allston Factors' Letters, SCHS).

6. "Memorial of the Wharf-holders of Charleston"; Petition, ND #1587, SCDAH. Also see Petitions, 1806 #98, 1806 #99, SCDAH.

7. Thomas Pinckney specifically argued that the hire of free white domestic workers would be more economical than owning slaves ("Reflections," 18–19).

8. Catterall, ed., *Judicial Cases* 2: 374.

9. *Southern Patriot*, May 1, 1835; July 23, 1846. *Charleston Courier*, August 21, 1841; also see September 1, 1841.

10. *Southern Patriot*, December 6, 1841.

11. Thomas Bennett Lucas informed his fellow owners of the Cannonsboro Wharf and Mill Company in August 1852 that, though the corporation had purchased slave workers in February, there had yet to be a reduction in disbursements for slave hire. Lucas explained that as many as twenty of the wharf and mill slaves had been contracted for an entire year, and that their masters insisted that the company continue to employ the hired bondsmen—and pay the masters their wages—until the agreements expired in November and December ("Report to the Owners of Cannonsborough Property," August 1852, James B. Campbell Business Papers, folder 11/102D/7, SCHS). Shipbuilding wharves and firms also utilized a combination of owned and hired labor. In May 1833, shipwrights James Marsh and James Poyas corresponded with Jesse D. Elliott of the U.S. Navy regarding the construction of a naval yard in Charleston. Marsh and

Poyas informed Elliott that there were eight master shipwrights or shipbuilding firms in the city, and that each owned between seven and nineteen slave ship carpenters. Marsh and Poyas reported, "These eight master carpenters own, in the aggregate, one hundred slave carpenters." In addition, "There are about seventy-five transient negroes that work out by the day in the ship carpenter yard, when business will admit of their being employed." Slave mechanics, such as house carpenters and joiners, also could be hired from their masters by the month, and common laborers could be hired by the day or by the month (U.S. Congress, 1st Session, 1833–34, House Report, no. 541, May 13, 1833, 19, Pease Papers, ARC).

    12. Vanderhorst Wharf Business Papers, folders 1–2, 17, SCHS.

    13. In a six-year rental agreement from January 1, 1827, through January 1, 1833, John Crawford agreed "to hire of said [Elias] Vanderhorst during s[ai]d. period of yrs. his two negro men, Will & Dublin and pay the yearly wages of one hundred dollars for each." The agreement for the year 1833 read, "And the said Crawford has also hired of said Vanderhorst, Two negro men, attached to the wharf (Will & Dublin) at yearly wages of fifty dollars each; the said Crawford finding said negroes in suitable clothes during said term of time" (Vanderhorst Wharf Business Papers, folders 2–3, 5–13, SCHS).

    14. Vanderhorst Wharf Business Papers, folders 11, 4; also see folders 5, 9, SCHS.

    15. Vanderhorst Wharf Business Papers, folder 3, SCHS.

    16. Vanderhorst Wharf Business Papers, folders 3, 6–13, SCHS.

    17. The City Council officially changed the terms "intendant" and "warden" to "mayor" and "alderman" on December 21, 1836. See Eckhard, *Digest of Ordinances of the City Council of Charleston From the Year 1783 to Oct. 1844,* 348.

    18. Vanderhorst Wharf Business Papers, folders 2–3, SCHS; South Carolina Will Transcripts 32: 925, SCHS; Vanderhorst Family Biographical and Genealogical Research Files, SCHS; Vanderhorst Family History and Genealogy Research Files, SCHS; Lapham, "'Vanderhorst Row,'" 59–61.

    19. Vanderhorst Wharf Business Papers, folders 4, 9, SCHS.

    20. Vanderhorst Wharf Business Papers, folders 3–14, SCHS. The Vanderhorsts purchased "Negro Clothing" from clothiers such as Matthiessen & O'Hara, which was located at 143 East Bay Street and specifically advertised clothing suitable to wharf hands. See July 12–November 5, 1856 account, Business and Household Receipts, folder 12/209/5, Vanderhorst Family Documents Series, SCHS; and *Charleston Mercury,* November 1 and 14, 1856; June 1, 1858; and October 27, 1859. In July 1862 a wharf hand named Nero owned by commission merchant John Burckmyer received twenty paddles and was subjected to three days of solitary confinement for "Taking the Coat of Pompy [belonging] to C. T. Lowndes during his Working Time on Atlantic Wharf." See Charleston Police Records, July 8, 1862, CLS; Gazlay, *Charleston City Directory . . . for 1855;* 1860 U.S. Census; and 1860 U.S. Census Slave Schedules.

    21. Vanderhorst Wharf Business Papers, folders 3, 6–7, SCHS.

    22. Vanderhorst Wharf Business Papers, folders 6, 11, 10, SCHS.

    23. Vanderhorst Wharf Business Papers, folders 6–7, 9–11, SCHS.

    24. Vanderhorst Wharf Business Papers, folder 11, SCHS. For examples of the family's pretensions to paternalism, see the following entries in the diary of Elias Vanderhorst's

wife: Ann Elliott Morris Vanderhorst Diary, July 12 and November 16, 1859; February 10, 1860; undated final entry in 1862, Ann Elliott Morris Vanderhorst Papers, SCHS. Also see the wills of Arnoldus and Elias Vanderhorst, South Carolina Will Transcripts 32: 924–36, SCHS; and Elias Vanderhorst Papers, SCHS.

25. Vanderhorst Wharf Business Papers, folders 11, 13, SCHS.

26. Charleston Death Records, CCPL; Vanderhorst Wharf Business Papers, folders 13–14, 12, SCHS. Also see correspondence between Charleston wharf owner Seth Lothrop and business associate Sylvanus Keith on September 18, 1804, and June 23, 1807, and the wharf account entitled "Mr. Sylvanus Keith in account Current with Lothrop's Wharf," Sylvanus Keith Papers, RL.

27. Slaves also manned the company's workshops in Charleston and maintained the rail line throughout the state.

28. Tupper added, "It is also important to have the eye of an owner to look to the treatment as well as the conduct of the slaves. If the Company owned them, the overseers might be cruel to them without redress; and it could not be expected they would attend much to their habits. But it is different where there is a master to appeal to, or to inquire after them, who feels nearly the same for them, [as] he does for his children, besides the protection of their value, which is a great stimulant to see they are not abused" (South Carolina Railroad Co. Semi-Annual Report, July 1840, 10–11, Pease Papers, ARC).

29. Gadsden argued that investing in slave laborers simultaneously would increase the value of the company's stock (James Gadsden to James Edward Calhoun, July 25, 1842, James Gadsden Papers, SCL).

30. A committee of stockholders supported Gadsden's recommendation to purchase slave laborers for the railroad in November 1840, but the matter was referred to another committee and was not approved ("Proceedings of the Stockholders," 13, 15, Pease Papers, ARC). Gadsden also noted that in 1846 the South Carolina Railroad suspended the purchase of slave laborers altogether (James Gadsden to James Edward Calhoun, August 20, [1846], James Gadsden Papers, SCL). The antebellum debate over whether to stretch rail lines to Charleston's waterfront was merely a component of a broader battle commencing in the early to mid-eighteenth century between the city's economic progressives advocating commercial development and diversification, and conservatives prioritizing defense and security. See Zierden and Reitz, "Excavations on Charleston's Waterfront," 13, 20–21.

31. Companies owning only male slaves could not benefit from natural reproduction, of course, since the progeny of female slaves became the property of female slaves' masters; At a meeting in October 1851, "The President was requested to investigate the subject of Labor in Charleston Cotton Yard: and apply such remedy, and make such Contracts, as in his opinion would best promote the Company Interest" (South Carolina Railroad Minute Book, September 20, 1850, 4; October 28, 1851, 33; November 20, 1850, 9, SCHS).

32. At the meeting on April 20, 1852, "The Double Track Committee were [*sic*] requested to attend the Sale of Negroes at Aiken on the 27th inst. and to exercise their discretion in purchasing." And at the meeting on May 20, 1852, "The purchase of 54

Negroes by the Committee on 'the Double Track' at the Sale at Aiken 27th ulto. was confirmed." The price paid for these slaves was not revealed, but a slave was purchased from J. C. Sproull in 1852 for $922.50. See South Carolina Railroad Minute Book, April 20, 1852, 42; May 20, 1852, 43; November 20, 1858, 215, SCHS. Also see Joyce, "Charleston Landscape," 176.

33. Rutledge and Young Miscellaneous Business Papers, SCHS. Records showed that Railroad Accommodation Wharf indeed paid taxes for ten slaves in 1861, 1862, and 1863, and for seven slaves in 1864 (Charleston Tax Records, CLS).

34. See Johnson, *Soul by Soul,* 1–44.

35. *Charleston Mercury,* November 10, 1837. The owners of shipbuilding wharves also sold their attached slave carpenters along with the other wharf property. When Robert Eason retired in 1835, for example, he advertised the sale of his wharf, ship yard, and ten slave mechanics, ship carpenters, and caulkers. The ad stated, "The wharf and Negroes to be sold together or separately." And a sale of the estate of shipwright John F. Knox in 1839 included a wharf (probably Knox's Wharf) and thirteen slave ship carpenters, "among whom are several prime Hands." See *Charleston Courier,* March 13, 1835; and *Charleston Mercury,* February 6, 1839.

36. Schirmer Diary, after July 1853, SCHS. Also see James B. Campbell Business Papers, folder 11/102D/7, SCHS.

37. Schirmer Diary, March 6 and 13, 1860, SCHS. Charleston's tax records revealed that West Point Mills owned ninety slaves in 1862, 1863, and 1864 (Charleston Tax Records, CLS). Also see the petition for the incorporation of West Point Mill Company (Petition, 1860 #106, SCDAH).

38. Henry, Elias, and Daniel Horlbeck to C. M. Furman, J. B. Campbell, and T. B. Lucas, February 14, 1859, James B. Campbell Business Papers, folder 11/102D/7, SCHS. The parties proceeded to debate the fate of Blum's share of the company's slaves, with the widow's agents urging immediate sale to ensure a substantial profit while slave prices remained high, and the mill arguing that these enslaved hands were absolutely vital to the operation of the firm and could not be spared until the end of the year. See Henry, Elias, and Daniel Horlbeck to J. B. Campbell, February 21, 1859, and J. B. Campbell to Henry, Elias, and Daniel Horlbeck, March 19, 1859, James B. Campbell Business Papers, folder 11/102D/7, SCHS. When Thomas Bennett Lucas and the other proprietors of Cannonsboro Mill and Wharf Company petitioned the state legislature for incorporation in 1857, they claimed ownership of fifty-four slaves to operate the rice and saw mills and work on the company's Ashley River wharves and storehouses. In 1858 the Cannonsboro Mills Company paid city taxes for forty-nine slaves, and in 1859 the Cannonsboro Wharf and Mill Company paid $150 in city taxes for fifty slaves. See Petition, 1857 #76, SCDAH; "List of the Tax Payers of the City of Charleston for 1858"; "List of the Tax Payers of the City of Charleston for 1859"; and Tuten, *Lowcountry Time and Tide,* 20–21, 96.

39. James B. Campbell Legal Case Papers, folder 11/102/8, SCHS; "List of the Tax Payers of the City of Charleston for 1858." The "List of the Tax Payers of the City of Charleston for 1859" recorded Otis Mills & Co. as owning seventeen slaves, and Mills, Beach & Co. as owning fifteen slaves. Also see Charleston Tax Records, CLS.

40. City death records offered further evidence about slaves owned by and attached to wharf and mercantile companies. Two of Hamilton & Co.'s enslaved wharf hands, for example, died in the early 1840s. Between 1850 and 1860, Boyce and Co.'s Wharves lost three of its slave laborers. Three slaves owned by Mills, Beach, & Co. and Otis Mills & Co.—including a sixty-five-year-old drayman named Primus—died in the five years before the Civil War. And in February 1857, a fifty-year-old slave owned by Savannah Wharf accidentally drowned. See Charleston Death Records, CCPL. Also see Charleston Tax Records, CLS; "List of the Tax Payers of the City of Charleston for 1858"; "List of the Tax Payers of the City of Charleston for 1859"; Kennedy and Parker, *Official Report*, 103–4, 108, 148–49; Starobin, ed., *Denmark Vesey*, 51; and Pearson, ed., *Designs against Charleston*, 196, 235, 273, 290–92, 297–309.

41. South Carolina Will Transcripts 32: 924–36, SCDAH.

42. South Carolina Will Transcripts 33: 1297–1301, SCDAH. William Pritchard Jr., a shipwright, also mentioned the use and income of his slave ship carpenters. In fact, it was common for white shipwrights to own wharves in or near the city and to include in their wills enslaved ship carpenters who were attached to their shipbuilding wharves. For example, in 1791 Paul Pritchard left his sons (William and Paul) thirteen slave ship carpenters and caulkers. And in 1852, James Marsh Sr. devised to his son "six Negro Carpenters and Caulkers." See South Carolina Will Transcripts 24: 963–66; 46: 219–23, SCDAH. When merchant and wharf owner Florian Charles Mey drafted his will in 1819, he specified that his "Wharf Servant" George be paid $50 within one year of Mey's death (South Carolina Will Transcripts 38: 538–40, SCDAH).

43. South Carolina Will Transcripts 40: 475–78, SCDAH.

44. South Carolina Will Transcripts 48: 338–50, SCDAH. In 1824 William Clarkson left his second son Kunhardt's Wharf along with the "Negroes Debts &c due to the Said Wharf" (South Carolina Will Transcripts 36: 1181–86, SCDAH). Also, in 1839 lumber merchant and wharf owner Robert Little bequeathed to his clerk, Robert Brodie, all of the lumber upon his wharf and in his waterfront stores at the time of his death, as well as his counting-house desk and other personal property on the wharf or in the stores, "Except my Slaves, my Books & Valuable papers" (South Carolina Will Transcripts 43: 565–79, SCDAH). And in 1840 William Smith Jr. instructed that "my Mansion house and Wharf property Should not be sold until the final division of my estates and I order and direct that my Executors and Trustees shall retain the Same with a sufficient Number of Negroes to manage the Wharf until the period of final distribution, unless some advantageous offer should be made for a sale" (South Carolina Will Transcripts 43: 490–97, SCDAH).

45. The 1850 U.S. Census Slave Schedules showed that, of the eighteen slaves, eleven were male and seven were female; "List of the Tax Payers of the City of Charleston for 1858," 3.

46. See wills of William Pritchard Jr., Florian Charles Mey, Arnoldus Vanderhorst (1748–1815), and William Clarkson (Kunhardt's Wharf), South Carolina Will Transcripts 33: 1297–1301; 38: 538–40; 32: 924–36; 36: 1181–86, SCDAH.

47. Smith, *Charlestonian's Recollections*, 5, 9–11.

48. This exchange was necessary since the Vanderhorsts required John Crawford to lease the family's two longtime dockhands, Will and Dublin, for $100 apiece per year along with the rental of the wharf. John Crawford received $11.50 from Elias Vanderhorst in April 1834 for "1 Month & 25 [days] of Dublin taking care of y[ou]r. House at $75 pr. Annum" (Vanderhorst Wharf Business Papers, folder 10, SCHS). Thomas H. Jones, a former slave stevedore from Wilmington, North Carolina, recalled that, despite his experience and aptitude for urban waterfront labor and the fact that he was among only a few of his master's slaves who "were kept at Wilmington," every spring he accompanied his master to his rural plantation, where he "acted as general waiter for the family." Jones was not put to work in the fields, but rather was assigned a task comparable in skill level to his work in the city (*Experience*, 49). Robert Smalls similarly explained in 1863, "I have never lived on a plantation except when I waited upon private families and they moved out for a few months in the Winter season" (Blassingame, ed., *Slave Testimony*, 373).

49. This is similar to how most skilled slaves on plantations, such as slave carpenters or boat hands, were separated from field hands and rarely if ever were employed in the fields. See Catterall, ed., *Judicial Cases* 2: 416, 431–32. Claudia Dale Goldin introduced the concept of "elasticity of demand" for urban slaves, meaning that slaveowners collectively increased or decreased the aggregate number of urban bondsmen as slave values fluctuated. According to Goldin, masters sold urban slaves to the countryside when slave prices rose during the 1830s and 1850s. Though Goldin's claims are applicable to temporarily hired or leased common waterfront workers in Charleston, the model is less useful when considering those skilled slaves designated as essentially permanent wharf hands (*Urban Slavery*).

50. Lambert, *Travels through Canada, and the United States* 2: 163–64; G. T. Fox Journal, November 5, 1834, Pease Papers, ARC.

51. Waring's estate received $34.34 for four months' hire of Frederick on August 3, 1841, and $13.33 for one month and ten days' hire on October 7, 1841. Married to Francis Malbone Waring until his death in 1839, Lydia also owned sixteen plantation slaves (Lydia Jane Waring Estate Book, 2–11, 19, 21, SCHS).

52. Juliet Georgiana Elliott Account Book, CLS. Also see Account Books of Benjamin Perry's Wards, SCHS.

53. Vanderhorst Wharf Business Papers, folder 13, SCHS.

54. Frederick William Davie Account Books, RL.

55. Cash Book, February 17, 1859, Legare, Colcock, and Company Records, SCHS. J. S. Lewis received the payment from the wharf on Mrs. Colcock's behalf.

56. Cash Book, July 31, 1856; January 1, 1857; July 29, 1857, Legare, Colcock, and Company Records, SCHS. These cash books furthermore showed that Mrs. J. J. Butler received $24 in July 1858 from a commission merchant named Salas for the hire of Ben for two months. Daniel Heyward also was paid $140 in August 1859 and $98 in September 1860 by W. C. Bee & Co. for the wages of George. William C. Bee was a factor on Vanderhorst's Wharf in 1855. See Cash Book, July 10, 1858; August 5, 1859, Legare, Colcock, and Company Records, SCHS; and Gazlay, *Charleston City Directory . . . for 1855*.

57. Cuffy was valued at £70, but Norton asked for more since the slave had provided such a substantial portion of her income. Norton received $122.44 from the legislature (Petitions, 1800 #189, 1801 #126, SCDAH; Committee Report, 1800 #143, SCDAH).

58. Charleston's intendant James Hamilton attached a note to Smith's petition attesting that "her situation is one peculiarly hard and well entitled to the compassionate consideration of the Legislature" (Petition, 1822 #128, SCDAH). Also see Kennedy and Parker, *Official Report*, 145–46, 160–61, 164; "Confession of Bacchus, the Slave of Mr. Hammet," in Starobin, ed., *Denmark Vesey*, 63; and Pearson, ed., *Designs against Charleston*, 256, 292–93. The legislature received a similar petition from wharf owner John C. Faber's widow, Catherine L. Faber, whose slave Polydor (a rope maker, sawyer, and "useful in all laboring branches") was executed for his supposed involvement in the Vesey conspiracy. See Petitions, 1822 #125, 1810 #181, 1810 #182, SCDAH; Negrin, *Negrin's Directory for the Year 1806*; Negrin, *Negrin's Directory for the Year 1807*; and Kennedy and Parker, *Official Report*, 127, 170–71. Other Charlestonians too lost income due to the death or impairment of a hired-out waterfront slave. Joseph Martin was indicted in the Court of General Sessions in 1829 for the cruel punishment of a slave with intent to kill after he was seen one evening on Fitzsimons's Wharf "pelting Archy, the slave of Miss Susan Evans, with stones, one of which hit the slave in the head and injured him badly thus harming Evans." And Mrs. Mary E. Boyden's slave drayman Jacob was killed when the brick wall of a warehouse on Magwood's South Wharf fell on him during a fire. See Court of General Sessions, Indictments, 1829-10A, SCDAH; Schirmer Diary, January 28, 1845, SCHS; *Boston Daily Atlas*, February 4, 1845; and Charleston Death Records, CCPL.

59. Pinckney, "Reflections," 13–14; Franklin and Schweninger, *Runaway Slaves*, 305–6. A petition from the early 1840s reiterated masters' consternation with the noxious "influence upon the docility and usefulness of our slaves" stemming from the mixture of local bondsmen with those in the port. See Petition, ND #2824, qtd. in Franklin and Schweninger, *Runaway Slaves*, 269, 272; Laurens qtd. in Carp, *Rebels Rising*, 165–66. Also see Chaplin, *Anxious Pursuit*, 125; and Young, "Ideology and Death," 678–79.

60. Charles Kershaw to Charlotte Anne Allston, February 8, 1819, Allston Factors' Letters, SCHS. Slaveowners, especially those residing on rural plantations, often entrusted their Charleston factors to collect and distribute the wages of their urban dock slaves. See, for example, John Schulz Account Books, SCL; and Legare, Colcock, and Company Records, SCHS. Sometimes other middlemen were used. Lewis W. Uttermahl, a "Collector of Accounts, and General Agent," announced in the 1835–36 city directory that he "Respectfully tenders his services in the above line of Business,— He will hire and collect Negro hire." John V. Holmes likewise advertised in the 1856 city directory as a "Collector of Accounts, House Rents, Servants' Hire, &c." Absentee masters also engaged men like Uttermahl and Holmes to identify and contract work for hired-out slaves. See Smith, *Charleston Directory and Register for 1835–6*, vi; and Purse, *Charleston City Directory . . . for 1856*, 80–81.

61. For a comprehensive discussion of the slave badge system in Charleston, see Greene et al., *Slave Badges*.

62. McCord, *Statutes* 7: 343, 363, 380, 408–9; Greene et al., *Slave Badges*, 15–16.

63. Greene et al., *Slave Badges*, 17–18.

64. Eckhard, *Digest of Ordinances of the City Council of Charleston From the Year 1783 to Oct. 1844*, 398; Greene et al., *Slave Badges*, 18.

65. Olwell, *Masters, Slaves, and Subjects*, 164. In November 1763 the *South Carolina Gazette* included "the want of a proper regulation of Negro Porters . . . (among many) Grievances, which the inhabitants of this town daily and loudly complain of" (November 5, 1763). According to historian Walter Fraser, "Venturesome black apprentice chimney sweeps, slave porters, and black common laborers sought to manipulate the local economy by combining to fix the pay for their services during the 1760s." Richard Walsh reported, "The tailors combined in 1760, and the Grand Jury complained that Negro apprentice chimney sweeps had joined together to raise their wages." Both Fraser and Walsh maintained that these were among the first unionizing and wage fixing efforts in American history, but neither scholar uncovered additional evidence or information (Fraser, *Charleston! Charleston!*, 105; Walsh, "Charleston Mechanics," 134).

66. Eckhard, *Digest of Ordinances of the City Council of Charleston From the Year 1783 to Oct. 1844*, 398; Greene et al., *Slave Badges*, 18–19.

67. Col. Othniel Beale's house was on the west side of East Bay Street, at the current location of Rainbow Row and nearly directly opposite North Adger's Wharf. The Watch House in 1764 was atop the Half Moon Battery on the site of the Old Exchange building at the intersection of East Bay and Broad streets.

68. Greene et al., *Slave Badges*, 18–19; Fraser, *Charleston! Charleston!*, 105.

69. Eckhard, *Digest of Ordinances of the City Council of Charleston From the Year 1783 to Oct. 1844*, 394–96; *South Carolina Gazette*, February 7, 1751, qtd. in Olwell, *Masters, Slaves, and Subjects*, 164.

70. See, for instance, Novak, *People's Welfare*; Hurst, *Law and the Conditions of Freedom*; Hurst, *Law and Markets*; and Friedman, *History of American Law*.

71. Writing about mid-to-late eighteenth-century Charleston, Robert Olwell argued, "This ongoing discrepancy between statute and custom suggests that the constant repetition of prohibitions by the legislature may actually have placated white resentment and allowed masters to accept the intrusion of the market into their everyday relations with their slaves. In this way, the law may have served as an ideological 'citadel,' a secure retreat, within which masters' absolute authority could be kept safe, while in practice and in the marketplace master-slave interactions were conducted on a very different and far more negotiated basis" (*Masters, Slaves, and Subjects*, 169–70). Also see Penningroth, *Claims of Kinfolk*.

72. A 1789 ordinance temporarily abolished the municipal badge system established by the 1783 ordinance and amended by a 1786 law. The slave badge system was revived in 1800, and once again slaves working out were required to visibly wear a badge. Ordinances passed in 1806 and 1843 consolidated existing badge laws. See Greene et al., *Slave Badges*, 22–30; and Eckhard, *Digest of Ordinances of the City Council of Charleston From the Year 1783 to Oct. 1844*, 21–23, 169–74.

73. For information regarding badge prices, see Greene et al., *Slave Badges*, 22, 29, 34, 48–50, 64–65.

74. Vanderhorst Wharf Business Papers, folders 6–11, SCHS; Juliet Georgiana Elliott Account Book, CLS; Frederick William Davie Account Books, RL. Lydia Jane Ball Waring's executors paid the Charleston City Treasurer $22 in January 1842 for seven slave badges (Lydia Jane Waring Estate Book, January 31, 1842, 24, SCHS).

75. Grimes, "Between the Tracks," 13.

76. Greene et al., *Slave Badges*, 82.

77. Greene et al., *Slave Badges*, 79–80, 128, 3, 80. Greene also referred to Bennett seeing an 1843 porter badge numbered 1,375. One of these reports may have been in error. See Greene et al., *Slave Badges*, 80.

78. U.S. Census records showed that 19,532 slaves resided in Charleston in 1850, and therefore roughly 23 percent (or 4,480 of 19,532) of the city's slaves engaged in hired-out occupations that required a badge, and approximately 7 percent (or 1,400 of 19,532) of the city's slaves worked out as porters; Greene estimated that only 4,135 of the 4,480 badges were sold (*Slave Badges*, 126–28).

79. Greene et al., *Slave Badges*, 136.

80. Eckhard, *Digest of Ordinances of the City Council of Charleston From the Year 1783 to Oct. 1844*, 32, 41–42, 394–96; Greene et al., *Slave Badges*, 127. Greene also reported that 700 dray and 400 cart tags were ordered in 1851 (*Slave Badges*, 136).

81. For cotton export statistics, see Dawson and DeSaussure, *Census of the City of Charleston . . . 1848*, 90–101; Van Deusen, *Economic Bases*, 333, appendix C; and Collins, "Charleston and the Railroads," 100, table 5.

82. South Carolina Railroad Stockholders Meeting Report, in Miscellaneous Communication, ND #169, SCDAH. The report noted that these figures were "exclusive of contract carts" and other vehicles, such as omnibuses.

83. *Charleston Times*, November 11, 1803.

84. *Charleston Times*, November 11, 1803.

85. *Charleston Times*, November 11, 1803.

86. See Coker, *Charleston's Maritime Heritage*, 171–76; Rogers, *Charleston*, 3–4, 11; Eaton, *History of the Old South*, 405; Letters of an American Traveler, 85, SCHS; Russell, *North America*, 162–63; and Thornbury, *Criss-Cross Journeys* 1: 278–79.

87. *Charleston Times*, November 11, 1803.

88. This provision was included within an ordinance passed in July 1807 defining the duties of city marshals (Eckhard, *Digest of Ordinances of the City Council of Charleston From the Year 1783 to Oct. 1844*, 158).

89. *Charleston Times*, November 11, 1803. The ordinance gave the owners or employers of offending slaves the option to pay $2 for the remission of the corporal punishment.

90. Eckhard, *Digest of Ordinances of the City Council of Charleston From the Year 1783 to Oct. 1844*, 172.

91. Unengaged porters and day laborers refusing an employer who offered the established wages now were to receive between twelve and twenty stripes on the bare back either at the workhouse or at the public market. The offending slave's owner still could pay $2 in lieu of this punishment, and a free offender could pay $5 to avert the whipping. Meanwhile, slaves receiving other than the fixed wages now also were subject to

between twelve and twenty lashes on the bare back. Free workers were fined at least $5 and confined in the workhouse until the sum was paid (Eckhard, *Digest of Ordinances of the City Council of Charleston From the Year 1783 to Oct. 1844*, 173).

92. Eckhard, *Digest of Ordinances of the City Council of Charleston From the Year 1783 to Oct. 1844*, 172.

93. Eckhard, *Digest of Ordinances of the City Council of Charleston From the Year 1783 to Oct. 1844*, 32–33, 158.

94. An 1801 city ordinance prohibited labor on the Sabbath and subjected those who employed slaves on Sundays to a twenty-dollar fine (Eckhard, *Digest of Ordinances of the City Council of Charleston From the Year 1783 to Oct. 1844*, 395, 32, 272–73). Liverpudlian G. T. Fox remarked in 1834, "The Negroes in the City . . . never work after dark, & Sunday is their own day" (G. T. Fox Journal, November 5, 1834, Pease Papers, ARC). Also see Olwell, *Masters, Slaves, and Subjects*, 166.

95. Charleston Chamber of Commerce Award Book, case 75, November 3, 1835, SCHS. See Smith, *Mastered by the Clock*.

96. The categories of goods for cartage included firewood, lumber, bricks, shingles, slate, tiles, dye wood or coal, and grain, lime, salt, or bush. The ordinance added, "That for every full cart or dray load of produce, or goods, wares, merchandise and commodities whatsoever, not heretofore particularly enumerated, to or from any place as above specified (not described in the above rates) a sum shall be paid proportionably to the rates for carting of lumber as mentioned in this ordinance." As for those relatively few dray loads not transported either to or from the waterfront, the measure similarly directed that workers conveying goods "to and from any other place not above mentioned" be compensated "in proportion with the above rates and distances." See Eckhard, *Digest of Ordinances of the City Council of Charleston From the Year 1783 to Oct. 1844*, 33–37; Hrabowski, *Directory for the District of Charleston* (1809), 123–28; Schenck and Turner, *Directory . . . for the City of Charleston . . . 1819*, 42–44; Schenck, *Directory . . . for the City of Charleston* (1822), 29–30; and Smith, *Charleston Directory and Register for 1835–6*, 128–29.

97. White or free black offenders were fined $5. If a guilty slave or his owner or employer refused to pay this fine, the slave faced corporal punishment (Eckhard, *Digest of Ordinances of the City Council of Charleston From the Year 1783 to Oct. 1844*, 37).

98. *Charleston Times*, November 11, 1803; Eckhard, *Digest of Ordinances of the City Council of Charleston From the Year 1783 to Oct. 1844*, 37.

99. Charleston's city directories between 1790 and 1860 included numerous livery stables and wagon yards, cart keepers, dray keepers and masters, proprietors and superintendents of drays, and at least two local delivery companies, Adams Express and T. & M. Geraghty City Express. An advertisement in the 1860 directory announced, "Geraghty's City Express, For the Conveyance of Packages and Baggage, To and from Rail Roads, Steamboats and all parts of the City, at Low Rates, and with Dispatch" (Ferslew, *Directory of the City of Charleston . . . 1860*). Also see an undated petition from approximately 120 companies and individuals with financial interests in "Drays, Carts, and other Vehicles which ply for hire in the City of Charleston and upon Charleston Neck," Petition, ND #4106, SCDAH; William Henry Vernon to John W. Mitchell, July

9, 1849, John Wroughton Mitchell Papers, SHC; and Cash Book, June 30, 1857, and April 2, 1859, Legare, Colcock, and Company Records, SCHS.

100. Ford, "Republics and Democracy," 124–27.

101. Charleston City Council, *Ordinances of the City of Charleston, 1833–1837*, 148.

102. Eckhard, *Digest of Ordinances of the City Council of Charleston From the Year 1783 to Oct. 1844*, 177. An hourly laborer therefore would have had to work on the docks for eight hours to earn the $1 given for a full day. Hourly workers were not paid for any meal time. But it is unclear whether those hired for a full day's labor but who worked for longer than eight hours between sunrise and twilight (especially during the summer) were compensated for overtime.

103. Eckhard, *Digest of Ordinances of the City Council of Charleston From the Year 1783 to Oct. 1844*, 39–40. Also see Dowling, *Dowling's Charleston Directory . . . for 1837 and 1838*, 19.

104. See City Council Minutes, November 4, 1839, *Charleston Courier*, November 6, 1839; and City Council Minutes, December 10, 1839, *Charleston Courier*, December 12, 1839; Charleston Police Records, January 10, 1862, CLS.

105. Thomas Napier to J. P. Deveaux, April 24, 1857, Thomas Napier Papers, SCL.

106. Eckhard, *Digest of Ordinances of the City Council of Charleston From the Year 1783 to Oct. 1844*, 40. According to the 1837 city ordinance, only those porters and day laborers who were hired for a full day's work were permitted an hour for breakfast and an hour for dinner. Hourly workers were compensated solely for the time they toiled. Being late April, there were about twelve hours of daylight between sunrise and twilight. Therefore, even after subtracting the two hours allowed for meals, it would have been much more economical for Napier to have hired these two day laborers for a full day's work at $1 per day. Instead, he paid them approximately $1.63 each for one day's labor.

107. Napier asked Deveaux if he would "oblige me by settling with the said men for the amount that you think right and I will refund you the money as soon as I hear from you the amount." He also recommended that "The Mate of the Schooner might inform [the draymen] when the Boxes would be out of the Vessel so that they need not be detained waiting for them at the wharf." This may explain in part why the three workers took nine hours to deliver the first four boxes. But it also shows that Napier was privy to workers' penchant for being paid during down time and for slowing the pace of the workday. Finally, Napier instructed Deveaux to send the additional boxes to the house "in the manner above mentioned" (Thomas Napier to J. P. Deveaux, April 27, 1857, Thomas Napier Papers, SCL).

108. Vanderhorst Wharf Business Papers, folders 2–3, SCHS.

109. John Crawford to Elias Vanderhorst, January 6, 1833; April 2, 1833, Vanderhorst Wharf Business Papers, folder 10, SCHS. Also see account from July 25 to October 15, 1825, folder 7.

110. For evidence of theft and running away among the Vanderhorsts' wharf hands, see Vanderhorst Wharf Business Papers, folders 3, 6, SCHS.

111. Vanderhorst Wharf Business Papers, folders 5–10, SCHS.

112. Elias Vanderhorst's wife, Ann, lamented in her diary the news in February 1860 that two of the family's schooner hands, Anthony and Scipio, were sick with typhoid

pneumonia. Characterizing these slaves as "careless negroes destitute of forethought" for selling their belongings, Mrs. Vanderhorst detailed Anthony's death before commenting that "Scipio is well now, but does not deserve it, for Mr. V always provides his Schooner hands with double clothing, but it is in vain & illness is the consequence of the miserable want to covering" (Ann Elliott Morris Vanderhorst Diary, February 10, 1860, Ann Elliott Morris Vanderhorst Papers, SCHS).

113. Though the connection is tenuous, Dublin missed a week of work in November 1822, just six months after being punished in the workhouse. Will and Dublin also may have gained through protest the intermittent right to a stipend for seeking their own food away from the wharf. Accounts from the summers of 1824 and 1825, when wharf repairs were taking place, included outlays for Will and Dublin "to find food." Then for twenty-three weeks between November 1833 and April 1834, there was a "Sum allowed Dublin to find himself," at first for 75 cents and then $1 each week (Vanderhorst Wharf Business Papers, folders 6–7, 10, SCHS). One dockhand, Robert, who was leased to Vanderhorst's Wharf for much of the 1820s, was sold in 1831 for frequent illness and drunkenness. See Vanderhorst Wharf Business Papers, folders 6–7, 9, SCHS; also see Camp, *Closer to Freedom.*

114. White, *American Negro Folk-Songs,* 290, 251.

115. See Krehbiel, *Afro-American Folksongs,* 46; and Fisher, *Negro Slave Songs,* 140.

116. James Carr Papers, SCL; N. M. Perkins to George W. Anderson, November 25, 1841, author's copy of privately owned letter. Seaman Charles Nordhoff described the cotton screwmen's songs in late antebellum Mobile as both "cheerful" and "generally plaintive and monotonous" (*Merchant Vessel,* 39–40).

117. This slave added, "It cheered me, however, to observe, as I went along, that my countrymen, who thronged the streets at every hand, seemed in general happy and contented. Some were driving drays, others drove fine and elegant carriages, and numbers were busy in the grog stores, or standing in groups at the doors of them; and their incessant laughing and chattering bespoke anything but misery" (Neilson, *Life and Adventures of Zamba,* 139, 109).

118. *The Nation* qtd. in Fisher, *Negro Slave Songs,* 12–13. Black abolitionist and novelist Martin Delany vividly described the "apparently cheerful but in reality wailing lamentations" of enslaved levee and river workers in 1850s New Orleans (*Blake,* 100–101). Actress and author Fanny Kemble variously described the work songs she heard in coastal Georgia as original, extemporaneous, agreeable, and pretty. But she also detected a measure of plaintiveness and lamentation in the lyrics, and suggested that the jovial tone of most slave work songs often did not accurately reflect the bondsmen's true sentiments: "I have heard that many of the masters and overseers on these plantations prohibit melancholy tunes or words, and encourage nothing but cheerful music and senseless words, depreciating the effects of sadder strains upon the slaves, whose peculiar musical sensibility might be expected to make them especially excitable to any songs of a plaintive character, and having any reference to their peculiar hardships. If it is true, I think it a judicious precaution enough—these poor slaves are just the sort of people over whom a popular music appeal to their feelings and passions would have an immense power" (*Journal,* 127–29). Krehbiel argued, "It is possible, of course, even likely, that

restrictions were placed upon the songs of the slaves," which helps explain "the general tone of cheer, not unmixed with pathos, which characterizes the music" (*Afro-American Folksongs*, 46).

119. White argued in 1928 that the workplace singing of gang laborers characteristically "reflects his immediate environment." Though White discussed modern rather than antebellum African American folk songs, he pointed out that labor gangs often expressed their "transient moods" about their employers, the difficulty, pace, or danger of the work, and wages. Workers had to take care that the boss did not hear certain lyrics, but other songs were meant for the ear of the employer: "Many of his remarks are intended for the captain to hear, or rather half-hear, in the manner familiar to most Southerners, wherein the Negro wishes to signify a state of disgruntlement but is unwilling to make a clear-cut issue of the matter" (*American Negro Folk-Songs*, 252–54).

120. Hill, *Jottings*, 19.

121. Grand Jury Presentment, Charleston District, January 1793, SCDAH; Grand Jury Presentment, Charleston District, September 1799, qtd. in Governors' Message, 1799 #744, SCDAH.

122. *Charleston Times*, November 11, 1803. For a description of Charleston's workhouse, see Redpath, *Roving Editor*, 50–62.

123. Eckhard, *Digest of Ordinances of the City Council of Charleston From the Year 1783 to Oct. 1844*, 173.

124. White, *American Negro Folk-Songs*, 251–52.

125. James Carr Papers, SCL. For a song with similar lyrics, see Hugill, *Shanties from the Seven Seas*, 8.

126. Gin also was purchased in April 1822, as was more "Liquor had of Mr. Cormich & others for Carpenters and Laborers" between July and December 1824 (Vanderhorst Wharf Business Papers, folders 4, 6, SCHS). Similarly, when the plantation boat hands of Col. Thomas Taylor arrived in Charleston, factor John Schulz usually paid their wages and provided them with meat and grog (Receipt Book/Business Ledger, September 22, 1813; October 6, 1813; Ledger, March 13, 1815, John Schulz Account Books, SCL).

127. The first published collection of American slave songs—*Slave Songs of the United States*—included the following comments from a man in Delaware: "Some of the best *pure negro* songs I have ever heard were those that used to be sung by the black stevedores, or perhaps the crews themselves, of the West India vessels, loading and unloading at the wharves in Philadelphia and Baltimore. I have stood for more than an hour, often, listening to them, as they hoisted and lowered the hogsheads and boxes of their cargoes; one man taking the burden of the song (and the slack of the rope) and the others striking in with the chorus. They would sing in this way more than a dozen different songs in an hour; most of which might indeed be warranted to contain 'nothing religious'—a few of them, 'on the contrary, quite the reverse'—but generally rather innocent and proper in their language, and strangely attractive in their music; and with a volume of voice that reached a square or two away" (Allen et al., *Slave Songs*, introduction, vii–viii).

128. The ordinance left it to the discretion of the warden of the workhouse whether to accept a payment of between one and five dollars from slaveowners or the guardians

of free blacks in lieu of this corporal punishment (Eckhard, *Digest of Ordinances of the City Council of Charleston From the Year 1783 to Oct. 1844*, 174–75).

129. An ordinance "to suppress riots and disturbances, at and in the vicinity of disorderly houses," enacted in 1821, prohibited "all clamorous singing, whooping, or other obstreperous, wanton and unnecessary noises, calculated to disturb the peace and quiet of the city." Another ordinance passed in 1838 punished "All indecent and disorderly conduct, cursing and swearing, clamorous noises, drunkenness, quarrelling, fighting, or profanity" committed on the Battery located at the end of the peninsula (Eckhard, *Digest of Ordinances of the City Council of Charleston From the Year 1783 to Oct. 1844*, 53–54, 24–25). Such decrees also may have been attempting to clamp down on street cries. One Charlestonian called for the regulation of the city's street criers (*Charleston Courier*, March 26, 1823, qtd. in Greene et al., *Slave Badges*, 43).

130. See, for example, *Charleston Mercury*, January 26, 1856.

131. *The Liberator* (Boston), April 18, 1835.

132. Schirmer Diary, June 23, 1834; April 18, 1839, SCHS.

133. Eckhard, *Digest of Ordinances of the City Council of Charleston From the Year 1783 to Oct. 1844*, 396, 33, 37; also see 40–41, and Walker, *Ordinances of the City of Charleston From the 19th of August 1844, to the 14th of September 1854*, 82, 99.

134. Ordinances passed in 1830 and 1838 also penalized those who "willfully break any lamp or part thereof," or "tye [*sic*], fasten, or secure any horse or mule, to any lamp post within the limits of the city" (Eckhard, *Digest of Ordinances of the City Council of Charleston From the Year 1783 to Oct. 1844*, 59, 132–33).

135. Adger, *My Life and Times*, 45.

136. Grand Jury Presentment, Charleston District, October 1821, SCDAH.

137. In the latter case, Mitchell reported the free black drayman to be Peter Devernier. This likely was Peter Desverneys, the former slave to whom the state granted both freedom and a lifelong pension for betraying the 1822 Denmark Vesey conspiracy. A sixty-year-old mulatto drayman named Peter Devineau appeared in the 1850 U.S. Census, and the 1852 city directory listed a Peter Deveneer as a proprietor of drays. Finally, a Peter P. Desverney successfully petitioned the City Council in April 1847 "for the remission of a fine imposed for employing on his dray a boy named Tom, contrary to Ordinance." See John Wroughton Mitchell Lawyer's Receipt Book, 15–16, 118, SCL; 1850 U.S. Census; Bagget, *Directory of the City of Charleston for the Year 1852*; City Council Minutes, April 5, 1847, *Southern Patriot*, April 6, 1847; and City Council Minutes, May 17, 1848, *Southern Patriot*, May 18, 1847. Also see Catterall, ed., *Judicial Cases* 2: 331.

138. City Council Minutes, January 6, 1840, *Charleston Mercury*, January 9, 1840. Similarly, see City Council Minutes, November 20, 1839, *Charleston Courier*, November 23, 1839; City Council Minutes, December 10, 1839, *Charleston Courier*, December 12, 1839; City Council Minutes, December 16, 1839, *Charleston Courier*, December 19, 1839; City Council Minutes, February 3, 1840, *Charleston Mercury*, February 6, 1840; City Council Minutes, February 27, 1840, *Charleston Mercury*, March 2, 1840; City Council Minutes, April 27, 1840, *Charleston Mercury*, April 30, 1840; City Council Minutes, May 11, 1840, *Charleston Mercury*, May 14, 1840; City Council Minutes, June 1, 1840,

Charleston Mercury, June 5, 1840; City Council Minutes, June 16, 1840, *Charleston Mercury,* June 18, 1840; City Council Minutes, August 3, 1840, *Charleston Mercury,* August 5, 1840; City Council Minutes, September 28, 1840, *Charleston Mercury,* October 1, 1840; and City Council Minutes, November 9, 1840, *Charleston Mercury,* November 11, 1840.

139. This Charlestonian, however, protested that the same ordinances were not being applied to the speedy and dangerous driving of omnibuses in the city. The City Council subsequently passed a measure regulating omnibuses in 1852. See *Charleston Courier,* September 15, 1841; and Walker, *Ordinances of the City of Charleston From the 19th of August 1844, to the 14th of September 1854,* 116–21.

140. City Council Minutes, November 14, 1848, *Southern Patriot,* November 16, 1848.

141. *Charleston Tri-Weekly Courier,* May 24, 1860; *Charleston Courier,* May 22, 1860; Schirmer Diary, June 1, 1859, SCHS. City police records showed that reckless driving along the city's thoroughfares continued during the early Civil War years. In December 1861 the driver of cart number 66 was arrested and fined eight dollars "for careles [*sic*] Driving in King Street"; a few days later a slave named Robert received 20 paddles for "Drunk and improper driving on East Bay" (Charleston Police Records, December 21 and 27, 1861, CLS).

142. *Daily Morning News* (Savannah), March 21, 1859.

143. *Charleston Mercury,* June 7 and August 23, 1799; *City Gazette and Commercial Daily Advertiser* (Charleston), May 7, 1812; May 17, 1821. A dockhand, office boy, and waiter named Billy, described as a tall, "well formed likely" twenty-one year old who was "very intelligent and plausible," ran away in May 1825. See *Charleston Mercury,* May 3, 1825; and Franklin and Schweninger, *Runaway Slaves,* 140. Also see the runaway ad for an enslaved drayman named March, in *Charleston Tri-Weekly Courier,* July 7, 1859.

144. Vanderhorst Wharf Business Papers, folders 3–4, SCHS; Christopher Fitzsimons to Mr. David Olivier, July 28, 1807, Christopher Fitzsimons Letterbook, SCL.

145. See Olwell, *Masters, Slaves, and Subjects,* 163, 165–66; Fraser, *Charleston! Charleston!,* 105; Chaplin, *Anxious Pursuit,* 123; and Morgan, "Black Life," 191. Laurens thereafter hired Ishmael to merchant Robert Pringle for £7 per month. See Greene et al., *Slave Badges,* 21.

146. *Charleston Times,* January 2, 1808.

147. *Charleston Mercury,* April 12, 1832. Also see Franklin and Schweninger, *Runaway Slaves,* 90–91.

148. Thomas C. Marshall to John W. Mitchell, October 10, 1839, John Wroughton Mitchell Papers, SHC.

149. Thomas C. Marshall to John W. Mitchell, December 18, 1839, John Wroughton Mitchell Papers, SHC. Also see correspondence of May 1, 1837, October 11 and December 11, 1838.

150. See Franklin and Schweninger, *Runaway Slaves,* 124–48.

151. This law, astonishingly, called for illegally hired slaves to be put to hard labor for a year and then sold, an excessive punishment that betrays the gravity of both the problem and the struggle for control over labor and laborers in late-eighteenth-century Charleston. The 1800 badge ordinance moderated the penalty. Though guilty slaves still were taken to the workhouse, if convicted they were publicly whipped and confined

in stocks. The 1786 ordinance is quoted in Greene et al., *Slave Badges*, 25. For the 1800 ordinance, see Greene et al., *Slave Badges*, 29–30.

152. *Charleston Times*, April 17, 1807.

153. Marshals likewise were required to examine once every quarter the licenses and numbers of drays, carts, and other vehicles let out for hire in the city (Eckhard, *Digest of Ordinances of the City Council of Charleston From the Year 1783 to Oct. 1844*, 158, 161). City Attorney John Wroughton Mitchell noted the "marshall's [*sic*] share" of a fine for "riding fast" in 1819. See John Wroughton Mitchell Lawyer's Receipt Book, 15, SCL.

154. Greene et al., *Slave Badges*, 101; City Council Minutes, October 6, 1834, CCPL manuscript.

155. See, for example, City Council Minutes, February 27, 1840, *Charleston Mercury*, March 2, 1840; City Council Minutes, May 11, 1840, *Charleston Mercury*, May 14, 1840; City Council Minutes, June 1, 1840, *Charleston Mercury*, June 5, 1840; City Council Minutes, June 16, 1840, *Charleston Mercury*, June 18, 1840; City Council Minutes, July 13, 1840, *Charleston Mercury*, July 16, 1840; City Council Minutes, December 12, 1842, *Charleston Mercury*, December 14, 1842; City Council Minutes, February 27, 1844, *Charleston Mercury*, February 29, 1844; City Council Minutes, May 1, 1848, *Southern Patriot*, May 3, 1848; and City Council Minutes, December 22, 1857, *Charleston Mercury*, December 24, 1857. Police reports to the City Council in 1859 detailed the monthly number of slaves arrested for "Working out without Badge." See, for instance, City Council Minutes, April 12, 1859, *Charleston Mercury*, April 14, 1859; and City Council Minutes, December 20, 1859, *Charleston Mercury*, December 22, 1859. Also see Charleston Police Records, March 11, 1862, CLS; and Catterall, ed., *Judicial Cases* 2: 361.

156. City Council Minutes, June 27, 1842, *Southern Patriot*, June 30, 1842.

157. *Charleston Mercury*, December 3, 1836. Richard Clark was listed as a pilot in the 1835–36 city directory, and as a captain and pilot in the 1840–41 directory. William Patton, the future owner of Patton's Wharf, was listed in the 1830–31 directory as a wharfinger, and in the 1835–36 directory as employed at the Steam Packet office on Fitzsimons's Wharf. See Smith, *Charleston Directory and Register for 1835–6*; Fay, *Charleston Directory and Strangers' Guide for 1840 and 1841*; and Goldsmith, *Directory and Strangers' Guide* (1831).

158. Greene et al., *Slave Badges*, 6–8.

159. *Charleston Mercury*, November 8, 1827. Also see Franklin and Schweninger, *Runaway Slaves*, 230.

160. *The Emancipator* (New York), October 18, 1838.

161. White Charlestonian qtd. in Fraser, *Charleston! Charleston!*, 105.

162. Grimes, "Between the Tracks," 12.

163. Laurens, "Address," 7–8. For a similar remark, see Henry W. DeSaussure qtd. in Ford, *Deliver Us from Evil*, 243.

Chapter Three: "Improper assemblies & conspiracies"

1. Jackson, *Experience of a Slave*. Also see Ashton, *I Belong to South Carolina*, 83–126. Like travel accounts, slave narratives cannot be read uncritically. In addition to

the imprecision and factual errors attributable to lapses in memory, the accounts of many former slaves were edited and published by abolitionists who oftentimes pursued their ideological objectives at the expense of the accuracy of the slaves' experiences. The evidence regarding waterfront work and workers utilized here, however, not only is plausible but also generally is confirmed by other, less potentially flawed sources.

2. Jackson, *Experience of a Slave*, 24–25.

3. When Jackson asked, "What did they put you in jail for?" the free black cook replied, "They put every free negro in jail that comes here, to keep them from going among the slaves" (Jackson, *Experience of a Slave*, 26).

4. Jackson, *Experience of a Slave*, 23–28; Ashton, *I Belong to South Carolina*, 4. Laboring temporarily in Boston, Jackson resided in Salem, Massachusetts; New Brunswick, Canada; and London, England, before returning to South Carolina following the Civil War. See Ashton, *I Belong to South Carolina*, 84. The slave stevedore in Wilmington, Thomas H. Jones, also successfully colluded with the steward of a vessel to stow away to New York in 1849. See Jones, *Experience*, 42–43.

5. Historian Jeffrey Bolster suggested the concept of antebellum southern waterfronts as "amphibious borderlands" while serving as a commentator for a panel session at the 2011 annual meeting of the Southern Historical Association in Baltimore.

6. For an introduction to many of this chapter's topics and themes during the eighteenth century, see Morgan, "Black Life," 187–232. Also see Goldfield, *Region, Race, and Cities*, 105–6, 112–13, 119, 143–44.

7. See, for example, Hamer, "Great Britain, the United States, and the Negro Seamen Acts, 1822–1848"; Hamer, "British Consuls and the Negro Seamen Acts, 1850–1860"; January, "First Nullification"; Fehrenbacher, *Dred Scott Case*; Bolster, *Black Jacks*; Linebaugh and Rediker, *Many-Headed Hydra*; Allen, *Origins of the Dred Scott Case*; Ford, *Deliver Us from Evil*; Wong, *Neither Fugitive Nor Free*; and Schoeppner, "Peculiar Quarantines."

8. Grand Jury Presentments, Charleston District, May 1851, Richland District, May 1852, SCDAH.

9. Kennedy and Parker, *Official Report*, 75, 115, 126. Robert Starobin pointed out that Vesey's co-conspirators were "mostly slave draymen, sawyers, stevedores, ricemillers, ropewalk workers, and artisans" (*Industrial Slavery*, 88). Recent works on the Vesey conspiracy have included Robertson, *Denmark Vesey*; Egerton, *He Shall Go Out Free*; and Pearson, ed., *Designs against Charleston*. Michael P. Johnson, however, prompted a reconsideration of the Vesey conspiracy. Johnson contended that scholars too uncritically have accepted the version of events as recorded in the official reports and trial transcripts, and argued that the Vesey plot in fact did not occur. See Wade, "The Vesey Plot: A Reconsideration"; Johnson, "Denmark Vesey and His Co-Conspirators"; Gross et al., "Forum"; Paquette, "From Rebellion to Revisionism"; and Spady, "Power and Confession."

10. For references to waterfront meetings, see Kennedy and Parker, *Official Report*, 93, 96–7, 103–4, 108, 125, 131, 139, 149, 152, 156, 162–63; and Pearson, ed., *Designs against Charleston*, 166, 196, 226, 267, 268, 272, 274–75. The black conspirators also planned to rendezvous at the docks—to "try to capture the shipping" and "to take every ship and

vessel in the harbour"—and flee the city by water. See "The Confession of Mr. Enslow's Boy John," in Starobin, ed., *Denmark Vesey,* 65; Kennedy and Parker, *Official Report,* 82–83; M. Richardson to James Screven, July 6, 1822, Arnold and Screven Family Papers, SHC; and Adger, *My Life and Times,* 52. The city's wharves also witnessed recruitment for free black pilot Thomas Jeremiah's supposed insurrection plot in 1775. According to historian Robert Olwell, "a slave named Sambo testified that, two months earlier, he had been approached by [Jeremiah] while working at the waterfront" and was encouraged to join with invading British soldiers to overthrow the institution of slavery (*Masters, Slaves, and Subjects,* 234–35).

11. Pearson, ed., *Designs against Charleston,* 265; "Confession of Bacchus, the Slave of Mr. Hammet," in Starobin, ed., *Denmark Vesey,* 61. Also see Kennedy and Parker, *Official Report,* 141.

12. Kennedy and Parker, *Official Report,* 146, 176; Pearson, ed., *Designs against Charleston,* 272.

13. Pearson, ed., *Designs against Charleston,* 273. Paris Ball, the slave of seamstress Ann Simons Ball, was identified as a stevedore in Egerton, *He Shall Go Out Free,* 144, 231. Nero was likely Nero Haig, a slave cooper owned by white cooper David Haig. See Pearson, ed., *Designs against Charleston,* 301–2; and Haig's petition for pecuniary compensation in the aftermath of the trials, Petition, 1822 #127, SCDAH.

14. Kennedy and Parker, *Official Report,* 94, 97, 172–73; Pearson, ed., *Designs against Charleston,* 261–62, 274–76.

15. Kennedy and Parker, *Official Report,* 116.

16. Kennedy and Parker, *Official Report,* 96–97.

17. "The Confession of Mr. Enslow's Boy John," in Starobin, ed., *Denmark Vesey,* 66. Also see Kennedy and Parker, *Official Report,* 146.

18. *Niles Register,* September 7, 1822. This free black steward's brother was said to be a general in St. Domingo. See Kennedy and Parker, *Official Report,* 153.

19. Qtd. from subtitle of Kennedy and Parker, *Official Report.*

20. Kennedy and Parker, *Official Report,* appendix, ii, iv–v. According to Charleston intendant James Hamilton, a free black man named Scott was responsible for detecting and reporting Allen's actions to city authorities (Petition, ND #2059, SCDAH).

21. Kennedy and Parker, *Official Report,* appendix, v–vi.

22. Kennedy and Parker, *Official Report,* appendix, ix–x, i–ii. Also see Rubio, "'Though He Had a White Face,'" 50–67.

23. Seabrook, "Concise View," 14. In the aftermath of the plot's discovery, lowcountry residents also blamed the "mis-guided philanthropy" of northern abolitionists. See Petition, 1823 #151, SCDAH, in Schweninger, ed., *Southern Debate* 1: 76–77.

24. Kennedy and Parker, *Official Report,* 98; "The Confession of Mr. Enslow's Boy John," in Starobin, ed., *Denmark Vesey,* 66. While "on the Bay," a free black carpenter named Saby Gailliard was accused of providing Monday Gell with a newspaper clipping concerning Boyer's battles against the Spanish in St. Domingo. See Kennedy and Parker, *Official Report,* 93, 125. Extant sources variously suggested that the black conspirators anticipated assistance to land at the city's docks from the countryside, James Island, St. Domingo, Africa, and even the northern states. See Kennedy and Parker, *Official*

Report, 62, 64, 68, 87. Also see M. Richardson to James Screven, July 6, 1822, Arnold and Screven Family Papers, SHC; Anna Johnson to Elizabeth Haywood, July 18, 1822, Ernest Haywood Collection of Haywood Family Papers, SHC; and "The Confession of Mr. Enslow's Boy John," in Starobin, ed., *Denmark Vesey,* 66.

25. Mary L. Beach to Elizabeth L. Gilchrist, July 5, 1822, Mary Lamboll Thomas Beach Papers, SCHS; *Niles Register,* September 7, 1822.

26. John Potter to Langdon Cheves, July 10, 1822, Langdon Cheves Papers, SCHS.

27. McCord, *Statutes* 7: 461–62.

28. Kennedy and Parker, *Official Report,* appendix, i. The acts also excluded black slaves, and were ambiguous in regards to many other free people of color. See Schoeppner, "Peculiar Quarantines," 560, 576–77.

29. *Charleston Southern Standard,* December 16, 1851, in "Law of Colored Seamen"; Governors' Message, 1824 #1362, SCDAH.

30. Petition, ND #1415, SCDAH. See January, "South Carolina Association," 191–201. Wharf owner Elias Vanderhorst, a member of the South Carolina Association, wrote to his wife in New York City in October 1835 that she could not bring her black nurse who accompanied her to the North back to South Carolina. Blacks who left South Carolina and thus were exposed to the knowledge and notions of freedom were barred from returning to the state. Vanderhorst wrote: "You must recollect that I told you directly I could not make any arrangement whatever for her return to this place. I am one of the Standing Committee of the S.C. Association & appointed for the express purpose of preventing mulattoes & negroes from returning to this place, therefore, you see that I cannot (without loss of reputation) have anything to do in the business. You can send her to Savannah, if that will suit her, & you can hire a white nurse to come on with you & send her back by the return of the boat" (Elias Vanderhorst to Ann Elliott Morris Vanderhorst, October 3, 1835, Vanderhorst Family Papers, SCHS). For the text of the 1820 law prohibiting South Carolina free blacks from leaving and then returning to the state, see McCord, *Statutes* 7: 459–60. Also see Johnson and Roark, *Black Masters,* 36. Edward Laurens argued in September 1832 that the presence of free blacks, northern and southern, among Charleston's slaves was dangerous because they encouraged thoughts of freedom and perhaps even insurrection (Laurens, "Address," 12–13). Also see Barra, *Tale of Two Oceans,* 161–62.

31. Governors' Message, 1824 #1362, SCDAH. Also see Catterall, ed., *Judicial Cases* 2: 323–24; "State v. Andrew Fletcher & Danl. Airs [Ayres], two free men of Colour," Charleston District Court, Record of Cases, Spring Term, 1823, RL; and Schoeppner, "Peculiar Quarantines," 563–70, 573–86.

32. Hildreth, *White Slave,* 312.

33. Petitions, 1826 #33, 1826 #34, SCDAH.

34. Grand Jury Presentment, Charleston District, May 1851, SCDAH. Also see Schoeppner, "Peculiar Quarantines," 575–78.

35. Levasseur dismissed South Carolinians' argument that the law was intended to prevent "all dangerous contact between the slaves of this state and free blacks from other places, who would not fail to talk to them of liberty!" Perhaps discerning tensions between local advocates of security and prosperity, he also remonstrated that "this state has

begun to suffer the inconveniences of slavery to such a degree, that measures of security have been adopted through fear, which at once are painful to humanity, and violate the right of property" (*Lafayette in America,* vol. 2, qtd. in Clark, ed., *South Carolina,* 85–86).

36. George Mathew also insisted in January 1852 that the Negro Seamen Acts "in their present shape" were unnecessary ("H.B.M.'s Consulate of N. and S. Carolina, Charleston, January 5, 1852," in "Law of Colored Seamen," 34). Also see Hamer, "Great Britain, the United States, and the Negro Seamen Acts, 1822–1848"; and Hamer, "British Consuls and the Negro Seamen Acts, 1850–1860."

37. See January, "South Carolina Association," 200; Hamer, "Great Britain, the United States, and the Negro Seamen Acts, 1822–1848," 21–23; Schoeppner, "Peculiar Quarantines," 580–86; Resolutions, 1844 #61, ND #1216, SCDAH; and Committee Report, 1845 #217, SCDAH.

38. See Ford, *Deliver Us from Evil,* 282–94; Wong, *Neither Fugitive Nor Free,* 183–239; Blumberg, *Repressive Jurisprudence,* 349–56; Schoeppner, "Peculiar Quarantines," 582–84; Hamer, "Great Britain, the United States, and the Negro Seamen Acts, 1822–1848"; and January, "First Nullification."

39. Governors' Message, 1824 #1362, SCDAH. Also see "Memorial of Sundry Masters," 3–4. For an account of a Boston captain upset by the seizure of his free black cook and five of eight of his sailors who were also free blacks born in Massachusetts, see Hildreth, *White Slave,* 309–14.

40. Briggs Thomas to Thomas Lamb, October 30, 1828, Thomas Lamb Papers, MHS. Thomas paid $22.75 for registry fees and three weeks' confinement for two free black seamen. See Pease Papers, ARC. Another Boston ship captain observed, "there is quite an expence [*sic*] attached to this unhuman [*sic*] law" (Erastus Sampson to Thomas Lamb, December 20, 1829, Thomas Lamb Papers, MHS).

41. This citizen also mentioned that the acts deprived ship masters of their crews, and suggested that since the City Guard was more observant and efficient than in the past, it was time to reconsider laws that arose "out of the transactions of 1822" (*Charleston Mercury,* August 8, 1837).

42. Petitions, 1826 #33, 1826 #34, 1830 #124, SCDAH. On December 6, 1830, the *Charleston Courier* reported, "The Bill to amend the law in relation to colored cooks and stewards, has been rejected, and the commercial interest of Charleston is therefore to be longer embarrassed by the existing law." Similarly, Charleston's grand jurors declared in January 1832 that the "Present law regarding colored stewards and seamen coming into Charleston port is injurious to merchants and the general interests of the city and the states," and recommended legislation amending the law (Grand Jury Presentment, Charleston District, January 1832, qtd. in *Charleston City Gazette,* January 20, 1832). Also see Schoeppner, "Peculiar Quarantines," 563, 570–72.

43. Georgia's 1829 Negro Seamen Acts quarantined free black sailors and passengers aboard their vessels while in port, jailing them only if caught going ashore or communicating with the state's black population. See Hamer, "Great Britain, the United States, and the Negro Seamen Acts, 1822–1848," 12–13; and Ford, *Deliver Us from Evil,* 332–33. For relative cotton export figures, see Collins, "Charleston and the Railroads," 100, table 5.

44. See Dawson and DeSaussure, *Census of the City of Charleston . . . 1848,* 60–71, 90–101; Van Deusen, *Economic Bases,* 333, appendix C; and Collins, "Charleston and the Railroads," 100, table 5.

45. Jeffrey Bolster argued, however, that northern free black seamen often were paid equal wages to those of white sailors (*Black Jacks,* 76, 161, 213).

46. Petition, ND #1415, SCDAH.

47. Barron also described making three trips to the city jail, where he saw fifty-two free black cooks and stewards, some of whom were for sale (Charles Barron to John Barron, November 30, 1839, Charles Barron Letters, SCL).

48. Petitions, 1826 #33, 1826 #34, SCDAH.

49. Opposing counsel countered that the federal government's constitutional "right to regulate Commerce gives a right with it of passing all laws in relation to seamen— both white & coloured." See "State v. Andrew Fletcher & Danl. Airs [Ayres], two free men of Colour," Charleston District Court, Record of Cases, Spring Term, 1823, RL. Also see Wong, *Neither Fugitive Nor Free,* 200–201.

50. Hill, *Jottings,* 21.

51. "H.B.M's Consulate of N. and S. Carolina, Charleston, January 5, 1852," in "Law of Colored Seamen," 34.

52. "H.B.M's Consulate of N. and S. Carolina, Charleston, January 5, 1852," in "Law of Colored Seamen," 34. While in Charleston in November 1838, seaman Henry P. Burr complained to his father that he was "worked as hard as possible—fair as poorly— abused from morning till night by the mate, and by him obliged to the hardest labor in company with a negro slave" (Henry Burr to Daniel Burr, November 11, 1838, Letters of Captain Henry P. Burr, CRCMS).

53. Kennedy and Parker, *Official Report,* appendix, vi. A young Frederick Douglass in slaveholding Baltimore was told about northern freedom and encouraged to run away by two white Irishmen who were unloading stone ballast from a scow and who had "the most decided hatred of slavery" (*My Bondage,* 169–70).

54. For the 1823 amendment, see McCord, *Statutes* 7: 463–66. For the 1835 amendment, see McCord, *Statutes* 7: 470–74, or Eckhard, *Digest of Ordinances of the City Council of Charleston From the Year 1783 to Oct. 1844,* 378–82.

55. McCord, *Statutes* 7: 466. See Court of General Sessions, Indictments, 1840–15A, SCDAH.

56. McCord, *Statutes* 7: 466–67. Members of Charleston's Chamber of Commerce maintained that the obligation to lighter goods between the wharves and vessels in the river was among the acts' chief inconveniences and subjected trade to "delays, damages, and vexations" (Petitions, 1826 #33, 1826 #34, 1830 #124, SCDAH). The lighterage of goods was far more demanding and costly, both in time and expense, than unloading and loading vessels when docked at a wharf. The judge of an 1806 maritime salvage case emphasized the relative difficulty and danger of "hoisting goods out of the hold of a vessel, and putting them on board another laying alongside" in open water. Captain Henry P. Burr noted when in Apalachicola in 1841 that his vessel's cargo was being discharged using lighters, "so that it comes out slowly, though we have plenty of time." And when the ship *Minnesota* was in Charleston in 1861, the vessel's owners were charged

$181.80 or 60 cents per bale for "Lighterage on 303 Bales [of] Cotton over [the] Bar," and then were billed $20 for a "Pilot Boat bringing back stevedore's hands" to the city. See Catterall, ed., *Judicial Cases* 2: 287–88; Henry Burr to Daniel Burr, January 10, 1841, Letters of Captain Henry P. Burr, CRCMS; and Cash Book, 135–36, Charles T. Mitchell Account Books, CLS. Also see Nordhoff, *Merchant Vessel,* 38–40.

57. *Charleston Southern Standard,* December 5, 1851, in "Law of Colored Seamen."

58. Scottish author Charles Mackay observed this amendment in action during his visit to Charleston in March 1858 (*Life and Liberty,* 195–96). For examples of ship captains and owners paying bonds for their free black crewmen after 1856, see Cash Book, November 26, 1858, 67; January 8, 1861, 135, Charles T. Mitchell Account Books, CLS; and Cash Book, Disbursement Account of the Hamburg Bark *Hamburg,* February 18, 1860, Charles O. Witte Estate Records, SCHS. Based on these factors' account books, the bond was only a dollar for each free black seaman.

59. City Council Minutes, March 2, 1858, *Charleston Mercury,* March 3, 1858. The council granted this captain relief from the fine at the meeting on April 20, 1858 (City Council Minutes, April 20, 1858, *Charleston Mercury,* April 21, 1858).

60. Henry C. Keene to Magon and Clapp, March 3, 1859, Henry C. Keene Letters, CRCMS. Scottish shipowner Charles Livingston reported in 1822 to his business associates in Greenock that the South Carolina port was "the worst place in the world I believe for sailors; in Charleston they do no work that deserves the name." Unable to secure replacement seamen when members of his crew deserted, Livingston was forced to hire local stevedores and laborers at great expense to unload and load his vessel. See Charles Livingston to Messrs. Livingston & Co., March 18 and 23, April 9, 1822, Letterbook, Charles Livingston Papers, RL. For a similar case, also see entries between March 21 and April 1, 1835, in Elisha L. Halsey Log, SHC.

61. An 1857 report from Charleston's sheriff listed the number of free black seamen who entered the port between December 1856 and December 1857, and included the date, name and origin of the vessel, and the number and occupation of the free black seamen on each vessel. According to Sheriff John E. Carew, registers of these free black seamen were kept in both the mayor's and harbor master's offices (Committee Report, 1857 #93, SCDAH; Miscellaneous Communication, 1857 #1, SCDAH). The General Assembly passed a resolution in 1856 requiring the sheriffs of Charleston, Beaufort, and Georgetown to report the number and origin of free blacks entering these ports from foreign or non-slaveholding states (Resolution, 1856 #16, SCDAH). In 1823 Harbor Master Thomas Paine petitioned the General Assembly asking for compensation for providing Charleston's sheriff with lists of free black seamen who entered the port. Paine argued that this task ought to be performed by the sheriff and asked to be relieved from the duty. His petition was rejected. See Petition, 1823 #39, SCDAH; Committee Report, 1823 #87, SCDAH.

62. City Council Minutes, November 23, 1858, *Charleston Mercury,* November 29, 1858. Prior to becoming mayor in 1857, Charles Macbeth owned Macbeth's Wharf north of Calhoun Street in Ward 5. Macbeth evidently sold this Cooper River wharf to the North Eastern Railroad. See Ward Books, CCPL.

63. Petition, ND #2916 Oversize, SCDAH. This petition was considered in the South Carolina Senate on December 5, 1859, and in the South Carolina House of Representatives on December 6, 1859. See *Charleston Tri-Weekly Courier,* December 8, 1859; and *Charleston Mercury,* December 8, 1859.

64. *Charleston Courier,* January 30, 1860.

65. Petition, 1797 #117, SCDAH. Also see Petition, 1797 #87, SCDAH.

66. Seabrook, "Concise View," 14; *New York Herald,* December 15, 1861; "State v. Andrew Fletcher & Danl. Airs [Ayres], two free men of Colour," Charleston District Court, Record of Cases, Spring Term, 1823, RL.

67. Laurens, "Address," 3–7.

68. "Declaration of the Immediate Causes Which Induce and Justify the Secession of South Carolina," 8–9.

69. Hildreth, *White Slave,* 312.

70. Laurens, "Address," 5–7.

71. Kennedy and Parker, *Official Report,* 18.

72. Pearson, ed., *Designs against Charleston,* 286. Discussed below is the oft-cited case of American Anti-Slavery Society pamphlets mailed to Charleston aboard the New York steamship *Columbia* in July 1835.

73. McCord, *Statutes* 7: 460. Also see Kennedy and Parker, *Official Report,* 18–19.

74. Court of General Sessions, Indictments, 1830-1A, SCDAH.

75. Court of General Sessions, Indictments, 1830-1A, SCDAH.

76. Walker, "Walker's Appeal." The free black Bostonian who supplied Smith with the pamphlets in March 1830 may have been David Walker himself, who died in Boston in late June 1830. Walker also is thought to have lived in Charleston during the time of the Denmark Vesey conspiracy. See Wilentz, ed, *David Walker's Appeal,* introduction, viii–xi; Hinks, ed., *David Walker's Appeal,* xx–xxii, 126; and Hinks, *To Awaken My Afflicted Brethren,* xi–xvii, 22–62, 116–72, 237–58.

77. Court of General Sessions, Indictments, 1830-1A, SCDAH; *Charleston Courier,* May 24, 1830. Also see *Charleston City Gazette,* May 26, 1830; and *Boston Daily Advertiser,* June 1, 1830. The *Charleston City Gazette* claimed in early March 1830 that local authorities had thwarted other recent attempts to circulate abolitionist pamphlets, perhaps including Walker's "Appeal" (*Charleston City Gazette,* March 3, 1830).

78. Court of General Sessions, Indictments, 1830–1A, SCDAH; Petition, ND #2916 Oversize, SCDAH; *Charleston Courier,* January 30, 1860. Charleston's City Council and Intendant Joseph Johnson petitioned the state legislature during the 1820s requesting the more stringent regulation of education for slaves and free blacks. Most slave occupations did not require literacy, the petitioners reasoned, and "It has been the policy of some evil minded persons to publish inflamatory [*sic*] writings and to circulate them among these people." Planter Edward Laurens similarly railed in 1832 against "all inflammatory publications vended in our country, whether written, or printed books, or pamphlets, or the yet more insidiously stamped calicoes and handkerchiefs, which made their appearance some time since." Echoing the call to prohibit slave literacy, Laurens contended that such a law would be necessary "until those of our negroes, who are

taught to read the bible, shall be unable to read Walker's pamphlet and other incendiary publications" (Petitions, ND #1799 Oversize, ND #207, SCDAH; Laurens, "Address," 5–7).

79. See Wilentz, *Rise of American Democracy,* 330; Eaton, "Dangerous Pamphlet," 323–34; Ford, *Deliver Us from Evil,* 330–38; Hinks, ed., *David Walker's Appeal,* xxxviii–xli, 92–106; Blumberg, *Repressive Jurisprudence,* 337–73; Pease and Pease, "Walker's Appeal," 287–92; and Schoeppner, "Peculiar Quarantines," 566.

80. Ford, *Deliver Us from Evil,* 337–38.

81. Court of General Sessions, Indictments, 1830–1A, SCDAH.

82. Many northern visitors, including known abolitionists, mingled with slaves in Charleston and throughout the South with impunity. According to historians Michael Johnson and James Roark, "City officials, assisted by assorted volunteer vigilance committees, were determined to rid the city of abolitionist sympathizers poisoning the minds of ignorant slaves with fanaticism. One Charlestonian pointed out that 'It is well known that our city is at the present time overrun with Abolition emissaries who are disseminating incendiary principles among our negros [*sic*]. . . .' The Charleston police were so ineffective at eliminating these 'Northern loiterers about our streets, without apparent occupation,' that the writer charged they did not even bother to hide their activities" (*Black Masters,* 275–76). Also see the letters written by "The Wandering Gentile" in William Lloyd Garrison's *The Liberator* (Boston), September 1 and 8, 1854; Redpath, *Roving Editor,* 45–47, 50–70; and Jones, *Experience,* 46–48.

83. See Hinks, ed., *David Walker's Appeal,* 93–94, 100; Ford, *Deliver Us from Evil,* 332; and Eaton, "Dangerous Pamphlet," 327.

84. See Hamer, "Great Britain, the United States, and the Negro Seamen Acts, 1822–1848," 14. The aforementioned experiences and observations of New England mariner Charles Barron demonstrated the laws' enforcement in the late 1830s.

85. Dawson and DeSaussure, *Census of the City of Charleston . . . 1848,* 60–80. See Cecelski, *Waterman's Song,* 121–51.

86. *Royal Gazette,* August 25–29, 1781, in Windley, comp., *Runaway Slave Advertisements* 3: 586.

87. *Charleston Royal South Carolina Gazette,* May 22–25, 1784, in Windley, comp., *Runaway Slave Advertisements* 3: 736.

88. *Royal Gazette,* October 31–November 3, 1781, in Windley, comp., *Runaway Slave Advertisements* 3: 590. G. Hooper likewise assumed that his slave Jupiter would "endeavour to get away by sea" (*Charleston South Carolina Gazette and General Advertiser,* March 20, 1784, in Windley, comp., *Runaway Slave Advertisements* 3: 730). Thomas Forbes of East Florida notified Charlestonians that his slave Mick, who was a skilled sailmaker and a good sailor, was thought to have "hired himself on board of some vessel in the harbour" and warned masters not to carry him away (*Royal Gazette,* September 21–28, 1782, in Windley, comp., *Runaway Slave Advertisements* 3: 698–99).

89. *Charleston South Carolina Gazette and General Advertiser,* May 20, 1783, in Windley, comp., *Runaway Slave Advertisements* 3: 715.

90. Stealing slaves was made a capital felony by an act passed on May 11, 1754. Another law enacted in the state legislature on December 20, 1821, prescribed punishments

for those who harbored or concealed runaway slaves. See McCord, *Statutes* 7: 426–27, 460–61.

91. For a copy of the Grand Jury Presentment, see Governors' Message, 1797 #703, SCDAH. Pinckney argued, "The personal property of our planters consists chiefly of slaves," and these "Instruments of our cultivation" were too vital to the wealth and commercial success of the state to allow them to be "clandestinely carried off." Pinckney also called for captains to present a pass signed by the governor and countersigned by the port collector (Governors' Message, 1797 #701, SCDAH). The committee noted that the previous laws fell by the wayside when the regulation of trade was transferred from the state to the federal government (Committee Report, 1797 #59, SCDAH).

92. Petition, ND #1415, SCDAH.

93. *Charleston Times,* April 5, 1821.

94. *Charleston Courier,* July 1, 1822. Originally appearing on June 27, 1822, in the *Darien Gazette* near Savannah, this incident was reprinted in Charleston as "a warning to others, who are in the habit of being employed on board our packets, in the Southern States," and who similarly might consider secreting slaves in the holds of coastal trading vessels. Unclear is whether this episode occurred in Charleston or Savannah. Also see Catterall, ed., *Judicial Cases* 2: 274, 338; and Court of General Sessions, Indictments, 1810-55A, 1825-15A, 1826-8A, 1839-22A-19, 1840-15A, SCDAH.

95. *Augusta Chronicle* (Georgia), July 28, 1824. According to an 1854 petition, lowcountry planter William Westcoat traced two of his runaways to Charleston only to be informed that "Colored Men" had hired the slaves aboard departing vessels (Franklin and Schweninger, *Runaway Slaves,* 131; also see 33, 118–19, 133–34).

96. *Charleston Courier,* January 30, 1860.

97. *The Emancipator* (New York), October 18, 1838. Also see Ashton, *I Belong to South Carolina,* 49–82.

98. As chronicled in the previous chapter, this former slave recalled a near run-in with city authorities for not possessing a badge. The fugitive described how he found a tag during a lunch break and successfully presented it to a policeman who was searching for runaways among black waterfront laborers.

99. *The Emancipator* (New York), October 18, 1838. This runaway did not settle permanently in Boston, however, his narrative having been recorded in Maine. See Ashton, *I Belong to South Carolina,* 50.

100. Rawick, *American Slave,* vol. 2, part 2, 233–34.

101. *Charleston Courier,* March 3, 1835; *The Emancipator* (New York), May 12, 1836. Charleston's 1855 city directory listed a stevedore named Benjamin Elliott living on Bogard Street, and the 1856 city directory included a free black stevedore named Benjamin Elliott living on Spring Street. There also was a forty-two-year-old mulatto drayman named Benjamin Elliot listed as residing in Charleston's Third Ward in the 1850 U.S. Census. This free black Charlestonian would have been approximately twenty-seven years old at the time slaveowner A. J. Huntington's 1835 advertisement described his runaway as being "about 25 years of age." It is possible that legally having gained his freedom, Elliott returned to Charleston in the 1850s to be reunited with his family and to labor as a free man on the city's wharves. See Gazlay, *Charleston*

City Directory . . . for 1855; Purse, *Charleston City Directory . . . for 1856;* and 1850 U.S. Census.

102. From September 1838 to August 1839, for instance, city authorities apprehended 115 runaway slaves, many of whom undoubtedly had planned to stow away (Phillips, *American Negro Slavery,* 418). Also see Powers, *Black Charlestonians,* 27.

103. Thomas C. Marshall to John W. Mitchell, December 18, 1839, John Wroughton Mitchell Papers, SHC.

104. Edward Pettingill to Langdon Cheves, June 22, 1837, Langdon Cheves Papers, SCHS.

105. *Savannah Georgian* qtd. in *The Liberator* (Boston), May 30, 1845. Williams and McBarney and Co. did not appear in the 1840–41 or 1849 city directories. There was, however, a William McBurnie in the 1840–41 directory, and a merchant named William McBurney appeared in the 1849 directory (Fay, *Charleston Directory and Strangers' Guide for 1840 and 1841;* Honour, *Directory of the City of Charleston and Neck for 1849*).

106. Equity Petition, 1846 #800, SCDAH. Also see Schweninger, ed., *Southern Debate* 2: 234–35.

107. Schirmer Diary, May 17, 1860, SCHS. Former slave Amie Lumpkin recalled the episode of "one big black man, who tried to steal a boat ride from Charleston" in or around 1856. This slave absconded from his master's plantation in Fairfield and made it to the city before being apprehended. According to Lumpkin, the returned runaway admitted to the overseer, "Sho', I try to git away from this sort of thing. I was goin' to Massachusetts, and hire out 'til I git 'nough to carry me to my home in Africa" (Rawick, *American Slave,* vol. 3, part 3, 130).

108. *Charleston Courier* qtd. in the *Savannah Morning News,* April 13, 1852.

109. *Charleston Courier,* October 27, 1836; *Charleston Mercury,* October 27, 1836.

110. The principal owner and master of the New Orleans-based *Robert Center* was Joseph Shepard (*Annual Report of the American Historical Association* 2: 425, 432–34, 443–44).

111. Valone, "William Henry Seward," 65; William Seward to [Virginia Lt. Governor] Henry Hopkins, October 24, 1839, in Baker, ed., *Works of William Seward* 2: 468. The three free black seamen's names were Isaac Gansey, Peter Johnson, and Edward Smith.

112. Committee Report, 1847 #237, SCDAH; Valone, "William Henry Seward," 65–66. Also see Marsh, ed., *Writings and Speeches of Alvan Stewart,* 219–33. Virginia governor Thomas W. Gilmer unsuccessfully offered a three-thousand-dollar reward to anyone who captured and delivered the three free black mariners to Virginia authorities. See Valone, "William Henry Seward," 75; and Marsh, ed., *Writings and Speeches of Alvan Stewart,* 220.

113. Historian Leslie Harris argued that, while serving as governor of New York between 1839 and 1843, William Henry Seward "provided abolitionists and blacks throughout the state with stronger legal tools in their struggles on behalf of accused fugitives. . . . Seward signed into law a series of bills passed by the Whig-dominated legislature that gave fugitives in New York State greater rights than ever before, and more rights than blacks had in any other northern state at the time" (*In the Shadow of Slavery,* 215).

114. Committee Report, 1847 #237, SCDAH.

115. Committee Reports, 1847 #130, 1847 #237, SCDAH; Petition, ND #2895, SC-DAH.

116. Ford, *Deliver Us from Evil*, 481–504; Freehling, *Prelude to Civil War*, 340–48; Harris, *In the Shadow of Slavery*, 238–39, 223, 215, 273–74. In addition, not only did New York City's 16,358 free black residents constitute one of the North's largest free black communities in 1840, but state law also permitted property-owning black men to vote. The South Carolina legislature, in contrast, passed laws in 1820 and then again in 1841—the same year this body enacted the New York Ship Inspection Law—aimed at limiting the state's free black population by prohibiting slaveholders from manumitting their slaves. See Harris, *In the Shadow of Slavery*, 7, 275; Johnson and Roark, *Black Masters*, 36, 169; Johnson and Roark, eds., *No Chariot*, 87–89, 102–3, 144–46; and Powers, *Black Charlestonians*, 39–40. Also see McCord, *Statutes* 7: 459–60. My thanks to Bernard Powers of the College of Charleston for reading an earlier version of this material and alerting me to this broader context in comments offered during a panel session at the 2011 annual meeting of the Southern Historical Association in Baltimore.

117. For the $120 figure, see Petitions, 1845 #30, ND #2823, SCDAH. Various other petitions from Charleston's shipowners claimed that this "Tax" collectively cost them the "large and enormous amount" of $1,000, $1,900, or $2,000 per year. See Petitions, 1853 #58, 1845 #30, ND #2823, 1847 #90, 1847 #91, SCDAH.

118. Committee Report, 1847 #237, SCDAH; Petitions, 1847 #90, 1847 #91, SCDAH. Also see Petitions, 1845 #30, ND #2823, SCDAH.

119. Petitions, 1847 #90, 1847 #91, 1845 #30, ND #2823, SCDAH.

120. Petitions, 1845 #30, ND #2823, 1847 #90, 1847 #91, SCDAH. The captains or owners of vessels departing the state without having undergone an inspection were fined $500 (Committee Report, 1847 #237, SCDAH).

121. Petitions, 1845 #30, ND #2823; also see 1847 #90, 1847 #91, SCDAH.

122. See Dawson and DeSaussure, *Census of the City of Charleston . . . 1848*, 60–79, 90–102; Van Deusen, *Economic Bases*, 333, appendix C; and Collins, "Charleston and the Railroads," 100, table 5.

123. Dawson and DeSaussure, *Census of the City of Charleston . . . 1848*, 66–67. The number of American-flagged steamboats—including those from New York—paddling in and out of Charleston Harbor also rose slightly between 1841 and 1842. See Dawson and DeSaussure, *Census of the City of Charleston . . . 1848*, 72, 74.

124. The collective tonnage of these vessels was 11,027, nearly equal that of all other ports' Charleston packet ships combined (Dawson and DeSaussure, *Census of the City of Charleston . . . 1848*, 80).

125. Dawson and DeSaussure, *Census of the City of Charleston . . . 1848*, 97.

126. Van Deusen, *Economic Bases*, 332, appendix B; Collins, "Charleston and the Railroads," 100, table 5. Charleston's proportion of cotton bales received for export from the four southern Atlantic states (presumably Virginia, North Carolina, South Carolina, and Georgia) dropped slightly from 46.67 percent between October 1840 and August 1841, to 42.90 percent between September 1841 and August 1842 (Dawson and DeSaussure, *Census of the City of Charleston . . . 1848*, 148).

127. Petitions, 1845 #30, ND #2823, 1847 #90, 1847 #91, 1853 #58, SCDAH.

128. Petition, 1853 #58, SCDAH.

129. Petitions, 1853 #58, ND #2895, SCDAH.

130. Committee Report, 1847 #237, SCDAH.

131. *Charleston Courier,* January 30, 1860. Jacob Schirmer noted the 1859 trial of Francis Michel "for stealing a Slave in endeavoring to take him away in one of the Steamers." Though the jury found Michel guilty in July 1859, it recommended mercy. The prisoner was sentenced on January 28 to be hanged in March, but the governor pardoned Michel in early February 1860. See Schirmer Diary, July 6, 1859; January 28 and February 4, 1860, SCHS. Also see *Charleston Courier,* July 9, 1859; Court of General Sessions, Criminal Dockets, January 1860 term, SCDAH; Court of General Sessions, Criminal Journals 1: 475, 561, SCDAH; and Johnson and Roark, eds., *No Chariot,* 128–29.

132. Assuming Withers indeed was referring here to the 1841 New York Ship Inspection Law, he mistakenly added, "The law provides for the supervision of every vessel arriving and departing from the port of Charleston." Though the author is unaware of any additional ship-inspection laws, this statement may suggest that the 1841 legislation was expanded in practice to vessels not owned or captained by New Yorkers (*Charleston Courier,* January 30, 1860).

133. See Committee Reports, ND #2548, 1847 #237, 1847 #130, 1853 #141, SCDAH.

134. Committee Report, 1847 #130, SCDAH.

135. Though the committee was "inclined to recommend" the law's repeal, this report came too late in the legislative session to take action (Committee Report, 1848 #235, SCDAH).

136. Catterall, ed., *Judicial Cases* 2: 418.

137. Committee Report, 1851 #16, SCDAH.

138. Committee Reports, 1853 #235, ND #2548, SCDAH.

139. Rogers, *Charleston,* 3, 138, 141, 145.

140. Grand Jury Presentment, Charleston District, May 1851, SCDAH.

141. Grand Jury Presentments, Charleston District, May 1852, January 1860, SCDAH. Also see Grand Jury Presentment, Charleston District, January 1859, SCDAH; Eckhard, *Digest of Ordinances of the City Council of Charleston From the Year 1783 to Oct. 1844,* 219–30; "Carolinian" in *Charleston Courier,* March 4, 1835; and "A Friend to Good Order" in *Charleston Courier,* March 14, 1835. Frederick Law Olmsted noted an item in the *Charleston Standard* from November 23, 1854, which stated, "This abominable practice of trading with slaves, is not only taking our produce from us, but injuring our slave property," adding that "the negroes will steal and trade, as long as white persons hold out to them temptations to steal and bring to them" (*Journey,* 441).

142. See Genovese, *Roll, Jordan, Roll,* 587–612; Lichtenstein, "'That Disposition to Theft,'" 413–40; Thompson, *Making of the English Working Class;* Linebaugh, *London Hanged;* Aptheker, *American Negro Slave Revolts;* Stampp, *Peculiar Institution;* Johnson, "Criminality on the Docks" 2: 721–45; Mars, "Dock Pilferage," 209–28; Grüttner, "Working-class Crime," 54–79; Hindus, *Prison and Plantation,* 140–41; and Douglass, *My Bondage,* 189–90. Also see Thompson, "'Some Rascally Business.'"

143. Grand Jury Presentment, Charleston District, May 1851, SCDAH.

144. Catterall, ed., *Judicial Cases* 2: 318.

145. Christopher Fitzsimons to Mr. David Olivier, July 28, 1807, Christopher Fitzsimons Letterbook, SCL.

146. Robert Pringle to John Erving, September 9, 1740, in Edgar, ed., *Letterbook of Robert Pringle* 2: 243–44. Also see a similar letter to Erving on December 7, 1743 (Edgar, ed., *Letterbook of Robert Pringle* 2: 616); Court of General Sessions, Indictments, 1809–53A, SCDAH; Charleston Chamber of Commerce Award Book, case 2, June 5, 1823, SCHS. Also see Henry Averell v. William Rindge, Charleston District Court, Record of Cases, May Term, 1816, RL.

147. State v. Francis Deignan, Charleston District Court, Record of Cases, January Term, 1823, RL; *Charleston Courier,* May 10, 1830. Jacob Schirmer similarly noted in December 1841 that on the "night of [the] 23rd a store on Boyce's Wharf was broken open and several Bags of Coffee stole [*sic*]" (Schirmer Diary, December 20, 1841; August 22, 1833, SCHS). The *Charleston Courier* reported that the back of the store was broken open "by wrenching off the pad lock," demonstrating that even locked-up waterfront goods were subject to theft (*Charleston Courier,* August 24, 1833); Goldsmith, *Directory and Strangers' Guide* (1831). The 1835–36 city directory listed Lafar as a cooper at 18 Vendue Range (Smith, *Charleston Directory and Register for 1835–6*).

148. Court of General Sessions, Indictments, 1823-55A, 1826-4A, SCDAH.

149. Van Deusen, *Economic Bases,* 333, appendix C. Also see Collins, "Charleston and the Railroads," 100, table 5; and Dawson and DeSaussure, *Census of the City of Charleston . . . 1848,* 90–101.

150. Court of General Sessions, Indictments, 1830-20A, SCHS. In August 1865 Elias Vanderhorst described the theft of three cotton bales from a building on Vanderhorst's Wharf (Vanderhorst Wharf Business Papers, folder 15, SCHS).

151. Court of General Sessions, Indictments, 1835-9A, SCDAH.

152. Though this petition is undated, it probably was written during the 1830s. It was not until the mid-1830s, for instance, that Ker Boyce and several other signers owned wharves (Petition, ND #1895, SCDAH).

153. Requesting exemption from militia duty to enable the protection of waterfront property during fires "and on all occasions where there is any sudden confusion in any portion of the City," Charleston's wharfingers stated in a petition to the state legislature in 1838 "that it frequently happens that goods of considerable value are allowed to remain on the wharf unstored during a part and often for the whole of a day" (Petition, 1838 #117, SCDAH).

154. Permitting slaves to independently cultivate cotton, complained South Carolina planters in 1816, enabled enterprising bondsmen to purchase and sell pilfered cotton "with impunity." Once entered onto the market, the petitioners argued, identifying and recovering the stolen cotton bales was "like looking [for] a drop of water lost in a river" (Petition, 1816 #95, SCDAH, qtd. in Franklin and Schweninger, *Runaway Slaves,* 90). Also see Schweninger, "Slave Independence," 101–25.

155. See McCord, *Statutes* 7: 407–8, 434–35, 454–55; Eckhard, *Digest of Ordinances of the City Council of Charleston From the Year 1783 to Oct. 1844,* 171–72; *Charleston Mercury,* December 24, 1839; and Lichtenstein, "'That Disposition to Theft,'" 428–30.

156. McCord, *Statutes* 7: 469. Also see Eckhard, *Digest of Ordinances of the City Council of Charleston From the Year 1783 to Oct. 1844*, 221, 224; and "A Friend to Morals" in *Charleston Courier*, June 25, 1835.

157. Court of General Sessions, Indictments, 1835-29A–1835-46A, SCDAH. Mary Daniels also pled guilty to further charges of trading cotton during the same session and was sentenced to an additional month imprisonment. Though the 1835–36 city directory confirmed that J. R. Daniels lived at 68 State Street, no occupation was given (Smith, *Charleston Directory and Register for 1835–6*). John Fraser & Co. owned one slave in 1858, 1859, 1860, and 1862, and sixteen slaves in 1864. In 1864 the company was involved heavily in running the Union blockade of Charleston Harbor (Charleston Tax Records, CLS; "List of the Tax Payers of the City of Charleston for 1858"; "List of the Tax Payers of the City of Charleston for 1859").

158. Court of General Sessions, Indictments, 1835-9A, SCDAH.

159. Charleston's "Lynch Club" wrote to abolitionist William Lloyd Garrison, "You son of a bitch: If you ever send such papers here again, we will come and give you a good Lynching; for the State will pay all expenses. So you had better keep them at home" (*The Liberator* [Boston], February 15, 1839). Also see Fraser, *Charleston! Charleston!*, 213. For references to the "Lynch Men," see Gatell, "Postmaster Huger," 201; Ford, *Deliver Us from Evil*, 483; Wyly-Jones, "1835 Anti-Abolition Meetings," 289–90; and John, *Spreading the News*, 257–59.

160. Schirmer Diary, August 21, 1835, SCHS; *Charleston Courier*, August 22, 1835. The 1830–31 and 1835–36 city directories both listed R. W. Carroll as a hairdresser at 4 Queen Street. See Goldsmith, *Directory and Strangers' Guide* (1831); and Smith, *Charleston Directory and Register for 1835–6*. Wood did not deal solely in stolen cotton. See *Charleston Courier*, August 24, 1835; and King, *Newspaper Press*, 150–51.

161. *Charleston Courier*, August 22, 1835. In May 1842 Jacob Schirmer remarked upon the trial and acquittal of John K. Brown "for receiving stolen cotton from a Mr. Howard" (Schirmer Diary, May 11, 1842, SCHS).

162. Petition, ND #5564, SCDAH; McCord, *Statutes* 7: 146; City Council Minutes, February 28, 1837, CCPL manuscript; City Council Minutes, April 4, 1837, *Charleston Courier*, April 18, 1837.

163. For examples of waterfront barriers, see Schirmer Diary, after July 1835, SCHS; City Council Minutes, August 25, 1840, *Charleston Mercury*, August 27, 1840; City Council Minutes, September 28, 1840, *Charleston Mercury*, October 1, 1840; and Vanderhorst Wharf Business Papers, folder 16, SCHS. For examples of night watchmen, see Patrick Scanlan in Gazlay, *Charleston City Directory . . . for 1855*, and P. McWee, P. Sheen, and W. S. Smith in Ferslew, *Directory of the City of Charleston . . . 1860*; Schirmer Diary, June 10, 1849, SCHS; and South Carolina Railroad Co. Semi-Annual Report, January 1, 1840, Pease Papers, ARC.

164. For information on waterfront street lamps, see City Council Minutes, August 3, 1840, *Charleston Mercury*, August 5, 1840; City Council Minutes, December 12, 1842, *Charleston Mercury*, December 14, 1842; City Council Minutes, August 9, 1848, *Southern Patriot*, August 11, 1848; City Council Minutes, September 26, 1848, *Southern Patriot*, September 28, 1848; City Council Minutes, August 3, 1858, *Charleston Mercury*, August

5, 1858; City Council Minutes, August 17, 1858, *Charleston Mercury,* August 19, 1858; and City Council Minutes, October 26, 1858, *Charleston Mercury,* October 28, 1858.

165. *Southern Patriot,* March 5, 1845; City Council Minutes, August 26, 1845, *Southern Patriot,* August 28, 1845. Also see City Council Minutes, September 14, 1846, *Southern Patriot,* September 15, 1846.

166. These guardsmen were said to report to their posts at twilight, which could be as early as 5 o'clock during the peak commercial season, and remain there until relieved at around half past nine at night, at which time they reported to the guard house unless impelled to return to the wharves by an emergency (City Council Minutes, February 15, 1847, *Southern Patriot,* February 16, 1847). Charleston police records revealed that these wharf patrols persisted into the 1850s. On February 26, 1856, for instance, Private Lyans "Could not be found on Post on Sunday Evenings [*sic*] Wharf Duty on Southern & Commercial Wharves between Bells and not returning to the Guard House." On the same day, Private Sullivan was caught "Lying a Sleep [*sic*] on post Atlantic Wharf on a Bale of Cotton at 3/4 past 10 oClock P.M." And on March 13, 1856, Private Daly "Could not be found on his Post No. 7 Frazers [*sic*] Wharf near 4 oClock A.M." All three guardsmen were fined three dollars, and Private Sullivan was dismissed from duty at his own request (Charleston Police Records, February 26 and March 13, 1856, CLS).

167. Petition, ND #1895, SCDAH. Also see Reeder and DeSaussure to A. H. Boykin, December 2, 1853; March 24, 1856; March 21, 1857; October 1, 1859, Boykin Family Papers, SHC.

168. K. Boyce & Company Account Book, January 17, 1837, 114, SCHS.

169. Walker, *Ordinances of the City of Charleston From the 19th of August 1844, to the 14th of September 1854,* 72–73. Cotton sometimes disappeared from cotton presses. On December 24, 1859, commission merchant Charles T. Mitchell made an entry of $46.64 in his cash book "for 1 Bale of Cotton Short from Union press & to be deducted from their Bill." Less than a year later, Charles O. Witte recorded $52.63 in cash "collected from Union Press for 1 Bale missing." See Cash Book, December 24, 1859, 106, Charles T. Mitchell Account Books, CLS; and Cash Book, November 1, 1860, Charles O. Witte Estate Records, SCHS.

170. Occasionally, when planters desired their cotton to be guarded on the wharves at night, Charleston factors hired the same worker to both repair and guard the bales, as when John Schulz paid a slave five dollars to mend and watch 100 bales owned by Wade Hampton on February 28, 1817 (Account Book, February 28, 1817, 22, John Schulz Account Books, SCL).

171. Horsey, *Ordinances of the City of Charleston from the 14th September, 1854, to the 1st December, 1859,* 16. The City Council also passed an ordinance in March 1858 to license and regulate second-hand or junk shops, several sections of which seemed to be aimed at preventing the traffic of stolen goods. One provision, for instance, declared that shops were to be kept open only between sunrise and sunset, and were subject to police inspection at any time. Another stipulated that keepers of such shops were not permitted to trade with minors, apprentices, slaves, or free blacks without the permission of their guardians or owners (Horsey, *Ordinances of the City of Charleston from the 14th September, 1854, to the 1st December, 1859,* 40–41).

172. Originally in the Mayor's Court, "The case was turned over to Magistrate Dingle for investigation." Officer Levy may have been either aforementioned police officer Moses E. Levy, or Orlando Levy, a second lieutenant in the guard. Regardless, Levy regularly patrolled the wharves. See *Charleston Mercury,* February 14 and 1, 1856; and Gazlay, *Charleston City Directory . . . for 1855.*

173. James B. Campbell Legal Case Papers, folder 11/102/8, SCHS; Charleston Tax Records, CLS. Also see Otis Mills & Co. in the 1855, 1859, and 1860 city directories, and in Ward Books, CCPL; Gazlay, *Charleston City Directory . . . for 1855;* Mears and Turnbull, *Charleston Directory* (1859); Ferslew, *Directory of the City of Charleston . . . 1860.*

174. Journal, February 28, 1857, 424; and Cash Book, July 19, 1859, 92, Charles T. Mitchell Account Books, CLS. Workers deliberately broke bottles and barrels of beer as well. In February 1861, for instance, the owners of the *Samoset* paid the grocer Bancroft five dollars for breakage on casks of ale (Cash Book, February 16, 1861, 138, Charles T. Mitchell Account Books, CLS). The rules of the Charleston Chamber of Commerce prescribed a standard "Allowance for Leakage and Breakage." See "New Tariff Amended," 24. Also see Johnson, "Criminality on the Docks" 2: 724, note 8.

175. See Johnson, "Criminality on the Docks" 2: 725; and Grüttner, "Working-class Crime," 59.

176. Logbook of the Ship *Robin Hood,* February 9, 1833, CRCMS.

177. John H. Graver v. Steamer *Palmetto,* February 15, 1853, Admiralty Final Record Books and Minutes of the District Court 5: 282–83, NAA.

178. "Rules for the Government of the Charleston Chamber of Commerce," 15.

179. Catterall, ed., *Judicial Cases* 2: 415. The 1849 city directory listed J. F. Tiedeman as a grocer on Elizabeth Street, and Otto Tiedeman as a grocer on Boundary Street (Honour, *Directory of the City of Charleston and Neck for 1849*).

180. Walker, *Ordinances of the City of Charleston From the 19th of August 1844, to the 14th of September 1854,* 45–8, 62–65, 159. Also see Mackay, Life and Liberty, 195; and McCrady Motte & Co. v. R. L. & W. E. Holmes, *Admiralty Journal,* 1–4, NAA.

181. See, for example, Court of General Sessions, Indictments, 1809-53A, 1823-55A, 1830-20A, SCDAH; Court of General Sessions, Criminal Journals 1: 160, 167, 198, SCDAH; and Court of General Sessions, Criminal Journals 2: 125, 129, 167, 433, 441, 463, SCDAH.

182. Genovese, *Roll, Jordan, Roll,* 599–600; Lichtenstein, "'That Disposition to Theft,'" 421.

183. Catterall, ed., *Judicial Cases* 2: 373.

Chapter Four: "Laborers from abroad have come to take their places"

1. Lambert, *Travels through Canada, and the United States* 2: 163; Petition, 1826 #33, SCDAH; Olmsted, *Cotton Kingdom* 1: 82.

2. An 1867 pamphlet recruiting immigrant labor to South Carolina stated, "It has been reported that manual labor was not honorable in the South. If this ever was a truth, hard work and steady employ have now become fashionable." See "South Carolina: A

Home for the Industrious Immigrant," 24. Also see Wyatt-Brown, *Southern Honor;* and Gillespie, *Free Labor in an Unfree World.*

3. Tower, *Slavery Unmasked,* 109.

4. Wood, *Black Majority,* 223–24, 229–30; Fraser, *Charleston! Charleston!,* 106; Berlin, *Slaves without Masters,* 234–35, 237–38; Silver, "New Look," 147. Among all free stevedores, porters, draymen, and carters—white and black—listed in Charleston's 1850 U.S. Census, only approximately 5 percent were native-born white southerners, and only 5.5 percent in 1860. The small number of white dock laborers born in the South furthermore constituted just 13.6 percent of all white waterfront and transportation workers—native and immigrant—in Charleston in 1850, but by 1860 they made up only about 7 percent of all such white laborers (1850 U.S. Census; 1860 U.S. Census).

5. Berlin and Gutman, "Natives and Immigrants," 1187.

6. Hine, "Black Organized Labor," 505.

7. Lyell, *Travels in 1841–2* 1: 151–52.

8. Qtd. in Fraser, *Charleston! Charleston!,* 106.

9. The 1790 city directory listed four draymen and nine carters (Milligan, *Charleston Directory* [1790]). The 1790 U.S. Census listed 8,089 whites in Charleston; therefore only about 20 percent of the city's white inhabitants appeared in the 1790 city directory (see table in introduction, above).

10. The 1816 city directory listed 3,181 whites, so only 0.063 percent were white porters. A third porter appearing in the 1816 directory, Amos Cruckshanks, was identified in the 1819 and 1822 guides as a free person of color (denoted as "FPC"). See Motte, *Charleston Directory and Stranger's Guide for the Year 1816;* Schenck and Turner, *Directory . . . for the City of Charleston . . . 1819;* and Schenck, *Directory . . . for the City of Charleston* (1822). Whites did not appear again as porters until the late 1840s, after the arrival of Irish and German immigrants. See Dawson and DeSaussure, *Census of the City of Charleston . . . 1848;* and Honour, *Directory of the City of Charleston and Neck for 1849.*

11. Archibald Cohler, listed as a stevedore in the 1830–31 city directory, was the first and only free black stevedore to appear prior to the 1850 U.S. Census (Goldsmith, *Directory and Strangers' Guide* [1831]). One white and one free black stevedore were listed in the 1848 municipal census, but no names were provided (Dawson and DeSaussure, *Census of the City of Charleston . . . 1848,* 33, 35); Dowling, *Dowling's Charleston Directory . . . for 1837 and 1838.*

12. Hazard and Ayrault employed a third drayman, named Henry Grimes. Though Grimes likely was also white, there was no evidence to corroborate his race. None of these three draymen was literate, and thus all accepted their payments by making their marks. But the firm's extant records revealed no payments to slave draymen for transporting goods to and from the waterfront (Hazard & Ayrault Company Receipt Book, SCL). Also see Bagnall, *Textile Industries* 1: 283–84. Both Woodmancy and Hyer also appeared in court records that affirmed their whiteness. See Court of General Sessions, Indictments, 1806-24A, 1809-7A, SCDAH. Hyer (also spelled Hire and Heir) resided on Boundary Street and was listed as a drayman in the 1801, 1802, 1807, 1809, and 1816 city directories. See Nelson, *Nelson's Charleston Directory . . . 1801;* Negrin, *New Charleston Directory and Stranger's Guide for the Year 1802;* Negrin, *Negrin's Directory for the Year*

1807; Hrabowski, *Directory for the District of Charleston* (1809); and Motte, *Charleston Directory and Stranger's Guide for the Year 1816.*

13. A Danish carter named John Johnson, who had resided in Charleston for five years, likewise was admitted to the alms house in December 1824. The alms house had an attached hospital for the medical care of both local and transient poor. Usually no slaves or free blacks were admitted (Register of Transient and City Poor, Charleston Alms House Records, CCPL). For more information about the alms or poor house, see Pinckney, "Report, 1837–1838," 39–40.

14. See Eckhard, *Digest of Ordinances of the City Council of Charleston From the Year 1783 to Oct. 1844,* 33, 37–38, 59, 394–96; and *Charleston Times,* November 11, 1803.

15. Native whites performing "Negro work" often were associated with blacks or persons with ambiguous racial backgrounds. The wife of John Cain, one of only two white draymen in the 1819 city directory, was granted seventy-eight dollars from the Charleston City Treasurer in July 1821 for taxes she paid from 1805 to 1820 under the "misapprehension" that she was a free woman of color. See John Wroughton Mitchell Lawyer's Receipt Book, 35, SCL; and Schenck and Turner, *Directory . . . for the City of Charleston . . . 1819.*

16. See Wood, *Black Majority,* 228.

17. Mills, *Statistics,* 427–28.

18. According to Pinckney, the city paid white laborers $1 per day. In all, the city's twenty-two white laborers cost $572 per month or $6,864 each year, whereas it cost $415 a month or $4,992 annually to employ twenty-six black slaves ("Report, 1837–1838," 11). Also see Pinckney's report in the *Charleston Mercury,* September 21, 1838. City records revealed that white laborers still were earning $1 per day in the early 1850s. See Charleston City Council, "Statement of Receipts and Expenditures by the City Council of Charleston From 1st July 1849, to 1st July 1850," and "Statement of Receipts and Expenditures by the City Council of Charleston From 1st Sept. 1850, to 1st Sept., 1851."

19. Mills, *Statistics,* 427–28; *Charleston Mercury,* August 5, 1846; *Southern Patriot,* August 5, 1846; Stuart, *Three Years* 2: 103–4. Also see Clark, ed., *South Carolina,* 162.

20. Wood, *Black Majority,* 228–29.

21. Greene et al., *Slave Badges,* 17; Snowden, "Notes," 5–6.

22. Wood, *Black Majority,* 229.

23. Eckhard, *Digest of Ordinances of the City Council of Charleston From the Year 1783 to Oct. 1844,* 398; Greene et al., *Slave Badges,* 20, 22–23.

24. Johnson and Roark, *Black Masters,* 176; Eckhard, *Digest of Ordinances of the City Council of Charleston From the Year 1783 to Oct. 1844,* 170–71.

25. Greene et al., *Slave Badges,* 17–18; Eckhard, *Digest of Ordinances of the City Council of Charleston From the Year 1783 to Oct. 1844,* 398.

26. Petitions, 1783 #159, 1783 #253, SCDAH.

27. Mills, *Statistics,* 427–28.

28. Petitions, 1793 #63, 1793 #64, SCDAH; Committee Report, 1793 #60, SCDAH.

29. Snowden, "Notes," 9.

30. Snowden, "Notes," 9.

31. Grand Jury Presentment, Charleston District, September 1795, SCDAH.

32. Petition, 1798 #45, SCDAH; Committee Report, 1798 #98, SCDAH.

33. Petition, 1803 #22, SCDAH.

34. In 1817 the society again requested that state legislators renew the organization's charter, and accentuated their "humane and benevolent views and intentions." The outcome of this petition is unknown. See Petition, 1817 #187, SCDAH.

35. Pinckney, "Reflections," 7, 9; Kennedy and Parker, *Official Report*, 26; Ford, *Deliver Us from Evil*, 240–42, 283. Several black draymen—including slaves William Garner, Caesar Smith, Smart Anderson, Perault Strohecker, and free person of color Prince Graham—were active participants in the Vesey conspiracy. Access to and the utilization of horses also were central to the plotting and planned execution of the revolt. See Kennedy and Parker, *Official Report*, 74, 116, 121, 126, 128–29, 145, 152, 154, 158, 165, 171–73; Pearson, ed., *Designs against Charleston*, 260–63, 268; John Potter to Langdon Cheves, July 20, 1822, Langdon Cheves Papers, SCHS; and M. Richardson to James Screven, September 16, 1822, Arnold and Screven Family Papers, SHC.

36. Pinckney, "Reflections," 9–11. When visiting Charleston in 1857, James Stirling noted that "the natural flow of immigration is damned back from these [southern] States by slavery." The Englishman conjectured that few Irish or other white immigrants settled in the South because "There is a natural aversion in the free labourer to put himself on a footing with a slave. Free labour, therefore, is scarce and dear in the Slave States" (*Letters*, 247, 230).

37. Pinckney argued that since all of the white mechanics, draymen, fishermen, and porters would be male, approximately 5,000 men would be added to the city's militia. An editor's note at the end of the essay sought to inform readers of the "expense attending the employment of Negro Slaves," and concluded that "it is probable that the labour of white men will, on the whole, be as cheap as that of the slave" ("Reflections," 10–26, 29–30).

38. Ireland, the author admitted, was not the only country from which the indigent yet industrious laborer could be induced to emigrate with the promise of profitable employment in Charleston. Pinckney also acknowledged that this migration of free white workers would only occur if past impediments to immigration were removed, namely labor competition with blacks and the impression of an unhealthy climate. The obstacle of black competition would "cease with their removal." As for the climate, once potential immigrants were "informed . . . that a considerable portion of our population consists of acclimatized foreigners" and that "the general salubrity of Charleston is scarcely surpassed by any city of great population, when not visited by yellow fever," this impediment too would be removed ("Reflections," 15–17).

39. Pinckney, "Reflections," 20, 26.

40. Petition, ND #2059, SCDAH; Grand Jury Presentment, Charleston District, October 1822, SCDAH; M. Richardson to James Screven, August 7, 1822, Arnold and Screven Family Papers, SHC. Pinckney's friend and protégé Henry W. DeSaussure, who resided in Columbia at the time of the Vesey affair, shared many of the former governor's views. See Ford, *Deliver Us from Evil*, 242–43.

41. McCord, *Statutes* 7: 461–62.

42. Kennedy and Parker, *Official Report*, 173.

43. Johnson and Roark, *Black Masters,* 176.

44. Petition, 1811 [ca. 1828] #48, SCDAH. This petition is misdated, and was in fact submitted in approximately 1828. Also see Schweninger, ed., *Southern Debate* 1: 101–3; and Franklin and Schweninger, *Runaway Slaves,* 371, note 25.

45. The petition concluded with a request for permission to form the "Charleston Mechanics' Association" (Petition, 1811 [ca. 1828] #48, SCDAH).

46. Laurens, "Address," 3, 7–9, 11–12.

47. In 1820 there were 14,127 blacks—both free and enslaved—and 11,229 whites residing in Charleston, a black advantage of 2,898. By 1830 there were 17,461 blacks and 12,828 whites in the city, a black majority of 4,633 (see table in introduction).

48. Laurens, "Address," 8. Laurens was referring to a city ordinance passed in 1830. See Eckhard, *Digest of Ordinances of the City Council of Charleston From the Year 1783 to Oct. 1844,* 176.

49. Laurens, "Address," 8, 11–12. Charleston ship carpenters James Marsh and James Poyas reported in 1833, "Many of our young mechanics have left Charleston to seek employment elsewhere" (U.S. Congress, 1st Session, 1833–34, House Report, no. 541, May 13, 1833, 19, Pease Papers, ARC).

50. Historian Jeffrey Young argued that this shift began decades before the 1830s. See his *Proslavery and Sectional Thought.*

51. An anonymous Charlestonian accused Mayor Jacob F. Mintzing of hiring his own slaves for municipal public works projects, "to the exclusion of our poor white laborers, who are our own fellow-citizens, and do militia duty, and fight for the country, and have families to support" (*Charleston Courier,* September 3, 1841). A white mechanic writing to the *Charleston Mercury* in May 1858 urged members of the community to support local white workingmen, but concluded, "There are some however (in office), who are of different opinion" (*Charleston Mercury,* May 31, 1858).

52. Laurens, "Address," 9–14. For an example of white South Carolinians calling on state legislators to restrict the rights and liberties of free blacks, see Petition, 1820 #143, SCDAH. Also see note 141, below.

53. South Carolina Railroad Stockholders Meeting Report, in Miscellaneous Communication, ND #169, SCDAH.

54. Ford, *Deliver Us from Evil,* 242. By the eve of the Civil War, over 1.6 million Irish natives resided in the United States (Gleeson, *Irish in the South,* 20). For other studies of immigration to and immigrants in Charleston, see Berlin and Gutman, "Natives and Immigrants"; Silver, "New Look"; Strickland, "Ethnicity and Race"; and Weaver, "Foreigners in Ante-Bellum Towns."

55. *Irish Immigrants: New York Port Arrival Records;* 1860 U.S. Census; *Charleston Mercury,* October 3, 1891; 1900 U.S. Census.

56. Torrent got married and had his first son, Joseph, in Maryland before moving to South Carolina. In addition to the two sons who worked as stevedores, John and his wife had five other children, all of whom were born in South Carolina. See 1850 U.S. Census; 1860 U.S. Census; 1860 U.S. Census Slave Schedules; Fay, *Charleston Directory and Strangers' Guide for 1840 and 1841;* Bagget, *Directory of the City of Charleston for the Year 1852;* Purse, *Charleston City Directory . . . for 1856;* Mears and Turnbull, *Charleston*

Directory (1859); and Ferslew, *Directory of the City of Charleston . . . 1860.* For horse own-ership figures, see John Torrent in "List of the Tax Payers of the City of Charleston for 1858"; "List of the Tax Payers of the City of Charleston for 1859"; and Charleston Tax Records, CLS.

57. William Doran was listed as a stevedore in the 1860 city directory, but City Council minutes revealed that he was working as a stevedore in 1857. See City Council Minutes, September 1, 1857, *Charleston Mercury,* September 3, 1857; City Council Min-utes, September 29, 1857, *Charleston Mercury,* October 1, 1857; Purse, *Charleston City Directory . . . for 1856;* and Ferslew, *Directory of the City of Charleston . . . 1860.*

58. See Gleeson, *Irish in the South,* 35, table 3, and 36, table 4.

59. Strickland, "How the Germans Became White Southerners." Of the 9,986 for-eign-born inhabitants of South Carolina in 1860, 6,311 or 63 percent were living in Charleston. There were 4,906 Irish and 2,947 Germans in the state in 1860. See Ballagh, ed., *South in the Building of the Nation* 5: 603, table 2 A; and 1860 U.S. Census.

60. Ford, *Census of the City of Charleston . . . 1861,* 11–12.

61. Pinckney pointed out that the financial reward of transients' hard work in Charleston must have outweighed not only competing with or working alongside black slaves, but also "the expense of two sea voyages in a few months" ("Reflections," 17).

62. Russell, *North America,* 162–63.

63. Gleeson, *Irish in the South,* 29; Silver, "New Look," 149–50.

64. Christopher Silver found that only 23 percent of Charleston's Irish population appearing in the 1850 U.S. Census still resided in the city in 1860. Among the city's unskilled Irish workers, only about 10 percent were in the city in both 1850 and 1860, whereas 25 percent of semiskilled and skilled workers and 50 percent of white-collar Irishmen remained ("New Look," 150, 154). Also see Bellows, *Benevolence among Slave-holders,* 102–3, 130.

65. Johnson and Roark, *Black Masters,* 227. Many of New York's poor and unskilled Irish had experience working on the wharves of New York City, thus increasing the likelihood that they would find work on Charleston's docks. Once in Charleston many working-class immigrants—from New York or otherwise—lived in shanties near the Cooper River waterfront, with unquestionably filthy and unhealthy living conditions, but also a short walk to work. See Silver, "New Look," 150–51.

66. For examples of cases in which the use of Irish immigrants was considered pref-erable to more valuable black slaves, see Silver, "New Look," 149–51; Niehaus, *Irish in New Orleans,* 48–49; Clark, *Irish in Philadelphia,* 66; and Gleeson, *Irish in the South,* 38, 53–54, 187. Also possibly rendering Irish workers expendable was the notion that Irish immigrants were not entirely white. Unlike the vast majority of native white southern-ers, after all, the Irish were willing not only to work unpleasant and hazardous jobs traditionally performed by blacks but also to labor alongside slaves on antebellum wa-terfronts. In mid-nineteenth century New York, as in most free-labor northern ports, Irish immigrant dockworkers were "becoming white" in part due to their disinclination to work shoulder to shoulder with blacks, as the 1863 Draft Riots later laid bare. Even in the border-state port of Baltimore, white ship carpenters who refused to continue laboring alongside black competitors nearly beat Frederick Douglass to death in the

mid-1830s. See Man, "Labor Competition," 375–405; Douglass, *Narrative,* 93–96; Roediger, *Wages of Whiteness;* Ignatiev, *How the Irish Became White;* Jacobson, *Whiteness of a Different Color;* and Kolchin, "Whiteness Studies," 154–73. Also see note 104, below.

67. Irish drayman Michael Lyons, for example, received payments in 1857 for unspecified work done on a local plantation. See Cash Book, April 13 and 16, 1857, Legare, Colcock, and Company Records, SCHS; Gazlay, *Charleston City Directory . . . for 1855;* Ferslew, *Directory of the City of Charleston . . . 1860;* and 1860 U.S. Census.

68. Regarding bids for city contracts, see City Council Minutes, October 27, 1857, *Charleston Mercury,* October 29, 1857; City Council Minutes, December 8, 1857, *Charleston Mercury,* December 10, 1857; City Council Minutes, October 26, 1858, *Charleston Mercury,* October 28, 1858; City Council Minutes, November 23, 1858, *Charleston Mercury,* November 29, 1858; City Council Minutes, December 21, 1858, *Charleston Mercury,* December 23, 1858; and City Council Minutes, December 6, 1859, *Charleston Mercury,* December 8, 1859. English stevedore John Symons was a member of the Palmetto Fire Company from its inception in 1841 and served as the president of the company in 1859. See Petitions, 1841 #33, 1841 #34, SCDAH; Gazlay, *Charleston City Directory . . . for 1855;* and Mears and Turnbull, *Charleston Directory* (1859). Regarding workers moonlighting as city guardsmen, see City Council Minutes, September 29, 1847, *Southern Patriot,* September 30, 1847.

69. Hunt, "Savannah's Black and White Longshoremen," 22–28; Hugill, *Shanties and Sailors' Songs,* 49–53; Nordhoff, *Merchant Vessel,* 43. Also see Doerflinger, *Songs of the Sailor and Lumberman,* xiv, 30, 32–34, 51, 80–81, 97–101; Barra, *A Tale of Two Oceans,* 54; and Erskine, *Twenty Years,* 296–98.

70. According to maritime scholar P. C. Coker, "On average two packet ships would leave Charleston each week during the 'cotton season.' During the summer months when there was little to haul, only about two departures per month were scheduled." By 1825 some packets left both Charleston and New York every four days. Also, "The packet ships quickly cut a normal New York to Charleston trip from ten days down to an average of six, depending upon the weather and the speed of the vessel" (*Charleston's Maritime Heritage,* 176–78). Also see Smith, *Charleston Directory and Register for 1835–6,* 159; Honour, *Directory of the City of Charleston and Neck for 1849,* 155; and Gazlay, *Charleston City Directory . . . for 1855,* 119.

71. Silver, "New Look," 149. Maritime historian Robert Greenhalgh Albion almost entirely ignored the working people who traveled on the packet lines. Albion instead focused on the elites of Charleston society, who in "large numbers sought to avoid the unhealthy and uncomfortable heat of the Southern cities" and escaped to summer homes in New Jersey or to patronize the shops and theaters of New York City. For example, Albion cited May 1825, when 164 cabin passengers departed Charleston for New York on two coastal packets. The cabin fare was thirty dollars and included food and wine. But according to Albion, only "A few steerage passengers were occasionally carried," and he did not note the cost of a steerage ticket (*Square-Riggers,* 229).

72. Pred, *Urban Growth,* 170–73. Further corroborating the presence in Charleston of significant numbers of transient workers from New York, records revealed that between September 1, 1848, and August 31, 1849, forty transient poor from New York—many of

whom were Irish immigrants—were admitted to the city's alms house, the most of any state excepting South Carolina. Since transient workers often arrived from New York and elsewhere without the assurance of employment and probably without having arranged for housing, those who found themselves unemployed or underemployed once they arrived in Charleston often had little choice but to turn to the alms house for shelter and sustenance. Only three transient paupers from New York, for instance, received outdoor support from the alms house, suggesting that these workers had another place to reside. See Committee Report, 1849 #27, SCDAH. The records of Charleston's charitable institutions, such as the Hibernian Society and the New England Society, included expenditures to enable indigent working-class immigrants to return to northern cities. See, for instance, Hibernian Society Minutes and New England Society Records, SCHS.

73. In 1859 steerage tickets cost $8 and cabin tickets cost $15. In 1860 steerage fares dropped to $7. One of the line's four steamships departed Adger's Wharf every Wednesday and Saturday at high tide, and the trip to New York took between forty-eight and fifty hours. Steerage passage between Charleston and Philadelphia was offered for only $5 in 1860. See Mears and Turnbull, *Charleston Directory* (1859), 7; and Ferslew, *Directory of the City of Charleston . . . 1860*. Also see Court of General Sessions, Indictments, 1830–17A, SCDAH; and Smith, *Charleston Directory and Register for 1835–6*, 159.

74. George A. Gordon to Krilla, July 27, 1858, George A. Gordon Correspondence, RL.

75. Silver, "New Look," 149–50.

76. 1860 U.S. Census. The 1850 U.S. Census was collected in Charleston between August 1 and December 22, 1850 (1850 U.S. Census). The 1861 municipal census, evidently, was conducted between late March and mid-May 1861 (Ford, *Census of the City of Charleston . . . 1861*, 3–4). Robert Mills argued in 1826 that the 1820 U.S. Census in Charleston was undercounted by 1,500–2,000 because the information had been collected when the city's population was "at the lowest computation." He estimated that there were 27,000 rather than 24,780 inhabitants in 1820, and pointed out that most of the absent citizens temporarily were in the North (*Statistics*, 396).

77. See Silver, "New Look," 149–51; and Gleeson, *Irish in the South*, 33–35, 38, 53.

78. The unspecified "laborers" employed on Charleston's antebellum wharves performed tasks corresponding to the work of longshoremen, a term that did not gain ascendancy in Charleston until after the Civil War. Waterfront laborers in antebellum Charleston often were referred to as wharf or dockhands, but they were not listed as such in the 1850 or 1860 U.S. Census. Christopher Silver counted 507 Irish laborers and 50 free black laborers in the 1850 U.S. Census, and 497 Irish laborers and 44 free black laborers in the 1860 U.S. Census ("New Look," 156, 160, table 1).

79. Census records reported that there were 2,336 laborers and only 31 stevedores and longshoremen in Charleston in 1870. And yet, in 1875 Charleston's mostly black Longshoremen's Protective Union Association counted an estimated 800–1,000 members. This supports the argument that many of those recorded as unspecified "laborers" both before and after the Civil War indeed worked on the city's docks and identified themselves as dockworkers (1870 U.S. Census figures in Powers, *Black Charlestonians*, 270–72, table 13; also see 128).

80. The entire free population of the city of Charleston as listed in the 1850 and 1860 U.S. Census schedules was evaluated for this study. In an undertaking of this magnitude, errors are inevitable despite my own most conscious efforts to avoid and eliminate them. Nevertheless, I am confident that any errors that are incorporated into the figures are few enough in number and limited enough in scope as to have a negligible impact upon my conclusions; Though the accuracy of the 1848 local census is highly dubious, it also tabulated the number of white and free black stevedores, porters, draymen, and laborers as follows: 1 white and 1 free black stevedore; 8 white and 5 free black porters; 18 white and 11 free black draymen; and 192 white and 19 male free black laborers (Dawson and DeSaussure, *Census of the City of Charleston . . . 1848,* 33, 35).

81. The 1850 U.S. Census listed three free black (James Cross, Francis Hale, and Andrew Sinclair) and three free mulatto (John Lovely, James Boudeau, and Charles Mikell) stevedores in Charleston. The Irish stevedores were Charles Farley, John Riley, Thomas Noland, Clark Raining, and William Farley. The other two white stevedores listed in 1850 were Emanuel Rosa, a native of Portugal, and William R. Green, a native of Connecticut. No German immigrants were listed as working as stevedores in Charleston in 1850.

82. Starobin, *Industrial Slavery,* 122. The Irish stevedores in Charleston in 1860 were Thomas Nolan (spelled Noland in 1850), Edward Fortune, Thomas Elliot, Thomas Carrol, John Conroy, Patrick Welsh, and Clark Leiky (spelled Leckie elsewhere). There were three Englishmen (William Palmer, William Smith, and John Symons), two Spaniards (Magna Rose and John Torrent), an Austrian (George Jefferson), a Canadian (William Watson), one Massachusettean (G. B. Stoddard), one Marylander (Joseph Torrent), and two white South Carolinians (Samuel Barr and John Torrent Jr.). The free black stevedore was Joseph Edmonston (1860 U.S. Census).

83. Johnson and Roark, eds., *No Chariot,* 101.

84. G. B. Stoddard appeared in the 1855 and 1856 city directories and in the 1860 U.S. Census; William Watson appeared in the 1856 and 1860 city directories and in the 1860 U.S. Census. See Gazlay, *Charleston City Directory . . . for 1855;* Purse, *Charleston City Directory . . . for 1856;* and Ferslew, *Directory of the City of Charleston . . . 1860.*

85. James Corcoran appeared as a drayman in the 1855 and 1859 city directories and in the 1860 U.S. Census; Thomas Green appeared as a drayman in the 1856 and 1860 city directories and in the 1860 U.S. Census; Miles Moran appeared as a porter in the 1855, 1856, and 1860 city directories and in the 1860 U.S. Census. See Gazlay, *Charleston City Directory . . . for 1855;* Purse, *Charleston City Directory . . . for 1856;* Mears and Turnbull, *Charleston Directory* (1859); and Ferslew, *Directory of the City of Charleston . . . 1860.*

86. The notice added, "The *Agamemnon* was loaded by C. A. Atkinson & Co.," which was a commission merchant firm located on Central Wharf. See *Columbus Times & Sentinel* (Georgia) qtd. in *Daily Morning News* (Savannah), March 23, 1858; *Daily Morning News* (Savannah), March 24, 1858; and Gazlay, *Charleston City Directory . . . for 1855.* Samuel Pervis did not appear in Charleston's city directories, death records, or the 1850 and 1860 U.S. Census records. A free black stevedore named William Purvis, however, did appear in the city's free black tax records in 1861, 1862, and 1863. William Purvis owned three slaves in 1861, and in 1862 and 1863 the stevedore owned two slaves.

See Charleston Free Black Capitation Tax Books, CCPL and CLS. Also see *Charleston Courier* qtd. in *Memphis Daily Appeal,* September 1, 1861.

87. Greene et al., *Slave Badges,* 3, 79–80, 126–28, 136. A local census taken in 1848, the accuracy of which scholars long have doubted, listed only 2 slave stevedores, 35 porters, 67 draymen, and 838 male laborers. Although many of these slave laborers surely were hired as dockworkers for at least part of the year, these figures failed to indicate how many. Carters were not counted separately in the 1848 census and did not appear under that title. See Dawson and DeSaussure, *Census of the City of Charleston . . . 1848,* 34. Also see Silver, "New Look," 156, 160, table 1.

88. John William DeForest to Andrew DeForest, November 9, 1855, qtd. in Johnson and Roark, *Black Masters,* 178.

89. Commissioners qtd. in Klebaner, "Public Poor Relief," 213, note 8. Also see *Charleston Courier,* January 1, 1840. The report went on to argue that, unlike many slaves, "The white Labourer in times of sickness, poverty, or distress has no one to provide for him, accustom'd to spend Weekly all that he makes, little or nothing is put up for future emergencies, and he is often compelled to seek the shelter of an Alms House or an Hospital" (Records of the Poor House, April 15, 1840, Pease Papers, ARC).

90. Dawson and DeSaussure, *Census of the City of Charleston . . . 1848,* 7–9, 11. Also see Bellows, *Benevolence among Slaveholders,* 106–7.

91. Later images that clearly were based on Crowe's 1853 sketch depicted blacks doing this work. For example, see the image that appeared on the front page of the *Illustrated London News* during the Secession Convention in Charleston in December 1860, in Rosen, *Confederate Charleston,* 43. When in Charleston on February 28, 1857, James Stirling wrote that the waiters employed at the Charleston Hotel were "partly Irish and partly slaves" (*Letters,* 230).

92. Mears and Turnbull, *Charleston Directory* (1859), 41; Jones et al., *Confederate Currency,* 102.

93. Nor were black waterfront workers north of the Mason-Dixon Line immune to foreign competition. "These impoverished and destitute beings—transported from the trans-atlantic shores, are crowding themselves into every place of business and of labor, and driving the poor colored American citizen out," one northern black man wrote in New York's *The Colored American.* "Along the wharves, where the colored man once done the whole business of shipping and unshipping . . . there are substituted foreigners or white Americans." A letter appearing in a Philadelphia newspaper in 1849 declared, "That there may be, and undoubtedly is, a direct competition between [the blacks and the Irish] as to labor we all know. The wharves and new buildings attest this fact, in the person of our stevedores and hod-carriers as does all places of labor; and when a few years ago we saw none but blacks, we now see nothing but Irish." And addressing northern free blacks in 1853, Frederick Douglass asserted, "Employments and callings formerly monopolized by us, are so no longer. White men are becoming house-servants, cooks and stewards on vessels—at hotels.—They are becoming porters, stevedores, woodsawers [*sic*], hod-carriers, bricklayers, white-washers, and barbers, so that the blacks can scarcely find the means of subsistence" (*The Colored American* [New York], July 28, 1838, qtd. in Litwack, *North of Slavery,* 163; Philadelphia newspaper letter qtd. in Hershberg,

"Free Blacks," 426–27; "From Frederick Douglass's Paper, 1853: 'Learn Trades or Starve,'" 388). Also see Ernst, *Immigrant Life,* 67, 69, 71, 104–7; Man, "Labor Competition," 377–78; and Wittke, *Irish in America,* 125–26.

94. Andrews, *Slavery and the Domestic Slave Trade,* 73; *Maryland Colonization Journal* 6 (October 1851): 71, qtd. in Berlin, *Slaves without Masters,* 231–32. Berlin pointed out that blacks long had dominated as stevedores and hod carriers on Baltimore's docks, but white immigrants successfully supplanted blacks from such waterfront occupations. Also see Rockman, *Scraping By.*

95. Lyell, *Second Visit* 2: 125; Olmsted, *Journey,* 589–90. Historian Earl Niehaus wrote, "the immigrant Irish draymen in New Orleans were the most striking example of the Irish forcing competition out of an employment field. Before they arrived Negroes, free men of color and hired-out slaves, were carting goods from wharves to the warehouses." But by the 1850s, the Irish "clearly monopolized this field of labor." See Niehaus, *Irish in New Orleans,* 43–58.

96. See Gleeson, *Irish in the South,* 38–39, 44–45. Also see Shoemaker, "Strangers and Citizens," 281–82.

97. *Charleston Mercury,* February 13, 1861. Also see Spratt, "Philosophy of Secession"; and Ford, "Republics and Democracy," 134–37.

98. Goldin also contended that, when urban slaves were sold away from cities, substitute laborers—such as native whites, free blacks, or immigrants—took their occupational places. Though some free black wage laborers filled slaves' vacated jobs, prior to the 1840s few immigrants performed waterfront work in Charleston, and the vast majority of native southern whites shunned waterfront labor. Both Wade's and Goldin's arguments are problematic because neither explained why the slave population in cities such as Savannah, Mobile, and Richmond increased during the same decade. See Wade, *Slavery in the Cities,* and Goldin, *Urban Slavery.* Also see chapter 2, note 49, above.

99. According to a study of Irish immigrants in antebellum Savannah, "By the mid-1840's Savannah's expanded transportation network brought more cotton, timber, lumber, and rice through the city than ever before. This increased trade brought to light labor shortages in the city which the Irish eventually filled. In 1845, the Savannah Chamber of Commerce acknowledged the 'serious embarrassment' of a shortage of black stevedores, a problem that slowed trade by forcing ships and freight cars alike to wait for crews to load and unload them" (Shoemaker, "Strangers and Citizens," 258–59).

100. *Charleston Mercury,* February 13, 1861.

101. Ford, "Republics and Democracy," 124–33; Huger qtd. on 133.

102. Gleeson, *Irish in the South,* 118–20; Cantwell, *History of the Charleston Police Force,* 13; Johnson and Roark, eds., *No Chariot,* 93, 105–6; Ford, "Republics and Democracy," 133–34; Bellows, *Benevolence among Slaveholders,* 174–75; Crowson, "Southern Port City Politics," 135–85.

103. William Henry Trescot qtd. in Bellows, *Benevolence among Slaveholders,* 183; Olmsted, *Journey,* 512.

104. Arnesen, *Waterfront Workers of New Orleans,* 20; Starobin, *Industrial Slavery,* 143. For instances of violence between Irish and free black dockworkers in northern ports,

see Adams, *South-Side View,* 120; *Milwaukee Daily Sentinel,* July 7, 1863; Man, "Labor Competition," 375–78, 380, 386, 392–94; and Spero and Harris, *Black Worker,* 17.

105. Niehaus, *Irish in New Orleans,* 50–54.

106. *Charleston Courier,* March 26, 1855. Several other incidents illustrated this supposed "proclivity to turbulence" among Charleston's late antebellum Irish. When a "converted Monk" named Mr. Leahey announced his plans in March 1852 to deliver a public lecture on "the gross immoralities of the Romish Church," he was denied access to the city's Masonic Hall since a "riot by the Irish was feared." A few months later the fire alarm was signaled at half past two in the morning, but the disturbance "proved to be a Riot between the Guard and some Irishmen in Chalmers Street" (Schirmer Diary, March 20, 1852; June 13, 1852, SCHS).

107. Schirmer added that a "Mr. Sanders also whipt [*sic*] him, and at the examination before the Mayor, some high words passed between Andrews & Sanders" (Schirmer Diary, August 7, 1846, SCHS; Honour, *Directory of the City of Charleston and Neck for 1849*). The 1850 U.S. Census Slave Schedules revealed that Andrews owned four slaves in Charleston in 1850, two of whom were adult black males.

108. This fight evidently took place on Sullivans Island near the ferryboat landing (Schirmer Diary, August 23, 1857, SCHS). Scott the carter may have been a slave. But there also were three free black carters or draymen named Scott in 1850s Charleston: James Scott, a free black carter in the 1856 city directory; Daniel Scott, a mulatto carter in the 1850 U.S. Census; and Joseph Scott, a free black drayman in the 1850 U.S. Census. See Purse, *Charleston City Directory . . . for 1856.*

109. James S. Bowie owned four slaves—two males and two female—in Charleston in 1850. See 1850 U.S. Census Slave Schedules; 1850 U.S. Census; and Gazlay, *Charleston City Directory . . . for 1855;* Grand Jury Presentment, Charleston District, October 1854, SCDAH. In this same presentment grand jurors complained about the practice of carrying deadly concealed weapons, which often led to "riots which frequently end in bloodshed."

110. City Council Minutes, February 14, 1854, *Charleston Mercury,* February 16, 1854; City Council Minutes, March 14, 1854, *Charleston Mercury,* March 16, 1854; Carson & Sons Daybook, SCHS; Reeder and DeSaussure to A. H. Boykin, March 21, 1857; November 27, 1856; March 2 and April 24, 1858, Boykin Family Papers, SHC. Also see Silver, "New Look," 156–57.

111. *Charleston Mercury,* November 1 and 22, 1856. Assault and battery offenses were so common in late antebellum Charleston that grand jury presentments from 1860 complained about the large number of these "petty and trifling cases" that were costly, time consuming, and required jurors to listen to "a history of midnight brawls amongst a number of inebriates" (Grand Jury Presentments, Charleston District, January, April, and June 1860, SCDAH).

112. Roach was found not guilty in April 1859, but co-defendant T. O'Brien—possibly livery stable keeper Thomas O'Brien—was found guilty. See Court of General Sessions, Criminal Journals 1: 334, 395, SCDAH; 1860 U.S. Census; Fay, *Charleston Directory and Strangers' Guide for 1840 and 1841;* Honour, *Directory of the City of Charleston and Neck for 1849;* and Bagget, *Directory of the City of Charleston for the Year 1852.*

113. Martin Murphy was indicted again for the same offense in April 1861, but the criminal journals did not reveal the result of the case. Patrick Carroll, recorded as P. Carroll, and the other convicted Irishmen appeared in the 1860 U.S. Census as confined in the Charleston city jail. See Court of General Sessions, Criminal Journals 1: 155, 498–99, 508, 511; 2: 8, 30–31, 34, 187, SCDAH; Court of General Sessions, Criminal Dockets, October 1859 term, April 1860 term, SCDAH; and Gazlay, *Charleston City Directory . . . for 1855.*

114. *The North American* (Philadelphia), March 5, 1847.

115. *Charleston TriWeekly Courier,* January 28, 1860.

116. *Charleston Mercury,* February 20, 1858; William Henry Trescot to William Porcher Miles, "Ye feaste of ye Nativite," 1855, William Porcher Miles Papers, SHC. In February 1856 white drayman Phillip McGuire "was reported for the improper driving of his dray and running against the wagon of Mr. Veronee" (*Charleston Mercury,* February 19, 1856). Also see City Council Minutes, December 16, 1839, *Charleston Courier,* December 19, 1839; and City Council Minutes, April 27, 1840, *Charleston Mercury,* April 30, 1840.

117. *Charleston Mercury,* September 16, 1859; 1860 U.S. Census; *Fayetteville Observer* (North Carolina), January 6, 1862. The *Charleston Mercury* reported in 1856, "The driver of a carriage belonging to the Mills House stables, was reported for overcharging the usual fare and retaining the baggage of the passenger who refused to pay the double fare. The case having been clearly made out to the satisfaction of the Mayor [Miles] by the testimony of the passenger, he imposed a fine of five dollars. The proprietor of the stables refused to pay the fine, and the case was turned over to the Recorder for prosecution" (*Charleston Mercury,* February 19, 1856).

118. Petitions, ND #2892 Oversize, ND #5649, SCDAH. For an advertisement of the meeting, see *Charleston Mercury,* October 8, 1858; also see *Charleston Courier,* October 11, 1858.

119. According to historians Michael Johnson and James Roark, about 80 percent of the signers were common laborers or tradesmen (such as carpenters, ship joiners, printers, and shoemakers), whereas only twenty of the petitioners were employed in nonmanual or white-collar occupations. Their analysis also found that more than three-quarters of the signers did not own property in the city, and only four were slaveowners (*Black Masters,* 173, 180–81). Stevedore G. B. Stoddard also may have signed this petition. An index at the South Carolina Department of Archives and History (SCDAH) listed Stoddard as a signer, but the signature on the petition does not match that of Stoddard's on a later petition (Petition, ND #2916 Oversize). Several scholars have maintained that John Symons (often misspelled Simmons or Symmons) employed Robert Smalls. In addition to working as a wharf hand, stevedore, rigger, wheelman, and pilot, Smalls evidently also directed hoist horses on the city's wharves. See Blassingame, ed., *Slave Testimony,* 373–79; Sterling, *Captain of the Planter,* 41–47, 52, 59, 156; Powers, *Black Charlestonians,* 11; Uya, *From Slavery to Public Service,* 6–8; Billingsley, *Yearning to Breathe Free,* 42–43, 52, 90; and "Short Sketch," 1–6.

120. Petition, ND #4744, SCDAH. Though the verbiage of this petition is very similar to that of Petition, ND #2892 Oversize, and Petition, ND #5649 (which was based

on the meeting on October 8, 1858), it was created from a meeting of the Charleston Mechanic Society held on November 1, 1858; Petition, 1858 #85, SCDAH.

121. The committee also considered, and rejected, two pieces of legislation proposed by the white mechanics: "A Bill to prevent slaves from hiring out their own time and carrying on mechanical pursuits," which included proposals to penalize both the employers and owners of illegally hired-out slaves, and to fine both a hundred rather than fifty dollars; and "A Bill to prevent negroes from carrying on mechanical pursuits." See "Report of the Committee on Colored Population," 3–4. This committee report also was printed in the *Charleston Mercury,* December 15, 1858. Also see Johnson and Roark, *Black Masters,* 181.

122. The committee conceded that the act passed in 1822 and a subsequent amendment in 1849 indeed prohibited slaves from hiring their own time. The 1849 amendment of the 1822 act added female slaves to the prohibition. It also decreased the fine for offending slaveowners to fifty dollars (Johnson and Roark, *Black Masters,* 177).

123. "Report of the Committee on Colored Population," 5; *Charleston Mercury,* December 15, 1858.

124. The proposed bill read: "That slaves working or employed in cities, towns, or villages as porters, common laborers, stevedores, cartmen, draymen, wagoners or hackmen, or drivers of licensed carriages or vehicles plying for freight or hire, which slaves shall have licenses or badges granted for such employments by the proper municipal authorities, shall not be included within the inhibitions of the acts heretofore passed to prevent slaves from hiring their own time." See "Report of the Committee on Colored Population," 5; and *Charleston Mercury,* December 15, 1858. Johnson and Roark observed, "In essence, the committee proposed to make the law conform to everyday practice. Rather than providing white mechanics with relief from slave competition, they offered slaveowners relief from inconvenient laws" (*Black Masters,* 182–83).

125. All three petitions noted that the ineffective and unenforced laws against slaves hiring their own time currently on the state statute books had been the topic of several recent grand jury presentments and had "gained the consideration of many influential [legislative] bodies." In October 1857, Charleston's Grand Jury indeed informed state legislators of "the alleged frequent infraction of the laws in relation to the hiring or employment of negroes otherwise than from their owners," and asked that an officer be appointed to enforce the law. In the spring of 1858 the City Council debated a new ordinance to outlaw slaves hiring their own time, but the aldermen effectively rejected the measure by voting to postpone it indefinitely. Then in October 1858 the grand jury again complained about "the privilege given by owners to their slaves of hiring their own time," which was deemed an evil demanding the "prompt intervention of the law" and "the most strenuous measures for [its] prevention." See Grand Jury Presentment, Charleston District, October 1857, SCDAH; City Council Minutes, March 16, 1858, *Charleston Mercury,* March 17, 1858; City Council Minutes, May 11, 1858, *Charleston Mercury,* May 12, 1858; and Grand Jury Presentment, Charleston District, October 1858, SCDAH. The foreman of the October 1857 grand jury was planter John Rutledge, who in 1860 owned seventy-one slaves in St. Peter's Parish (Beaufort) and thirteen slaves in Charleston. The foreman of the October 1859 body was Vanderhorst's Wharf factor

John P. Deveaux, who owned eleven slaves in Charleston in 1860. As demonstrated by Thomas Pinckney and Edward R. Laurens, however, not all slaveowners were champions of prevailing slave-hiring practices. Two slaveowning white stevedores, John Torrent and William Doran, sat on the grand jury in early 1859 even as they railed against slave competitors who were permitted to hire out their own time on the docks. Non-slaveholders sometimes may have outvoted self-interested slaveowning grand jurors, resulting in presentments critical of slaves hiring out their own time in Charleston. See Gazlay, *Charleston City Directory . . . for 1855;* 1860 U.S. Census; 1860 U.S. Census Slave Schedules; and *Charleston Mercury,* January 11, 1859.

126. *Charleston Tri-Weekly Courier,* December 8, 1859; *Charleston Mercury,* December 8, 1859.

127. Petition, ND #2916 Oversize, SCDAH.

128. Petition, ND #2916 Oversize, SCDAH. After Charleston's Grand Jury complained about free blacks and slaves assembling, a legislative committee in 1791 deemed this behavior dangerous to the public safety and recommended that another body be appointed "to revise the negroe [*sic*] Law and to provide particularly against the assemblage of free negroes & Slaves in great numbers under any pretext whatsoever." An ordinance from 1836 stated, "No slaves or free persons of color being more in number than seven, shall be allowed to assemble and meet together (except when attending funerals or fires, or when engaged in their owners [*sic*] or employers [*sic*] business, under the direction of such owner or employer) unless some responsible white person is actually present, and for some lawful purpose." The exceptions enumerated seemingly would have included slave work gangs stowing cargo in the holds of vessels. Then in 1856, a grand jury presentment complained that many of Charleston's row houses or tenements were filled with between fifty and a hundred slaves and free blacks, and pointed out the illegality of a gathering of seven or more slaves without the supervision of a responsible person. See Committee Report, 1791 #145, SCDAH; Eckhard, *Digest of Ordinances of the City Council of Charleston From the Year 1783 to Oct. 1844,* 176–77; and Grand Jury Presentment, Charleston District, March 1856, SCDAH. Also see Eckhard, *Digest of Ordinances of the City Council of Charleston From the Year 1783 to Oct. 1844,* 93–94, 170, 223–24, 228, 376–78; and Laurens, "Address," 7–8.

129. Petition, ND #2916 Oversize, SCDAH.

130. With a shared history, ethnicity, religion, and culture, Charleston's Irish at times presented a united front against a common political enemy. The challenge from the nativist Know-Nothing Party during the mid-1850s, for instance, brought together Irishmen irrespective of socioeconomic status in many southern cities. But as the stevedores' petition demonstrated, when the Know-Nothing challenge faded and the menace of slave competition reclaimed center stage, this interclass harmony dwindled as well. See Gleeson, *Irish in the South,* 118–20.

131. Committee Report, 1859 #104, SCDAH.

132. This contemplated ordinance would have subjected both the offending slaveowner and employer to fifty-dollar fines (City Council Minutes, January 17, 1860, *Charleston Mercury,* January 19, 1860).

133. *Charleston Evening News,* January 20, 1860, qtd. in *Charleston Courier,* January 30, 1860.

134. *Charleston Courier,* January 30, 1860.

135. Two stevedores were identified on the census schedules as married, but did not have wives listed as residing with them in Charleston. The two unmarried white stevedores were John Torrent's relatively young sons, Joseph and John Jr. (1860 U.S. Census).

136. Charleston Tax Records, CLS; "List of the Tax Payers of the City of Charleston for 1858"; "List of the Tax Payers of the City of Charleston for 1859." Also see John Torrent in the 1860 U.S. Census Slave Schedules.

137. In a series of letters written by a northern abolitionist and published in *The Liberator* in 1854, the author spoke to a German immigrant in Wilmington who maintained that many nonslaveowners in southern cities, such as laborers, mechanics, and storekeepers, were abolitionists. See *The Liberator* (Boston), September 1, 1854. Also see Gleeson, *Irish in the South,* 121–40.

138. *Charleston Courier,* January 30, 1860. Brakes were the handles or levers used to pump water from contemporary fire engines.

139. *Charleston Courier,* January 30, 1860.

140. City Council Minutes, February 28, 1860, *Charleston Mercury,* March 1, 1860. The special committee consisted of John Kenifick, E. W. Edgerton, and William Ravenel. Johnson and Roark concluded that the City Council consented to this special committee report, thus granting "semiofficial local approval to the existing black market in slave hiring" (*Black Masters,* 184).

141. Free blacks comprised approximately only 14.7 percent of Charleston's free population and 8 percent of the city's total population in 1850. They made up 12.2 percent of the free population and 8 percent of the total population in 1860 (see table in introduction). Free blacks in South Carolina and throughout the antebellum South stood tenuously betwixt and between slavery and freedom. Unlike slaves, whose urban occupations were safeguarded by a large and influential master class, free blacks often relied upon the kindness and generosity of a smaller group of sympathetic whites for the preservation of their vocations, rights, and liberty. The future treasury secretary of the Confederacy, Christopher G. Memminger, for example, argued that free blacks were "entitled to the protection of our laws" and pointed out that it was a free black man who while still a slave blew the whistle on the Vesey plot. The chairman of the legislature's Committee on Colored Population, John Harleston Read Jr., described South Carolina's free persons of color as "good citizens, and patterns of industry, sobriety and irreproachable conduct." As with the white stevedores' appeals on their own behalf, Read and others cited tax payments and property holdings as evidence of free blacks' orderly and responsible disposition. Johnson and Roark termed prominent white Charlestonians' protection of the city's free blacks the "Charleston defense." See Johnson and Roark, *Black Masters,* 167–73, 184–94; Johnson and Roark, eds., *No Chariot,* 13–15, 132–7; and Petition, ND #2801, SCDAH.

142. The South Carolina Mechanics Association appealed to state authorities for relief from competition with free blacks in 1858: "Your petitioners would further request

that Your Honorable body would take into consideration the class of negroes known amongst us as Free Negroes and that a tax be imposed upon them or that some other remedy be made that shall at least place us in such a position that we may be able to compete with them if they are to be on an equality with us" (Petition, 1858 #85, SC-DAH).

143. Petitions, ND #1799 Oversize, ND #207, SCDAH. Intendant Joseph Johnson, who served from 1825–1826, signed this petition. Also see Powers, *Black Charlestonians,* 14–15.

144. According to the petitioners, "The merchant is not allowed to employ his slave or a free negro or colored person as his clerk; so too is it of the Wharfinger, of the Lawyer, of the Doctor, the Tradesman, and the Shop-keeper; all these avocations and all others whatever they may be, are as your petitioners understand it, protected by law from the intrusion of the colored race. The law does not allow them the chance of an equality, and it makes it a penal offense for those who attempt it in any other pursuit, except in the Mechanic arts." What's more, since blacks were excluded from these occupations, they turned increasingly to the unprotected employments of the petitioners (Petition, ND #4330, SCDAH). Though free blacks and slaves could not work independently at occupations such as wharfingers, clerks, lawyers, doctors, and shopkeepers, they often were permitted to serve under white persons so employed. An ordinance passed in 1806, for instance, stated, "No person or persons whatever, vending goods, wares, and other merchandize [*sic*], or retailing spirituous liquors in a public or open shop within the city, shall on any pretense employ or permit any negro or other slave to sell any such goods, wares, merchandize [*sic*] or liquors, unless the owner thereof or another white person in the employ of such owner be present" (Eckhard, *Digest of Ordinances of the City Council of Charleston From the Year 1783 to Oct. 1844,* 172).

145. Schirmer Diary, November 5, 1853, SCHS. The offending merchant was H. W. Kuhntmann or Kuhtman. See Bagget, *Directory of the City of Charleston for the Year 1852.*

146. Petition, ND #4330, SCDAH. Also see *Charleston Mercury,* December 12, 1860.

147. Johnson and Roark, *Black Masters,* 266–70, 276–81; Johnson and Roark, eds., *No Chariot,* 132–42; Committee Report, 1861 #90, SCDAH. Also see *Charleston Mercury,* December 6 and 18, 1860; and Bellows, *Benevolence among Slaveholders,* 186–87.

148. Since the collection of the 1860 U.S. Census in Charleston was completed on August 2—before the announcement of the new policy on August 9—it accurately reflected the shifting racial and ethnic composition that had taken place on Charleston's waterfront prior to this crackdown on free blacks. Newspaper reports indicated that stevedores indeed were among those free blacks who made their way northward in the late summer and fall of 1860. Charleston's free black tax records, meanwhile, listed three stevedores—John Chavis, William Turpin, and William Purvis—in 1861. But only Purvis retained his position on the docks in 1862–64; Turpin was listed as a laborer in 1862 before disappearing from these records; and Chavis did not appear from 1862 to 1864. See Johnson and Roark, *Black Masters,* 236–37, 274–75, 290–92; Johnson and Roark, eds., *No Chariot,* 85–116, 128–49; *The North American* (Philadelphia) qtd. in *The Liberator* (Boston), November 16, 1860; and *The Liberator,* November 23, 1860. Also see Committee Reports, ND #2183, 1860 #10, SCDAH; and Charleston Free Black Capitation Tax

Books, CCPL and CLS. Amid this enslavement scare one free person of color ironically sneaked back into Charleston by stowing away aboard a northern steamer in violation of the 1820 statute against the reentry of free blacks into South Carolina after departing the state for the North. See Johnson and Roark, eds., *No Chariot*, 110, 114–15, note 23. Finally, there is no city directory or census evidence to support the argument that the "Charleston defense" shielded the stevedoring jobs of light-skinned free blacks while abandoning the supposedly less respectable dark-skinned blacks to withering white competition. Among the six free black stevedores in the 1850 U.S. Census, for instance, three were categorized as black and three as mulatto. The one remaining free black stevedore appearing in the 1860 U.S. Census was listed as black.

149. See note 38, above.

Chapter Five: "The unacclimated stranger should be positively prohibited"

1. Kiple and King, *Another Dimension*, 69–78; Waring, *History of Medicine in South Carolina, 1825–1900*, 9–11.
2. See Young, "Ideology and Death," 681, 693–96.
3. See, for instance, Wood, *Black Majority*, 63–91.
4. Kiple, ed., *Cambridge World History*, 642–49; Curtin, *Death by Migration*, 71–76.
5. Petition, 1827 #31, SCDAH; Committee Report, 1827 #42, SCDAH.
6. Chambers, *Conquest of Cholera*, 64, 113, 118; Rosenberg, *Cholera Years*, 37; Schirmer Diary, August 1, 1832, SCHS. Regarding the quarantine, see Goldfield, *Region, Race, and Cities*, 214–15; and Rosenberg, *Cholera Years*, 14–15.
7. City Council Minutes, June 25, 1832, *Charleston Courier*, July 2, 1832. The City Council similarly resolved in June 1833 to employ four additional scavenger carts. See City Council Minutes, June 18, 1833, *Charleston Courier*, June 20, 1833.
8. Schirmer Diary, August 1, 1832, SCHS.
9. Pinckney, "Report, 1837–1838," 7, 46, 50; Petition, 1832 #30, SCDAH; Committee Reports, 1832 #84, 1838 #214, 1838 #271, SCDAH; *Report of Law Cases*, 123–41; Chambers, *Conquest of Cholera*, 82.
10. Waring, "Asiatic Cholera," 459–60; Rosenberg, *Cholera Years*, 37; Goldfield, *Region, Race, and Cities*, 215; Gaillard and Kinloch, "Report on the Cholera," 27.
11. *Report of Law Cases*, 124.
12. Waring, "Asiatic Cholera," 459; Waring, *History of Medicine in South Carolina, 1825–1900*, 41–42. Also see Petition, 1832 #30, SCDAH.
13. Kiple and King, *Another Dimension*, 25–57, 147–57; Cooper, "Cholera in Brazil," 235–56. Also see note 67, below.
14. *Charleston Courier*, August 8, 1832.
15. Kiple and King, *Another Dimension*, 148, 151.
16. Carson, ed., *Life, Letters, and Speeches of James Louis Petigru*, 161. Also see Waring, "Asiatic Cholera," 460; Waring, *History of Medicine in South Carolina, 1825–1900*, 42–43; and Pollitzer, *Gullah People*, 80.
17. *Charleston Courier*, August 20 and 23, 1834; Waring, "Asiatic Cholera," 460; Waring, *History of Medicine in South Carolina, 1825–1900*, 43; Gaillard and Kinloch, "Report

on the Cholera," 27. Charleston's maritime quarantine laws were strengthened on December 20, 1832. See Eckhard, *Digest of Ordinances of the City Council of Charleston From the Year 1783 to Oct. 1844,* 373–74.

18. "Facts and Speculation on Cholera," 290, 293; Goldfield, *Region, Race, and Cities,* 215.

19. Schirmer Diary, August 20, 1836, SCHS. Later in August, Schirmer noted, "Cholera rumored to be here, and 29 Physicians officially announced its appearance, increasing every day and as yet principally confined among the Blacks" (Schirmer Diary, August 27, 1836, SCHS). Also see Schirmer Diary, September 3 and 27, 1836; after October 1836, SCHS.

20. Contending that the Board of Health's official mortality reports far underreported the actual number of cholera deaths in the city, Porcher—who "live[d] in sight of 3 Negro burial grounds"—found convincing some local physicians' deduction that the disease had claimed 300 victims by mid-September. See William Mazyck Porcher to Robert Marion Deveaux, September 15 and 17, 1836, William Mazyck Porcher Letters, SCL.

21. During this week ending on October 2, the Board of Health reported the deaths of 118 Charlestonians, exclusive of the Neck north of Boundary Street. Of these, only 4 of the deceased were white and the remaining 114 were black. All of the whites died from cholera, whereas 80 of the 114 blacks died from the disease (Schirmer Diary, October 4, 1836, SCHS).

22. Richard Bacot to Robert Dewar Bacot, September 7, 1836, Bacot Family Collection, SCHS.

23. Bachman et al., *John Bachman,* 137–40.

24. Kiple and King, *Another Dimension,* 152.

25. "Facts and Speculation on Cholera," 293–94; Dawson and DeSaussure, *Census of the City of Charleston . . . 1848,* 198–99; Rosenberg, *Cholera Years,* 55–64, 133, 137; Kiple and King, *Another Dimension,* 151–52; Young, "Ideology and Death," 691–92.

26. *Report of Law Cases,* 125.

27. Richard Bacot to Robert Dewar Bacot, September 7, 1836, Bacot Family Collection, SCHS; William Mazyck Porcher to Robert Marion Deveaux, September 15 and 17, 1836, William Mazyck Porcher Letters, SCL. Also see Bachman et al., *John Bachman,* 139–40; Schirmer Diary, December 31, 1852, SCHS; and Kiple, ed., *Cambridge World History,* 648.

28. Kiple and King, *Another Dimension,* 147, 156.

29. Waring, "Asiatic Cholera," 463–64; Waring, *History of Medicine in South Carolina, 1825–1900,* 46–47; Kiple and King, *Another Dimension,* 152. In an 1852 study of the "life statistics" of southern blacks, J. D. B. De Bow reported, "The greatest mortality ever known in Charleston in the colored class, was in 1836, when it was raised by the cholera to 1 in 19, more than double the average; but even cholera and slavery combined here," De Bow contended, "are far less destructive to the negro than liberty and climate in Boston, where the mortality is said to average 1 in 15" (*Industrial Resources* 2: 294).

30. "Facts and Speculation on Cholera," 292.

31. Wharf owners William Bird, George Chisolm, James Marsh, and William P.

Knox, as well as rice mill owner Thomas Bennett, also lost slaves in the 1836 cholera epidemic (Charleston Death Records, CCPL).

32. Eckhard, *Digest of Ordinances of the City Council of Charleston From the Year 1783 to Oct. 1844*, 263–70, 113–17, 123–25. Also see Eckhard, 254–60; Waring, "Asiatic Cholera," 461–62; Waring, *History of Medicine in South Carolina, 1825–1900*, 43–44; and Goldfield, *Region, Race, and Cities*, 214–17.

33. Charleston City Council, *Ordinances of the City of Charleston, 1833–1837*, 94–97. At a City Council meeting in late August or early September 1837, the aldermen further resolved, "that it shall hereafter be the duty of the Harbour Master to examine the Fruit and Vegetables, which may from time to time be brought by any vessel into this Harbour, and when he shall find any unsound Fruit or Vegetables on Board of any Vessel, he shall report the same to the Port Physician whose duty it shall be to have the same destroyed" (City Council Minutes, undated, CCPL manuscript). Also see Eckhard, *Digest of Ordinances of the City Council of Charleston From the Year 1783 to Oct. 1844*, 79–80; and Schirmer Diary, September 13, 1836, SCHS.

34. "Facts and Speculation on Cholera," 290–95.

35. "Facts and Speculation on Cholera," 294–95.

36. Concerning the applicability of the plantation evacuation plan to Charleston, the *Southern Literary Journal* admitted, "unfortunately it can rarely be adopted in the city" ("Facts and Speculation on Cholera," 294).

37. So many wealthy white Charlestonians fled, in fact, that "The prevalence of the Cholera,—the absence of many of our citizens" was blamed in October 1836 for the disappointing number of subscriptions in support of the Louisville, Cincinnati, and Charleston Railroad. See *Charleston Mercury*, October 24, 1836; Johnson and Roark, eds., *No Chariot*, 9, 101. In the aftermath of Charleston's 1852–53 cholera epidemic, Unitarian minister Charles M. Taggart apprised his congregants that they were "free moral agents," and "The supreme power performs no miracles, to correct our mistakes or supply our ignorance, but leaves us free, to work out our own preservation or deliverance, both from ignorance and sin" ("Virtue of Fasting and Prayer," 10).

38. *Charleston Mercury*, October 31, 1836.

39. *Charleston Courier*, October 27, 1836; *Charleston Mercury*, October 27, 1836. Bill was returned to Charleston on a schooner sailing from Boston to Key West. He was owned by "Miss Ball," perhaps referring to Lydia Jane Ball Waring, who hired out one of her urban slaves to Southern Wharf in the early 1840s.

40. *Charleston Courier*, October 26, 1836. The cholera epidemic, along with the low level of the region's waterways, also curtailed the influx of cotton from the port's hinterlands in September and October 1836. Plantation owners understandably were reluctant to send their enslaved boatmen, carters, and wagoners to Charleston in the midst of the prevailing illness. See the "Review of the Market" section of the *Charleston Mercury*, October 1 and 22, 1836, and the "Charleston Markets" section of the *Charleston Courier*, October 15, 1836. Whereas there were only nineteen vessels in the port on the eve of the new commercial season on September 30, 1836, that number increased to thirty-four on October 21, and to forty-seven on November 4. See *Charleston Courier*, October 1 and 22, and November 5, 1836.

41. Charles Hunt to Thomas Lamb, November 5, 1836, Thomas Lamb Papers, MHS. The ship *Switzerland,* along with its captain Charles Hunt, was reported to be in the stream of the Cooper River on October 14, 1836, shortly after arriving from Boston. After docking at Boyce & Co.'s Wharf for nearly a month, the vessel returned to the stream and was awaiting departure for Le Havre on November 11. See *Charleston Courier,* October 15, 22, and 29, and November 5 and 12, 1836. Regarding the *Switzerland,* also see *Charleston Courier,* October 26, 1836.

42. *Charleston Courier,* November 4, 1836. Three weeks earlier the *Charleston Mercury* conveyed the suggestion "that a Report from the Board of Heath in relation to the health of the city, would tend to the restoration of its business, as the few scattering cases of Cholera which are said to prevail, appear to cause no apprehension" (*Charleston Mercury,* October 14, 1836). Throughout October 1836, local newspapers published reports intimating the epidemic's abatement in the city and state. See, for instance, *Charleston Mercury,* October 6 and 10, 1836; and *Charleston Courier,* October 18 and 28, 1836. On November 10, 1836, Intendant Robert Y. Hayne proclaimed November 17 as a day of thanksgiving and prayer to mark the end of the cholera epidemic and the restoration of health and prosperity (*Charleston Courier,* November 11, 1836; *Charleston Mercury,* November 11, 1836).

43. Gaillard and Kinloch, "Report on the Cholera," 27.

44. Goldfield, *Region, Race, and Cities,* 215.

45. *Charleston Courier,* October 29–November 22, 1836. Another wharf sought four or five dockhands for at least five months of waterfront labor. See *Charleston Mercury,* October 14–24, 1836.

46. "Facts and Speculation on Cholera," 292.

47. Rosenberg, *Cholera Years,* 116; Waring, "Asiatic Cholera," 464; Gaillard and Kinloch, "Report on the Cholera," 27; Kiple, ed., *Cambridge World History,* 647; Chambers, *Conquest of Cholera,* 193–259. Though "13 cases of cholera" were recorded at the Orphan House in 1837, scholars have dismissed this episode as "cholera morbus," that is, gastrointestinal disorders resembling the epidemic disease. See Waring, "Asiatic Cholera," 462; and Waring, *History of Medicine in South Carolina, 1825–1900,* 47. City death records failed to confirm one historian's unsubstantiated claim that cholera appeared in Charleston in December 1842. See Farley, *Account of the History of Stranger's Fever,* 76; and Charleston Death Records, CCPL. Prompted by the appearance of cholera in both New York City and New Orleans, Charleston's City Council passed resolutions in December 1848 implementing local sanitation measures and enforcing the quarantine regulations for vessels arriving from those cities. At a meeting in early March 1849, the City Council concurred with Port Physician Thomas Y. Simons's recommendation that the quarantine be lifted for vessels arriving from New Orleans, since it was reported that the disease had subsided in the Crescent City. See City Council Minutes, December 14, 1848, *Charleston Mercury,* December 15, 1848; City Council Minutes, December 30, 1848, *Charleston Mercury,* January 1, 1849; City Council Minutes, January 2, 1849, *Charleston Mercury,* January 3, 1849; and City Council Minutes, March 2, 1849, *Charleston Mercury,* March 3, 1849; also see Schirmer Diary, July 28, 1849, SCHS.

48. Gaillard and Kinloch, "Report on the Cholera," 27–28; Waring, *History of Medicine in South Carolina, 1825–1900,* 47.

49. Gaillard and Kinloch, "Report on the Cholera," 28–29; Waring, "Asiatic Cholera," 464.

50. Gaillard and Kinloch, "Report on the Cholera," 31, 32–33.

51. Gaillard and Kinloch, "Report on the Cholera," 29–34. Among Thomas Bennett's mill hands who died of cholera in 1852–53 were a fifty-year-old black slave named Dick and a sixty-year-old bondsman named Calamiel. Lucas's enslaved black victims included a forty-five-year-old named Adam, a forty-eight-year-old named Jacob, a twenty-five-year-old named Primus, and a forty-five-year-old named Simon (Charleston Death Records, CCPL). Also see Schirmer Diary, December 18, 26, and 31, 1852; and January 5 and 15, 1853, SCHS.

52. Of the 419 cholera fatalities listed in Charleston's death records from the 1836 and 1852–53 epidemics, the vast majority were born in Charleston or elsewhere in the South. Only 3 Irish-born immigrants died from cholera in Charleston in 1836, and only 9 in 1852–53. Among the 8 other immigrant deaths from cholera in 1836 were 1 German, 2 Englishmen, 1 Scotsman, and 4 Frenchmen. The 5 non-Irish immigrant cholera deaths in 1852–53 included 3 Germans and 2 Englishmen (Charleston Death Records, CCPL; Gaillard and Kinloch, "Report on the Cholera," 32; Waring, "Asiatic Cholera," 464–65). Charleston physician Samuel Henry Dickson observed in early January 1853, "Thus far [cholera] has attacked very few except the lowest class of White labourers and Negroes." See Waring, "Asiatic Cholera," 465; and Kiple and King, *Another Dimension,* 152, 154.

53. According to one study, "the impression that cholera was essentially a black man's disease still prevailed" at the time of the last major cholera epidemic in U.S. history in 1866 (Kiple and King, *Another Dimension,* 152).

54. "Yellow Fever in Charleston in 1852," 142–43.

55. Among other names, yellow fever was known as the "disease of acclimation," "patriotic fever," and "yellow jack" (Kiple, ed., *Cambridge World History,* 1100–1101).

56. As scholar Charles Rosenberg argued, "Yet popular convictions must not be dismissed as merely crude, or inconsistent, or even irrational. The ideas which men have held in the past become, through their belief, truth—at least historical truth. . . . With almost nothing known of cholera and its cause, physicians, especially in 1832 and 1849, clearly reflected the values and preconceptions of their class and time in the discussion of what are ostensibly medical problems. A careful study of their writings on cholera discloses as well something of the slow and complex way in which scientific ideas change, not necessarily in the minds of a few great men, but in that substrate of assumption and accepted wisdom which constitutes the intellectual texture of an age" (*Cholera Years,* introduction, 7–9).

57. See Curtin, *Death by Migration,* 44–47, 66, 109–11; and Kiple, ed., *Cambridge World History,* 1101–2. Dr. William Hume distinguished between the protections of "acclimation" to a location versus "habitude" to a disease ("Yellow Fever of Charleston," 23–31).

58. See Simons, "Essay on the Yellow Fever," 782; Cain, "History of the Epidemic of Yellow Fever," 12; and Kiple, ed., *Cambridge World History,* 1101, 1104. For contemporary

views on the acclimation status of children, see Pinckney, "Report . . . During the Late Epidemic," 26; "Editorial and Miscellaneous: Letter to the Late Editors," 137; and Cain, "History of the Epidemic of Yellow Fever," 11.

59. See, for example, Strobel, *Essay on the Subject of the Yellow Fever,* 201–2; and Chisolm, "Brief Sketch of the Epidemic Yellow Fever of 1854," 439.

60. Kiple, ed., *Cambridge World History,* 1101, 1104; James Carr Papers, SCL; Kinloch, "Brief Description of the Yellow Fever," 10, 16; Johnson, "Some Account of the Origin and Prevention of Yellow Fever," 158; Strobel, *Essay on the Subject of the Yellow Fever,* 142–43, 190–91.

61. Samuel Henry Dickson to B. B. Strobel, in Strobel, *Essay on the Subject of the Yellow Fever,* 128–29; "Editorial and Miscellaneous: Yellow Fever in Charleston," 846. Frederick Law Olmsted deemed 1850s Charleston "The worst climate for unacclimated whites of any town in the United States" (*Cotton Kingdom* 2: 259). Also see Schirmer Diary, August 31, 1852, SCHS; Alfred Huger in 1856, qtd. in Farley, *Account of the History of Stranger's Fever,* 111; and the letters of Henry Gourdin on August 20, 1858, and Louis Gourdin Young on August 27 and September 1, 1858, in Racine, ed., *Gentlemen Merchants,* 340, 345, 347.

62. Pinckney, "Report . . . During the Late Epidemic," 10. Also see John Moultrie Jr. in 1749, qtd. in Farley, *Account of the History of Stranger's Fever,* 40; Simons, "Report on the History and Causes of the Strangers or Yellow Fever," 13; Cain, "History of the Epidemic of Yellow Fever," 23; and "Editorial and Miscellaneous: Yellow Fever in Charleston," 846. For a contrary view, see Henry Gourdin to Robert Newman *Gourdin,* October 7, 1854, in Racine, *Gentlemen Merchants,* 283.

63. For instance, see Strobel, *Essay on the Subject of the Yellow Fever,* 201–2, 128–29; Bird, "Observations on Yellow Fever," 333; Chisolm, "Brief Sketch of the Epidemic Yellow Fever of 1854," 434; Johnson, "Some Account of the Origin and Prevention of Yellow Fever," 158; "Review of R. LaRoche," 831; Simons, "Report on the History and Causes of the Strangers or Yellow Fever," 21; and Simons, "Essay on the Yellow Fever," 782. Just as some argued that immigrants could acquire acclimated status, many professed the notion that native Charlestonians who had been away from the city for an extended period of time could lose their acclimation. See Ramsay, "Dissertation on Preserving Health," 30; John Perrier to Thomas Lamb, April 1, 1833, Thomas Lamb Papers, MHS; Simons, "Observations in Reply to Hume," 185; and Ann Elliott Morris Vanderhorst Diary, June 15, 1859, Ann Elliott Morris Vanderhorst Papers, SCHS.

64. Kiple, ed., *Cambridge World History,* 1101–2.

65. Waring, "John Moultrie Jr., M.D., . . . His Thesis on Yellow Fever," 772–77; Chisolm, "Brief Sketch of the Epidemic Yellow Fever of 1854," 446–47; Dickson, "Yellow Fever," 745; Cain, "History of the Epidemic of Yellow Fever," 11, 20–21; Williman, "Account of the Yellow Fever Epidemic in Norfolk," 333–34.

66. Hume, "On the Introduction, Propagation, and Decline of the Yellow Fever in Charleston," 21; Dawson, "Report of the Cases of Yellow Fever," 701. Regarding black vomit, see Dickson, "Yellow Fever," 747; and Kiple, ed., *Cambridge World History,* 1100, 1102.

67. For a discussion of relative black immunity to yellow fever, see Curtin, "Epidemiology of the Slave Trade," 190–216; Kiple and Kiple, "Black Yellow Fever Immunities," 419–36; Kiple, ed., *Cambridge World History*, 1100–1107; Kiple and King, *Another Dimension*, 29–49; Kiple, "Survey of Recent Literature," 7–34; Watts, "Yellow Fever Immunities," 955–67; Kiple, "Response to Sheldon Watts," 969–74; and Watts, "Response to Kenneth Kiple," 975–76.

68. Adams qtd. in Farley, *Account of the History of Stranger's Fever,* 34; also see 93–94; and Wood, *Black Majority,* 80–83, 90–91. According to *The Cambridge World History of Human Disease,* the first visitation of yellow fever in Charleston occurred in 1690 (Kiple, ed., *Cambridge World History,* 1103). For a good, albeit brief, overview of the history of yellow fever in South Carolina, see Waring, *History of Medicine in South Carolina, 1670–1825,* and *History of Medicine in South Carolina, 1825–1900,* 30–35.

69. Horlbeck, "Maritime Sanitation," 9. Also see "Facts and Speculation on Cholera," 292; Dawson and DeSaussure, *Census of the City of Charleston . . . 1848,* 200; "Review of R. LaRoche," 831; Simons, "Report on the History and Causes of the Strangers or Yellow Fever," 14; Simons, "Essay on the Yellow Fever," 782, 780; Dawson, "Report of the Cases of Yellow Fever," 701; and Cain, "History of the Epidemic of Yellow Fever," 10. This greater degree of acclimation among blacks prompted some white Charlestonians during the 1850s to petition the state legislature to reconsider a bill aimed at driving free blacks from the state: "Their labor is indispensable to us in this neighborhood. They are the only work men who will, or can, take employment . . . in the summer. We cannot build or repair a house in that season without the aid of the colored carpenter or bricklayer." The petition's signatories, among many others, included Mayor Charles Macbeth, suggesting that the document was written during the late 1850s (Petition, ND #2801, SCDAH).

70. Ramsay qtd. in Horlbeck, "Maritime Sanitation," 7.

71. Strobel, *Essay on the Subject of the Yellow Fever,* 130, 11. Also see Dickson, "Yellow Fever," 753; Hume, "Report to the City Council," 154; and Lebby et al., "Report of the Committee of the City Council of Charleston, on the Origin and Diffusion of the Yellow Fever," 28. A few eighteenth-century physicians, such as Dr. James Killpatrick, occasionally posited the importation theory of yellow fever. See Farley, *Account of the History of Stranger's Fever,* 38. For brief biographies of many of the physicians noted in this chapter, see Waring, *History of Medicine in South Carolina, 1670–1825,* 173–330; and Waring, *History of Medicine in South Carolina, 1825–1900,* 199–319.

72. Regarding Rush's views and influence on yellow fever's origins debate, see Simons, "Report on the History and Causes of the Strangers or Yellow Fever," 15; "Review of R. LaRoche," 833; Hume, "Report to the City Council," 148; Simons, "Report Read Before the City Council," 342; Hume, "On the Introduction, Propagation, and Decline of the Yellow Fever in Charleston," 1; Simons, "Observations in Reply to Hume," 175; Hume, "On the Introduction of Yellow Fever into Savannah," 10, 15, 18–19; and Strobel, *Essay on the Subject of the Yellow Fever,* 8.

73. Hume, "Meteorological and Other Observations in Reference to the Causes of Yellow Fever in Charleston," 2–3, 27.

74. Simons, "Report on the History and Causes of the Strangers or Yellow Fever," 18; Strobel, *Essay on the Subject of the Yellow Fever,* 34, 210.

75. *Charleston Mercury,* November 5, 1858.

76. Simons, "Report on the Epidemic Yellow Fever," 363–64; Hume, "Inquiry into Some of the . . . Causes to Which the Endemic Origin of Yellow Fever Has Been Attributed," 727; Hume, "On the Introduction, Propagation, and Decline of the Yellow Fever in Charleston," 5; Petition, ND #5557, SCDAH. Also see Committee Report, ND #5866, SCDAH; Walker, *Ordinances of the City of Charleston From the 19th of August 1844, to the 14th of September 1854,* 149, 185, 187; and Grand Jury Presentments, Charleston District, January 1824, May 1824, SCDAH.

77. John Lining to Robert Whytt, December 11, 1753, qtd. in Hume, "Report to the City Council," 148–49; Hume, "Report to the City Council," 162. Hume, who colleagues eventually characterized as "the archbishop of contagion," converted from the localist to the importationist cause. See Waring, *History of Medicine in South Carolina, 1825–1900,* 249; Hume, "Sequel to Meteorological and Other Observations," 60; and Hume, "Inquiry into Some of the . . . Causes to Which the Endemic Origin of Yellow Fever Has Been Attributed," 727. Dr. Dickson too migrated from the localist to the importationist camp. See Dickson, "Account of the Epidemic," 64–77; and Dickson, "Yellow Fever," 754–55.

78. Though scholars have disagreed whether yellow fever originated in Africa or the Americas, the virus was endemic in the tropical regions of both following the escalation of the Atlantic slave and commercial trades in the mid-seventeenth century. The disease never has been endemic in the United States, but trade with the Caribbean exposed American port cities to yellow fever beginning in the 1660s. During the nineteenth century, according to *The Cambridge World History of Human Disease,* "Cuba became the yellow fever capital of the Caribbean." On August 21, 1856, "A Citizen" wrote to the *Charleston Mercury* that St. Jago de Cuba "is notoriously the most unhealthy port in the Island," and that the sickness of Trinidad de Cuba "ought to be taken for granted, that when Yellow Fever prevails as an epidemic, every haunt of commerce in Cuba is infected." See Kiple, ed., *Cambridge World History,* 1100–1105; and *Charleston Mercury,* August 21, 1856. Also see Vainio and Cutts, "Yellow Fever," 5, 10, 16.

79. Kiple, ed., *Cambridge World History,* 1100–1101.

80. *Charleston Mercury,* November 10, 1858. Also see McCrady, *Series of Articles upon the Means of Preventing the Recurrence of Yellow Fever;* Dickson, "Yellow Fever," 749; and Hume, "On the Germination of Yellow Fever," 177. Many importationists adhered to the concept of "contingent contagion." See, for instance, Johnson, "Some Account of the Origin and Prevention of Yellow Fever," 154–63; and Gaillard, "Essay on the Importability and Diffusion of Yellow Fever," 460.

81. Simons, "Essay on the Yellow Fever," 795–96; Hume, "Meteorological and Other Observations in Reference to the Causes of Yellow Fever in Charleston," 28; Hume, "Sequel to Meteorological and Other Observations," 65; "Review of R. LaRoche," 838; Simons, "Report on the History and Causes of the Strangers or Yellow Fever," 22. Also see Waring, *History of Medicine in South Carolina, 1825–1900,* 66–69.

82. Eckhard, *Digest of Ordinances of the City Council of Charleston From the Year 1783 to Oct. 1844*, 129, 305, 254–59, 263–68; Walker, *Ordinances of the City of Charleston From the 19th of August 1844, to the 14th of September 1854*, 17. Englishman John Lambert observed the bodies of deceased slave imports being thrown into the Cooper River in early 1808 (*Travels through Canada, and the United States* 2: 166).

83. Simons, "Observations in Reply to Hume," 171–72. Also see Simons, "Essay on the Yellow Fever," 794–95; and Simons, "Report Read Before the City Council," 333.

84. For a brief history of Charleston's quarantine and the origins debate, see Farley, *Account of the History of Stranger's Fever*, 42, 48–49, 90–93, 128–41. An updated treatment of these and other related topics can be found in McCandless, *Slavery, Disease, and Suffering*, 61–83, 106–24, 226–48.

85. Strobel, *Essay on the Subject of the Yellow Fever*, preface, 171–74, 223–24.

86. On December 20, 1832, the South Carolina state legislature passed "An Act to Enlarge and Extend the Powers of the Governor, and of the City Council of Charleston, Over Quarantine." Under the authority of this legislation, the Charleston City Council passed the June 1840 quarantine ordinance. See Eckhard, *Digest of Ordinances of the City Council of Charleston From the Year 1783 to Oct. 1844*, 373–74, 211–14.

87. Hume, "Report to the City Council," 162. Also see Farley, *Account of the History of Stranger's Fever*, 91. Simons—who described himself as "the principal officer to whom the external and internal medical police of the city has been entrusted"—served as the port physician from 1821 until his death in 1857. The 1840 ordinance called for "infected" cargo to be removed and the hold to be cleaned as well. But Simons explained, "The cargo could not properly be taken out to disinfect the hold of the vessels, there being neither ware-houses nor lighters, nor any means for such purposes" at the quarantine ground. British Consul William Ogilby confirmed Simons's claim that Charleston lacked the means to disinfect the holds of vessels at quarantine. See Simons, "Report Read Before the City Council," 334, 350; Simons, "Observations in Reply to Hume," 171, 172, 174–75; and Ogilby, "British Counsel Report," no. 18, SCL. The lax enforcement of the quarantine during this period also was enabled by the relative absence of yellow fever in Charleston between the 1839 and 1849 epidemics. One New England ship captain was so impressed by the health of the city in 1845 that he wrote to his father, "The keeper of a grave yard here who has been dependent upon his funeral fees for support has applied to the city government for aid as his business will not keep him from starving!" (Henry Burr to Daniel Burr, September 4, 1845, Letters of Captain Henry P. Burr, CRCMS). Also see Henry Burr to Daniel Burr, August 28, 1847; and Honour, *Directory of the City of Charleston and Neck for 1849*, preface, iv.

88. Hume argued that the "Transhipment [*sic*] of the cargo, in order to ventilate and purify the hold of the vessel, is indispensable to an efficient quarantine." Hume also recommended that to "guard against the failure of complete disinfection" of either the cargo or the vessels, "it would be prudent to assign an especial and separate wharf . . . removed to the greatest possible distance" from the eastern Cooper River wharves ("Report to the City Council," 160–64). Regarding the use of lighters, also see City Council Minutes, June 8, 1858, *Charleston Mercury*, June 9, 1858. For reaction to Hume's

proposals, see Simons, "Observations in Reply to Hume," 171, 174; and Simons, "Report Read Before the City Council," 334.

89. Hume, "Report to the City Council," 163–64, 157. For a brief history of the Marine Hospital, see Waring, *History of Medicine in South Carolina, 1825–1900*, 15–19.

90. Hume, "Report to the City Council," 158; Charleston Death Records, CCPL.

91. Hume, "Inquiry into Some of the . . . Causes to Which the Endemic Origin of Yellow Fever Has Been Attributed," 728–29; Charleston Death Records, CCPL.

92. City Council Minutes, February 14, 1854, *Charleston Mercury,* February 16, 1854.

93. Hume, "Report to the City Council," 160, 147.

94. City Council Minutes, April 21, 1854, *Charleston Mercury,* April 25, 1854; City Council Minutes, May 23, 1854, *Charleston Mercury,* May 27, 1854. Hume went much further in 1860, calling for the annual prohibition of the West Indies trade between June and September ("Yellow Fever of Charleston," 1–32).

95. Kiple, ed., *Cambridge World History,* 1102.

96. Hume, "Report to the City Council," 164; City Council Minutes, May 23, 1854, *Charleston Mercury,* May 27, 1854. Hume's quarantine bill also proposed that the port physician be granted a number of new powers. See City Council Minutes, April 21, 1854, *Charleston Mercury,* April 25, 1854.

97. City Council Minutes, May 9, 1854, *Charleston Mercury,* May 11, 1854; City Council Minutes, May 23, 1854, *Charleston Mercury,* May 27, 1854.

98. Ramsay, "Dissertation on Preserving Health," 29; Strobel, *Essay on the Subject of the Yellow Fever,* 7. Echoing Ramsay, Hume declared in January 1855, "Health and wealth have been arrayed against each other in hostile attitude" ("On the Introduction, Propagation, and Decline of the Yellow Fever in Charleston," 35; also see Hume, "Yellow Fever of Charleston," 1–32). Frequently unmentioned, however, was the damage that epidemic diseases exacted on Charleston's economy. At the end of 1852, Jacob Schirmer lamented in his diary that "the appearance of yellow fever this last summer has partially blasted the prospects of the Merchants," and then how just as commerce and prosperity "were again reviving the Cholera made its appearance on our borders and partially visited our City, which again threw us back" (Schirmer Diary, after December 1852, SCHS). Also see Kiple, ed., *Cambridge World History,* 648.

99. City Council Minutes, May 23, 1854, *Charleston Mercury,* May 27, 1854; City Council Minutes, June 6, 1854, *Charleston Mercury,* June 9, 1854. Writing on May 30 to the editors of the *Charleston Mercury,* "A Merchant" spurned Hume's importation theory and accused the doctor of attempting "to prevent any vessel from coming to Charleston till 1st Nov. next." Ratifying the quarantine bill would "be like putting a chain cable across the Bar [of Charleston Harbor]," the writer argued, since the measures would strangle the port's substantial summer rice trade with Cuba and New Orleans and burgeoning summer cotton trade with Spain (*Charleston Mercury,* May 30, 1854). Regarding the relative difficulty and expense of utilizing cargo lighters, see chapter 3, note 56, above.

100. City Council Minutes, May 23, 1854, *Charleston Mercury,* May 27, 1854. The last quote appeared in the *Charleston Mercury* as follows: "as time wears on, the disease may arrive before we are ready to oppose any impediment to its entrance in to our city." It

reasonably can be assumed that the word "oppose" was a misprint, and thus the word "impose" has been substituted. On May 11 the steamship *Isabel* arrived in Charleston Harbor from Havana, and three days later one of its steerage passengers—who had been taken on board at Key West where yellow fever already was prevailing—was taken to the Marine Hospital with symptoms of the disease. Fortunately, this man recovered and the malady did not spread. Charleston dodged a bullet, but this scare may have prompted the City Council to pass the proposed quarantine bill at the May 23 meeting (Hume, "On the Introduction, Propagation, and Decline of the Yellow Fever in Charleston," 13–14). Also see Hume, "Yellow Fever of Charleston," 4, in which Hume blamed the watering down of the quarantine law for the "calamities of 1858."

    101. City Council Minutes, June 6, 1854, *Charleston Mercury,* June 9, 1854.

    102. City Council Minutes, June 13, 1854, *Charleston Mercury,* June 15, 1854; Simons, "Observations in Reply to Hume," 175–76; Simons, "Report Read Before the City Council," 334–36, 348, 350; Simons, "Essay on the Yellow Fever," 795–96. Simons also pointed out the long-held opinion of the South Carolina Medical Society that a stringent enforcement of quarantine laws was not necessary to prevent yellow fever. In 1854 Simons and Hume debated whether the South Carolina Medical Society maintained this view of quarantine laws. See Simons, "Report on the History and Causes of the Strangers or Yellow Fever," 16–17; Hume, "Report to the City Council," 148, 153, 162; Simons, "Report Read Before the City Council," 344–45; and Farley, *Account of the History of Stranger's Fever,* 90–91.

    103. Sources varied on the *Aquatic's* Irish destination, whether its fore and aft cabins were cleansed and disinfected before or after arriving in Charleston, the composition and health status of the crew, and the precise date and location of the vessel's docking at the city's wharves. See Cain, "History of the Epidemic of Yellow Fever," 4–5, 30; Chisolm, "Brief Sketch of the Epidemic Yellow Fever of 1854," 436; "Editorial and Miscellaneous: Yellow Fever [September 1854]," 710–11; Simons, "Observations in Reply to Hume," 180–81; Hume, "On the Introduction, Propagation, and Decline of the Yellow Fever in Charleston," 18–19; Hume, "On the Introduction of Yellow Fever into Savannah," 3; and Schirmer Diary, July 10, 1854, SCHS. Captain Magee was probably Captain Arthur Magee, who lived at 101 Broad Street in 1852 (Bagget, *Directory of the City of Charleston for the Year 1852*). For a contemporary medical theory regarding the link between yellow fever and ships' holds containing bilge water and molasses, see Johnson, "Some Account of the Origin and Prevention of Yellow Fever," 156.

    104. There is no known evidence to suggest the regular segregation of black and white work gangs on Charleston's antebellum waterfront. See Hugill, *Shanties and Sailors' Songs,* 50.

    105. Olmsted, *Journey,* 550–51. Also see Phillips, *American Negro Slavery,* 301–3.

    106. Hume, "Report to the City Council," 160; Hume, "On the Introduction, Propagation, and Decline of the Yellow Fever in Charleston," 12, 35. Also see Hume, "Meteorological and Other Observations in Reference to the Causes of Yellow Fever in Charleston," 11; and Hume, "Yellow Fever of Charleston," 1–2, 29–30. Dr. B. B. Strobel similarly exclaimed in 1840, "These are questions that involve the interest and lives of others, and which we have no right to jeopardize! Dare we place the life-blood of our

fellow men in one scale, and coldly calculate how many pounds, shillings and pence in the other shall preponderate?" (*Essay on the Subject of the Yellow Fever*, 9–10).

107. Simons, "Observations in Reply to Hume," 181; Hume, "On the Introduction, Propagation, and Decline of the Yellow Fever in Charleston," 22; Schirmer Diary, July 10, 1854, SCHS.

108. For instances of labor activism among Irishmen elsewhere in the antebellum South, see Gleeson, *Irish in the South*, 51–54, 125.

109. Hume, "On the Introduction, Propagation, and Decline of the Yellow Fever in Charleston," 22; Cain, "History of the Epidemic of Yellow Fever," 6, 31; Charleston Death Records, CCPL; "Editorial and Miscellaneous: Yellow Fever [September 1854]," 711; Chisolm, "Brief Sketch of the Epidemic Yellow Fever of 1854," 437; Simons, "Observations in Reply to Hume," 182. Garvey also was referred to as Garrie, and he appeared in the death records as M. Garvin. McNeal also was spelled McNeall. Many medical experts believed that getting wet or sleeping in open air, and thus being exposed to dew, were contributing causes of yellow fever. See Cain, "History of the Epidemic of Yellow Fever," 14; Simons, "Report on the Epidemic Yellow Fever," 369; and *Charleston Courier*, September 6, 1854. Dr. Cain reported that Garvey died "of coma." Some physicians reported congestion of the brain as a symptom of those stricken with yellow fever, especially among the intemperate. For example, see Williman, "Account of the Yellow Fever Epidemic in Norfolk," 333.

110. Cain, "History of the Epidemic of Yellow Fever," 6, 31.

111. Simons, "Observations in Reply to Hume," 182.

112. Hume, "On the Introduction, Propagation, and Decline of the Yellow Fever in Charleston," 22. The names of these two deceased workers were not disclosed. But an examination of Charleston's death records from August 1854 revealed that Patrick Loone, a forty-year-old Irishman, died of yellow fever at the poor or alms house on August 25, 1854, and that Francis Long, a twenty-six-year-old Irishman, died of yellow fever on Tradd Street on August 26, 1854. In addition, two other Irishmen died of yellow fever at the Marine Hospital (which normally was reserved for seamen) on August 20 and 22, and two more Irishmen died of the disease on August 31, one at the alms house and the other on Calhoun Street (Charleston Death Records, CCPL).

113. Hume, "On the Introduction, Propagation, and Decline of the Yellow Fever in Charleston," 22.

114. During the City Council meeting on July 20, 1858, Alderman James H. Taylor articulated "the theory that woolen, linen or hemp fabrics are capable of carrying the seeds of [yellow fever] from one locality to another," and revealed that "it is the opinion of some physicians of good reputation, 'that persons employed on lighters, whose clothes become impregnated with disease, might, under certain circumstances, communicate it to others'" (City Council Minutes, July 20, 1858, *Charleston Mercury*, July 22, 1858). An Irish dockworker named Anthony Howe similarly was blamed for spreading yellow fever to his family and neighborhood after unloading a vessel during the 1853 epidemic in New Orleans (Gaillard, "Essay on the Importability and Diffusion of Yellow Fever," 480).

115. Dr. Cain referred to Mr. and Mrs. Gorman as Gorham, and the city death records referred to Mrs. Gorman as Mrs. German. Cain claimed that Mary Gorman was stricken with the fever on August 17 and died on August 20, but the death records (which referred to Mary Gorman as Mary Gooman) indicated that the infant indeed died on August 23 from yellow fever. Hume reported in March 1858 that Mr. Gorman "is still alive and well," and the 1859 city directory listed a laborer named Joseph Gorman living on Nunan Street near Rutledge. The same directory included a watchman named George McNeil residing on Smith Street opposite Marion Street. See Cain, "History of the Epidemic of Yellow Fever," 6, 32, 34; Charleston Death Records, CCPL; "Editorial and Miscellaneous: Yellow Fever [September 1854]," 712; Hume, "On the Introduction, Propagation, and Decline of the Yellow Fever in Charleston," 6–8, 26; Chisolm, "Brief Sketch of the Epidemic Yellow Fever of 1854," 437; Hume, "On the Germination of Yellow Fever," 146; and Mears and Turnbull, *Charleston Directory* (1859).

116. Simons, "Report Read Before the City Council," 334. Also see Lebby et al., "Report of the Committee of the City Council of Charleston, on the Origin and Diffusion of the Yellow Fever," 36.

117. Cain, "History of the Epidemic of Yellow Fever," 4–7, 28–34; "Editorial and Miscellaneous: Yellow Fever [September 1854]," 710–12; Hume, "On the Introduction, Propagation, and Decline of the Yellow Fever in Charleston," 22; Charleston Death Records, CCPL.

118. Cain, "History of the Epidemic of Yellow Fever," 34. Not realizing that Mr. Gorman had worked on the *Aquatic,* Hume attempted to trace Mrs. Gorman's movements during the days leading up to her attack. "We have no reason to believe that she ever visited the immediate neighborhood of the infected vessels," Hume puzzled. On a trip to and from the city market it was estimated that she must have come within 1,200 feet of the *Aquatic* and within 900 feet of the tainted Spanish polacre *Concha,* and that "if she went to the market on or after the 12th [of August], she must have passed within one hundred and fifty feet of [Garvey's] house, in Pinckney-st., where the Irishman who worked on board of the Aquatic died." Of course, according to the prevailing medical beliefs of the day, Mrs. Gorman did not have to go to the disease; the disease came to her via her husband's clothing. Hume finally concluded that "we attribute the origin of Mrs. Gorman's case to the lowness and moisture" of her house, conditions which enabled the propagation of the imported disease ("On the Introduction, Propagation, and Decline of the Yellow Fever in Charleston," 8, 26–27).

119. The *Aquatic* was not the only West Indies vessel permitted to come up to the city's wharves during the summer of 1854. The two Spanish polacres *Concha* and *Columbus* sailed into Charleston Harbor from Havana on July 21, and subsequently were linked to the yellow fever illness of Mr. F. Salus (a clerk for Hall & Co. on Central Wharf and a native of Barcelona who had been in Charleston for only six months) and the death of Mr. Friday (a clerk for factor and commission merchant Rice Dulin on Central Wharf and a native of Columbia, South Carolina). See Cain, "History of the Epidemic of Yellow Fever," 5–6, 29, 32; Simons, "Observations in Reply to Hume," 179–80; Chisolm, "Brief Sketch of the Epidemic Yellow Fever of 1854," 436–37; "Editorial

and Miscellaneous: Yellow Fever [September 1854]," 711–12; Hume, "On the Introduction of Yellow Fever into Savannah," 12–13; Hume, "On the Introduction, Propagation, and Decline of the Yellow Fever in Charleston," 21–22; and Bagget, *Directory of the City of Charleston for the Year 1852.* The 1855 city directory listed Mr. Salus as F. Salas (Gazlay, *Charleston City Directory . . . for 1855*). The above sources varied both on the Spanish vessels' precise date of arrival and the wharves at which they docked. Both Dr. Hume and Dr. Cain argued that the *Aquatic, Concha,* and *Columbus* were simultaneously "three distinct centres of the disease." See Hume, "On the Introduction, Propagation, and Decline of the Yellow Fever in Charleston," 17–19; and Cain, "History of the Epidemic of Yellow Fever," 30–31. The disease also claimed the lives of a number of seamen from healthy northern vessels docked next to or near West Indies vessels. The bark *Vesta,* for example, arrived from Boston on July 16, 1854, and lay in the same dock as the *Aquatic.* Two of the *Vesta*'s seamen were stricken with yellow fever, and one died on August 9, the other on August 15. Similarly, the ship *Sullivan* from New York arrived in Charleston on July 21, and shared a dock with the *Columbus.* Two of this northern vessel's seamen soon were sickened with yellow fever, and one died with black vomit on August 10. Additionally, an Irish woman residing on East Bay Street—nearly opposite North Commercial Wharf where the *Aquatic* had been for two days—was struck down on August 16, and two German men living at the foot of Hasell Street near Dry Dock Wharf were sickened on August 19 and died on August 22 and August 23. See Cain, "History of the Epidemic of Yellow Fever," 5–7; "Editorial and Miscellaneous: Yellow Fever [September 1854]," 711–12; and Chisolm, "Brief Sketch of the Epidemic Yellow Fever of 1854," 436–37.

120. Cain, "History of the Epidemic of Yellow Fever," 32, 7; Hume, "On the Introduction, Propagation, and Decline of the Yellow Fever in Charleston," 19; Schirmer Diary, August 23, 1854, SCHS; "Editorial and Miscellaneous: Yellow Fever [September 1854]," 710. Also see Schirmer Diary, September 1854, SCHS; and Strobel, *Essay on the Subject of the Yellow Fever,* 9, 215–16.

121. Dickson, "Yellow Fever," 745. At the end of September 1854, an estimated 445 people had died. See Horlbeck, "Maritime Sanitation," 9; Cain, "History of the Epidemic of Yellow Fever," 7–8; "Editorial and Miscellaneous: Yellow Fever [November 1854]," 851; and Dawson, "Statistics Relative to the Epidemic," 200.

122. Hume, "On the Introduction, Propagation, and Decline of the Yellow Fever in Charleston," 20, 2–3, 31–32, 35. Also see Schirmer Diary, July 10, 1854, SCHS; and Simons, "Observations in Reply to Hume," 181. The editors of the *Charleston Medical Journal and Review* largely concurred with Hume's quarantine recommendations. See "Editorial and Miscellaneous: Yellow Fever in Charleston," 850.

123. "CHARLESTON" in *Charleston Mercury,* August 20, 1856. Vessels arriving from April 1 to November 1 (exclusive of May 31 to October 1) from the same ports or having fever on board during the voyage were "subject to such quarantine and other rules and regulations, as the Port Physician shall prescribe." See Horsey, *Ordinances of the City of Charleston from the 14th September, 1854, to the 1st December, 1859,* 7–14.

124. Gleeson, *Irish in the South,* 118–19; Miles, "Mayor's Report," 25. During the 1857 mayoral race, Macbeth's opponent campaigned against "the horrors of Catholicism, Germanism, Irishism, Policeism, Drainage, and Quarantine, and all the rest of

the thirteen deadly sins" attributed to Miles's brief tenure (Bellows, *Benevolence among Slaveholders*, 174–75).

125. The Spanish vessel *Columbus,* noted above, was permitted to dock at the Cooper River wharves under identical circumstances two years earlier.

126. Wragg, Hume, and Eason, "Report of the Committee on Health and Drainage," 2–3, 8, 11; Dawson, "Report of the Cases of Yellow Fever," 698–99; Lebby et al., "Report of the Committee of the City Council of Charleston, on the Origin and Diffusion of the Yellow Fever," 7.

127. Wragg, Hume, and Eason, "Report of the Committee on Health and Drainage," 15, 14; Lebby et al., "Report of the Committee of the City Council of Charleston, on the Origin and Diffusion of the Yellow Fever," 8–9.

128. Denning did not appear in the 1850 U.S. Census or the city directories, rendering it likely that he only recently had arrived in Charleston. Denning also was referred to in reports as Dening and Denner, but these names were not included in other local records. Dawson noted that Denning lived at 125 East Bay Street, and the 1856 Committee on Health and Drainage reported 142 East Bay Street. In March 1858 William Hume claimed that the *Industria* "lost six of her crew at the Lazaretto," but the 1856 Committee on Health and Drainage report suggested that six total passengers and crew members sickened, and only three died at the Lazaretto. See Dawson, "Report of the Cases of Yellow Fever," 699; Hume, "On the Germination of Yellow Fever," 160–61; and Wragg, Hume, and Eason, "Report of the Committee on Health and Drainage," 3–4, 7, 11, 14. For a brief history of Roper Hospital, see Waring, *History of Medicine in South Carolina, 1825–1900,* 19–23.

129. Hume, "On the Germination of Yellow Fever," 160; Wragg, Hume, and Eason, "Report of the Committee on Health and Drainage," 16; Charleston Death Records, CCPL.

130. Dr. Dawson's city register report stated that John Abbott and Michael Denning were the first and second Charlestonians to sicken with yellow fever in 1856. Dawson also reported that the first case in 1856 occurred on July 14 aboard the schooner *Exchange* at Palmetto Wharf, and that the second case was Mr. Collens, a man from Savannah who had been in Charleston for only ten days when he took ill on the same day as Abbott, and thus hardly could be considered a Charleston resident any more than a visiting seaman ("Report of the Cases of Yellow Fever," 698–99).

131. Wragg, Hume, and Eason, "Report of the Committee on Health and Drainage," 16; Hume, "On the Germination of Yellow Fever," 160; Charleston Death Records, CCPL; Horlbeck, "Maritime Sanitation," 9; Lebby et al., "Report of the Committee of the City Council of Charleston, on the Origin and Diffusion of the Yellow Fever," 64.

132. *Charleston Mercury,* August 13, 15, 18, and 21, 1856. Also see "Editorial and Miscellaneous: Yellow Fever in Charleston," 845; and Hume, "Yellow Fever of Charleston," 18, 30.

133. City Council Minutes, April 14, 1857, *Charleston Mercury,* April 18, 1857.

134. *Charleston Mercury,* August 13, 1856.

135. Horsey, *Ordinances of the City of Charleston from the 14th September, 1854, to the 1st December, 1859,* 9.

136. *Charleston Mercury,* August 18, 1856. Simons also presented a statement from five of Charleston's commission merchant firms regarding "men coming from vessels at Quarantine for provisions." The certificate, dated August 13, 1856, stated, "We herby [*sic*] certify that the Captains arriving from the different ports of Cuba have been acclimated, and that the permit of the Port Physician has been to allow an officer and four men to come, when necessary, to the city for provisions. One man to go to the market, the others to remain in the boat or consignee's office; that they came in the morning, and returned after obtaining their marketing." Simons made no further comment concerning the acclimation status of these four crew members who typically accompanied the vessels' supposedly acclimated captains.

137. *Charleston Mercury,* August 21, 1856.

138. In March 1854 Simons quoted Hume as warning, "That the crew and passengers of a vessel arriving at quarantine may be well, and after coming to the city, cases of fever may occur, and thus cause an epidemic" (Simons, "Report Read Before the City Council," 334). The Committee on Health and Drainage report referred to Pellighon as Pettijohn. See Wragg, Hume, and Eason, "Report of the Committee on Health and Drainage," 16; Charleston Death Records, CCPL.

139. *Report of Law Cases,* 126, 128, 136, 140. One scholar made the unsubstantiated claim that, "When it was discovered that the wreckers had been in contact with the cholera patients, they were sent back to Charleston in quarantine or kept on Folly Island" (Waring, *History of Medicine in South Carolina, 1825–1900,* 42). Also see Johnson, "Some Account of the Origin and Prevention of Yellow Fever," 159–60.

140. See Strobel, *Essay on the Subject of the Yellow Fever,* 190–96.

141. *Charleston Mercury,* August 13 and 15, 1856. Though "A Citizen" was not identified, he likely was an editor for the *Charleston Medical Journal and Review.* In September 1855 the editors candidly acknowledged their support for the theory of importation of yellow fever and rejection of localist explanations, stating about the latter, "The readers of this Journal are aware that we do not subscribe to this opinion." And in November 1856 an editorial in the journal almost exactly echoed the complaints put forth by "A Citizen" in the pages of the *Charleston Mercury* a few months earlier. See "Editorial and Miscellaneous: Yellow Fever in Norfolk and Portsmouth," 733; and "Editorial and Miscellaneous: Yellow Fever in Charleston," 846–47. Also see "Yellow Fever and Quarantine," 706–7.

142. Dickson, "Yellow Fever," 755.

143. Denying that such communication could have introduced yellow fever into the city, the same report maintained that, although Brown's Wharf "had by far the most intercourse with the vessels and cargoes arriving from infected Ports," such as that of the *St. Andrews,* "it should not be forgotten that among the numerous laborers and others employed about Brown's wharf not a single case of fever occurred." And even though an Italian seaman on a vessel from New York became fatally ill while at the wharf next to Brown's, the committee reasoned that, if this unacclimated sailor "did contract his disease from the intercourse of the wharf with vessels from infected ports, others equally subject to the disease and exposed to it for a longer time," such as unacclimated Irish dock workers, "failed to suffer." That may have been so in 1856, when the afflicted

Irish workers had been employed at the quarantine ground on lighters; but it had not been the case for Mr. Garvey and Mr. McNeal in 1854, who had worked on what were thought to be contaminated ships tied up at the city's wharves (Wragg, Hume, and Eason, "Report of the Committee on Health and Drainage," 8, 9, 15).

144. Hume, "Report to the City Council," 164; City Council Minutes, January 19, 1854, *Charleston Mercury*, January 23, 1854; Eckhard, *Digest of Ordinances of the City Council of Charleston From the Year 1783 to Oct. 1844*, 373; Walker, *Ordinances of the City of Charleston From the 19th of August 1844, to the 14th of September 1854*, 213; Horsey, *Ordinances of the City of Charleston from the 14th September, 1854, to the 1st December, 1859*, 12. The 1832 act granted the governor or Charleston City Council the power to "cause all persons arriving in or going on board of [a quarantined] vessel, or handling such infected cargo, to be removed to such place as may be designated by the Governor or City Council, there to remain under the orders of the Governor or City Council." For information regarding New York's quarantine policies and stevedores, see *New York Herald*, August 27 and September 5, 1856; *Charleston Mercury*, September 20, 1858; "Editorial and Miscellaneous: Yellow Fever in Charleston," 851–53; and "Proceedings and Debates," 219–20.

145. Taylor even worried about acclimated lightermen, who he mistakenly believed might introduce yellow fever into the city upon their clothing. See City Council Minutes, July 20, 1858, *Charleston Mercury*, July 22, 1858. Also see note 114, above.

146. Hume, "Report to the City Council," 164.

147. The April 1855 quarantine ordinance only vaguely declared, "No lighter shall be employed to load or unload vessels at quarantine, without permission of the Port Physician and Mayor, and subject to such restrictions as they shall impose" (Horsey, *Ordinances of the City of Charleston from the 14th September, 1854, to the 1st December, 1859*, 9).

148. "Editorial and Miscellaneous: Quarantine Regulations," 596–97; City Council Minutes, May 15, 1855, *Charleston Mercury*, May 17, 1855. The resolution also required passengers desiring to leave a quarantined vessel and come to the city to obtain certificates of acclimation, and declared that those who did not qualify but on their way to cities outside of South Carolina could, "at the discretion of the Port Physician, and with the concurrence of the Mayor, if in health, be transported to the Railroad Depot, by way of the uppermost wharf, with the *bona fide* intent to depart from the city, and not return within twenty-one days, nor to remain within the State." Also see City Council Minutes, June 11, 1857, *Charleston Mercury*, June 12, 1857.

149. *Charleston Mercury*, August 18, 1856.

150. *Charleston Mercury*, August 18, 1856. Simons defiantly informed the City Council in April 1857 that "the law instructed me . . . to have cargos discharged by lighters with crews acclimated, to be brought to the city," adding that, "If the course pursued . . . as regards persons going in lighters and laborers to discharge cargo of vessels and load them, is defective . . . you have full information so as to guide you in making improvements" (City Council Minutes, April 14, 1857, *Charleston Mercury*, April 18, 1857).

151. *Charleston Mercury*, August 20, 1856.

152. *Charleston Mercury,* August 18, 1856. The steamship *Isabel*—implicated in the 1849 and 1854 epidemics, and later used to evacuate U.S. Major Robert Anderson from Fort Sumter in April 1861—plied regularly between Charleston and Havana during the 1850s. According to the *Charleston Mercury,* the vessel departed Charleston for Havana via Key West on the fourth and nineteenth of each month, and departed Havana for Charleston on the tenth and twenty-fifth of each month. Since it typically took three days for the *Isabel* to complete the trip between Havana and Charleston, and since the testimony of the commission merchants was recorded on August 13, 1856, it is assumed that the last trip of the steamship referred to by Mordecai & Co. was that which departed Havana on July 25, 1856, and arrived in Charleston on approximately July 28, 1856. This was over three weeks after the arrival of the *St. Andrews* from Havana, and about two and a half weeks after the arrival of the *Industria* from the same port. Also, the 1856 Committee on Health and Drainage report stated, "On the 13th of July the steamship Isabel, with an assorted cargo, arrived in two and a half days from Havana, with a crew of 40 men, and with 49 passengers. She had two sick on board, but their diseases did not prove to be serious. She did not come to the city." The report further stated that on "July 12th, a boat came from the Isabel once or twice during her stay at Quarantine, on this trip, to the Savannah Packet Wharf, but she was soon ordered off, and on one occasion, probably this same trip of the Isabel, some clothing was brought from her up to Adger's wharf." See *Charleston Mercury,* April 14, 1856; and Wragg, Hume, and Eason, "Report of the Committee on Health and Drainage," 3, 11.

153. Simons, "Observations in Reply to Hume," 181. Hume stated, "We have searched in vain for the propagation of the disease by the labourers engaged in discharging and loading the Concha and Columbus," and concluded that none was found precisely because acclimated blacks performed the loading of the vessels ("On the Introduction, Propagation, and Decline of the Yellow Fever in Charleston," 22).

154. *Charleston Courier,* January 30, 1860.

155. *Charleston Mercury,* April 7, 1857. Critics of these policies later pointed out that, notwithstanding the race or acclimation status of the draymen, the "infected" cargo necessitated conveyance from the western quarantine warehouses "across the city, through its narrow streets, and among its unacclimated inhabitants, and delivered to those who, in handling or using, may be in danger of receiving the poison into their systems" (City Council Minutes, August 3, 1858, *Charleston Mercury,* August 5, 1858).

156. *Charleston Mercury,* April 7, 1857.

157. City Council Minutes, May 12, 1857, *Charleston Mercury,* May 14, 1857. This policy was continued under Charles Macbeth, who served as Charleston's mayor from 1857 to 1865. See *Charleston Mercury,* July 21, 1858. In his final "Mayor's Report on City Affairs" presented to the council in late September 1857, Miles articulated the position of many Charlestonians when he wrote that, although "it is obviously the duty of the city authorities in carrying out measures for the public good, to see that they work as little individual injury as possible. Still the general interest of the community must override the convenience and advantage of any special interest." Though in context Miles evidently was addressing merchants' complaints regarding the city's stringent quarantine measures, the mayor stated that the general interest of the community ought to come

before *any* special interest, which in mid-nineteenth-century Charleston politics included the Irish and other white workingmen (Miles, "Mayor's Report," 25). According to one scholar, "The strengthening of the quarantine in the summer of 1857 was given as the reason for few cases of yellow fever that year, which saw only thirteen deaths being reported." See Farley, *Account of the History of Stranger's Fever*, 100; also see "Yellow Fever and Quarantine," 706–7.

158. City Council Minutes, June 23, 1857, *Charleston Mercury*, June 25, 1857; City Council Minutes, June 26, 1857, *Charleston Mercury*, June 29, 1857. Also see the petition from six of the city's West Indies merchant firms asking the City Council on May 12, 1857—the same day the body adopted updated quarantine measures—to allow vessels arriving prior to June 1 with no sick persons on board to come to the city's wharves and discharge their cargoes of sugar or molasses (City Council Minutes, May 12, 1857, *Charleston Mercury*, May 14, 1857).

159. City Council Minutes, August 4, 1857, *Charleston Mercury*, August 6, 1857; City Council Minutes, June 22, 1858, *Charleston Mercury*, June 23, 1858. Also see City Council Minutes, September 1, 1857, *Charleston Mercury*, September 3, 1857; City Council Minutes, September 15, 1857, *Charleston Mercury*, September 18, 1857; City Council Minutes, June 8, 1858, *Charleston Mercury*, June 9, 1858; City Council Minutes, July 6, 1858, *Charleston Mercury*, July 8, 1858; City Council Minutes, August 17, 1858, *Charleston Mercury*, August 19, 1858; City Council Minutes, September 14, 1858, *Charleston Mercury*, September 18, 1858; City Council Minutes, April 26, 1859, *Charleston Mercury*, April 28, 1859; City Council Minutes, May 10, 1859, *Charleston Mercury*, May 12, 1859; City Council Minutes, July 2, 1859, *Charleston Mercury*, July 4, 1859; City Council Minutes, August 2, 1859, *Charleston Mercury*, August 5, 1859; City Council Minutes, August 30, 1859, *Charleston Mercury*, September 1, 1859; and City Council Minutes, September 20, 1859, *Charleston Mercury*, September 22, 1859.

160. City Council Minutes, July 16, 1858, *Charleston Mercury*, July 17, 1858; City Council Minutes, August 31, 1858, *Charleston Mercury*, September 2, 1858.

161. Dickson, "Yellow Fever," 755; Miles, "Mayor's Report," opposite 88; Lebby et al., "Report of the Committee of the City Council of Charleston, on the Origin and Diffusion of the Yellow Fever," 5, table C. Though approximately thirty-six vessels arrived from infected West Indies ports between May 1 and July 30, 1839, at this time black slaves still dominated waterfront work and thus few unacclimated laborers would have been seeking employment on Charleston's wharves during that summer (Strobel, *Essay on the Subject of the Yellow Fever*, 171).

162. Horlbeck, "Maritime Sanitation," 9. Lebby et al. reported 717 deaths in 1858 ("Report of the Committee of the City Council of Charleston, on the Origin and Diffusion of the Yellow Fever," 67, table D, 6, 13). Also see Farley, *Account of the History of Stranger's Fever*, 114–23.

163. Charleston Death Records, CCPL. Lebby et al. and the editors of the *Charleston Medical Journal and Review* reported that Abbott died on July 18. Assuming that John Abbott's cause of death in 1858 was indeed yellow fever, this evidence suggested that the attending physician and Dr. J. L. Dawson mistakenly diagnosed Abbott with the disease in July 1856, since a veritable recovery from the illness would have afforded the Irishman

lifelong immunity. The events of 1858 also supported Thomas Y. Simons's 1856 claim that Abbott was ill from sun exposure rather than yellow fever, and substantiated that John Abbott was hired to work aboard quarantine lighters and the *St. Andrews* during the summer of 1856 despite his unacclimated status. City authorities tried to explain that Abbott's illness in 1858 "must have been of city origin, as he had, in 1856, the Havana *imported fever.*" The editors of the *Charleston Medical Journal and Review* stated after the 1858 epidemic that "the charmed circle of acclimation has been unusually contracted, and not a few, who little suspected their danger, have discovered, when too late, that they were beyond its pale." See Lebby et al., "Report of the Committee of the City Council of Charleston, on the Origin and Diffusion of the Yellow Fever," 7; "Editorial and Miscellaneous: Yellow Fever Epidemic of 1858," 843, 842; and Hume, "Yellow Fever of Charleston," 4–13.

164. Charleston Death Records, CCPL. An Irish carter named E. Coffine who lived on Linguard Street and "was employed in carting materials to fill up Tradd Street"—both locations mere blocks from the Cooper River waterfront—died from yellow fever in August 1858 and was blamed for spreading the disease. See Hume, "Yellow Fever of Charleston," 9–10, 12.

165. Buckingham, *Slave States* 1: 70–71; Farley, *Account of the History of Stranger's Fever*, 89.

166. About the 1838 yellow fever epidemic, Simons observed that the disease did not attack "even those who were loading and unloading the said-to-be infected [*Lord Glenelg*]," a British bark that arrived from Demerara in British Guiana on July 4 and was docked at Boyce & Co.'s Wharf. Likewise, Simons inquired about the 1839 epidemic, which claimed 134 lives, "If the infectious principle was so powerful, why should it be confined so long to the [seamen], when a free intercourse was had with them by laborers." See Simons, "Report Read Before the City Council," 345; and Simons, "Report on the History and Causes of the Strangers or Yellow Fever," 11. Also see Hume, "Report to the City Council," 154; and Strobel, *Essay on the Subject of the Yellow Fever*, 124.

167. Captain Parker to Robert Lebby, March 2, 1840, and Daniel Wells to Robert Lebby, February 26, 1840, Lebby Family Papers, SCL. Also see Strobel, *Essay on the Subject of the Yellow Fever*, 192–95.

168. Horlbeck, "Maritime Sanitation," 9.

169. Pinckney, "Report . . . During the Late Epidemic," 26. As Henry Gourdin wrote to his brother Robert Newman Gourdin on August 20, 1858, yellow fever "will exist most probably in such a climate as ours, wherever there is a dense and crowded population of working people such as the Irish and Germans" (Racine, ed., *Gentlemen Merchants*, 340).

170. Mrs. Porcher to Mrs. Allston, October 16, 1854, Allston Family Papers, SCHS. Also see Taggart, "Virtue of Fasting and Prayer," 10–11. *The Cambridge World History of Human Disease* supported this interpretation, stating that "in the years immediately prior to the outbreak of the 1849 epidemic, Brazil had been the recipient of a sizable influx of European immigrants; in addition, the population of Rio de Janeiro still included a number of individuals on their way to California. Thus in this epidemic, as in the countless ones to follow, it would be the newcomers who were the chief sufferers of

the illness." Yellow fever, on the other hand, "treated local blacks and whites far more gently, suggesting, of course, that the disease may have been present in the region all along—in its jungle or sylvan form—quietly immunizing the population by periodically producing mild cases in the young." The text went on to explain, "Without doubt, however, yellow fever gained its most fearsome reputation in the Caribbean because of Europeans on hand to host it, often in the form of military personnel who provided the disease with a seemingly endless stream of nonimmunes." Later in the nineteenth century in Cuba, for example, "the influx of Spanish soldiers sent since 1876 to end the Ten Years' War had provided the tinder for an epidemic that raged on that island from 1876 until 1879" (Kiple, ed., *Cambridge World History*, 1101, 1104–5).

171. For a discussion of unconfirmed cases of yellow fever in 1864, see Farley, *Account of the History of Stranger's Fever*, 156–62; Waring, *History of Medicine in South Carolina, 1825–1900*, 34–35; Kiple, ed., *Cambridge World History*, 1105–6; and Horlbeck, "Maritime Sanitation," 9.

Postscript

1. Reeder and DeSaussure to A. H. Boykin, December 8, 1860, Boykin Family Papers, SHC; Johnson and Roark, *Black Masters*, 289–90; *New York Tribune*, January 4, 1861, qtd. in Johnson and Roark, *Black Masters*, 290; *New York Herald*, March 1, 1861; *Philadelphia Inquirer*, March 14, 1861.

2. *Philadelphia Inquirer*, March 14, 1861.

3. Though the Union blockade of Charleston officially began on May 28, 1861, Schirmer reported in late April that all but one of the New York–Charleston steamers had been detained in the northern port to be converted into warships, further choking off the regular shipment of essential provisions into Charleston and eliminating waterfront labor opportunities (Schirmer Diary, April 27, 1861, SCHS). Also see Adger Family Correspondence, folder 8, Adger Family Papers, SCHS.

4. Schirmer Diary, June 29, 1861, SCHS.

5. Corsan, *Two Months*, 65–66. Between October 1 and December 31, 1862, only seven vessels arrived at the docks and only thirteen exited the harbor (Corsan, *Two Months*, 65, note 14).

6. On November 30, 1860, *The Liberator* reported that the packet vessels *Nashville* and *James Adger*, both of the New York Steamship Line, had not been allowed to land in Charleston and were forced to return to New York. Eighty-one steerage passengers aboard these two ships, described as "mostly mechanics and laborers," were "treated with politeness" by Charleston's authorities, who even paid for the transient workers' return voyage to New York. Also in late November, the *New York Journal of Commerce* announced that the proprietors of the steamship *Marion* "were obliged to refuse a large number of applications for steerage tickets." As a result, "many poor mechanics and workmen who have been employed to go South, and others who think that their chances for employment will be quite as good there, notwithstanding political troubles, as they will be [in New York] during the winter," were forced to seek passage to other southern ports. The pro-trade newspaper bitterly concluded, "Abolitionists have made

Northern people almost universally hated and shunned at the South." See *The Liberator* (Boston), November 30, 1860; and *New York Journal of Commerce* qtd. in *The Liberator,* November 30, 1860; Johnson and Roark, *Black Masters,* 275–76. For a case of two northern workingmen hanged as alleged abolitionist spies near Charleston, see *Bangor Daily Whig and Courier,* February 12, 1861.

7. Williams, *Shamrocks and Pluff Mud,* appendixes 6 and 7; Mears and Turnbull, *Charleston Directory* (1859); Ferslew, *Directory of the City of Charleston . . . 1860;* 1860 U.S. Census.

8. Miscellaneous Communication, 1862 # 25 Oversize, SCDAH.

9. The announcement of Mills's death appeared on an undated clipping from an unknown newspaper found in the index of Jacob Schirmer's diary. Otis Mills died, however, on October 23, 1869.

10. South Carolina Railroad Minute Book, April 19, 1861, 277, SCHS.

11. Schirmer Diary, May 27, 1861, SCHS.

12. Schirmer was referring to Confederate Brigadier General Roswell Sabine Ripley (Schirmer Diary, April 28, 1862, SCHS).

13. See chapter 4, note 119, above.

14. "Calendar of Events in the Defense of Charleston, South Carolina," in *Yearbook City of Charleston 1888;* Johnson, *Defense of Charleston Harbor,* 116–17.

15. Rawick, *American Slave,* vol. 3, part 3, 216.

16. *Charleston Post and Courier,* April 7, 1980.

17. Aleckson, *Before the War,* 91.

18. See, for instance, "Some Charleston Wharves," in *Yearbook City of Charleston 1936,* 184, 189.

19. Schirmer Diary, September 18, 1864; after July 1864, SCHS. Also see R. M. Mitchell to John W. Mitchell, July 22, 1865, John Wroughton Mitchell Papers, SHC; and Reminiscence, 1864, William King Smith Papers, SHC.

20. Ann Elliott Morris Vanderhorst Diary, May 30, 1862, Ann Elliott Morris Vanderhorst Papers, SCHS. Also see Vanderhorst Wharf Business Papers, folders 15, 16, SCHS. Jacob Schirmer similarly wrote after the conflict, "The War is ended and we are not only a Conquered People, but degraded and crushed. All the labor and toil of years have been swept away in one fell Sweep [*sic*], and we are now a perfectly ruined people. Business is perfectly prostrate" (Schirmer Diary, December 31, 1865, SCHS).

21. Powers, *Black Charlestonians,* 127; Spero and Harris, *Black Worker,* 182–83.

22. 1870 U.S. Census.

23. Doran's oldest son, James, born in South Carolina in 1849, was working as a stevedore in Charleston in 1870 (1870 U.S. Census). Also see Doran Family Papers, SCHS; and Jowitt, *Jowitt's Illustrated Charleston City Directory and Business Register, 1869–70.*

24. *Charleston Mercury,* October 3, 1891.

25. Stoddard's sons, Franklin and John, also joined their father as stevedores on Charleston's postbellum wharves. See Lea, *Charleston City Directory for 1867–68;* Jowitt, *Jowitt's Illustrated Charleston City Directory and Business Register, 1869–70;* 1870 U.S. Census; and Atlantic Wharves Records, box 2, folder 7, SCHS.

Bibliography

PRIMARY SOURCES

Manuscript Collections

Avery Research Center for African American History and Culture, College of Charleston, Charleston, South Carolina

Jane H. and William H. Pease Papers, 1804–1992.

Charleston County Public Library, Charleston, South Carolina

Charleston Alms House Records, 1794–1917.
Charleston Death Records, 1819–70.
Charleston Free Black Capitation Tax Books, 1852, 1861, 1864.
City Council Minutes, 1821–1980.
Ward Books, 1852–56.

Charleston Library Society, Charleston, South Carolina

Charleston Free Black Capitation Tax Books, 1862, 1863.
Charleston Police Records, 1853–56, 1861–63.
Charleston Tax Records, 1860–65.
Juliet Georgiana Elliott Account Book, 1844–74.
Charles T. Mitchell Account Books, 1850–62.

Collections Research Center, Mystic Seaport, Mystic, Connecticut

Abstract Logbook of the Bark *Edward*, 1845–46.
Journal of the Schooner *Ganges*, 1842–45.
Journal of the Schooner *Nameaug*, 1854–57.
Henry C. Keene Letters, 1859.
The Letters of Captain Henry P. Burr and His Family, 1837–89.
Logbook of the Schooner *Amazon*, 1837–38.
Logbook of the Schooner *Hopewell*, 1843–45.
Logbook of the Ship *Robin Hood*, 1832–33.

Massachusetts Historical Society, Boston, Massachusetts

Thomas Lamb Papers, 1795–1865.

National Archives at Atlanta, Morrow, Georgia

Admiralty Final Record Books and Minutes of the District Court, District of South Carolina, 1790–1857.
Admiralty Journal, U.S. District Court, Eastern District of South Carolina, Charleston, 1857–61.

David M. Rubenstein Rare Book and Manuscript Library, Duke University, Durham, North Carolina

Charleston District Court, Record of Cases, 1816–23.
Frederick William Davie Account Books, 1850–71.
George A. Gordon Correspondence, 1850–66.
Sylvanus Keith Papers, 1798–1880.
Charles Livingston Papers, 1812–29.

South Carolina Department of Archives and History, Columbia, South Carolina

Committee Reports of the General Assembly, 1776–1879.
Court of General Sessions, Criminal Dockets, Charleston District, 1859–63.
Court of General Sessions, Criminal Journals, Charleston District, 1857–92.
Court of General Sessions, Indictments, Charleston County, 1786–1840.
Equity Petitions, Charleston District, 1791–1868.
Governors' Messages, 1783–1870.
Grand Jury Presentments, 1783–1877.
Miscellaneous Communications to the General Assembly, 1777–1877.
Petitions to the General Assembly, 1776–1883.
Resolutions of the General Assembly, 1779–1879.
South Carolina Will Transcripts, 1782–1868.

South Carolina Historical Society, Charleston, South Carolina

Account Books of Benjamin Perry's Wards, 1841–64.
Adger Family Papers, 1796–1893.
Charlotte Anne Allston Factors' Letters, 1808–24.
Allston Family Papers, 1730–1901.
Atlantic Wharves Records, 1869–71.
Bacot Family Collection, 1752–1973.
Mary Lamboll Thomas Beach Papers, 1822–90.
K. Boyce & Company Account Book, 1836–41.
James Butler Campbell Papers, 1814–97.
Carson & Sons Daybook, 1854–55.
Charleston Chamber of Commerce Award Book, 1823–39.
Langdon Cheves Papers, 1777–1864.
Doran Family Papers, 1890–1934.

Hibernian Society Minutes, 1827–1967.

Legare, Colcock, and Company Records, 1855–65.

Letters of an American Traveler, 1810–12.

New England Society Records, 1819–1995.

Reynolds, Clark G. "Fort Sumter National Monument 'Dockside II Study,' 1987."

Robertson, Henry Clay. "Personal Recollections of Henry C. Robertson While Engaged in a Sea Island Cotton Factor's Office, 1898–1923."

Rutledge and Young Miscellaneous Business Papers, 1860–61.

Jacob F. Schirmer Diary, 1826–80.

South Carolina Railroad Minute Book, 1850–68.

Thomas J. Tobias Papers, 1716–1968.

Ann Elliott Morris Vanderhorst Papers, 1859–82.

Elias Vanderhorst Papers, 1818–76.

Vanderhorst Family Biographical and Genealogical Research Files.

Vanderhorst Family History and Genealogy Research Files.

Vanderhorst Family Papers, 1689–1942.

Lydia Jane Waring Estate Book, 1840–47.

Charles O. Witte Estate Records, 1851–71.

South Caroliniana Library, University of South Carolina, Columbia, South Carolina

Anonymous Charleston Merchant Account Book, 1849–52.

Charles Barron Letters, 1839.

James Carr Papers, 1811–16.

Daniel Deshon Letters, 1796.

Christopher Fitzsimons Letterbook, 1799–1813.

James Gadsden Papers, 1820–58.

Hazard & Ayrault Company Receipt Book, 1796–1805.

Edward Hudson Papers, 1823.

Lebby Family Papers, 1826–1940.

John Lucas Letters, 1840–43.

Simon Magwood Papers, 1810–70.

Marine School Ship *Lodebar* Log Book, 1861–62.

John Wroughton Mitchell Lawyer's Receipt Book, 1817–35.

Thomas Napier Papers, 1803–60.

Ogilby, William. "British Counsel Report on Trade and Shipping in Charleston, S.C., 1833 June 29."

William Mazyck Porcher Letters, 1836.

John Schulz Account Books, 1812–24.

Southern Historical Collection, Louis Round Wilson Special Collections Library, University of North Carolina at Chapel Hill, Chapel Hill, North Carolina

Arnold and Screven Family Papers, 1762–1903.

Boykin Family Papers, 1748–1932.

John Matthew Winslow Davidson Papers, 1853–73.

Elisha L. Halsey Log, 1833–35.

Ernest Haywood Collection of Haywood Family Papers, 1752–1967.

Samuel C. Jackson Diary, 1832–33.

William Porcher Miles Papers, 1784–1906.

John Wroughton Mitchell Papers, 1817–65.

William King Smith Papers, 1845–1901.

Published Sources

Abbott, John S. C. *South and North; or, Impressions Received During a Trip to Cuba and the South.* New York: Abbey & Abbot, 1860.

Adams, Nehemiah. *A South-Side View of Slavery.* Boston: Ticknor and Fields, 1860.

Adger, John B. *My Life and Times, 1810–1899.* Richmond, Va.: Presbyterian Committee of Publication, 1899.

Aleckson, Sam. *Before the War, and After the Union.* Boston: Gold Mind Publishing Co., 1929.

Allen, William Francis, et al. *Slave Songs of the United States.* New York: A. Simpson & Co., 1867.

Andrews, Ethan A. *Slavery and the Domestic Slave Trade in the United States.* Boston: Light & Stearns, 1836.

Arfwedson, Carl David. *The United States and Canada, in 1832, 1833, and 1834.* Vol. 1. London: Richard Bentley, 1834.

Ashton, Susanna, ed. *I Belong to South Carolina: South Carolina Slave Narratives.* Columbia: University of South Carolina Press, 2010.

Bachman, C. L., et al. *John Bachman: The Pastor of St. John's Lutheran Church, Charleston.* Charleston: Walker, Evans, & Cogswell Co., 1888.

Bagget, J. H. *Directory of the City of Charleston for the Year 1852: Containing the Names, Occupation, Place of Business & Residence of the Inhabitants Generally: With Other Information of General Interest.* Charleston: Printed by Edward C. Councell, 1852.

Baker, George E., ed. *The Works of William Seward.* Vol. 2. New York: Redfield, 1853.

Barra, E. I. *A Tale of Two Oceans; A New Story by an Old Californian: An Account of a Voyage from Philadelphia to San Francisco, Around Cape Horn, Years 1849–50.* San Francisco: Press of Eastman & Co., 1893.

Bird, H. L. "Observations on Yellow Fever." *Charleston Medical Journal and Review* 10 (May 1855): 329–33.

Blassingame, John W., ed. *Slave Testimony: Two Centuries of Letters, Speeches, Interviews, and Autobiographies.* Baton Rouge: Louisiana State University Press, 1977.

Buckingham, James. *The Slave States of America.* Vol. 1. London, Fisher, Son & Co., 1842.

Burlin, Natalie Curtis. *Negro Folk-Songs.* New York: G. Schirmer, 1918.

Cain, D. J. "History of the Epidemic of Yellow Fever in Charleston, S.C., in 1854." Philadelphia: T. K. and P. G. Collins, 1856.

Carson, James Petigru, ed. *Life, Letters, and Speeches of James Louis Petigru: The Union Man of South Carolina.* Washington, D.C.: H. L. & J. B. McQueen, 1920.

Catterall, Helen Tunnicliff, ed. *Judicial Cases Concerning American Slavery and the Negro.* Vol. 2. Buffalo: W. S. Hein, 1998.

Charleston Chamber of Commerce. "Report of a Special Committee Appointed by the Chamber of Commerce, to Inquire into the Cost, Revenue, and Advantages of a Rail Road Communication Between the City of Charleston and the Towns of Hamburg & Augusta." Charleston: A. E. Miller, 1828.

Charleston City Council. *Ordinances of the City of Charleston: From the 5th Feb., 1833, to the 9th May, 1837. Together with Such of the Acts and Clauses of Acts of the Legislature of South Carolina as Relate to Charleston, Passed Since December, 1832.* Charleston: A. E. Miller, 1837.

———. "Statement of Receipts and Expenditures by the City Council of Charleston From 1st July 1849, to 1st July 1850." Charleston: A. E. Miller, 1850.

———. "Statement of Receipts and Expenditures by the City Council of Charleston From 1st Sept. 1850, to 1st Sept., 1851, With a List of the Tax Paying Citizens in the Upper and Lower Wards—Separated." Charleston: A. E. Miller, 1851.

Chisolm, J. J. "A Brief Sketch of the Epidemic Yellow Fever of 1854, in Charleston." *Charleston Medical Journal and Review* 10 (July 1855): 433–56.

Clapp, Edwin J. "Charleston Port Survey." Charleston: Walker, Evans & Cogswell Co., ca. 1921.

Clark, Thomas D., ed. *South Carolina: The Grand Tour, 1780–1865.* Columbia: University of South Carolina Press, 1973.

Corsan, W. C. *Two Months in the Confederate States: An Englishman's Travels through the South.* Ed. Benjamin H. Trask. Baton Rouge: Louisiana State University Press, 1996.

Crowe, Eyre. *With Thackeray in America.* New York: Charles Scribner's Sons, 1893.

Dawson, J. L. "Report of the Cases of Yellow Fever Which Have Occurred in Our City, and on Ship-board in Our Harbor, up to August 25th." *Charleston Medical Journal and Review* 11 (September 1856): 698–702.

———. "Statistics Relative to the Epidemic Yellow Fever of 1854, in the City of Charleston." *Charleston Medical Journal and Review* 10 (March 1855): 198–200.

———, and H. W. DeSaussure. *Census of the City of Charleston, South Carolina, for the Year 1848.* Charleston: J. B. Nixon, 1849.

De Bow, James D. B. *The Industrial Resources, Etc., of the Southern and Western States: Embracing a View of Their Commerce, Agriculture, Manufactures, Internal Improvements; Slave and Free Labor, Slavery Institutions, Products, Etc., of the South.* Vol. 2. New Orleans: Office of De Bow's Review, 1852.

"Declaration of the Immediate Causes Which Induce and Justify the Secession of South Carolina from the Federal Union; and the Ordinance of Secession." Charleston: Evans & Cogswell, 1860.

Delany, Martin R. *Blake; or, The Huts of America.* Ed. Floyd J. Miller. Boston: Beacon Press, 1970.

Dickson, Samuel Henry. "Account of the Epidemic Which Prevailed in Charleston, S.C. during the Summer of 1827." *American Journal of the Medical Sciences* 3 (May 1828): 64–77.

———. "Yellow Fever." *Charleston Medical Journal and Review* 11 (November 1856): 743–58.

Douglass, Frederick. *My Bondage and My Freedom*. New York: Miller, Orton & Co., 1857.

———. *Narrative of the Life of Frederick Douglass, An American Slave; Written by Himself.* Boston: Anti-Slavery Office, 1845.

Dowling, D. J. *Dowling's Charleston Directory and Annual Register for 1837 and 1838.* Charleston: D. J. Dowling, 1837.

Eckhard, George B., ed. *A Digest of Ordinances of the City Council of Charleston From the Year 1783 to Oct. 1844.* Charleston: Walker and Burke, 1844.

Edgar, Walter, ed. *The Letterbook of Robert Pringle.* 2 vols. Columbia: University of South Carolina Press, 1972.

"Editorial and Miscellaneous: Letter to the Late Editors." *Charleston Medical Journal and Review* 10 (January 1855): 136–37.

"Editorial and Miscellaneous: Quarantine Regulations for the Port of Charleston, Ratified May '55." *Charleston Medical Journal and Review* 10 (July 1855): 594–97.

"Editorial and Miscellaneous: Yellow Fever." *Charleston Medical Journal and Review* 9 (September 1854): 710–12.

"Editorial and Miscellaneous: Yellow Fever." *Charleston Medical Journal and Review* 9 (November 1854): 850–51.

"Editorial and Miscellaneous: Yellow Fever in Charleston." *Charleston Medical Journal and Review* 11 (November 1856): 845–50.

"Editorial and Miscellaneous: The Yellow Fever Epidemic of 1858." *Charleston Medical Journal and Review* 13 (November 1858): 841–45.

"Editorial and Miscellaneous: Yellow Fever in Norfolk and Portsmouth." *Charleston Medical Journal and Review* 10 (September 1855): 733–66.

Erskine, Charles. *Twenty Years Before the Mast: With the More Thrilling Scenes and Incidents while Circumnavigating the Globe under the Command of the Late Admiral Charles Wilkes, 1838–1842.* Philadelphia: George W. Jacobs & Co., 1896.

"Facts and Speculation on Cholera." *Southern Literary Journal and Monthly Magazine* 3 (December 1836): 290–95.

Fay, T. C. *Charleston Directory and Strangers' Guide for 1840 and 1841, Embracing Names of Heads of Families—Firms, and the Individuals Composing Them.* Charleston: T. C. Fay, 1840.

Ferslew, W. Eugene. *Directory of the City of Charleston, to Which Is Added a Business Directory, 1860.* Savannah: J. M. Cooper and Co., 1860.

Folker, Joseph. *A Directory of the City and District of Charleston and Stranger's Guide for the Year 1813.* Charleston: Printed by G. M. Bounetheau, 1813.

Ford, Frederick A. *Census of the City of Charleston, South Carolina, For the Year 1861.* Charleston: Evans & Cogswell, 1861.

"From Frederick Douglass's Paper, 1853: 'Learn Trades or Starve.'" In *The Education of the Negro Prior to 1861: A History of the Education of the Colored People of the United States from the Beginning of Slavery to the Civil War*, ed. Carter G. Woodson, 388–91. Washington, D.C.: Associated Publishers, Inc., 1919.

Gaillard, P. C. "An Essay on the Importability and Diffusion of Yellow Fever." *Charleston Medical Journal and Review* 14 (July 1859): 457–91.

Gaillard, P. C., and R. A. Kinloch. "Report on the Cholera in Charleston in 1852–'53." In *Proceedings of the South Carolina Medical Association at the Annual Meeting, in the City of Charleston, S.C., Held on the 30th January, 1854*, 26–36. Charleston: Steam Power Press, 1854.

Gazlay, David M. *The Charleston City Directory and General Business Directory for 1855*. Charleston: David M. Gazlay, 1855.

Glascock, W. N. *The Naval Officer's Manual, for Every Grade in Her Majesty's Ships*. London: Parker, Furnivall, & Parker, 1848.

———. *The Naval Service: or, Officer's Manual for Every Grade in His Majesty's Ships*. London: Saunders and Otley, 1836.

Goldsmith, Morris. *Directory and Strangers' Guide, for the City of Charleston and Its Vicinity, From the Fifth Census of the United States*. Charleston: Printed at the Office of the Irishman, 1831.

Hall, Basil. *Travels in North America, in the Years 1827 and 1828*. Vol. 2. Philadelphia: Carey, Lea & Carey, 1829.

Harrison, T. P., ed. "Journal of a Voyage to Charlestown in So. Carolina by Pelatiah Webster in 1765." *Publications of the Southern History Association* 2 (January 1898): 1–18.

Hildreth, Richard. *The White Slave, or Memoirs of a Fugitive*. Boston: Tappan and Whittemore, 1852.

Hill, Henry B. *Jottings from Memory, from 1823 to 1901*. N.p., 1910.

Hinks, Peter P., ed. *David Walker's Appeal to the Coloured Citizens of the World*. University Park: Pennsylvania State University Press, 2002.

Honour, John H. *A Directory of the City of Charleston and Neck for 1849; Containing the Names, Residences and Occupations of the Inhabitants Generally*. Charleston: Printed by A. J. Burke, 1849.

Horlbeck, H. B. "Maritime Sanitation at Ports of Arrival." Concord, N.H.: Republic Press Association, 1891.

Horsey, John R., ed. *Ordinances of the City of Charleston from the 14th September, 1854, to the 1st December, 1859*. Charleston: Walker, Evans & Co., 1859.

Hrabowski, Richard. *Directory for the District of Charleston*. Charleston: Printed by John Hoff, 1809.

Hume, William. "An Inquiry into Some of the General and Local Causes to Which the Endemic Origin of Yellow Fever Has Been Attributed by Myself and Others." *Charleston Medical Journal and Review* 9 (November 1854): 721–30.

———. "On the Germination of Yellow Fever in Cities, in Contrast with the Incubation of Fever in Individuals." *Charleston Medical Journal and Review* 13 (March 1858): 145–79.

———. "On the Introduction of Yellow Fever into Savannah in the Year 1854, in Reply to a Letter to the Editor from R. C. Mackall, M.D., Late Health Officer of the City of Savannah." *Charleston Medical Journal and Review* 11 (January 1856): 1–22.

———. "On the Introduction, Propagation, and Decline of the Yellow Fever in Charleston, during the Summer of 1854." *Charleston Medical Journal and Review* 10 (January 1855): 1–35.

———. "Meteorological and Other Observations in Reference to the Causes of Yellow Fever in Charleston, with an Outline of a Plan for its Prevention." *Charleston Medical Journal and Review* 5 (January 1850): 1–67.

———. "Report to the City Council of Charleston, on a Resolution of Inquiry Relative to 'the Source and Origin of Yellow Fever, as It Has Occasionally Prevailed in Charleston, and the Means of Prevention or Exclusion, as May Seem Worthy of Adoption, in Order to Obviate Its Future Occurrence.'" *Charleston Medical Journal and Review* 9 (March 1854): 145–64.

———. "Sequel to Meteorological and Other Observations in Reference to the Causes of Yellow Fever in Charleston, Brought Forward to 1852." *Charleston Medical Journal and Review* 8 (January 1853): 55–67.

———. "The Yellow Fever of Charleston, Considered in Its Relation to the West India Commerce." *Charleston Medical Journal and Review* 15 (January 1860): 1–32.

Jackson, John Andrew. *The Experience of a Slave in South Carolina*. London: Passmore & Alabaster, 1862.

Johnson, Joseph. "Some Account of the Origin and Prevention of Yellow Fever in Charleston, S.C." *Charleston Medical Journal and Review* 9 (March 1849): 154–69.

Johnson, Michael P., and James L. Roark, eds. *No Chariot Let Down: Charleston's Free People of Color on the Eve of the Civil War*. Chapel Hill: University of North Carolina Press, 1984.

Jones, Thomas H. *The Experience of Rev. Thomas H. Jones, Who Was a Slave for Forty-Three Years. Written by a Friend, as Related to Him by Brother Jones*. New Bedford: E. Anthony & Sons, Printers, 1885.

Jowitt, Thad. C. *Jowitt's Illustrated Charleston City Directory and Business Register, 1869–70*. Charleston: Walker, Evan & Cogswell, 1869.

Kemble, Frances Anne. *Journal of a Residence on a Georgian Plantation in 1838–1839*. New York: Harper & Brothers, 1864.

Kennedy, Lionel H., and Thomas Parker. *An Official Report of the Trials of Sundry Negroes, Charged with an Attempt to Raise Insurrection in the State of South Carolina*. Charleston: James R. Schenck, 1822.

Kinloch, R. A. "A Brief Description of the Yellow Fever as It Prevailed at Mount Pleasant and in Charleston Harbor during the Summer of 1857, with a Critical Inquiry into Its Probable Origin." *Charleston Medical Journal and Review* 13 (January 1858): 3–34.

Lambert, John. *Travels through Canada, and the United States of North America, in the Years 1806, 1807, & 1808. To Which Are Added, Biographical Notices and Anecdotes of Some of the Leading Characters in the United States*. Vol. 2. London: C. Cradock and W. Joy, 1814.

Laurens, Edward R. "An Address Delivered in Charleston, Before the Agricultural Society of South Carolina, on September 18th, 1832." Charleston: A. E. Miller, 1832.

"The Law of Colored Seamen." Charleston: n.p., 1852?

Lea, Jno. Orrin, & Co. *Charleston City Directory for 1867–68. Containing the Names of the Inhabitants of the City; Their Occupations, Places of Business, the Dwelling Houses; Business Register; Public Institutions, Banks, &c. &c.* Charleston: Jno. Orrin Lea, 1867.

Lebby, Robert, et al. "Report of the Committee of the City Council of Charleston, on the Origin and Diffusion of the Yellow Fever in Charleston, in the Summer of 1858." Charleston: Walker, Evans & Co.'s Steam Power Press, 1859.

Leiding, Harriette Kershaw. "Street Cries of an Old Southern City." Charleston: Daggett Printing Co., 1910.

"List of the Tax Payers of the City of Charleston for 1858." Charleston: Steam Press of Walker, Evans & Co., 1859.

"List of the Tax Payers of the City of Charleston for 1859." Charleston: Steam-Power Press of Walker, Evans & Co., 1860.

Lyell, Charles. *A Second Visit to the United States of North America.* Vol. 2. New York: Harper and Brothers, 1850.

———. *Travels in North America in the Years 1841–2: With Geological Observations on the United States, Canada, and Nova Scotia.* Vol. 1. New York: Wiley and Putnam, 1845.

MacElwee, Roy S., and Henry F. Church. "A Comprehensive Handbook on the Port of Charleston." Charleston: Bureau of Foreign Trade and Port Development, ca. 1924.

Mackay, Alexander. *Western World, or, Travels in the United States in 1846–47.* Vol. 2. London: R. Bentley, 1849.

Mackay, Charles. *Life and Liberty in America: or, Sketches of a Tour in the United States and Canada in 1857–8.* New York: Harper & Brothers, 1859.

Marsh, Luther Rawson, ed. *Writings and Speeches of Alvan Stewart, on Slavery.* New York: A. B. Burdick, 1860.

McCord, David J., ed. *The Statutes at Large of South Carolina; Edited, Under Authority of the Legislature.* Vol. 7. Columbia: A. S. Johnston, 1840.

McCrady, Edward. *A Series of Articles upon the Means of Preventing the Recurrence of Yellow Fever in Charleston, Addressed to the Citizens of Charleston: Published in the Charleston Mercury over the Signature of "E. McC."* Charleston: Steam Power Press of Walker, Evans & Co., 1858.

Mears, Leonard, and James Turnbull. *The Charleston Directory: Containing the Names of the Inhabitants, a Subscribers' Business Directory, Street Map of the City, and an Appendix of Much Useful Information.* Charleston: Evans, Walker, & Co., 1859.

"Memorial of Sundry Masters of American Vessels, Lying in the Port of Charleston, S.C." Washington, D.C.: Printed by Gales & Seaton, 1823.

"Memorial of the Wharf-holders of Charleston to the General Assembly of South Carolina." Charleston: Walker, Evans, & Co., 1859.

Michaux, François André. *Travels to the West of the Alleghany Mountains, in the States of Ohio, Kentucky, and Tennessee, and Back to Charleston, By the Upper Carolines.* Ed. Reuben Gold Thwaites. Vol. 3. Cleveland: A. H. Clark, 1904.

Miles, William Porcher. "Mayor's Report on City Affairs: Submitted to Council at a Meeting Held Tuesday, September 29th, 1857." Charleston: Walker, Evans, and Co., 1857.

Milligan, Jacob. *The Charleston Directory.* Charleston: W. P. Young, 1794.

———. *The Charleston Directory and Revenue System.* Charleston: T. B. Bowen, 1790.

Mills, Robert. *Statistics of South Carolina, Including a View of its Natural, Civil, and Military History, General and Particular.* Charleston: Hurlbut and Lloyd, 1826.

Motte, Abraham. *Charleston Directory and Stranger's Guide for the Year 1816; Including the Neck to the Six Mile House.* Charleston: Printed for the Publisher, 1816.

Murphy, John McLeod, and W. N. Jeffers. *Nautical Routine and Stowage, with Short Rules in Navigation.* New York: Henry Spear, 1849.

Negrin, J. J. *Negrin's Directory and Almanac for the Year 1806; Containing Every Article of General Utility.* Charleston: J. J. Negrin, 1806.

———. *Negrin's Directory for the Year 1807: Containing Every Article of General Utility.* Charleston: J. J. Negrin, 1807.

———. *New Charleston Directory and Stranger's Guide for the Year 1802.* Charleston: John A. Dacqueny, 1802.

Neilson, Peter, ed. *The Life and Adventures of Zamba, an African Negro King; and His Experience of Slavery in South Carolina.* London: Smith, Elder & Co., 1847.

Nelson, John Dixon. *Nelson's Charleston Directory and Strangers Guide for the Year of Our Lord, 1801. Being the Twenty Fifth Year of the Independence of the United States of America, until July Fourth.* Charleston: Printed by John Dixon Nelson, 1800.

"New Tariff Amended, or Duties Payable on Goods, Wares & Merchandize Imported into the United States of America: Likewise the Rates of Tonnage, Drawback, Tares, &c." Charleston: A. E. Miller, 1823.

Nordhoff, Charles. *The Merchant Vessel: A Sailor Boy's Voyages to See the World.* Cincinnati: Moore, Wilstach, Keys & Co., 1856.

Olmsted, Frederick Law. *The Cotton Kingdom: A Traveller's Observations on Cotton and Slavery in the American Slave States.* 2nd ed. 2 vols. New York: Mason Brothers, 1862.

———. *A Journey in the Seaboard Slave States: With Remarks on Their Economy.* New York: Dix & Edwards, 1856.

Pearson, Edward A., ed. *Designs against Charleston: The Trial Record of the Denmark Vesey Slave Conspiracy of 1822.* Chapel Hill: University of North Carolina Press, 1999.

Pinckney, Henry L. "Report; Containing a Review of the Proceedings of the City Authorities, from the 4th September, 1837, to the 1st August, 1838. With Suggestions for the Improvement of the Various Departments of the Public Service. Presented to the City Council, August 6, 1838, By Henry L. Pinckney, Mayor." Charleston: Thomas J. Eccles, 1838.

———. "A Report, Relative to the Proceedings for the Relief of the Sick Poor, During the Late Epidemic; and on the Subject, Generally, of the Public Health; to Which Is Annexed the Report of the Commissioners of the Temporary Hospital; Presented to the City Council on the 5th of November, 1838." Charleston: W. Riley, 1838.

Pinckney, Thomas [Achates]. "Reflections, Occasioned by the Late Disturbances in Charleston." Charleston: A. E. Miller, 1822.

"Proceedings and Debates of the Third National Quarantine and Sanitation Convention, Held in the City of New York, April, 1859." *Charleston Medical Journal and Review* 15 (March 1860): 213–25.

"Proceedings of the Stockholders of the South-Western R. Road Bank, and of the Stockholders of the Louisville, Cincin. and Charleston Rail-Road Company. At Their Annual Meetings, in Their Banking Institution, on the 17th, 19th, and 20th November, 1840." Charleston: A. E. Miller, 1840.

Purse, R. S. *Charleston City Directory and Strangers Guide for 1856.* New York: J. F. Trow, 1856.

Racine, Philip N., ed. *Gentlemen Merchants: A Charleston Family's Odyssey, 1828–1870.* Knoxville: University of Tennessee Press, 2008.

Ramsay, David. "A Dissertation on the Means of Preserving Health, in Charleston, and the Adjacent Low Country. Read Before the Medical Society of South Carolina, on the 29th of May, 1790." Charleston: Markland & McIver, 1790.

Rawick, George P., ed. *The American Slave: A Composite Autobiography.* 41 vols. Westport, Conn.: Greenwood Publishing Co., 1972–79.

Redpath, James. *The Roving Editor; or, Talks with Slaves in the Southern States.* New York: A. B. Burdick, 1859.

Report of Law Cases, Determined in the Court of Appeals of South Carolina, January Term, 1836, April Term, 1836, and February Term, 1837. Charleston: W. Riley, 1839.

"Report of the Committee on Colored Population, on the Petition of the South Carolina Mechanics' Association; also, the Petition of the Mechanics and Working Men of the City of Charleston; also, the Memorial of the Charleston Mechanics' Society; also, the Presentment of Grand Jury for Charleston District; also, on Two Bills; All in Reference to the Enactment of Laws Preventing Negroes from Hiring Out Their Own Time, &c." Columbia: Steam-Power Press, Southern Guardian, 1858.

"Review of R. LaRoche, M.D., Yellow Fever, Considered in its Historical, Pathological, Etiological, and Therapeutical Relations." *Charleston Medical Journal and Review* 10 (November 1855): 826–40.

"Rules for the Government of the Charleston Chamber of Commerce, Revised and Adopted December 26, 1842: Together with the Tariff of Commissions and Other Regulations, Adopted by the Chamber. To Which Is Added a List of the Officers and Members of the Chamber in May, 1844." Charleston: Burges & James, 1844.

Russell, Robert. *North America, Its Agriculture and Climate; Containing Observations on the Agriculture and Climate of Canada, the United States, and the Island of Cuba.* Edinburgh: A. and C. Black, 1857.

Schenck, James R. *Directory and Stranger's Guide for the City of Charleston.* Charleston: A. E. Miller, 1822.

———, and Turner. *The Directory and Stranger's Guide for the City of Charleston . . . for the Year 1819.* Charleston: A. E. Miller, 1819.

Schweninger, Loren, ed. *The Southern Debate over Slavery.* 2 vols. Urbana: University of Illinois Press, 2001, 2008.

Seabrook, Whitemarsh Benjamin. "A Concise View of the Critical Situation and Future Prospects of the Slave Holding States in Relation to Their Colored Population." Charleston: A. E. Miller, 1825.

"A Short Sketch of the Military and Political Career and Public Service of General Robert Smalls, of South Carolina." Washington, D.C.: E. G. Nalle, 1882.

Simons, Thomas Y. "An Essay on the Yellow Fever as It Has Occurred in Charleston, Including Its Origins and Progress up to the Present Time. Read Before the So. Ca. Medical Association, at Its Anniversary Meeting, 1851, and Published by Their Request." *Charleston Medical Journal and Review* 6 (November 1851): 777–802.

———. "Observations in Reply to William Hume, M.D." *Charleston Medical Journal and Review* 10 (March 1855): 170–85.

———. "A Report on the Epidemic Yellow Fever as It Occurred in Charleston in 1852, with Statistical and Other Observations." *Charleston Medical Journal and Review* 8 (May 1853): 363–76.

———. "A Report on the History and Causes of the Strangers or Yellow Fever of Charleston: Read Before the Board of Health." Charleston: W. Riley, 1839.

———. "A Report Read Before the City Council of Charleston, and Ordered to be Printed with the Proceedings; with an Appendix, in Reply to the Report of Wm. Hume, M.D." *Charleston Medical Journal and Review* 9 (May 1854): 329–51.

Smith, Daniel E. Huger. *A Charlestonian's Recollections, 1846–1913.* Charleston: Carolina Art Association, 1950.

Smith, James. *The Charleston Directory and Register for 1835–6. Containing the Names, Occupations, and Residences of Persons in Business, &c. Collected by James Smith and the City Register; Consisting of a Variety of Useful Information, Connected with Our Trade and Commerce.* Charleston: Daniel J. Dowling, 1835.

"South Carolina: A Home for the Industrious Immigrant." Charleston: Joseph Walker, 1867.

Spratt, L. W. "The Philosophy of Secession; A Southern View, Presented in a Letter Addressed to the Hon. Mr. Perkins of Louisiana, in Criticism on the Provisional Constitution Adopted by the Southern Congress at Montgomery, Alabama, by the Hon. L. W. Spratt." Charleston: n.p., 1861.

Starobin, Robert S., ed. *Denmark Vesey: The Slave Conspiracy of 1822.* Englewood Cliffs, N.J.: Prentice-Hall, 1970.

Stevens, Robert White. *On the Stowage of Ships and Their Cargoes.* Plymouth, Mass.: Published by Stevens, 1858.

Stirling, James. *Letters from the Slave States.* London: J. W. Parker, 1857.

Strobel, B. B. *An Essay on the Subject of the Yellow Fever, Intended to Prove Its Transmissibility.* Charleston: Printed by Asa J. Muir, 1840.

Stuart, James. *Three Years in North America.* Vol. 2. Edinburgh: Printed for R. Cadell, 1833.

Taggart, Rev. Charles M. "The Virtue of Fasting and Prayer: A Discourse, Preached on Thursday, Oct. 13, 1853, a Day of Fasting, Humiliation, and Prayer, Appointed by the Governor of South Carolina." Charleston: Steam-Power Press of Walker & James, 1853.

Thornbury, Walter. *Criss-Cross Journeys.* Vol. 1. London: Hurst and Blackett, 1873.

Tower, Philo. *Slavery Unmasked: Being a Truthful Narrative of a Three Years' Residence and Journeying in Eleven Southern States.* Rochester, N.Y.: E. Darrow & Brother, 1856.

Vessey, John Henry. *Mr. Vessey of England: Being the Incidents and Reminiscences of Travel in a Twelve Weeks' Tour through the United States and Canada in the Year 1859.* Ed. Brian Waters. New York: Putnam, 1956.

Walker, David. "Walker's Appeal, in Four Articles; Together with a Preamble, to the Coloured Citizens of the World, but in Particular, and Very Expressly, to Those of the United States of America, Written in Boston, State of Massachusetts, September 28, 1829." Boston: David Walker, 1830.

Walker, H. Pinckney, ed. *Ordinances of the City of Charleston From the 19th of August 1844, to the 14th of September 1854; and the Acts of the General Assembly Relating to the City of Charleston, and City Council of Charleston, During the Same Interval.* Charleston: A. E. Miller, 1854.

Washington, Booker T. Preface. *Twenty-four Negro Melodies Transcribed for the Piano by S. Coleridge-Taylor.* Boston: Oliver Ditson Co., 1905.

Wilentz, Sean, ed. *David Walker's Appeal, to the Coloured Citizens of the World, but in Particular, and Very Expressly, to Those of the United States of America.* New York: Hill and Wang, 1995.

Willard, Benjamin J. *Captain Ben's Book: A Record of the Things Which Happened to Capt. Benjamin J. Willard, Pilot and Stevedore, During Some Sixty Years on Sea and Land, as Related by Himself.* Portland, Maine: Lakeside Press, 1895.

Williman, A. B. "An Account of the Yellow Fever Epidemic in Norfolk during the Summer of 1855." *Charleston Medical Journal and Review* 11 (May 1856): 331–43.

Windley, Lathan A., comp. *Runaway Slave Advertisements: A Documentary History from the 1730s to 1790.* Vol. 3. Westport, Conn.: Greenwood Press, 1983.

Wragg, William T., William Hume, and James M. Eason. "Report of the Committee on Health and Drainage, on the Origin and Diffusion of Yellow Fever in Charleston in the Autumn of 1856." Charleston?: n.p., 1856.

Yearbook City of Charleston 1888. Charleston: News and Courier Book Presses, 1889.

Yearbook City of Charleston 1936. Charleston: News and Courier Book Presses, 1937.

"Yellow Fever and Quarantine." *Charleston Medical Journal and Review* 12 (September 1857): 706–7.

"Yellow Fever in Charleston in 1852." *Southern Quarterly Review* 7 (January 1853): 140–78.

Electronic Resource

Irish Immigrants: New York Port Arrival Records, 1846–1851. http://search.ancestry.com/search/db.aspx?dbid=5969. Provo, Utah: Generations Network, Inc., 2001 (accessed May 19, 2009).

Periodicals

Augusta Chronicle (Georgia).
Bangor Daily Whig and Courier.
Boston Atlas.
Boston Daily Advertiser.
Boston Daily Atlas.
Charleston City Gazette.
Charleston Courier.
Charleston Mercury.
Charleston Post and Courier.
Charleston Times.
Charleston Tri-Weekly Courier.
City Gazette and Commercial Daily Advertiser (Charleston).

Daily Morning News (Savannah).
Daily National Intelligencer (Washington, D.C.).
Emancipator (New York).
Fayetteville Observer (North Carolina).
Frank Leslie's Illustrated Newspaper.
Globe (Washington, D.C.).
Harper's Weekly.
Hornet, or Republican Advocate (Maryland).
Illustrated London News.
Independence Chronicle & Boston Patriot.
Liberator (Boston).
Memphis Daily Appeal.
Milwaukee Daily Sentinel.
New Hampshire Statesman and Concord Register.
New York Herald.
New York Tribune.
Niles Register.
North American (Philadelphia).
Philadelphia Inquirer.
Savannah Morning News.
South Carolina Gazette.
Southern Patriot (Charleston).
State (Columbia).

SECONDARY SOURCES

Books and Edited Collections

Albion, Robert Greenhalgh. *The Rise of New York Port, 1815–1860.* New York: Charles Scribner's Sons, 1939.

———. *Square-Riggers on Schedule: The New York Sailing Packets to England, France, and the Cotton Ports.* Princeton, N.J.: Princeton University Press, 1938.

Allen, Austin. *Origins of the Dred Scott Case: Jacksonian Jurisprudence and the Supreme Court, 1837–1857.* Athens: University of Georgia Press, 2006.

Annual Report of the American Historical Association for the Year 1907. Vol. 2. Washington, D.C.: Government Printing Office, 1908.

Aptheker, Herbert. *American Negro Slave Revolts.* New York: International Publishers, 1993.

Arnesen, Eric. *Waterfront Workers of New Orleans: Race, Class, and Politics, 1863–1923.* Urbana: University of Illinois Press, 1994.

Bagnall, William R. *The Textile Industries of the United States.* Vol. 1. Cambridge, Mass.: Riverside Press, 1893.

Ballagh, James Curtis, ed. *The South in the Building of the Nation: A History of the Southern States Designed to Record the South's Part in the Making of the American Nation;*

to Portray the Character and Genius, to Chronicle the Achievements and Progress and to Illustrate the Life. Vol. 5. Richmond: Southern Historical Publication Society, 1909.

Bellows, Barbara L. *Benevolence among Slaveholders: Assisting the Poor in Charleston, 1670–1860.* Baton Rouge: Louisiana State University Press, 1993.

Berlin, Ira. *Slaves without Masters: The Free Negro in the Antebellum South.* New York: Pantheon Books, 1974.

Billingsley, Andrew. *Yearning to Breathe Free: Robert Smalls of South Carolina and His Families.* Columbia: University of South Carolina Press, 2007.

Blumberg, Phillip I. *Repressive Jurisprudence in the Early American Republic: The First Amendment and the Legacy of English Law.* New York: Cambridge University Press, 2010.

Bolster, W. Jeffrey. *Black Jacks: African American Seamen in the Age of Sail.* Cambridge, Mass.: Harvard University Press, 1997.

Buchanan, Thomas. *Black Life on the Mississippi: Slaves, Free Blacks, and the Western Steamboat World.* Chapel Hill: University of North Carolina Press, 2004.

Camp, Stephanie M. H. *Closer to Freedom: Enslaved Women and Everyday Resistance in the Plantation South.* Chapel Hill: University of North Carolina Press, 2004.

Cantwell, Edward P. *A History of the Charleston Police Force from the Incorporation of the City, 1783 to 1908.* Charleston: J. J. Furlong, 1908.

Carp, Benjamin L. *Rebels Rising: Cities and the American Revolution.* New York: Oxford University Press, 2007.

Cecelski, David S. *The Waterman's Song: Slavery and Freedom in Maritime North Carolina.* Chapel Hill: University of North Carolina Press, 2001.

Chambers, J. S. *The Conquest of Cholera: America's Greatest Scourge.* New York: Macmillan Co., 1938.

Chaplin, Joyce E. *An Anxious Pursuit: Agricultural Innovation and Modernity in the Lower South, 1730–1815.* Chapel Hill: University of North Carolina, 1993.

Clark, Dennis. *The Irish in Philadelphia: Ten Generations of Urban Experience.* Philadelphia: Temple University Press, 1973.

Coclanis, Peter A. *The Shadow of a Dream: Economic Life and Death in the South Carolina Low Country, 1670–1920.* New York: Oxford University Press, 1991.

Coker, P. C., III. *Charleston's Maritime Heritage, 1670–1865: An Illustrated History.* Charleston: CokerCraft Press, 1987.

Curtin, Philip D. *Death by Migration: Europe's Encounter with the Tropical World in the Nineteenth Century.* New York: Cambridge University Press, 1989.

Dance, Daryl Cumber, ed. *From My People: 400 Years of African-American Folklore.* New York: Norton, 2002.

Doerflinger, William Main. *Songs of the Sailor and Lumberman.* Glenwood, Ill.: Meyerbooks, 1990.

Eaton, Clement. *A History of the Old South.* New York: Macmillan, 1949.

Edgar, Walter. *South Carolina: A History.* Columbia: University of South Carolina Press, 1998.

Egerton, Douglas R. *He Shall Go Out Free: The Lives of Denmark Vesey.* Madison, Wis.: Madison House, 1999.

Erem, Suzan, and E. Paul Durrenberger. *On the Global Waterfront: The Fight to Free the Charleston 5*. New York: Monthly Review Press, 2008.

Ernst, Robert. *Immigrant Life in New York City, 1825–1863*. Port Washington, N.Y.: I. J. Friedman, 1965.

Farley, M. Foster. *An Account of the History of Stranger's Fever in Charleston, 1699–1876*. Washington, D.C.: University Press of America, 1978.

Fehrenbacher, Don. *The Dred Scott Case: Its Significance in American Law and Politics*. New York: Oxford University Press, 1978.

Fisher, Miles Mark. *Negro Slave Songs in the United States*. New York: Carol Publishing Group, 1990.

Fletcher, Bill Jr., and Fernando Gapasin. *Solidarity Divided: The Crisis in Organized Labor and a New Path toward Social Justice*. Berkeley: University of California Press, 2008.

Ford, Lacy K. *Deliver Us from Evil: The Slavery Question in the Old South*. New York: Oxford University Press, 2009.

Franklin, John Hope, and Loren Schweninger. *Runaway Slaves: Rebels on the Plantation*. New York: Oxford University Press, 1999.

Fraser, Walter. *Charleston! Charleston! The History of a Southern City*. Columbia: University of South Carolina Press, 1989.

Freehling, William W. *Prelude to Civil War: The Nullification Controversy in South Carolina, 1816–1836*. New York: Harper & Row, 1965.

Friedman, Lawrence M. *A History of American Law*. New York: Simon and Schuster, 2005.

Frothingham, Robert. *Songs of the Sea & Sailors' Chanteys: An Anthology*. Freeport, N.Y.: Books for Libraries Press, 1969.

Genovese, Eugene D. *Roll, Jordan, Roll: The World the Slaves Made*. New York: Vintage Books, 1974.

Gilje, Paul A. *Liberty on the Waterfront: American Maritime Culture in the Age of Revolution*. Philadelphia: University of Pennsylvania Press, 2004.

Gillespie, Michele. *Free Labor in an Unfree World: White Artisans in Slaveholding Georgia, 1789–1860*. Athens: University of Georgia Press, 2000.

Glass, Paul, and Louis C. Singer. *Songs of the Sea: Chanteys, Historical Songs, and Ballads*. New York: Grosset & Dunlap, 1966.

Gleeson, David T. *The Irish in the South, 1815–1877*. Chapel Hill: University of North Carolina Press, 2001.

Goldfield, David. *Region, Race, and Cities: Interpreting the Urban South*. Baton Rouge: Louisiana State University Press, 1997.

Goldin, Claudia Dale. *Urban Slavery in the American South: A Quantitative History*. Chicago: University of Chicago Press, 1976.

Greene, Harlan, et al. *Slave Badges and the Slave-Hire System in Charleston, South Carolina, 1783–1865*. Jefferson, N.C.: McFarland & Co., 2004.

Harris, Leslie M. *In the Shadow of Slavery: African Americans in New York City, 1626–1863*. Chicago: University of Chicago Press, 2003.

Hindus, Michael Stephen. *Prison and Plantation: Crime, Justice, and Authority in Massachusetts and South Carolina, 1767–1878.* Chapel Hill: University of North Carolina Press, 1980.

Hinks, Peter P. *To Awaken My Afflicted Brethren: David Walker and the Problem of Antebellum Slave Resistance.* University Park: Pennsylvania State University Press, 1997.

Horton, James O., and Lois E. Horton. *In Hope of Liberty: Culture, Community and Protest Among Northern Free Blacks, 1700–1860.* Cambridge, U.K.: Oxford University Press, 1997.

Hugill, Stan. *Shanties and Sailors' Songs.* London: H. Jenkins, 1969.

———. *Shanties from the Seven Seas: Shipboard Work-Songs and Songs Used as Work-Songs from the Great Days of Sail.* Mystic, Conn.: Mystic Seaport, 1994.

Hurst, James Willard. *Law and the Conditions of Freedom in the Nineteenth-Century United States.* Madison: University of Wisconsin Press, 1964.

———. *Law and Markets in United States History: Different Modes of Bargaining Among Interests.* Madison: University of Wisconsin Press, 1982.

Ignatiev, Noel. *How the Irish Became White.* New York: Routledge, 1995.

Jacobson, Matthew Frye. *Whiteness of a Different Color: European Immigrants and the Alchemy of Race.* Cambridge, Mass.: Harvard University Press, 1998.

John, Richard R. *Spreading the News: The American Postal System from Franklin to Morse.* Cambridge, Mass.: Harvard University Press, 1998.

Johnson, John. *The Defense of Charleston Harbor, Including Fort Sumter and the Adjacent Islands, 1863–1865.* Charleston: Walker, Evans, & Cogswell, 1890.

Johnson, Michael P., and James L. Roark. *Black Masters: A Free Family of Color in the Old South.* New York: W. W. Norton & Co., 1984.

Johnson, Walter. *Soul by Soul: Life Inside the Antebellum Slave Market.* Cambridge, Mass.: Harvard University Press, 1999.

Jones, John W., et al. *Confederate Currency: The Color of Money, Images of Slavery in Confederate and Southern States Currency.* West Columbia, S.C.: Olive Press, 2002.

King, William L. *The Newspaper Press of Charleston, S.C.: A Chronological and Biographical History, Embracing a Period of One Hundred and Forty Years.* Charleston: Edward Perry Book Press, 1872.

Kiple, Kenneth F., ed. *The Cambridge World History of Human Disease.* New York: Cambridge University Press, 1993.

Kiple, Kenneth F., and Virginia H. King. *Another Dimension to the Black Diaspora: Diet, Disease, and Racism.* New York: Cambridge University Press, 1981.

Krehbiel, Henry Edward. *Afro-American Folksongs: A Study in Racial and National Music.* New York: Frederick Ungar Publishing Co., 1967.

Linebaugh, Peter. *The London Hanged: Crime and Civil Society in the Eighteenth Century.* London: Verso, 2003.

Linebaugh, Peter, and Marcus Rediker. *The Many-Headed Hydra: Sailors, Slaves, Commoners, and the Hidden History of the Revolutionary Atlantic.* Boston: Beacon Press, 2000.

Litwack, Leon F. *North of Slavery: The Negro in the Free States, 1790–1860*. Chicago: University of Chicago Press, 1961.

McCandless, Peter. *Slavery, Disease, and Suffering in the Southern Lowcountry*. New York: Cambridge University Press, 2011.

Niehaus, Earl F. *The Irish in New Orleans, 1800–1860*. Baton Rouge: Louisiana State University Press, 1965.

Novak, William J. *The People's Welfare: Law and Regulation in Nineteenth-Century America*. Chapel Hill: University of North Carolina Press, 1996.

Olwell, Robert. *Masters, Slaves, and Subjects: The Culture of Power in the South Carolina Low Country, 1740–1790*. Ithaca: Cornell University Press, 1998.

Parrish, Lydia. *Slave Songs of the Georgia Sea Islands*. Hatboro, Pa.: Folklore Associates, 1965.

Pease, William H., and Jane H. Pease. *The Web of Progress: Private Values and Public Styles in Boston and Charleston, 1828–1843*. New York: Oxford University Press, 1985.

Penningroth, Dylan C. *The Claims of Kinfolk: African American Property and Community in the Nineteenth-Century South*. Chapel Hill: University of North Carolina Press, 2002.

Phillips, U. B. *American Negro Slavery*. New York: D. Appleton and Co., 1918.

Pollitzer, William S. *The Gullah People and Their African Heritage*. Athens: University of Georgia Press, 2005.

Powers, Bernard E., Jr. *Black Charlestonians: A Social History, 1822–1885*. Fayetteville: University of Arkansas Press, 1994.

Pred, Allan R. *Urban Growth and the Circulation of Information: The United States System of Cities, 1790–1840*. Cambridge, Mass.: Harvard University Press, 1973.

Robertson, David. *Denmark Vesey*. New York: Alfred A. Knopf, 1999.

Rockman, Seth. *Scraping By: Wage Labor, Slavery, and Survival in Early Baltimore*. Baltimore: Johns Hopkins University Press, 2009.

Roediger, David. *The Wages of Whiteness: Race and the Making of the American Working Class*. London: Verso, 2007.

Rogers, George C., Jr. *Charleston in the Age of the Pinckneys*. Columbia: University of South Carolina Press, 1980.

Rosen, Robert N. *Confederate Charleston: An Illustrated History of the City and the People During the Civil War*. Columbia: University of South Carolina Press, 1994.

Rosenberg, Charles E. *The Cholera Years: The United States in 1832, 1849, and 1866*. Chicago: University of Chicago Press, 1962.

Rosenberg, Daniel. *New Orleans Dockworkers: Race, Labor, and Unionism, 1892–1923*. Albany: State University of New York Press, 1988.

Rowe, Charles R. *Pages of History: 200 Years of the Post and Courier*. Charleston: Evening Post Publishing Co., 2003.

Sellers, Charles. *The Market Revolution: Jacksonian America, 1815–1846*. New York: Oxford University Press, 1991.

Smith, Mark M. *Mastered by the Clock: Time, Slavery, and Freedom in the American South*. Chapel Hill: University of North Carolina Press, 1997.

Spero, Sterling D., and Abram L. Harris. *The Black Worker: The Negro and the Labor Movement.* New York: Columbia University Press, 1931.

Stampp, Kenneth M. *The Peculiar Institution: Slavery in the Ante-Bellum South.* New York: Alfred A. Knopf, 1956.

Starobin, Robert S. *Industrial Slavery in the Old South.* New York: Oxford University Press, 1970.

Sterling, Dorothy. *Captain of the Planter: The Story of Robert Smalls.* Garden City, N.Y.: Doubleday & Co., Inc., 1958.

Taylor, George Rogers. *Transportation Revolution, 1815–1860.* Armonk, N.Y.: M. E. Sharpe, 1989.

Thompson, E. P. *The Making of the English Working Class.* New York: Vintage, 1966.

Tuten, James H. *Lowcountry Time and Tide: The Fall of the South Carolina Rice Kingdom.* Columbia: University of South Carolina Press, 2010.

Uya, Okan Edet. *From Slavery to Public Service, Robert Smalls, 1839–1915.* New York: Oxford University Press, 1971.

Van Deusen, John G. *Economic Bases of Disunion in South Carolina.* New York: Columbia University Press, 1928.

Wade, Richard C. *Slavery in the Cities: The South, 1820–1860.* New York: Oxford University Press, 1964.

Walsh, Richard. *Charleston's Sons on Liberty: A Study of the Artisans, 1763–1789.* Columbia: University of South Carolina Press, 1968.

Waring, Joseph I. *A History of Medicine in South Carolina, 1670–1825.* Columbia: South Carolina Medical Association, 1964.

———. *A History of Medicine in South Carolina, 1825–1900.* Columbia: South Carolina Medical Association, 1967.

White, Newman I. *American Negro Folk-Songs.* Hatboro, Pa.: Folklore Associates, Inc., 1965.

White, Shane, and Graham J. White. *The Sounds of Slavery: Discovering African American History Through Songs, Sermons, and Speech.* Boston: Beacon Press, 2005.

Wilentz, Sean. *The Rise of American Democracy: Jefferson to Lincoln.* New York: W. W. Norton, 2005.

Williams, Donald M. *Shamrocks and Pluff Mud: A Glimpse of the Irish in the Southern City of Charleston, South Carolina.* Charleston: BookSurge Publishing, 2005.

Wittke, Carl. *The Irish in America.* Baton Rouge: Louisiana State University Press, 1956.

Wong, Edlie L. *Neither Fugitive Nor Free: Atlantic Slavery, Freedom Suits, and the Legal Culture of Travel.* New York: New York University Press, 2009.

Wood, Peter. *Black Majority: Negroes in Colonial South Carolina from 1670 through the Stono Rebellion.* New York: Alfred A. Knopf, 1974.

Wyatt-Brown, Bertram. *Southern Honor: Ethics and Behavior in the Old South.* New York: Oxford University Press, 1982.

Young, Jeffrey R. *Proslavery and Sectional Thought in the Early South, 1740–1829: An Anthology.* Columbia: University of South Carolina Press, 2006.

Journal Articles, Book Chapters, and Pamphlets

Berlin, Ira, and Herbert Gutman. "Natives and Immigrants, Free Men and Slaves." *American Historical Review* 88 (December 1983): 1175–1200.

Cooper, Donald B. "The New 'Black Death': Cholera in Brazil, 1855–1856." In *The African Exchange: Toward a Biological History of Black People*, ed. Kenneth F. Kiple, 235–56. Durham: Duke University Press, 1987.

Curtin, Philip D. "The Epidemiology of the Slave Trade." *Political Science Quarterly* 83 (June 1968): 190–216.

Eaton, Clement. "A Dangerous Pamphlet in the Old South." *Journal of Southern History* 2 (August 1936): 323–34.

Ford, Lacy K. "Republics and Democracy: The Parameters of Political Citizenship in Antebellum South Carolina." In *The Meaning of South Carolina History: Essays in Honor of George C. Rogers Jr.*, ed. David R. Chesnutt and Clyde N. Wilson, 121–45. Columbia: University of South Carolina Press, 1991.

Gatell, Frank Otto. "Postmaster Huger and the Incendiary Publications." *South Carolina Historical Magazine* 64 (October 1963): 193–201.

Grimes, Kimberly M. "Between the Tracks: The Heritage of Charleston's East Side Community." Charleston: Charleston Museum, 1987.

Gross, Robert A., et al. "Forum: The Making of a Slave Conspiracy, Part 2." *William and Mary Quarterly* 59 (January 2002): 135–202.

Grüttner, Michael. "Working-class Crime and the Labour Movement: Pilfering in the Hamburg Docks, 1888–1923." In *The German Working Class, 1888–1933: The Politics of Everyday Life*, ed. Richard J. Evans, 54–79. Totowa, N.J.: Barnes & Noble, 1982.

Hamer, Philip M. "British Consuls and the Negro Seamen Acts, 1850–1860." *Journal of Southern History* 1 (May 1935): 138–68.

———. "Great Britain, the United States, and the Negro Seamen Acts, 1822–1848." *Journal of Southern History* 1 (February 1935): 3–28.

Hershberg, Theodore. "Free Blacks in Antebellum Philadelphia." In *Plantation, Town, and County: Essays on the Local History of American Slave Society*, ed. Elinor Miller and Eugene D. Genovese, 415–40. Urbana: University of Illinois Press, 1974.

Hine, William C. "Black Organized Labor in Reconstruction Charleston." *Labor History* 25 (Autumn 1984): 504–17.

Hirsch, Arnold R. "On the Waterfront: Race, Class, and Politics in Post-Reconstruction New Orleans." *Journal of Urban History* 21 (May 1995): 511–17.

January, Alan F. "The South Carolina Association: An Agency for Race Control in Antebellum Charleston." *South Carolina Historical Magazine* 78 (July 1977): 191–201.

Johnson, Linda Cooke. "Criminality on the Docks." In *Dock Workers: International Explorations in Comparative Labour History, 1790–1970*, vol. 2, ed. Sam Davies et al., 721–45. Burlington, Vt.: Ashgate Publishing Ltd., 2000.

Johnson, Michael P. "Denmark Vesey and His Co-Conspirators." *William and Mary Quarterly* 58 (October 2001): 915–76.

Joseph, J. W., et al. "The Vendue/Prioleau Project: An Archaeological Study of the Early Charleston Waterfront." Stone Mountain, Ga.: New South Associates, 2000.

Joyce, Dee Dee. "The Charleston Landscape on the Eve of the Civil War: Race, Class, and Ethnic Relations in Ward Five." In *Carolina's Historical Landscapes: Archaeological Perspectives,* ed. Linda F. Stine et al., 175–85. Knoxville: University of Tennessee Press, 1997.

Kiple, Kenneth F. "Response to Sheldon Watts, 'Yellow Fever Immunities in West Africa and the Americas in the Age of Slavery and Beyond: A Reappraisal.'" *Journal of Social History* 34 (Summer 2001): 969–74.

———. "A Survey of Recent Literature on the Biological Past of the Black." In *The African Exchange: Toward a Biological History of Black People,* ed. Kenneth F. Kiple, 7–34. Durham: Duke University Press, 1987.

———, and Virginia H. Kiple. "Black Yellow Fever Immunities, Innate and Acquired, as Revealed in the American South." *Social Science History* 1 (Summer 1977): 419–36.

Klebaner, Benjamin J. "Public Poor Relief in Charleston, 1800–1860." *South Carolina Historical Magazine* 55 (October 1954): 210–20.

Kolchin, Peter. "Whiteness Studies: The New History of Race in America." *Journal of American History* 89 (June 2002): 154–73.

Lapham, Samuel, Jr. "'Vanderhorst Row,' Charleston, South Carolina (A.D. 1800): A Prototype of the Modern Apartment House." *Architectural Forum* 39 (August 1923): 59–61.

Lichtenstein, Alex. "'That Disposition to Theft, with Which They Have Been Branded': Moral Economy, Slave Management, and the Law." *Journal of Social History* 21 (Spring 1988): 413–40.

Man, Albon P., Jr. "Labor Competition and the New York Draft Riots of 1863." *Journal of Negro History* 36 (October 1951): 375–405.

Mars, Gerald. "Dock Pilferage." In *Deviance and Social Control,* ed. Paul Rock and Mary McIntosh, 209–28. London: Tavistock Publications Ltd., 1974.

Morgan, Philip D. "Black Life in Eighteenth-Century Charleston." *Perspectives in American History* (1984): 187–232.

Northrup, Herbert. "The New Orleans Longshoremen." *Political Science Quarterly* 57 (December 1942): 526–44.

Paquette, Robert L. "From Rebellion to Revisionism: The Continuing Debate about the Denmark Vesey Affair." *Journal of the Historical Society* 4 (Fall 2004): 291–334.

Pease, William H., and Jane H. Pease. "Walker's Appeal Comes to Charleston: A Note and Documents." *Journal of Negro History* 59 (July 1974): 287–92.

Poliakoff, Eli A. "Charleston's Longshoremen: Organized Labor in the Anti-Union Palmetto State." *South Carolina Historical Magazine* 103 (July 2002): 247–64.

Rubio, Philip F. "'Though He Had a White Face, He Was a Negro in Heart': Examining the White Men Convicted of Supporting the 1822 Denmark Vesey Slave Insurrection Conspiracy." *South Carolina Historical Magazine* 113 (January 2012): 50–67.

Schoeppner, Michael. "Peculiar Quarantines: The Seamen Acts and Regulatory Authority in the Antebellum South." *Law and History Review* 31 (August 2013): 559–86.

Schweninger, Loren. "Slave Independence and Enterprise in South Carolina, 1780–1865." *South Carolina Historical Magazine* 93 (April 1992): 101–25.

Silver, Christopher. "A New Look at Old South Urbanization: The Irish Worker in Charleston, South Carolina, 1840–1860." In *South Atlantic Urban Studies,* vol. 3, ed. Samuel M. Hines and George W. Hopkins, 141–72. Columbia: University of South Carolina Press, 1979.

Snowden, Yates. "Notes on Labor Organizations in South Carolina, 1742–1861." Columbia: University Press, 1914.

Spady, James O'Neil. "Power and Confession: On the Credibility of the Earliest Reports of the Denmark Vesey Slave Conspiracy." *William and Mary Quarterly* 68 (April 2011): 287–304.

Strickland, Jeffery. "How the Germans Became White Southerners: German Immigrants and African Americans in Charleston, South Carolina, 1860–1880." *Journal of American Ethnic History* 28 (Fall 2008): 52–69.

Thompson, Michael D. "'Some Rascally Business': Thieving Slaves, Unscrupulous Whites, and Charleston's Illicit Waterfront Trade." In *Capitalism by Gaslight: Illuminating the Economy of Nineteenth-Century America,* ed. Brian Luskey and Wendy Woloson. Philadelphia: University of Pennsylvania Press, 2015.

Vainio, Jari, and Felicity Cutts. "Yellow Fever." Geneva: World Health Organization, 1998.

Valone, Stephen J. "William Henry Seward, the Virginia Controversy, and the Anti-Slavery Movement, 1839–1841." *Afro-Americans in New York Life and History* 31 (January 2007): 65–80.

Wade, Richard C. "The Vesey Plot: A Reconsideration." *Journal of Southern History* 30 (May 1964): 143–61.

Walsh, Richard. "The Charleston Mechanics: A Brief Study, 1760–1776." *South Carolina Historical Magazine* 60 (July 1959): 123–44.

Waring, Joseph I. "Asiatic Cholera in South Carolina." *Bulletin of the History of Medicine* 40 (September–October 1966): 459–66.

———. "John Moultrie Jr., M.D., Lieutenant Governor of East Florida: His Thesis on Yellow Fever," n.p. Rpt. from *Journal of the Florida Medical Association* 54 (August 1967): 772–77.

Watts, Sheldon. "Response to Kenneth Kiple." *Journal of Social History* 34 (Summer 2001): 975–76.

———. "Yellow Fever Immunities in West Africa and the Americas in the Age of Slavery and Beyond: A Reappraisal." *Journal of Social History* 34 (Summer 2001): 955–67.

Weaver, Herbert. "Foreigners in Ante-Bellum Towns of the Lower South." *Journal of Southern History* 13 (February 1947): 62–73.

Wyly-Jones, Susan. "The 1835 Anti-Abolition Meetings in the South: A New Look at the Controversy over the Abolition Postal Campaign." *Civil War History* 47 (December 2001): 289–309.

Young, Jeffrey R. "Ideology and Death on a Savannah River Rice Plantation, 1833–1867: Paternalism amidst 'a Good Supply of Disease and Pain.'" *Journal of Southern History* 59 (November 1993): 673–706.

Zierden, Martha A., and Elizabeth J. Reitz. "Excavations on Charleston's Waterfront: The Atlantic Wharf Garage Site." Charleston: Charleston Museum, 2002.

Dissertations and Theses

Collins, Frederick Burtrumn, Jr. "Charleston and the Railroads: A Geographic Study of a South Atlantic Port and Its Strategies for Developing a Railroad System, 1820–1860." MA thesis, University of South Carolina, 1977.

Crowson, Brian Edward. "Southern Port City Politics and the Know Nothing Party in the 1850s." PhD diss., University of Tennessee, 1994.

Farrington, Clifford. "Biracial Unions on Galveston's Waterfront, 1865–1925." PhD diss., University of Texas, 2003.

Hunt, Monica. "Savannah's Black and White Longshoremen, 1856–1897." MA thesis, Armstrong State College, 1993.

January, Alan F. "The First Nullification: The Negro Seamen Acts Controversy in South Carolina, 1822–1860." PhD diss., University of Iowa, 1976.

Shoemaker, Edward. "Strangers and Citizens: The Irish Immigrant Community of Savannah, 1837–1861." PhD diss., Emory University, 1990.

Strickland, Jeffery. "Ethnicity and Race in the Urban South: German Immigrants and African-Americans in Charleston, South Carolina during Reconstruction." PhD diss., Florida State University, 2003.

Index